WITHDRAWN BY THE
UNIVERSITY OF MICHIGAN

THE AMERICAN ELECTORATE

Undergraduate
Library

JK
1764
.C331
cop. 3

THE AMERICAN ELECTORATE
Attitudes and Action

Bruce A. Campbell
University of Georgia

Holt, Rinehart and Winston
New York   Chicago   San Francisco   Dallas
Montreal   Toronto   London   Sydney

For Kirsten and Robbie

Library of Congress Cataloging in Publication Data

Campbell, Bruce A   1945–
   The American electorate.

   Bibliography: p. 300
   Includes index.
   1. Political participation—United States.
2. Political socialization—United States. 3. Public opinion—United States. 4. Voting—United States. I. Title.
JK1764.C33   324'.2   78–31154
ISBN 0–03–038451–6

Copyright © 1979 by Holt, Rinehart and Winston
Printed in the United States of America
All rights reserved
9 0 1 2 090 9 8 7 6 5 4 3 2 1

PREFACE

I have tried to do three things in this book: (1) to present in a single volume of modest length a discussion of the three major topics in the study of mass political behavior: political socialization, public opinion, and political participation; (2) to provide a framework, based on the concept of attitude, that will integrate these three areas and enhance understanding of any one or all of them; and (3) to present the most current data available from national surveys, placing particular emphasis on two of the most important political events of our generation: Vietnam and Watergate.

These three goals are all empirical and analytical: my discussions are based on a wide selection from the literature in political science, sociology, and psychology. However, there is a fourth element present, a theme that is interwoven with the analytical material throughout the book. This is a normative concern. It asks what role the electorate *should* play in the political life of our country, whether or not it actually *does* play that role, and to what extent the situation that we find is a desirable one.

Clearly, these questions cannot be answered by citing survey data. They can be answered only through the application of judgment, which rests ultimately on ideology. I think, therefore, that the reader deserves to know what my ideology is, so that any confusion between my facts and my judgments will be minimized. I am a reformer. I believe that the interests of the mass electorate are often poorly served by government and that the common man should have more to say about what happens in the political world. I also believe that the electorate has the power to assert itself more forcefully. That it fails to do so is essentially the fault of its own ignorance and neglect. Indeed, if this book does no more than persuade its readers that political self-awareness can overcome the effects of ignorance and neglect, it will have achieved no small success.

I have written *The American Electorate* for a variety of audiences. Its primary mission is to serve as the core text in upper-division undergraduate courses on mass political behavior: political socialization, public opinion, electoral behavior, and general survey courses on political behavior. In addition, the book also provides a supplement for teachers of introductory courses in American government or American politics which will enable them to stress the behavioral aspects of their respective topics. I have made a considerable effort to keep my vocabulary simple and free of jargon. Also, I have tried not to use any concept without first explaining it. In short, the reader should be able to derive maximum benefit from this book without any specific formal preparation.

My desire not to impose prerequisites extends almost as completely to my presentation of empirical material as it does to the substantive content of the book. The most complex analytical technique which I have used is the two-dimensional contingency table. I have also tried, when appropriate, to use charts to illustrate patterns. Overall, the level of methodological sophistication required to read the book, while not zero, is certainly at a manageably low level.

This book reports data from a large number of sources. I have made particularly heavy use of the facilities of the Inter-University Consortium for Political and Social Research. Their archive made available to me the Presidential Election Studies for the years 1952–1976, as well as the Jennings Political Socialization Study. Neither the original collectors of these data nor the Consortium bear any responsibility for the analyses or interpretations presented here. In addition, the data from the Atlanta Student Study, reported in Part III, were collected with the support of the National Institute of Education (Grant Number NE-G-00-3-0188).

Books are rarely written without considerable help, and this one is no exception. Parts of the manuscript were read by numerous undergraduates at the University of Georgia. I also want to acknowledge the efforts of Bonnie Browne, Hendrik Van Dalen, and Sarah Morehouse for their useful comments. I was assisted in my work by Cheryl Bilgin and Chris Dennis, both of whom deserve my commendation. Leah Wilds served as editor during the final revision and helped Ginny Hailey, Sharron Devane, and Stephanie Buffington with a collectively excellent job of typing and preparing the manuscript. Finally, the University of Georgia and the University of California at Berkeley contributed to my efforts by providing both time and a congenial environment in which to work.

Athens, Georgia B.A.C.
January 1979

CONTENTS

Preface *v*

PART I: SETTING THE STAGE 1

1. Introduction 3

The Organization of the Book *6*

2. The Development of the Modern Electorate *11*

Universal White Male Suffrage *11*
Women's Suffrage *14*
Black Suffrage *21*
Summary *32*

3. An Approach to Political Behavior 35

What Is an Attitude? *36*
Attitude Sets *40*
Attitudes and Behavior *45*
Summary *49*

PART II: THE ACQUISITION OF ATTITUDES: POLITICAL SOCIALIZATION 51

4. The Processes of Political Socialization 53

The Psychoanalytic Approach *53*
The Cognitive-Developmental Approach *57*
Social Learning Theory *63*
Summary *68*

5. Political Culture I: Attachments to the Political System 70

The Concept of Culture *71*
The Content of American Political Culture: The Political System *75*
Summary *84*

6. Political Culture II: Views of Politicians and Citizens 86

The Government 86
Attitudes toward the Political Self 95
Deviant Subgroups 102
Summary 107

7. The Sources of Political Learning 110

The Agents of Political Socialization 110
Summary 128
Group Differences in Political Socialization 129
Summary 134

PART III: THE EXPRESSION OF ATTITUDES: PUBLIC OPINION 139

Presence of an Issue 140
The Complex of Preferences in the Public 140
Number of Persons Involved 141

8. The Acquisition of Opinion: Intrapersonal Processes 143

A Model of Opinion Formation 143
The Dynamics of Attitude Formation and Change 145
The Perceptual Screen 156
The Personality 160
Summary 162

9. The Acquisition of Opinion: Interpersonal Processes 165

Social Reality 165
Summary 176
The Impact of the Media 177
Summary 185

10. The Distribution of Opinion in the Electorate 189

The Concept of Distribution 189
Types of Distributions and Public Policy 193
The Major Dimensions of Political Opinion in the Electorate 196
Public Opinion Polling 204
Summary 206

PART IV: ATTITUDES IN ACTION: POLITICAL PARTICIPATION 209

Modes of Active Conventional Political Participation *210*

11. The Demographic Bases of the Vote *215*

Primary Groups *217*
Secondary Groups *218*
Summary *229*

12. The Attitudinal Bases of the Vote *232*

Turnout *232*
Party Choice *240*
Summary *257*

13. The Voting Outcome: Attitudes Combined *259*

The Combination of Party Identification and the Vote *259*
Directions in the Electorate *265*
Summary *277*

PART V: EPILOGUE: THE IMPACT OF THE AMERICAN ELECTORATE ON PUBLIC POLICY 281

The Structure of Demand: How Political Socialization Influences Policy *285*
The Structure of Communication: How Public Opinion Influences Policy *287*
The Structure of Alternatives: How Participation Influences Policy *291*

Bibliography *300*

Name Index *313*

Subject Index *317*

THE AMERICAN ELECTORATE

Part **I**

Setting the Stage

Most Americans don't think they have much to do with the way government operates. During the Carter–Ford campaign, almost three out of every five people contacted in a nationwide survey said they thought that the government is pretty much run by a few big interests looking out for themselves, rather than for the benefit of all the people. About two out of five felt that they had no say about what the government does.[1]

These are alarming statistics. Democracy means popular government, where sovereignty resides with the common citizens. And yet many, if not most, Americans say they have no power over their own government. What is more, they may have good reason to believe as they do. Vietnam and Watergate have convinced many of us that government no longer reflects the national will. The enormous expansion of the federal bureaucracy, coupled with the celebrated difficulties of certain branches like the CIA or the postal service, make bureaucrats appear remote and inaccessible. The continuing inequities of poverty and discrimination suggest strongly that the common man does not get a fair shake in America.

I believe that the common man *has* lost control of his government, at least at certain times and in certain areas. Some people have said that this has happened because control has been "stolen" from the people, either by the politicians, the bureaucrats, or the rich.[2] I reject that view of politics. I tend instead to agree with Benjamin Franklin, who, when asked what form of government the Continental Congress had selected, is supposed to have said: "a republic ... if you can keep it." These were wise words, for in fact governmental abuse of the popular will in a democracy is primarily the result of the negligence of the people themselves. Through ignorance, or complacency, or the distractions of "making it" in today's world, we have abdicated our political responsibilities. The politicians, the bureaucrats and the wealthy have not stolen control of our government from us; they have simply taken it over as the people have let it default.

For many people, unfortunately, it makes little difference whether political control has been "stolen" or simply "lost." Large numbers of citizens have given up trying to make democracy work. But the distinction is important. I believe that since the common people have lost political control through their own neglect, they can regain it by virtue of their own actions. It is to this idea that this book is dedicated. If ignorance is at the base of political impotence, then knowledge is the key to revitalization.

In the pages to follow, I shall discuss with you the phenomenon of mass political behavior. We shall examine the basic values that underlie our political beliefs, the various influences that create our political opinions, and the ways in which we choose to translate these opinions into political action. If we understand ourselves and our place in the political system, our potential for exercising the sovereignty granted to us under the Constitution should become more clear. Our ability to be citizens and to see our wishes carried out by government should be strengthened.

NOTES

1. These and many other results reported in this book are drawn from the studies of the American electorate conducted at the University of Michigan by the Survey Research Center (SRC), and subsequently by the Center for Political Studies (CPS). These results come from the CPS 1976 Presidential Election Study. These data are available from the Inter-University Consortium for Political and Social Research (ICPSR).

2. See Walter Dean Burnham, "The Changing Shape of the American Political Universe, *The American Political Science Review*, vol. 59, no. 1 (March 1965), 7–28.

1
Introduction

It is said that in a democracy the people rule, yet we know that many times this is not the case. Why have the people allowed their power over government to slip away? I think that much of the cynicism expressed by Americans, much of the feeling of powerlessness, has been produced by an unreasonable and mistaken view of what it means to exercise popular control. For many people, to exercise political control means that a *single* person has a *direct* effect on government. Occasionally, to be sure, a single common citizen does have such an impact, but this is not the way the mass electorate can most effectively assert its sovereignty. The nature of popular control is quite different in two ways. Political influence of the common man tends to be *aggregate* and *indirect*, as contrasted to the *single* and *direct* power of congressmen, high-level bureaucrats, the President, or other political elites.

These two words, aggregate and indirect, convey two simple ideas. The aggregate nature of influence means that control by the common man is generally wielded by groups, or aggregates, of people acting together. The most obvious form of aggregate influence is the vote, when the aggregate we call the electorate chooses its representatives. Another use of the vote is the referendum, a procedure used by some states to allow the voters to pass or repeal laws or even amendments to the state constitution. The power of the referendum is well illustrated by the recent California vote on the so-called Jarvis-Cann initiative. Among other things, this new law limits property taxes to a maximum of 1 percent of the property's assessed valuation. Since the average California property tax before the vote was more than 2½ percent, in one stroke the voters have reduced their property taxes (and revenue to local governments in California) by some 60 percent, which amounts to about 7 *billion* dollars a year!

There are many ways other than voting by which the people exercise influence by banding together. Our local county commission met recently to consider the request of the biggest real estate developer in the area to change the zoning so that he could build a huge shopping center in the midst of several residential areas. The meeting room was filled with people who lived in those areas and were unanimously opposed to the shopping center. Although there were probably not more than 200 citizens present, the commission, which had been suspected of favoring the developer's request, voted unanimously to deny the rezoning.

An aggregate of common citizens can be influential in even more subtle ways. The profile of public opinion in the electorate, for instance, may have a profound influence on decision making in all branches of government. This has been most clearly exposed in the Watergate affair, where it was quite obvious that Congress would pursue impeachment of President Nixon only if it was assured that the voters back home felt that this drastic step was necessary.

The second aspect of popular control is that it is generally indirect. The people rarely make policy directly. Instead, they set up boundaries within which those who do make decisions must stay. Again, Watergate exemplifies this idea quite well. Under most circumstances, the American people hold their President in very high esteem. This means that the boundaries set on his behavior are quite broad; he can do virtually anything and continue to enjoy the support of the bulk of the people. However, there are certain limits which even the President cannot trespass. Apparently, covering up illegal acts lies outside of those boundaries.

The preceding examples can be most conveniently organized as shown in Figure 1.1. We can clearly see that there are four basic types of political action: single-direct, single-indirect, aggregate-direct, and aggregate-indirect. The examples reviewed above all fall into the bottom row of

		Type of Action	
		Direct	Indirect
Number of Actors	Single	Presidential Veto	Litigation Assassination
	Aggregate	Elections Referenda	Petitions Attending Meetings "Boundary Setting"

Figure 1.1. A Typology of Political Action.

Figure 1.1. In fact, aside from voting, all of them would be classified in the lower-right-hand cell: the aggregate-indirect type of action.

Since this book deals with the entire electorate, I shall simply mention in passing the two cells in the upper row of the table. When the President vetoes a bill, we have the classic single-direct political activity; as a direct consequence of one person's action, public policy will be one thing and not another. In certain narrower areas, the head of one of the federal bureaucracies may also exercise this type of political influence. The example of the attorney general comes to mind. When John Mitchell took over that post in 1968, the attitude of the Department of Justice in the area of civil rights changed from the aggressive problack policy of the Johnson years to one of much greater restraint. In Congress, we can point to the chairmen of the major committees who have the power to exercise single-direct action by killing bills through their refusal to report them for debate.

While single-direct action almost always involves members of the political elite, single-indirect action is much more open to input from the common man. Anyone (anyone who has enough money and a good case, at least) can bring suit in court, and may ultimately see a law ruled unconstitutional by the Supreme Court.[1] Another type of single-indirect action that, tragically, is open to anyone is assassination. Who can say what sort of country this would be if John Kennedy, Robert Kennedy, or Martin Luther King had lived, or if George Wallace had not been crippled? Indirectly, the removal of these individuals from U.S. government has had a profound effect on policy.

To summarize briefly, I have made four points in these opening paragraphs. First, popular control of government is weaker than it should be. Second, this weakness arises not only from the acts of isolated elites but also from the simple neglect, by the people, of their own political sovereignty. Third, popular control tends to be exercised not by individuals but by groups. Finally, popular control tends to be exercised indirectly, although direct control, especially by voting, is also common.

From these four points, two important conclusions may be drawn. First, because of the indirect nature of popular control, the common citizen is much more engaged in the political process than he or she thinks. We are continually involved in the business of setting boundaries. The less attention we pay to politics, the wider are the boundaries within which our political leaders may move. The logical conclusion of this argument is that *doing nothing* is an important political act. It is precisely this sort of behavior that allows the government the maximum freedom from popular control. When we acquiesce, when we accept the decisions of government, even decisions we believe are wrong, we are providing support for the government. In effect, by doing nothing we say to government, "It's all right for you to make the decisions." From this springs the truth of the motto "not to decide is to decide." Although it sounds threateningly like a phrase from George Orwell's book, *1984*, we can reasonably conclude that nothing *is* something in popular politics.

The second conclusion we draw from our argument is that even though the people have forfeited much of their control over government, there is no logical reason why they cannot regain it. Remember, I claimed earlier that no one had stolen political control from the people. The ability to control still exists; it is simply not used effectively. Our constitutional system contains the same guarantees for popular sovereignty that it had when it was originally written; in fact, it has been amended several times to increase those guarantees. Our representatives are still elected by popular ballot. As long as that is true, the people may reassert themselves any time they wish.

These two conclusions suggest that aggregate-indirect action may be much more effective than it presently appears to be. It is easy to be cynical and to believe that circulating petitions or attending meetings won't do any good because nobody is listening. Many times this is true. But the reason is *not* that the elites don't have to listen, rather it is that the attempt to influence them is not sufficiently well organized or sufficiently persuasive. The basic truth remains that ultimately, the elites *do* have to listen. It is up to the people to make it plain that if they do not, there will be consequences.

THE ORGANIZATION OF THE BOOK

The basic goal of this book is to present under one cover the essential information about the three major areas of mass political behavior: socialization, public opinion, and participation. These three sections are linked together through the use of an attitudinal approach. That is, the basic factor to understand in political behavior is the individual's political attitudes. This concept is presented in Chapter 3. The remainder of the book is divided into three parts. The first of these, Part II, deals with the origins of political attitudes (the process of socialization); Part III turns to the expression of those attitudes (public opinion); and Part IV considers the action which flows from those attitudes (political participation). This focus is obviously psychological in orientation. However, the sociology of political behavior cannot be neglected. At appropriate places the links between political sociology and political psychology are pointed out, and group differences are presented at some length in several instances. Schematically, this organization appears in Figure 1.2. Here, each of the three major divisions is subdivided into two parts, labeled "individual" and "aggregate." The distinction resembles the difference between a motion picture and a snapshot. In the individual-level chapters, our concern will

	PART II The Origins of Political Attitudes	PART III The Expression of Political Attitudes	PART IV Political Attitudes to Political Action
Individual	Socialization The Process of Learning Chap. 4 The Agents of Learning Chap. 7	The Formation of Public Opinion Interpersonal Processes Chap. 8 Intrapersonal Processes Chap. 10	Political Participation The Demographic Bases of the Vote Chap. 11 The Attitudinal Bases of the Vote Chap. 12
Aggregate	Political Culture The Content of Learning, I Chap. 5 The Content of Learning, II Chap. 6	Distribution and Trends of Public Opinion in the Electorate Chap. 10	Patterns of Change in the Electorate The Evolution of Presidential Voting Chap. 13

Figure 1.2. The Organization of the Book.

be with *processes,* the flow of events over time. These processes involve attitude acquisition, expression and action, and are best discussed in the context of individual members of the electorate.

The aggregate-level chapters present the snapshots. Here we are not concerned with "how" but with "what." We look at *content* rather than process. The distinction is blurred a bit because several of these chapters present trends over time, but the concern remains focused on content, and the entire electorate forms the basis of discussion.

Part II focuses on the origins of political attitudes, or political socialization. Chapter 4 is devoted to a discussion of the process of political learning. The discussion is based on three major approaches to learning: social learning theory, psychoanalytic theory, and cognitive-developmental theory.

After setting out the basic process, the two succeeding chapters on political culture describe the major attitudes and values that make up the content of political learning in the American electorate. The final chapter in this section returns to the concern with process, this time combining it with content. In this chapter, I discuss the major agents of socialization, those actors in society who seem to send the most persuasive political messages to most Americans. These are the parents, the school, and the peer group. I also deal here with major group differences in socialization.

Part III presents the topic of public opinion, or the expression of political attitudes. The focus on process reappears in Chapters 8 and 9. Chapter 8 deals with interpersonal processes—that is, the way external forces, particularly the media, influence opinion. Chapter 9 focuses on intrapersonal processes: the ways that the individual's personality determines how his or her opinions form in reaction to issues and events.

The section that describes the content of American public opinion, Chapter 10, attempts to communicate a feeling not only for what the state of American public opinion is today, but also to trace the patterns of change that have come about since 1952.

Part IV is organized very similarly to Parts II and III. We shall focus our attention first on an individual-level discussion of voting, with one chapter about the demographic, or group bases of the vote, and a second about the attitudinal bases of the vote. Chapter 13 shifts over to the aggregate level of analysis. In it we shall look at the behavior of the entire electorate over the past decades, and perhaps say some meaningful things about future trends.

Difficulties of the Attitudinal Approach

Throughout this book you will discover that the discussion of one topic or another often rests on untested assumptions. This means that in order to draw a particular conclusion from a set of data, we have to assume that something is true. We may feel intuitively that our assumption is correct, but in fact we have little or no evidence to back us up.

The presence of untested assumptions is bad enough, but the failure to realize their existence is worse, for it precludes understanding. Since the goal of this book is to give you an understanding of mass political behavior, I want to set out with some care the major assumptions we must make.

In general, these assumptions revolve around the supposition that mass political behavior is produced by mass political attitudes, which are in turn somehow related to the political attitudes that individuals acquired as children. As Easton and Dennis put it: "We . . . hold to the theory that what is learned early in life tends to be retained and to shape later attitudes and behavior."[2]

The schema that appears in Figure 1.3 presents a typical progression of events. At the beginning we find a stimulus, which is simply an event occurring in the life of a child. Our first major assumption (link 1) is that these experiences and the consequent learning do in fact relate to the attitudes that the child acquires. This is a crucial assumption for the study of political socialization. Any statement about what society must do to encourage political outlooks favorable to the established government, for instance, must rest on this assumption.

The second assumption (link 2) states that the attitudes an individual holds as a child are the same as, or at least relate to, those he holds as an adult. This is another assumption upon which rests much of the validity of political socialization research. The enormous stress on childhood learn-

INTRODUCTION   9

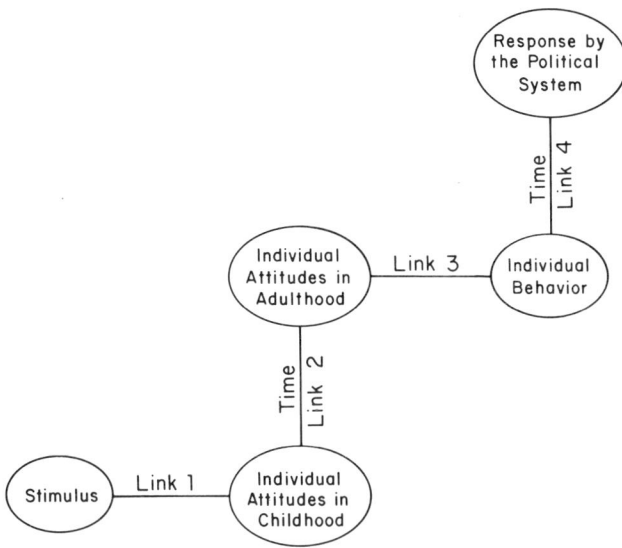

Figure 1.3. Schematic View of the Major Assumptions in the Study of Mass Political Attitudes and Behavior.

ing would have little meaning indeed if the individual eventually abandoned that learning in favor of something entirely new.

The third assumption links adult attitudes to behavior. Clearly, the entire attitudinal approach depends on this assumption. The major importance of the attitude concept, after all, is that it helps us to understand and predict what people *do*. There are psychologists, however, who point out that attitudes often cannot be reliably matched with particular behaviors. Even if we continue to accept the assumption, the lack of strong attitude-behavior relationships leads to a great deal of uncertainty about which of several attitudes actually produces a given behavior. Candidates for office, for instance, are very anxious to know which issue positions will produce a favorable vote, and much of the time the conclusions they draw are highly inaccurate.

The final assumption (link 4) states that individual behavior has some influence on the behavior of the political system. Do the elites respond when the people speak? This question lies outside the range of concerns with which this book deals, but to eliminate the question entirely would be an act of sheer cowardice. Consequently, the last chapter reviews the evidence, which suggests that the American electorate does indeed have a say in the way government operates. More important, I hope to point out how a little self-awareness on the part of the electorate can increase that power greatly.

NOTES

1. In practice, although there is usually an individual litigant, such suits are nearly always supported by a large organization such as the NAACP or by the Department of Justice itself.

2. David Easton and Jack Dennis, *Children in the Political System: Origins of Political Legitimacy* (New York: McGraw-Hill, 1969), p. 9. See also the excellent piece by David Marsh, "Political Socialization: The Implicit Assumptions Questioned," *British Journal of Political Science,* vol. 1, pt. 4 (October 1971), 453–465.

2
The Development of the Modern Electorate

The struggle for the vote occupies an important place in the discussion of modern mass political behavior for two reasons. First, each of the major concepts of this book has played a vital role as different groups in society have fought to gain the right to vote. Women and blacks both won the vote in spite of the fact that the political culture initially opposed it. A variety of types of political participation, from gentle letter-writing to armed insurrection, were used, first to alter public opinion and ultimately to achieve the changes in policy which they sought.

The second reason that this chapter is important relates to the loss of political control experienced by the modern electorate. Reading of the struggles, and finally of the victories of landless white males, women, and blacks, should fill us with feelings of both shame and hope—shame that we have wasted the privilege that was won by the struggle and suffering of our ancestors and hope that their example will mean that we may in turn win our own struggle to have our voices heard in government.

UNIVERSAL WHITE MALE SUFFRAGE

It is a surprising truth that the nation that emerged on the Eastern seaboard of the American continent in the 1780s was no democracy. It is even more shocking to learn that many of our founding fathers had no intention of creating a democracy; in fact they opposed the idea bitterly. Democracy was generally seen as an evil menace to the stability and prosperity of the nation. Give the commoner (the man who owned no property) the vote and he would immediately use it to deprive the wealthy of their riches. What the delegates at the Constitutional Convention were trying to achieve "was to keep the country republican, which was a sufficiently radical idea in 1787, without the risk of having it collapse into that feared condition, democracy." John Jay, a New York delegate, reflected the sympathies of many when he wrote that "the mass of men are neither wise nor good—those who own the country ought to govern it."[1]

In due course the defenders of property and a limited franchise (that is, the right to vote) came to rally under the leadership of Alexander Hamilton and the Federalist party. It seems confusing, perhaps, that the names we traditionally associate with our country's birth, and our very Constitution, should be linked here with a position that to our twentieth-century eyes seems to be patently un-American. In 1787, however, this was not the case. These men—Hamilton, Adams, and their partisans—were ardent revolutionaries. They sought, no less than anyone, to throw off the yoke of royal authority and achieve independence. But to them the Revolution was never intended to give political control to the mass of the people. Their expectation was to create a nation which would be guided by the wise and experienced hands of men of property. It was to be England without a king.

To be sure, there were strong forces arrayed against the Federalists. These individuals, who coalesced around the leadership of James Madison, were called the Republicans. This group would probably have found more approval in contemporary America. They felt, for instance, that the Revolution was fought by all manner of men, and that these same men should share in the government of the state that their victory had won. Their central bond, however, was the belief in the philosophical view that good government could be achieved only if all men could participate. Their leaders, in addition to Madison, were people like Franklin, Paine, and Jefferson. Jefferson, for example, believed that the control of government should belong to "all who had a permanent intention of living in the country."[2] Because of such views, Jefferson is remembered as the most consistently radical of our early leaders.

The Constitutional Convention of 1787 could reach no conclusion about what should be done regarding the right to vote; therefore, the delegates determined that the issue would be left to the states. Each of the states had written a constitution after independence was declared, and 12 of the 13 had inserted limitations on the franchise that reflected the Federalist position. For the most part, the restrictions placed upon entry into the electorate revolved around the possession of property, commonly called a freehold. Some states, primarily in the South, demanded that a voter own a certain number of acres of land. In the North, where land was scarcer and cities larger, the individual needed simply to prove that his property had a certain value.[3] Only three of the new states—New Hampshire, Pennsylvania, and Georgia—admitted adult males into the electorate without a stipulation for ownership of a certain minimum amount of property, reckoned either in value or acres. They did require, however, that the individual be a taxpayer in order to vote.[4]

Although the variety of laws that the 13 states adopted to govern voting makes interesting reading, the point concerning us here is this: How large was the electorate in the early days of our country's existence? Just how democratic was the "home of democracy" in 1789, the year George Washington was elected to be our first President?

The question defies an easy answer. We can only guess at the number of freeholders in the different states, and of course different proportions of these people qualified to vote because of the variety in state laws. The best estimate seems to be that between one-half and three-quarters of white adult males living in the United States in 1789 were qualified to vote.[5] However, only about 20 percent of the total population were white adult males. So the electorate in 1789 must have been limited to about 10 to 15 percent of the total population.

Of course, as is true today, not everyone who was eligible actually voted. It appears likely that only 20 to 30 percent of the eligible electorate went to the polls in 1789. That is, about 3 percent of the population voted in the first election held under the American Constitution.[6]

From the very beginning, the pressure to expand this limited franchise was intense. In the original colonies the landed economic elites of the coastal counties were able to resist the demands of the inhabitants of the cities and the hinterlands with some success. North Carolina, Virginia, and Rhode Island maintained some type of property qualification until the 1840s. (The last holdout, North Carolina, did not abandon the freehold criterion until 1859.)

The major thrust toward universal male suffrage came from the frontier. There was no landed gentry in the western reaches of the 13 states, and by consequence, perhaps, there was a very strong sense of social equality and a commitment to democratic government (by white male adults, at least). While 10 of the 13 original states imposed a freehold qualification on their electorate, not one state to enter the Union subsequently did so. Furthermore, only three of the states to join the Union after 1789 imposed a taxpaying qualification. All the others rejected both property and taxation as qualifications for voting.

The dual pressure of the cities and the western frontier (where "West" meant just over the Appalachian Mountains) produced a gradual expansion of the electorate, which began to have a meaningful effect after 1824. In that year, about 4 percent of the total population voted for President, not much above the 3 percent estimate of 1789.[7] However, Andy Jackson's election in 1828 witnessed a near-tripling of the vote, to over 11 percent of the total population. By 1840, the consensus in favor of universal white male suffrage was nearly complete; 17 percent of the population went to the polls in that year.[8]

The experience of Rhode Island, one of the last states to yield in the struggle against the freehold requirement, gives us an excellent illustration of the power of aroused public opinion. Sympathy for universal male suffrage was widespread in Rhode Island when Thomas Dorr, a wealthy and prominent citizen, set out to speak for those who "did military duty and worked the fire engines," but who could not vote. His Rhode Island Suffrage Association soon had organized followings in nearly every township in the state. On April 17, 1841, this organization proclaimed "People's Day," and assembled some 3000 men wearing badges proclaiming "I am an American citizen" in a prosuffrage procession.

This early success was followed by a much bolder move. The Suffrage Association declared that in October a meeting, called the People's Convention, would assemble for the purpose of writing a new state constitution. All white males could send delegates. In due order these plans were carried out and in December the new constitution was ratified, again by universal male suffrage. Dorr and his supporters believed they were at that moment the legal government of Rhode Island.

The General Assembly failed to agree. It branded the new constitution illegal, which it certainly was, but could not prevent the Suffrage Association from holding elections for state offices the following April. As a result, in 1842, two elections were held in Rhode Island and two governors were elected, one of whom was Thomas Dorr.

This episode of our history does not lack comic elements, but obviously a state cannot have two governments, and the issue was eventually resolved by armed conflict. Dorr, who never really had a chance, was driven from the state, and his association was disbanded. The Dorr War was not without consequence, however. Within a year of the rebellion, Rhode Island freeholders had revised their constitution to abolish the ownership of property as a voting qualification for native white males. They clearly had no taste for a second confrontation with an aroused public and instead yielded to the popular will.

WOMEN'S SUFFRAGE

The arrival of universal manhood suffrage probably did not increase the size of the electorate by more than 50 percent in any state, and the increase may have been as little as 10 percent.[9] Giving the vote to women was quite another matter, since in a single blow the size of the electorate would be more than doubled. This fact was only one of the hurdles that stood in the way of women's suffrage, however. By the time women finally won the right to vote, nearly 300 years of effort had been expended.

To the mind of the wealthy colonial freeholder, the gift of the vote to men without property seemed a radical and dangerous thing, as we have seen. It is safe to say that giving the vote to women never crossed his mind at all. Indeed, one of the rare instances of unanimity recorded in a colonial legislature was occasioned by the petition of Mistress Margaret Brent of Maryland in 1647. Mistress Brent had inherited her husband's estate and was an immensely wealthy woman. Since Maryland's law stipulated only that voters own property, she petitioned the legislature for "place and voyce."[10] The unanimous denial she received served other legislatures, which had neglected to exclude women from the franchise in their own constitutions, as a convenient precedent in the ensuing decades.

Another of the early advocates of women's suffrage was the redoubtable Abigail Adams. As her husband was struggling for a declaration of independence from Great Britain, she wrote to him these words:

> I long to hear that you have declared an independency, and by the way, in the new code of laws which I suppose it will be necessary for you to make, I desire you would remember the ladies.... If particular care and attention are not paid to the ladies we are determined to foment a rebellion, and will not hold ourselves bound to obey any laws in which we have no voice or representation.[11]

We can easily suppose that these sentiments were regarded as a joke by John Adams and the others in Philadelphia. Certainly no proposal was made in 1776 to include women in the electorate. Nonetheless, Abigail Adams' words proved prophetic by nearly 150 years.

Voting by women was not totally unknown in the early years of our country's history. However, most of the colonies did not exclude women from voting for the simple reason that no one seriously supposed that women would ever be likely to attempt it. Thus, in local instances, voting by prominent female members of the community was a common occurrence, and it became a sufficiently noticeable phenomenon that by the beginning of the nineteenth century all the states except New Jersey had formally outlawed voting by women. New Jersey had twice endorsed its suffrage law, which referred to "all free inhabitants," in 1790 and again in 1797. But when it became clear that the women's vote might actually be influencing elections, New Jersey followed the example of the other states and in 1807 outlawed women's suffrage.[12]

Thus matters rested at the beginning of the nineteenth century. This was a time when, if he thought about it at all, the male of the species regarded the opposite sex as a distinctly inferior one. Oberlin College, the first institution of higher education to open its doors to men and women on an equal basis, would not do so until 1833. Men generally believed that Greek and higher mathematics, which formed the basis of the collegiate curriculum at that time, were utterly beyond the capacity of women to comprehend.

The legal status of women reflected this belief. Once a woman married, she became "dead in law." Her legal existence was suspended.

> Husband and wife were one, and that one the husband. He assumed all her debts and she was not capable of maintaining legal relationships independent of him. Her property became his, her earnings were his, she could bring no action at law without his aid, and all her dealings with the government had to be through him. Not only could she hold no property in her own right, but she had no rights with regard to her children.[13]

Judging from these circumstances, it is small wonder that the women's suffrage movement got its start through a close identification with the antislavery movement. The more emotional advocates on the side of the women in what was to become a very emotional dispute did in fact refer to themselves as "little better than slaves."

Whatever the truth of this argument, it is possible to date the beginning of the organized women's suffrage movement in the United States from 1840, the year of the World's Anti-Slavery Convention held in London. The American abolitionist movement was strongly supported by women, both in in its own right and out of a hope that civil rights for blacks would be accompanied by similar gains by women. The delegation sent from the United States therefore included several women. The arrival of the female delegates threw the London conference into an uproar. With crushing irony, the male abolitionists refused to seat the American women!

As things turned out, this act by the London Conference gave to the American women's suffrage movement a tremendous impetus. It demonstrated to Lucretia Mott and Elizabeth Cady Stanton, who had been delegates, that no male-dominated organization would champion their cause. They would have to found their own, and in 1848, they did precisely that. At Seneca Falls, New York, they called a Women's Rights Convention, and framed a Declaration of Women's Rights that listed women's grievances against government as the Declaration of Independence had listed grievances against the king. The first of the grievances named was "the denial of the electoral franchise."

The reaction to the 1848 convention can easily be guessed. A newspaper of the period editorialized as follows:

> This bolt is the most shocking and unnatural incident ever recorded in the history of humanity; if the demands were effected, it would set the world by the ears, make confusion worse confounded, demoralize and degrade from their high sphere and noble destiny women of all respectable and useful classes, and prove monstrous injury to all mankind.[14]

In these early years, the women's suffrage movement not only endured unfair treatment by the press, but was vilified as well by politicians, and in particular by southern politicians, who connected the suffragists most intimately with the hated abolitionist movement. Spoke Senator Brown of Georgia in 1884:

> The Creator intended that the sphere of the males and females of our race should be different ... how could the wife, with all the heavy duties of citizen, politician and office-holder resting on her shoulders ... attend to the more sacred, delicate and refining trust ... for which she is peculiarly fitted by nature? Who is to care for and train the children while she is absent in the discharge of these masculine duties?[15]

These pronouncements from the press and the government set the tone for the popular reception given to the women's suffrage movement throughout the nineteenth century. It was such as to make meetings for the purpose of discussing the topic an often dangerous endeavor. Independence Hall in Philadelphia was torn up and set on fire by a mob in 1837 as one early suffragist, Angelina Grimke, was speaking there. And in 1835, a meeting of the Boston Female Anti-Slavery Society, which totaled 15 or 20 women, was stormed and disrupted by a mob of from six to ten *thousand* men.[16]

While the women were greeted with derision and hostility in many instances, there occurred in 1838 the first of a long series of changes in state law which were to continue until 1920. In that year, Kentucky gave women the first vote in the United States (not counting New Jersey's earlier experience), when widows with children obtained the franchise in school elections.

The Civil War amendments, most particularly the Fifteenth, which guaranteed the right to vote to blacks (and which was then generally ignored for 100 years), were a stunning disappointment for the women's movement. The movement had supported the abolitionists ardently, both out of principle and out of the hope that their own cause would attract some of the luster that the slavery issue had come to possess. Indeed, the leading male abolitionists of the time, Horace Greeley and Senators Sumner and Stevens for instance, had assured the women that their cause and the Negroes' were one.

Unfortunately, in the cold political world that followed Appomattox, these erstwhile champions of women's suffrage began to fade away. They realized, perhaps, that simply to gain what they wanted for the blacks would not be easy. In any event, one by one they abandoned the women. "It is the Negro's hour," they said, "the women will be next." It was 55 years before the women's hour finally came.

The main thrust for women's suffrage in the second half of the nineteenth century came not from the older, eastern states, where most of the prominent suffragists lived (New York, home of many of these, and site of the founding of the first women's suffrage organization, did not give women the vote until 1917), but from the West. The Wyoming Territory became the first place in recorded history where women went to the polls on equal terms with men, in 1869.[17] By 1896, seven states had adopted some form of women's suffrage, and all of them were in the West.[18]

Why the West? Two reasons seem apparent. First, these territories were very sparsely settled in the late nineteenth century, and extending political rights to women was seen as a way in which people could be encouraged to make the long trip from the East to settle in new areas.

A second reason reflects the harsh realities of life on the frontier. The women of the wealthier classes in the East, and especially in the South, because of the leisure their stations provided, were expected to do nothing more than care for the home and tend the children. But there was very little leisure on the frontier. Women helped with the plowing and the harvesting, the building of cabins and the fighting of Indians. The image of woman as a gentle creature with limited abilities whose existence revolved around subservience to her husband failed to correspond with reality, and the men knew it. The arguments of the suffragists, both men and women, were much more persuasive here than they could ever have been in the East.

As the result of the enfranchisement of women by the various western states, women's suffrage began to attract serious opponents. The ridiculous fulminations of men whose only reaction to women voting was a gut-level emotional one, gave way to more sinister antagonists. Three major interests aligned themselves against women's suffrage around the beginning of this century. These were the major corporations, who had no use for the huge increases in the working class vote that women's enfranchisement would bring; the brewers and distillers, who saw in the women the fatal ally of the prohibition movement; and the southern delegation in Congress, which continued to identify the women's movement with the abolitionist cause.

The women were quick to comprehend that their early successes in the western states could never lead to a satisfactory outcome nationwide. After nearly 50 years of effort before state legislatures, only 17 percent of the total population lived in suffrage states (in 1915).[19] Therefore, the focus was increasingly placed on attempts to amend the federal constitution. The work of women to secure the vote continued in the states after 1900, and they enjoyed some notable success. However, the final chapter of the fight for women's vote was written in Washington. Susan B. Anthony was an early leader of this move, and in 1878, what became known as the

Anthony Amendment was introduced in Congress. Section I read: "The right of citizens of the United States to vote shall not be denied or abridged by the United States or by any state on account of sex."

The opposition arrayed its forces impressively. One estimate claims that the brewers and distillers alone collected between $4 and $10 *million* each year to fight the Anthony Amendment.[20] Although the amendment was introduced in each session of Congress beginning in 1878, it was brought to a vote only once before 1914. The combination of corporate funding and the southern bloc's intransigence made the women's goal seem remote indeed.

Woodrow Wilson was elected President in 1912, and the women hoped that he might use his influence in favor of their cause. They were disappointed. Early in his administration, he declared himself to be uninformed on the women's issue. The women thereupon deluged the White House with deputation after deputation, until an exasperated President declared that he would receive no more women who wanted to speak about voting. Instead, he passed responsibility for getting results on the Anthony Amendment to his party, and accordingly advised the women to devote their attention to "concerting public opinion."

How to achieve this concert of public opinion was a question that divided the women's movement from one end to the other. The traditional, and by far the larger, wealthier part, the National American Women's Suffrage Association, determined that it would continue its conventional lobbying efforts. The second group, which broke away from the NAWSA, took the name of the National Women's Party. The difference that led to this split was the choice by the NWP to employ radical tactics to gain the approval of the Anthony Amendment.

The NWP began to carry out its plans on January 10, 1917, when a small group of women began to picket the White House. For five months, these pickets maintained their vigil, undisturbed by District police. However, in June, a change occurred. Between then and November 1917, over 500 suffragists were arrested, and 168 served prison terms, primarily for convictions on the charge of obstructing traffic.[21] This occurred in spite of the fact that there was no law in the District of Columbia that forbade picketing and the fact that the sidewalk in front of the White House where the pickets stationed themselves was 40 feet wide.

The actions of the NWP were hotly debated both inside and outside the women's movement. Because of the NWP picketing and the accompanying violence, many groups, especially the NAWSA, speculated that the entire suffrage movement would be set back 20 years or more. But one thing was assured, the picketing and arrests gained literally acres of newsprint for the women. The District police unwittingly abetted the women's cause by mistreating their prisoners in a variety of ways. A leader of the NWP wrote:

> The jail in which the pickets were first imprisoned was unspeakably dirty and was infested with vermin and rats ... the rats were so large and strong that prisoners at night could actually hear the light cell-chairs being moved by them. One night [a prisoner] beat three of the rats, one after another, off [her] bed ... the poison used by the prison officials did not decrease the rats, and the dog that was brought in seemed afraid of them.[22]

An officer of the workhouse where the women were held filed an affidavit in 1917 that contained the following:

> Officers are warned not to touch any of the bedding. The one officer who has to handle it is compelled by the regulations to wear rubber gloves while she does so ... the beans, hominy, rice, cornmeal ... and cereal have all had worms in them. Sometimes the worms float on top of the soup.[23]

Many of the women were kept for as long as five weeks in solitary confinement and several went on hunger strikes to demonstrate their belief that they were being held as political prisoners. All told, it is a wonder that these events failed to produce a martyr for the women's cause.

Whether the picketing and imprisonments of the members of the NWP during the summer and fall of 1917 were critical to the fight for the ballot cannot be determined. They probably helped. But other forces were loose in the land that also came to the women's aid. The Eighteenth (Prohibition) Amendment to the Constitution was ratified in 1919, and suddenly the brewers and distillers had lost their battle. Their primary motive for opposing women's suffrage vanished, and their forces dwindled.

A second great event, one that unwittingly gave a tremendous boost to the women's cause, was the First World War. In the beginning, this may have been a military war only, but in the end, it was a war fought for the forces of democracy, equal rights, and national self-determination. The women, particularly the NAWSA, threw themselves wholeheartedly into the war effort. They did not neglect, however, to point out to the politicians the rankling injustice that arose when one contrasted the fine democratic principles for which Americans died in Europe with the naked fact that at home half the population did not share in that democracy.

Finally, after fighting a political war without political weapons for so many years, by the 1916 election 11 states had given women the vote, and they began to cast it to elect proamendment senators and representatives. Woodrow Wilson endorsed the 1916 Democratic Party platform plank on women's suffrage, which supported the principle, but held that it was up to the states to enfranchise women. Women knew that this philosophy meant their defeat, and brought considerable pressure to bear on Charles Evans Hughes, the Republican nominee, to endorse the Anthony Amendment.

This he did, and lost the election. However, Wilson's victory in 1916 was much narrower than it had been four years earlier, and the Republicans began to see that it would be to their distinct political advantage if they could capture the banner as the champion of women's suffrage and lead millions of new Republican women into the electorate.

Wilson naturally realized this possibility too, and finally, on January 9, 1918, he changed his position on the Anthony Amendment. He instructed the Democratic delegation from the House, which had come to him for advice, to support the amendment. The following day, January 10, 1918, which was 40 years to the day after Susan B. Anthony had first submitted her amendment, and one year to the day after the first pickets appeared at the gates of the White House, the House of Representatives approved the measure by the necessary two-thirds majority, with one vote to spare.

The Senate, however, was not quite ready. It was not until a year later that the necessary vote emerged from the upper house. By that time, however, ratification was a foregone conclusion. The only question remaining was whether women across the country would be able to vote for President in 1920. The necessary 36 states voted to ratify within 15 months, and Warren G. Harding became the first man to be elected President by a vote of both men and women in every state in the union.

BLACK SUFFRAGE

Harding came into office with a vote of a vastly increased electorate, but one major group of Americans still stood outside. The story of the struggle for black suffrage is a great deal more complicated than was the struggle for women's suffrage. The women fought one long battle over a period of three-quarters of a century. They overcame heavy odds, and when they had won, the vote was theirs, and the country was ready to give it to them.

Blacks followed quite a different path, and a far more arduous one. The story of black suffrage in the United States begins in the early history of the abolitionist movement in the North. Prior to the Civil War, six New England states had granted all males, regardless of race, equality at the polls.[24] However, few blacks resided in these areas, and there was certainly no black presence in public policy anywhere in the United States before the 1860s.

As we all know, the Civil War resulted in the sudden *de jure* enfranchisement of nearly all black males, through the Reconstruction Act of 1867 and the Fifteenth Amendment, which was ratified in 1870. The process by which this monumental change in the electorate took place is less well understood, however. The war began not as a conflict that aimed at giving the vote to blacks; some historians doubt that its aim was even to emancipate the slaves.[25] It was not until 1863, after more than two years of war, that Lincoln issued the Emancipation Proclamation, out of a combination of humanitarian, political, and military motives.

Of course, Lincoln did not live to achieve the reunification of the nation; that task fell to his Vice President, Andrew Johnson. The Thirteenth Amendment had been ratified in December 1865, so there was no question of any continuation of slavery. Beyond this, Johnson demanded very little. The states had abolished slavery, repealed the ordinances of secession and recognized the Union. As far as the new President was concerned, the constitutions of the states that had been in force before the war continued to be the legal documents of government. He felt in 1866 that the task of reconstruction was finished.

Congress refused to accept this position. While Lincoln had been a Republican at the head of a Republican Congress, Johnson was a Democrat. His relationship with Congress, which was dominated by the radical Republicans who were bent on punishing the South, was hostile and bitter in the extreme. The issues of reconstruction led to a series of more than 20 vetoes, 12 of which were overridden, as well as impeachment proceedings against Johnson himself, which fell short of actual conviction in the Senate by a single vote.

The position taken by Congress was simple. "No senator or representative shall be admitted to either branch of Congress from any of said [southern] States until Congress shall have declared such state entitled to representation."[26] Being entitled to representation meant in turn that the states were expected to amend their constitutions to include black males in the electorate.

With the exception of Tennessee, the southern states refused, at first, to comply with this demand. However, Congress had the authority of a victorious army behind it, and in 1867, the Reconstruction Act mandated these states to accept blacks into the electorate by treating them not as states but as conquered territory. These new voters were quickly organized by Northerners who arrived in the South with their belongings packed in the typical suitcase of the time, the carpet bag. The white electorate was at the same time severely diminished by the exclusion of Confederate soldiers and officeholders (including such trivial posts as coroner).

These reconstruction legislatures were naturally compliant with the wishes of the radical Republican Congress in Washington and during the years 1867 and 1868, all the remaining states of the South amended their constitutions to include male Negroes. A point of great bitterness was created by the fact that Congress imposed no such requirement on the states of the North, many of which continued to exclude blacks. In fact, in 1868 the Ohio legislature passed its notorious "Visible Admixture Law," which required election officials to challenge the ballot of any person who displayed "visible admixture" of Negro blood and white blood.[27] At the end of the War, 18 states of the North and West continued to deny the vote to blacks.[28]

Congress proceeded to readmit the states of the Confederacy, and by 1868, the Union was once again complete. For a variety of reasons, however, the radical Republicans remained dissatisfied. Their goal may have been motivated by an honest devotion to the ideal of equality of the races, but it is also clear that they had down-to-earth political motives as well. They saw the black vote as the force that would bring the South into the Republican Party permanently, thus assuring the political dominance of the party nationwide.

The Republicans' insecurity led to the final Civil War amendment, the Fifteenth. This incorporated into the U.S. Constitution the right of the black man to vote, and placed this right beyond the reach of any state legislature to alter. It was ratified with the help of the reconstruction legislatures of the South, and became part of the Constitution in 1870.

While the military occupation of the South continued for six more years, the Fifteenth Amendment marked the end of the efforts of the Reconstruction Congress on behalf of the Negro. He had been brought into the electorate, into the state legislatures, and into the United States Congress. Fourteen black representatives and two black senators served in Washington between 1869 and 1876.[29] Reconstruction had enfranchised more than 703,000 blacks at a time when the total white registration in the reconstructed states was 627,000.[30]

The withdrawal of federal troops from the South hinged on a political question, just as their stationing had been in large part a political move. Hayes and Tilden contested the presidency in 1876, and the result was extremely close. After considerable bargaining, Hayes, the Republican, got the White House, and the South got the removal of the troops. The fact that Tilden had won the popular vote was conveniently ignored.[31]

With the departure of federal authority, however, blacks could not expect to remain in the positions of influence to which that authority had brought them. They lacked education and experience, and the same class of whites who had governed the South before the war—the planters, the merchants and the professionals, the so-called conservative, or "bourbon" Democrats—returned to the centers of influence throughout the South with reasonably little difficulty.

It would be a mistake to assume, however, that the black population was immediately resubjugated. In fact, this did not occur during the 20-year period after 1876, which has come to be known as the Redemption Period.[32] It is true that the white "bourbons" had regained political control. They did not repress the black population, however. Theirs was a conservative view of race, a highly paternalistic one in which the black was treated as one would a child in need of guidance. Most significantly, blacks maintained their right to vote. In Mississippi in 1890, some 71,000 more blacks than whites were registered to vote, and 130,000 blacks were registered to vote in Louisiana in 1896.[33] Black representatives continued to take their seats in the various state legislatures, and a black was sent to Washington from a North Carolina constituency until 1901. While it was far from a golden age of race relations, neither did it resemble the period of segregation and racial violence that was to follow.

Around the turn of the century, the Redemption Period came rather abruptly to an end, to be followed by nearly a half-century of utter and complete subjugation of blacks by the "lower instincts of the worst class of whites in the South."[34] This shift, during which blacks lost all their political rights, along with their very dignity as human beings, came about as a direct result of the Populist movement, which sought to unite rural and agrarian interests against eastern money trusts, corporations, and monopolies. Tom Watson, a foremost leader of southern Populism, imagined a platform which both races would benefit from supporting. "You are made to hate each other," he said, "because upon that hatred is rested the keystone of the arch of financial despotism which enslaves you both."[35] It may well be that during the brief Populist upheaval of the 1890s, Negroes and native whites reached a greater common understanding and harmony of political purpose than ever before or since in the South.

The reaction of the conservative Democrats, whose financial despotism gave rise to Watson's reference, was swift. A union of poor whites and blacks in the voting booth threatened their power. They therefore confronted the challenge by removing the blacks from all political influence. And so it was. The Mississippi Constitution of 1890 is generally accepted as the model document that set out the various legal entrapments that succeeded in disenfranchising the black man.[36] It, and later refinements, included the poll tax, which required not only payment but also the retention of the receipt, and which could accumulate so that if an individual did not vote regularly, he could be saddled with a tax of 20 or 30 dollars. They included a literacy test, requiring the ability to read the constitution, and an understanding clause, which required the prospective voter to interpret passages from various legal documents. There was also a "good character clause," in which the potential voter was required to present a registered voter who would vouch for his moral qualities. The effect of these measures cannot be questioned. Nearly three-quarters of a million blacks had been registered to vote during Reconstruction. In 1890 hundreds of thousands remained on the voting lists, in spite of the reestablishment of white rule. Then, in the ten-year period from 1896 to 1905, the black voter vanished from the South. The state of Louisiana provides an example. In 1896, 130,334 blacks were registered. In 1904, 1342 blacks remained on the rolls.[37] In the former year, black registrants were in the majority in 26 parishes. By 1900, no parish had a black majority.[38]

The awkward thing about these legal entrapments was not that they failed to remove blacks from the voting rolls. In this they succeeded very well. Rather, they also eliminated a great number of white voters, who were nearly as poor and illiterate as the blacks. It was only through a grossly discriminatory application of these standards that the desired outcome could be obtained.

In order to avoid the necessity of indulging in dishonesty, the southern states turned to two other mechanisms that offered a much neater solution. They were the "grandfather clause" and the white primary. The grandfather clause was variously applied, but in essence it gave automatic registration to anyone who was eligible to vote before 1867, or who was a descendent of such a person. Naturally, no black qualified, while most of the whites who would ordinarily have been unable to pay a poll tax or pass a literacy test could be registered.

The grandfather clause had a short life-span. Although the Supreme Court had consistently upheld the various techniques for disenfranchisement discussed above, the grandfather clause proved too much, and it was declared unconstitutional in 1915.[39]

Fortunately for those who were inconvenienced by the 1915 decision, the political reform movement of the turn of the century provided them with what proved to be the most effective technique for disenfranchising blacks, the primary system. The primary was conceived as a way of opening up the selection of candidates. However, the southern states soon found that it could serve another purpose. They took the position that the Democratic Party was not a creature of the state, controlled by state law, but rather a private organization. As such, it could restrict its membership, and therefore the participation in its elections, without violating the Fourteenth and Fifteenth Amendments. Since nearly the entire white population in the South voted Democratic, whether the blacks voted against them on election day was immaterial; the Democrat would win. The Democratic primary, therefore, became the election which actually selected the eventual winner.

As was the case with earlier efforts to prevent the southern black from voting, the white primary had its day before the Supreme Court. In fact, it had two of them. The first, *Grovey* v. *Townsend,* which was heard in 1935, ended in the manner so familiar to civil rights lawyers of that time; the court upheld the white primary.[40]

But the times were changing. The Great Depression had worked a political transformation on the land. Franklin Roosevelt became President in 1932, the first Democrat since Woodrow Wilson. He made it clear that he intended to make his party the defender of the little man, the man who had been thrown into the soup lines by the stock market crash of 1929.

While Roosevelt made very few direct gestures to the blacks, they could scarcely be excluded from New Deal ideology. Just as the cause of women's suffrage had won the approval of public opinion at the turn of the century, now the hour of the Negro would come, 50 years afterward.

The first major event in the demolition of the Jim Crow laws, those legal barriers that had been erected to keep the black man out of the electorate (and out of virtually every other place occupied by whites), came in 1944. Since the *Grovey* decision of 1935, Roosevelt's appointments to the Supreme Court had come into the majority. This new Court, only nine years after affirming the white primary, reversed itself in *Smith* v. *Allwright*, declaring the white primary to be unconstitutional.[41]

Yet the demise of the white primary did not result in any dramatic increase in black registration. About five percent of voting-age blacks in the southern states were registered in 1940; yet by 1947, which was three years after the *Smith* decision, the figure had advanced only to 12 percent.

There are three major reasons for the failure of southern blacks to take greater advantage of the situation. First, public opinion, in the North as well as the South, had not yet coalesced. Blacks who desired to register found few white allies. The federal government, outside of the Supreme Court, sensed no public mandate to act, and did virtually nothing for black voting rights for 13 years following the 1944 decision.

The lack of public support had a second consequence which was far more serious from the southern black's personal point of view. It meant

TABLE 2.1. Southern Blacks and Whites Registered to Vote: 1940–1976

	Percent of Voting Age Individuals Registered	
Year	Black	White
1940	5	NA
1952	20	NA
1956	25	NA
1960	29	NA
1962	29	53
1964	43	63
1966	53	64
1968	62	71
1970	58	65
1972	64	70
1974	55	61
1976	56	67

Sources: Adapted from Donald R. Matthews and James W. Protho, *Negroes and the New Southern Politics*, © 1966 by Harcourt Brace Jovanovich, Inc. Reprinted by permission of the publisher; and Current Population Reports, *Population Characteristics*, Voter Participation in November 1976 (advance report), Series P–20, No. 304 (December 1976), p. 2.

that no restraint was placed on the small minority of southern whites who acted out their racial prejudices in the most nauseating kind of violence. Racial violence is nothing new, of course, in the North or the South. Over 3400 blacks were lynched in this country between 1882 and 1927.[42] Perhaps it is only because the violence directed at southern blacks who sought their right to vote was eventually laid open to such public scrutiny that we find it so abhorrent. Whatever the case, physical intimidation was one of the major techniques that kept the blacks away from southern voting booths in the decades following 1944.

I can hardly begin to document the scope and nature of the violence that befell so many blacks during this time. In literally hundreds and thousands of isolated incidents, blacks, as well as whites who took their side, were harassed, terrorized, beaten, and killed by the uncontrolled element of southern white society. It was not only the Ku Klux Klan that precipitated incidents of physical brutality against blacks. Often enough, those responsible were officials of local government.

> An example of physical intimidation, surprising even in the South for its openness, involved the registrar of Walthall County, Mississippi. A young civil rights worker accompanied two local residents who were seeking to register. The registrar drove them from his office, striking the leader on the head with a pistol butt. After stopping the bleeding, the assaulted youth reported the incident to the sheriff, who responded by arresting the victim for disturbing the peace.[43]

Slowly, however, the majority of whites began to take notice of the blacks' plight. Slowly, blacks began to organize to demand their rights. Physical intimidation of blacks one at a time could easily be accomplished by local hoodlums, hidden from the view of the world outside. But intimidating 100 or 200 blacks who might appear at the courthouse to register at the same time was another matter. To be sure, Sheriff Eugene "Bull" Conner in Birmingham and others elsewhere did not flinch from the task. Blacks demonstrating for their right to vote were beaten by the hundreds, but this time people took notice. The sight of one of Bull Conner's dogs attacking a black man could be obtained in every city in the country for the price of a newspaper. National leaders emerged at the head of the black cause. When Martin Luther King was jailed in Montgomery and John Kennedy telephoned his condolences, the entire country knew.

The climax of the organized confrontation between blacks demanding their civil rights, and whites defending the old order, came in Selma, Alabama, in March 1965.[44] Selma was intended to be the culmination of the civil rights movement, the catalyst that would transform blacks overnight into full participants in the political system.

Selma had been the scene of voter registration activity for two years. In 1963 there were 200 blacks registered out of a possible 15,115. The registration office was open two Mondays a month, and even when the movement began to bring blacks in to register, they found the registrar unable to process more than 30 a day. Even going on the incredible assumption that all blacks would be accepted, it would have taken more than ten years to enroll as many blacks as whites.

Throughout the winter of 1964–1965, demonstrations were organized around Selma. In January, Martin Luther King arrived to open the voter drive of his organization, the Southern Christian Leadership Conference. In February, 105 black teachers lined up to register, and were shoved away with nightsticks. A young people's march resulted in the arrest of 165 children, some of whom were under 12. They were taken on a forced march, at a pace somewhere between a fast walk and a run, two miles to the jail.

On March 6 a band of 70 white Alabama citizens marched in support of the blacks' right to vote in Selma. It was the first all-white demonstration by Southerners in the history of the movement. It was a brave act, and it carried a signal, which few in Selma could see: The cause of civil rights had begun to spread beyond the southern blacks and the few whites who were involved in the movement. In only three days' time, the whole nation would be drawn in.

It was on March 9 that 525 blacks attempted to march from Selma to Montgomery in direct defiance of Governor George Wallace's order that they refrain from so doing. The march resulted in the attack on them at the Edmund Pettus Bridge on the edge of downtown Selma.

> The nation saw their line on television standing there, orderly, asking the 50 state troopers up ahead for a word, and heard Major John Cloud say, "There is no word to be had . . ." And: "You have two minutes to turn around and go back to your church." Then the awful moment of their just standing there, the troopers and Sheriff Clark's volunteer posse advancing on them with clubs, with horses, with whips, and with tear gas, and routing them the six blocks back to their church in helpless, defenseless terror, with attacks made again and again. This kind of thing had happened before—how many times in the voter effort alone across the South? But now the nation saw it, as it never had before, and responded, as it never had before. People dropped everything, many of them, that very Sunday night and flew to Selma, not planning ahead, just determined to do something about the outrage.[45]

Four days after the violence at the Edmund Pettus Bridge, on March 13 President Johnson announced that he would send a voting rights bill to Congress. On March 26 a 58-mile march from Selma to Montgomery ended successfully under the protection of the U.S. Army. That night, as she returned to Montgomery after ferrying marchers back to Selma, Viola Liuzzo, a white housewife from Detroit, was murdered.[46] Her death culminated a series of events which galvanized sympathy for the civil rights movement nationwide. Civil rights became a popular cause in 1965, a fact that weighed heavily in the ultimate resolution of the blacks' struggle.

The third impediment that stood between the blacks and the vote in the South after 1944 was the fact that although the white primary had ceased to exist, a multitude of other laws still enabled county registrars to discriminate. Many of these laws were identical to those passed after 1890. They included the literacy test, the understanding clause, the good character clause, and the poll tax.

Examples of the discriminatory application of these techniques abound in the documents assembled by the Civil Rights Division of the Department of Justice during the 1960s. Six blacks with doctorates were ruled illiterate in Alabama and five black teachers, three of whom held master's degrees, were judged to be illiterate in a Mississippi city in which no whites had ever failed the examination.[47] In Mississippi, whites were often given Section 240 of the state constitution to interpret, which reads: "All elections by the people shall be by ballot." Blacks, on the other hand, were often confronted with Section 182, which states:

> The power to tax corporations and their property shall never be surrendered or abridged by any contract or grant to which the state or any political subdivision thereof may be a party, except that the legislature may grant exemption from taxation in the encouragement of manufacturers and other new enterprises of public utility extending for a period not exceeding five years, the time of such exemptions to commence from the date of charter, if to a corporation; and if to an individual enterprise, then from the commencement of work; but when the legislature grants such exemptions for a period of five years or less, it shall be done by general laws, which shall distinctly enumerate the classes of manufacturers and other new enterprises of public utility entitled to such exemptions, and shall prescribe the mode and manner in which the right to such exemptions shall be determined.[48]

As public awareness of the civil rights movement began to grow, and as the blacks' cause began to be viewed with greater sympathy (a sympathy produced in large measure by the tales of violence that filtered out of the South), Congress finally began to act. Between 1957 and 1964, three acts were passed, over the increasingly loud objections of the southern delegations. The first of these, the Civil Rights Act of 1957, created the Civil Rights Division in the Department of Justice. It also gave the attorney general the right to defend blacks who were denied the vote for reasons of race, where previously the suits had to be brought privately.[49]

The chief flaw of the 1957 act was that when confronted by federal legal actions, registrars simply resigned and registration boards were abolished. The government was left with nothing to sue.[50] The Civil Rights Act of

1960 addressed these problems in four ways. First, the attorney general was allowed to proceed against not only the individual registrars, but the states themselves. Second, the states were required to preserve voting records for 22 months. Third, voting records were declared subject to federal inspection. Fourth, if federal judges found "pattern or practice" of discrimination, a federal referee could be named with the power to register voters.

The Civil Rights Act of 1964 begins to reveal a bit of congressional impatience. Investigations by the Department of Justice had begun to show that blacks were being refused registration for such errors as failing to calculate their age correctly to the exact day, while whites who made similar errors were allowed to register. The 1964 act forbade rejections of applicants for such immaterial errors or omissions. It also declared that anyone who possessed a sixth-grade education was to be presumed literate for the purpose of voting.[51]

Unfortunately, these three acts had a disappointing effect on black registration. Table 2.1 shows that by 1964 a significant increase had come about, but fewer than half of the blacks of voting age in the South had registered. The President's Commission on Civil Rights summarized the situation as follows:

> The Civil Rights Acts of 1957, 1960, and 1964 . . . were unsuccessful attempts to compel state registration officials to apply their state voting standards fairly. Progress under these acts was painfully slow, partly because of the intransigence of state and local officials and partly because of the delays inherent in the case-by-case litigation required under these statutes.[52]

It may have been for political reasons that the commission failed to mention another reason for this slow progress: the intransigence of federal judges. Particularly under the provisions of the 1960 act, the willingness of these men to find "pattern or practice" of discrimination affected the progress of blacks quite directly.

One of the most notorious judges to confront this act was William Harold Cox of Mississippi. Cox was a Kennedy appointee, but philosophically felt much closer to his old law school roommate, Senator James Eastland. He once revealed his feelings in an unguarded comment in which he likened some Negroes to "chimpanzees" who "ought to be in the movies rather than being registered to vote."[53]

With such an attitude, one can imagine that a decision finding "pattern or practice" of discrimination would not be one which Judge Cox would make lightly. For example, in spite of a record of consistent reversals by the Fifth Circuit Court of Appeals, Cox managed to delay for more than four years any federal action whatsoever in Clarke County, Mississippi. He found no pattern or practice of discrimination, in spite of the fact that not a single Negro out of a population of 3000 had registered to vote for 30 years.[54]

In spite of delays and setbacks, the tide of the civil rights movement gained strength with each passing year, and in 1965 the dam broke. Selma had implanted sympathy for the black struggle in the mind of white America. The Voting Rights Act of 1965, submitted to Congress four days after the confrontation at Pettus Bridge, was designed to sweep away once and for all the mechanisms which the southern states and counties had erected to delay the registration of black voters. At the heart of the 1965 act was the "trigger clause," which declared in part that its provisions were to apply to all states and counties in which less than 50 percent of the voting age population was registered or had voted in 1964. This affected six southern states, Alaska, and some counties in North Carolina. In those areas covered by the act all tests and devices used to screen potential registrants were prohibited, except for age, length of residence, and criminal record.

Most important, the act provided that federal registrars could go into the affected counties and register people, in place of the elected officers of the county. This clause was accompanied by a 95 percent increase in the budget of the Civil Rights Division of the Department of Justice.

The 1965 act did make important inroads on the problems of black voting. Over 130,000 persons were registered by federal registrars in the first year of the act.[55] Many more blacks found themselves able to register in counties that had not been visited by the federal registrars, evidently because of the desire of the local officials to avoid being taken over by these authorities from the outside.

However, the 1965 act was not the millennium that some had predicted. Enormous numbers of blacks remained unregistered. This may have been due to the fact that registrants in the early years were the "easy" ones. These were the highly educated, highly motivated individuals, who lived in urban areas, away from the intimidation of possible physical violence or economic retaliation on the part of whites. By 1965 those who remained unregistered came from the segment of the population that would be difficult to reach under the best of conditions, the poor, the elderly, or the very young, and those who lived in isolated rural areas.

Successes in the registration of blacks continued after 1966 until 1970, when approximately two-thirds of the black voting-age population of the South was registered. (The decline that can be seen after 1972 is produced primarily by the passage of the Twenty-sixth Amendment, which brought politically inactive 18–20-year-olds into the electorate.) Most of the old laws that deprived the black of his franchise have now been banished permanently. The literacy test was banned by Congress in the 1975 amendments to the Voting Rights Act. The poll tax was outlawed through the ratification of the Twenty-fourth Amendment in 1966. The 1965 Civil

Rights Act has been reaffirmed twice, once in 1970 and again in 1975. The effect has been to make certain of its provisions permanent and to extend them to the entire country.

This chapter of history is not quite over. We find that resistance to black political power has in some cases fallen back to a second line of defense, centered in the creation or maintenance of at-large constituencies, for instance. Nonetheless, it is in its last pages. The rule of law has come to most of the South, and there is no turning back.

SUMMARY

We have seen in this chapter how, in three separate instances, large groups of ordinary people have achieved a goal that the political system initially refused to grant. Men without property, women, and finally blacks have demanded the right to vote, and using techniques that were primarily aggregate and indirect, have won this right.

Consider the example of the women's suffrage movement. Of course, the women who captured the headlines were the pickets who were arrested and thrown in jail. Perhaps it may be said that they were acting in a single, indirect manner. It is significant to remember, however, that these women were backed up by an immense national organization. When a picket was arrested, this fact was immediately communicated to the editors of hundreds of newspapers across the country. Every senator and representative was contacted, and virtually every organization that would listen received the news. Without this organization, the White House pickets would never have been able to exercise the influence that they did. So an analysis of women's suffrage should go beyond the pickets to reveal the true core of the movement, which existed in the broadly based organization that backed up the demonstrators. It is much more accurate to label this an *aggregate,* not single, influence.

The civil rights movement also illustrates the indirect nature of popular influence. Blacks held only a few congressional seats in the 1960s, and made up only a small fraction of the national electorate. They could accomplish very little in a direct way, to achieve the vote. Virtually the only political resource available to them was to sway public opinion in their favor. The powerful force that finally made the vote a reality for most blacks was the perception by millions of people that the cause of civil rights was basically just.

All told, these three cases of struggle for the vote should remind us all of the possibilities that are open to efforts at influence of the aggregate and indirect kind. They stand as witness to the potential power of the common people.

NOTES

1. Marchette Chute, *The First Liberty: A History of the Right to Vote in America, 1619–1850* (New York: Dutton, 1969), pp. 253 and 223.
2. *Ibid.*, p. 209.
3. These laws differed from state to state and value was expressed in pounds. We therefore do not make any attempt to detail what the restrictions were. Chute, *op. cit.*, provides an excellent summary.
4. Since there was no income tax in the 1780s, these laws were still tantamount to a property requirement. However, individuals could qualify to vote by possessing even the smallest amount of property, and that property did not need to be in land; it could be a house in one of the towns, for instance. It is also interesting to note that the vote was granted outright to members of the militia in many states. These were often poor men without property, who would otherwise have been excluded from government. The Conservative power brokers of the eastern seaboard, while they did not favor such expansions of the suffrage in principle, thought it prudent not to offend the army, which had recently brought Great Britain to defeat.
5. Chilton Williamson, *American Suffrage from Property to Democracy: 1760–1860* (Princeton, N.J.: Princeton University Press, 1960), pp. 24–38
6. Harold F. Gosnell, *Democracy: The Threshold of Freedom* (New York: Ronald, 1948), p. 36.
7. This estimate is from Robert Lane, *Political Life: Why People Get Involved in Politics* (New York: Free Press, 1959), p. 19.
8. Albert Bushnell Hart, "The Exercise of the Suffrage," *Political Science Quarterly*, vol. 7, no. 2 (June 1892), 307–329.
9. Williamson, *op. cit.*, p. 283.
10. Caroline Katzenstein, *Lifting the Curtain* (Philadelphia: Dorrance, 1955), p. 14.
11. *Ibid.*
12. Carrie Chapman Catt and Nellie Rodgers Shuler, *Woman Suffrage and Politics* (New York: Scribner's, 1926), p. 9. Although it seems unbelievable today, this exclusion was justified on the grounds that women "had not supported the right candidates in the election" and had thereby demonstrated their incompetence to assume this public trust.
13. Kirk Harold Porter, *A History of Suffrage in the United States* (New York: AMS Press, Inc., 1971), p. 138.
14. Katzenstein, *op. cit.*, p. 19.
15. V. O. Key, Jr., *Politics, Parties and Pressure Groups*, 5th ed. (New York: Crowell, 1964), p. 613.
16. Catt and Shuler, *op. cit.*, p. 14.
17. Katzenstein, *op. cit.*, p. 29.
18. Montana, North Dakota, South Dakota, and Washington in 1889; Idaho and Wyoming in 1890 (Wyoming became a state in 1890); and Utah in 1896.
19. Gosnell, *op. cit.*, p. 52.
20. Catt and Shuler, *op. cit.*, p. 141.
21. Katzenstein, *op. cit.*, p. 206.
22. *Ibid.*, p. 245.
23. *Ibid.*, pp. 246–247.
24. Forrest G. Wood, *Black Scare: The Racist Response to Emancipation and Reconstruction* (Berkeley: University of California Press, 1968), p. 82.
25. Key, *op. cit.*, p. 602; Porter, *op. cit.*, pp. 150ff.; Gosnell, *op. cit.*, p. 94.
26. Porter, *op. cit.*, p. 166.
27. Wood, *op. cit.*, p. 83.

34   SETTING THE STAGE

28. *Ibid.*, 85–86.
29. *Ibid.*, pp. 90–91.
30. Pat Watters and Reese Cleghorn, *Climbing Jacob's Ladder: The Arrival of Negroes in Southern Politics* (New York: Harcourt, 1967), p. 9.
31. Key, *op. cit.*, p. 602.
32. For further information on this period see C. Vann Woodward, *The Strange Career of Jim Crow* (New York: Oxford, 1955).
33. Harrell R. Rodgers and Charles S. Bullock, III, *Law and Social Change: Civil Rights Laws and Their Consequences* (New York: McGraw-Hill, 1972), p. 17
34. Woodward, *op. cit.*, p. 32.
35. *Ibid.*, pp. 44–45.
36. Porter, *op. cit.*, pp. 208ff.
37. Rodgers and Bullock, *op. cit.*, p. 17.
38. Woodward, *op. cit.*, p. 68.
39. *Guinn and Beal* v. *United States,* 238 U.S. 348 (1915).
40. *Grovey* v. *Townsend,* 295 U.S. 45 (1935).
41. *Smith* v. *Allwright,* 321 U.S. 649 (1944).
42. Gerald M. Pomper, *Elections in America: Control and Influence in Democratic Politics* (New York: Dodd, Mead, 1970), p. 219.
43. Rodgers and Bullock, *op. cit.*, pp. 19–20. Quoted from Anthony Lewis, *Portrait of a Decade* (New York: Random House, 1964), pp. 126–128.
44. The following paragraphs are drawn from Pat Watters and Reece Cleghorn, *op. cit.*
45. *Ibid.*, p. 253.
46. In spite of the bestiality of some acts in the fight for the black vote, it should not be impossible to understand the anguish that many southern whites faced. Many whites believed two things about the civil rights movement and believed them with religious fervor. First, they believed that if the black was ever recognized as the social equal of the white, a terrible fate would befall the South; life would be forever and irredeemably changed in ways which were unknown, and therefore feared. Second, many southern whites believed that those whites who arrived in their towns to help the blacks were Communists who had embarked on the civil rights movement as one step in their master plan to subvert the government and bring the entire country under the hammer and sickle.

It may be difficult for today's readers, especially if they are not southern, to accept that people could actually believe those things. But they did, and they believed them sincerely. Some still do, although the course of events makes it more difficult with each passing year. And believing those things made it extremely difficult, indeed impossible, for many Southerners to take the side of the blacks against the violence of the police and the Klan.

47. Rodgers and Bullock, *op. cit.*, pp. 21ff. Quoted from the U.S. Commission on Civil Rights, 1959 Report (Washington, D.C.: GPO, 1960), p. 80, and *U.S.* v. *Lynd,* 301 F.2d 818 (1962).
48. Quoted from the U.S. Commission on Civil Rights, *Voting in Mississippi* (Washington, D.C.: GPO, 1965), pp. 14–15.
49. It has been estimated that the Brown case on school desegregation cost the NAACP $300,000.
50. Watters and Cleghorn, *op. cit.*, pp. 211–212.
51. Rodgers and Bullock, *op. cit.*, p. 26.
52. *Ibid.*, p. 28. Quoted from U.S. Commission on Civil Rights, *The Voting Rights Act* (Washington, D.C.: GPO, 1965), p. 8.
53. Watters and Cleghorn, *op. cit.*, p. 216.
54. *Ibid.*, pp. 216–217. This is not to imply that there were no forthright or courageous federal judges in the South, for indeed there were.
55. *Ibid.*, p. 244.

3
An Approach to Political Behavior

I see political behavior as a great mosaic, a picture made up of thousands of multicolored, glittering little chips. We can appreciate its beauty by standing back and looking at its total form, just as we can sit by the television on election night and watch the returns come in, all added up and packaged by the networks. But really to understand the process that produced the mosaic, we have to move in closer, and study how the artist placed each individual chip.

The equivalent of the mosaic chip in political behavior is the attitude. The overall picture has its own message, but true understanding can come only when we see how all of those thousands of attitudes have come together to produce it. This view has led me to use the concept of attitude as the basic structural component of this book. Most of the questions I address ask how attitudes are formed, what their content is, how and why they change, or how they influence behavior. I find that the concept is sufficiently general that it can be applied to a variety of phenomena that on the surface are rather different. This is a tremendous advantage, for it allows us to develop a frame of reference within which much of what happens in the political world can be understood.

A second advantage of an attitudinal approach to political behavior is that we can all identify with it. This is no dusty theory without any personal relevance for today's student. We all have attitudes, and moreover most of us have *political* attitudes of one kind or another. So when we begin talking about party identification, you will probably be able to see yourself in the discussion. And when I assert that if a person's parents are both Democrats, then he or she is probably also a Democrat, you might even find yourself there as well, or at least you will have the satisfaction of saying, "Aha, not me!" Whatever the case, I hope that by presenting politics in this way, you will see that you really are a part of the American electorate, and by studying and understanding that electorate, you will come to understand your own political identity, your obligations, and your potential.

WHAT IS AN ATTITUDE?

Clearly enough, we can't go very far with an attitudinal approach without defining what an attitude is. Psychologists agree (most of them do, anyway), that the attitude is the basic building block of the personality and hence of behavior. They disagree, however, when it comes to definition. For our own purposes, I have adopted a definition that is fairly broad and seeks to avoid excessive psychological jargon.

> An attitude is an individual's readiness or disposition to respond in a favorable or unfavorable manner to some object.[1]

I can discuss this definition by breaking it down into its constituent parts. By "object," for instance, we may mean physical objects that we can touch and see. My attitude toward a policeman will lead me to do certain things when I am in the presence of one. My attitude toward a man who is running for President will contribute to whether or not I pull the lever next to his name on voting day.

But we must expand our definition to include not only physical objects, but "psychological" objects as well. "Democracy," "free enterprise," or "Communism" are not physical objects, but they are certainly objects to which many Americans respond. Suppose the opponents of national health insurance were to succeed in convincing some Americans that the legislation was "Communist" in inspiration. Many people, accepting this argument, would oppose the proposal on the spot. Their position would not be based on any judgment of the pros or cons of national health insurance, but would arise from their overwhelming reaction to the psychological object "Communism."

The second element of the definition involves the notion of response. A response is simply behavior. This may include overt actions like demonstrating or rioting, secret behaviors like voting, or simply spoken statements. The response of many to the supposedly Communist national health insurance proposal mentioned above might be to speak against it, to write letters to the editor, or to vote against a candidate who advocated it.

Finally, the definition contains the idea of "readiness." We can think of the individual as a bundle of potential behaviors. At any moment one of them may be triggered by an encounter with a particular object. An extreme example was portrayed in the 1962 film, *The Manchurian Candidate*, in which the character Raymond Shaw was brainwashed to react to the sight of the queen of hearts from a deck of cards with a series of behaviors that was supposed to result in his assassinating the President.[2] On a more prosaic level, all of us are "primed" by our attitudes to react in certain ways to certain objects. The sight of the American flag generally elicits feelings of pride and patriotism among Americans. The label "Democrat," when attached to a political candidate, will also trigger a positive or negative reaction among many of us. Significantly, such a reaction can occur without any knowledge of the candidate's ideology or positions on various issues, just as many Americans would oppose legislation about which they know nothing, except that it is accused of being Communist inspired.

I am going to carry out this discussion of attitudes at three levels. As Figure 3.1 shows, we first look at the constituent elements that make up attitudes. These include beliefs or cognitions, and evaluation or affect.

Once we have built a single attitude, we shall discuss three concepts which help us to describe and understand each of our attitudes. They are direction, intensity, and centrality. Next, whole attitudes are integrated into sets of attitudes, which are characterized by their constraint and balance. Finally, we shall discuss the nature of the relationships between attitudes and behavior.

Cognition and Affect

Psychologists have conventionally broken attitudes into two components. The first of these is the cognitive component. Part of what we mean when we talk about an attitude toward an object is simply the set of beliefs, or factual information (called cognitions), which we possess about it. We

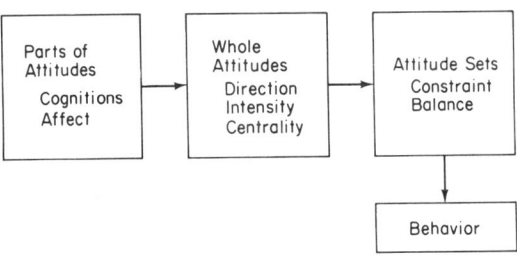

Figure 3.1. Organizational Schema for the Discussion of Attitudes.

know, for instance, that Jimmy Carter is a Southerner and a Democrat; he grows peanuts, smiles a lot, and likes to play softball. We also know that he is the President, and, as we shall see, this one belief probably outweighs all our other bits of factual information in forming our attitude toward the man.

Before a set of beliefs can become a "readiness to react," it must be linked with the second component of attitude, called affect. Associated with many of our beliefs about Jimmy Carter, we also possess a judgment. That is, we have a fact: Jimmy Carter is a Southerner. We (might) also have a judgment: Southerners are nice people. We would therefore say that to this particular cognition of the object "Jimmy Carter," we have associated a *positive affect.*

Not all cognitions have associated affective components. There are a lot of people who know that President Carter likes to play softball, but they couldn't care less. Also, not all belief-affect pairs have the same importance in determining the nature of our overall attitude. Jimmy Carter's characteristics of being a Southerner with an incandescent smile may turn some people off. But there is almost no one in the United States who does not also know that this man is the President, and there are relatively few who fail to consider this fact to be of overwhelming importance. The combination of all these cognitions and their associated affects generates the overall attitude.

I have illustrated this idea in Table 3.1, which lists a few of the beliefs that a person might have about President Carter. Next to each of these, I have indicated whether the belief is associated with a positive or negative affect (signified by a "+" or a "−"). In the third column, I have provided a measure of the importance that each belief-affect pair possesses for this particular hypothetical individual.

We see that on the first five characteristics, this person evaluated Carter negatively. However, none of these beliefs was given much importance in

TABLE 3.1. Elements of a Hypothetical Person's Attitude toward President Carter

Belief	Affect	Importance
He is a Southerner	−	3
He is a Democrat	−	5
He grows peanuts	−	1
He smiles a lot	−	1
He likes softball	−	1
He is President	+	20
		+9

the overall attitude. Only the last piece of information was really considered important in the attitude this person held of Carter. So in spite of five negatively evaluated beliefs, the overall attitude is positive.

Direction and Intensity and Centrality

To describe the nature of political attitudes, we need to distinguish the direction of an attitude from its intensity. In order to do this, we must take the attitude as a whole, neglecting the fact that numerous belief-affect pairs have produced it.

The direction of an attitude may be positive or negative. Clearly, when an individual has a positive attitude toward an object, he or she will act favorably if a situation is encountered where a reaction to that object is appropriate. A favorable attitude may produce a vote for a candidate, a contribution to a campaign, or a signature on a petition. It is the direction of people's attitudes that the Gallup poll attempts to measure the day before the election. For the politician, this is critical information, for it reveals the basic knowledge of whether a majority of the electorate favors a certain candidate or a certain policy.

For those who are a little more thoughtful about public opinion, however, the second characteristic of attitudes holds far greater interest. This characteristic is the intensity of the attitude. The more intensely a person holds an attitude, the more likely he or she is to put that attitude into action when given the opportunity. For example, two fathers may hold attitudes that are identical in their direction: They both oppose busing for purposes of school integration. Yet one may send his children to school on the bus, while the other may withdraw his children from the public school and enroll them, at great expense, in a private school. This difference in behavior cannot arise from differences in the favorability or unfavorability of the attitudes toward school busing. They can only be explained by considering the intensity with which the attitudes are held. The first man opposes school busing, but in his overall scheme of things, this attitude is relatively unimportant. He may also feel that integration is a good thing in principle, or that he doesn't want to separate his children from their friends, or that he can't afford the private school. The second man, on the other hand, feels so strongly about busing that he will act upon that attitude even though it may conflict with others he holds.

Closely related to the intensity of an attitude is its centrality. The most central attitudes tend to be acquired early in life; and, by definition, the more central an attitude, the more closely it is related to the individual's self-concept. The attitude "I am a good person" is one that most of us hold quite centrally. It is part of our essential identity. You can well imagine that a change in this attitude, or in one closely related to it, would be a very traumatic event for most people. Consequently, a central attitude will be held most intensely and will be difficult to change, whereas a peripheral attitude will be changed more easily since it is less intensely held.

Party identification is a commonly held attitude among members of the electorate, and it serves nicely to illustrate how both direction and intensity are incorporated into the measurement of attitude. Typically, when public opinion polls are conducted, the people contacted are asked not only to reveal whether they are Republicans or Democrats (or Independents), but also to say how strong their loyalty is. This questioning produces a scale such as the one which appears in Table 3.2, with strong Democrats at one end, then weak Democrats, Independents, weak Republicans and strong Republicans at the other end. The most intensely held loyalties belong to the strong Republicans and Democrats, and the Independents are the least intense in their sense of partisanship.

Now, if we had settled for the direction of the party identification attitude in conducting our poll, we would have found that 82 percent of Democrats voted for Carter, while only 18 percent of Republicans did so. However, the information in Table 3.2 contains the intensity component as well, and this clearly adds to our information about the relationship between party identification and the vote for President. It illustrates the general principle that intensely held attitudes are more likely to be put into action: Strong Democrats are more likely to have voted for Carter than weak Democrats (92 percent versus 75 percent), and strong Republicans are more likely to have voted for Ford than weak Republicans (97 percent versus 78 percent).

ATTITUDE SETS

We must now face the fact that attitudes do not exist in isolation. Not only do we all hold many attitudes simultaneously, but these attitudes are more or less strongly interrelated in logical terms. If you approve of social welfare legislation, for instance, then you should also approve of Carter as President (all else notwithstanding). And, if your attitude about one of these objects changes, that change should affect the other attitude as well.

TABLE 3.2. The Relationship between Party Identification and the Vote in 1976

	Percent for Carter	*N*
Strong Democrat	92	(270)
Weak Democrat	75	(374)
Independent	45	(532)
Weak Republican	22	(251)
Strong Republican	3	(201)

Source: ICPSR Archive: CPS 1976 Presidential Election Study.

Belief Systems

A set of attitudes that is characterized by an interlocking web of logical relationships is called a belief system. Those attitudes that have political objects are organized into a political belief system. Figure 3.2 presents schematic drawings of two possible belief systems. The circles in these figures represent attitudes, and the lines connecting them represent the logical interlinkages existing between those attitudes.

Constraint. Constraint refers both to the number of linkages in a given belief system, and to the strength of the linkages. People who are well educated, attend to the media, and invest a good deal of effort in understanding their political world should have a highly constrained belief system. That is, these individuals should understand the implications and interdependencies of their attitudes. We all have attitudes about domestic affairs (say, balancing the budget) as well as on foreign affairs (for instance, a belief in the necessity for strong defense). Now, an individual who is careless about his or her attitudes might very easily believe that the budget should be balanced *and* that we should have the strongest possible military force. The more insightful person will realize, however, that such attitudes are inconsistent, since spending more money on the military will increase the federal deficit just as rapidly as anything else. The *constrained* political belief system, which we might call an ideology, will not contain such internal inconsistencies. The ideologue will adopt attitudes according

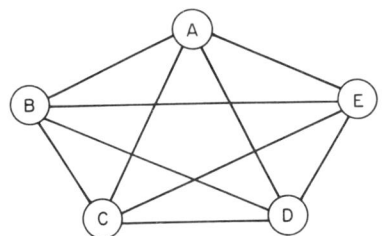

A Highly Constrained Belief System

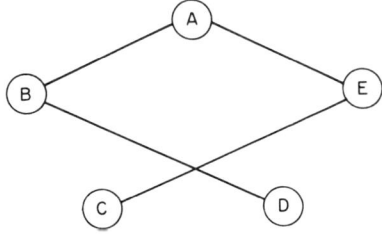

An Unconstrained Belief System

Figure 3.2. Schematic Drawings of Two Belief Systems.

to a certain overall plan or structure and will be sure that he or she achieves a logical interconnectedness among them. In advocating a balanced budget, this individual will either oppose additional defense spending or else believe that the budget should be cut elsewhere in order to make room for the additional military appropriation which he or she favors.

The importance of the constraint concept becomes clear when we turn to the question of the stability and change of attitudes. In general, the attitudes in a well-constrained belief system will resist change more strongly than those in a poorly constrained belief system. The two schematic drawings in Figure 3.2 help to illustrate why. Each of these attitude sets contains five attitudes. However, in the poorly constrained set, there are only four linkages, while in the well-constrained set, there are ten. Consider what happens if the poorly constrained individual comes upon some information that seems to contradict attitude C. While this attitude belongs to a five-attitude set, it is related in the person's mind to only one other of them, namely E. In order to incorporate the new information, the only price this person must pay is to sacrifice the linkage originally constructed between C and E. (He could also change E, but then he would have to deal with the A–E linkage, and so on.)

The well-constrained individual, on the other hand, has a more difficult task. His attitude C is the same in content, but this time it is linked to *all* the other attitudes in the set. In order to change C to fit the new information, this person must either alter four linkages, or change all of his other attitudes. Clearly, such a task would require a very high psychological cost. Such a person would be far more likely to ignore the new information.

Balance. Implicit in the discussion of constraint is the idea that people naturally seek to keep their belief systems logically ordered. One is not likely, for instance, to dislike Southerners intensely, and also to hold President Carter in high esteem. Since Carter is a Southerner, those two attitudes are not logically related. The point I wish to make is that in all of us there exists what Heider has called a "strain for consistency."[3] That is, we feel uncomfortable if our belief system contains mutually contradictory attitudes. Furthermore, we seek to remove the inconsistency, usually by changing one of the offending attitudes.

Let me use an example to illustrate the concept of balance and the strain for consistency. Suppose that you were an enthusiastic Nixon supporter in 1968 and also in 1972. This attitude can be illustrated by drawing a positive link between that person and the object, Richard Nixon.

YOU ——————— + ——————— NIXON

Now, throughout 1973 and early 1974, a great deal of evidence of wrongdoing had begun to be amassed by the special Watergate prosecutor and by the Senate and House Watergate committees. You are naturally horrified by these revelations, and this creates another object and linkage, which is added to your belief system.

Now you are lacking one element of a complete belief system: The link between Nixon and the events of Watergate. What will this link be? If you think about it for a moment, you have only one choice. If you like Nixon and dislike Watergate, you must believe that Nixon was not involved and would have rejected the various Watergate activities had he known about them. This is the only logically consistent pattern. So we complete the triangle.

This is an example of a "balanced" belief system.

But there is one final step in this little drama. On July 24, 1974, the Supreme Court ordered Nixon to turn over to the House committee certain tape recordings that had been made of conversations in which Nixon had discussed Watergate. Suddenly you are confronted with evidence that part of your belief system is incorrect. The link between Nixon and Watergate should not be negative, but positive. That is, Nixon *was* associated with the Watergate affair. Now, since you feel a "strain for consistency," this turn of events causes a problem. Somehow, you must bring your various attitudes back into balance. Suppose you simply can't abandon your respect for Nixon. In that case you have two choices. You may choose to deny the evidence. You might conclude, for instance, that the tapes were faked by Nixon's enemies, or that the things which he said were taken out of context and really meant something different. This denial would allow you to maintain the negative link between Watergate and Nixon.

The second alternative open to you would be to change your attitude about Watergate. Instead of considering it to be an enormous wrong and a threat to our democratic system, you could decide that after all, it was really no different from what politics has always been. And besides, the Democrats have done their share of dirty tricks. Such a conclusion could restore balance to your belief system by shifting the link between yourself and Watergate from negative to positive (or at least neutral).

However, for most Americans, Watergate was too serious a crisis to judge lightly, and Richard Nixon's complicity in it was too overt to be denied. The final way to restore consistency to this belief system, therefore, is the one that most people came to adopt. The link between you and Nixon probably changed from positive to negative. In the electorate as a whole, this shift led in turn to an increased willingness in Congress to consider impeachment, which ultimately resulted in Nixon's resignation.

While the concept of balance often proves useful as we attempt to understand attitudes and attitude change, it is not infallible. Often, an inconsistency is not resolved, or it is resolved in an unexpected way.

A common example of this comes from voting. While the choice of a presidential candidate often reflects a voter's party loyalty, such is not always the case. A simple belief system illustrates this possibility.

In spite of the fact that the person's party loyalty would have indicated a vote for Carter in 1976, this voter prefers Ford. Clearly, this is an inconsistent pattern; yet hundreds of thousands of people fell precisely into this category in 1976. Do we therefore reject the concept of balance as useless?

No, of course not. This example illustrates an important point, however, and one that may already have occurred to many readers. It is that we all have more than three elements in our belief system. Rarely do we make a judgment about something by consulting only one element. In the case of our voter, we can easily imagine that in spite of his loyalty to the Democratic party, he preferred the stands that the Republicans took on the issues. This factor is illustrated by adding another triangle to our diagram.

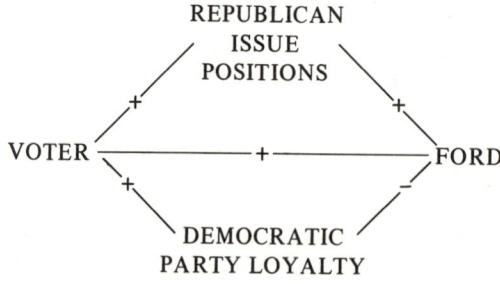

Now we are dealing with two simple three-element belief systems. One is balanced (the triangle on top), and the other is not. In terms of the example, if the voter chooses to give greater weight to his preferences on the issues, he must sacrifice his party loyalty to vote for Ford. Obviously, in each election many people do exactly that and simply live with the inconsistency that it produces.

ATTITUDES AND BEHAVIOR

We have simply assumed, up to this point, that attitudes are in fact related to behavior. However, I would be remiss to let this question pass unexamined. It turns out that there is a great deal of evidence that attitudes do not predict behavior very well. We shall take just a brief glance at some of this evidence and attempt to place the attitude-behavior link in greater perspective.

The classic study of the attitude-behavior problem was conducted in the 1930s by Richard LaPiere.[4] LaPiere had had the occasion to travel with a well-to-do Chinese couple and was surprised by the cordial and unhesitating reception the three of them received in the hotel where they stopped (remember that in the 1930s racial prejudice was not restricted to those with black skins). He was even more surprised when some months later he telephoned the hotel to ask whether they would accept "an important Chinese gentelman" as a guest. Their answer was a flat refusal, which blatantly contradicted the behavior he had earlier observed.

This experience led LaPiere to expand his study, and in the course of time, he stopped in over 200 hotels and restaurants with his two Chinese friends. They were almost never refused service. But when he wrote to the proprietors of those same establishments, they nearly all replied that they would refuse service to the hypothetical Chinese gentleman.

What do we make of this? It seems as though the hotel and restaurant proprietors were prejudiced, because they *said* they would refuse to serve Chinese. Yet when put to the test, very few of them actually behaved in a prejudiced manner. Wicker, for instance, has suggested that this and other examples should lead us to reject the idea that attitudes and behaviors are linked.[5]

My own position is more moderate. I feel that there is no reason to expect that a particular attitude will *always* lead to a given behavior. The bulk of the discussion in this chapter has, in fact, suggested that we *won't* obtain perfect prediction. In LaPiere's example, the hotel manager may well have responded to a prejudiced attitude in answering the letter. When the Oriental couple actually walked in the door, however, his situation was totally different. He may still have been prejudiced, but now he would have had to offend the affluent and well-educated white who accompanied them and would have had to create a scene if he had refused service. Other factors may also have complicated the situation and may have served to short-circuit the behavior that would have followed had the attitude of racial prejudice alone determined that behavior. The key idea is that *many* attitudes may contribute to a behavior simultaneously, and a single one of them may or may not be the determining one in any particular case.

A concluding example will illustrate how a single attitude may not succeed completely in predicting behavior, but when several attitudes are taken into account, the attitude-behavior link becomes quite clear. In 1976 there were certain positions which were identified with the two candidates. Without getting too much into the details of the matter, we might say that Carter was seen as the liberal on tax policy, poverty, and federal intervention to guarantee jobs and a good standard of living, while Ford was seen as the conservative. Now, according to our approach, if a voter was liberal on one of these issues, he should have voted for Carter, since the two shared similar ideological positions. In other words, the issue attitude should have led to a certain behavior.

Consider the first issue: tax policy. Table 3.3 shows that while the voters' positions on this issue related to their choice for President, the relationships were far from perfect. We can see that of those who were liberal on the tax policy issue, 59 percent did vote for Carter. But there was another 41 percent who failed to act on this particular attitude and voted for Ford. On the other side, 56 percent of the conservatives voted according to their attitude by choosing Ford, but 44 percent deviated and voted for Carter.

How do we explain these deviations? An obvious possibility is that voters who fail to follow their attitude have other attitudes that may be more important to them. In Table 3.4, I add a second issue attitude to check this idea out. I have used the poverty issue, where the liberal position is the belief that poverty exists because society doesn't give people an equal chance.

Now things become a bit more clear. In the case where the voter was conservative or liberal on *both* of his issue attitudes, the tendency to vote for Ford or Carter was strengthened noticeably. The liberals supported Carter 71 percent of the time, and the conservatives voted for Ford 63 percent of the time.

The interesting part of this table contains the conflicted voters. Since they possess two attitudes which push them in opposite directions, we can make no prediction about which candidate they will choose. As we can see, they split just about down the middle, 54 percent for Carter and 46 percent for Ford.

TABLE 3.3. Relationship between Attitude on Taxes and the 1976 Vote for President

		Attitude on Taxes		
		Liberal Response (Tax the Rich)	Neutral	Conservative Response (Tax All Equally)
1976 Vote	Carter	59%	49%	44%
	Ford	41	51	56
		100%	100%	100%
	N:	(582)	(251)	(605)

Question: As you know, in our tax system people who earn a lot of money already have to pay higher rates of income tax than those who earn less. Some people think that those with high incomes should pay even more of their income into taxes than they do now. Others think that rates shouldn't be different at all—that everyone should pay the same portion of their income, no matter how much they make. Where do you place yourself on this scale, or haven't you thought much about this?

Source: ICPSR Archive: CPS 1976 Presidential Election Study.

TABLE 3.4. Relationship between Attitude on Tax Policy and Attitude on Poverty and the 1976 Vote for President

		Attitude on Taxes and Poverty		
		Liberal on Both	Mixed	Conservative on Both
1976 Vote	Carter	71%	54%	37%
	Ford	39	46	63
		100%	100%	100%
	N:	(181)	(423)	(347)

Question: "The poor are poor because the American way of life doesn't give all people an equal chance?"

Source: ICPSR Archive: CPS 1976 Presidential Election Study.

48   SETTING THE STAGE

However, we note that in Table 3.4, there are still deviants, voters who vote against their attitudes. Clearly, by taking only two attitudes into account, we still have plenty of room for inconsistency with other elements of the belief system. The final step in this example will be to add a third attitude relating to federal job guarantees.

The addition of the third issue does eliminate a further degree of inconsistency from the behavior of those who are liberal or conservative on all three. The liberals voted 84 percent in favor of Carter, and 70 percent of the conservatives backed Ford. By combining issues in this way, we have been able to distill these two relatively pure groups of voters. Their attitudes about the three issues all agreed (all liberal or all conservative), and consequently, their behavior followed their attitudes fairly closely.

However, there is a gaping hole in the argument I have just made. It is obviously possible to create purer and purer groups by adding additional issues, but these groups become smaller and smaller parts of the total electorate. In our example, by the time we had included three issues, we had left only 74 pure liberals and 216 pure conservatives, out of a total of 613. That is, only 47 percent of this sample qualified as pure liberals or pure conservatives. For the remaining 53 percent, we are still confronted

TABLE 3.5.   Relationship between Attitude on Taxes, Poverty, and Government Guarantee of a Job and a Good Standard of Living, and the 1976 Vote for President

		Attitude on Taxes, Poverty, and Government Guarantees			
		Liberal on All Three	Liberal on Two, Conservative on One	Conservative on Two, Liberal on One	Conservative on All Three
1976 Vote	Carter	84%	64%	40%	30%
	Ford	16	36	60	70
	N:	100% (74)	100% (116)	100% (207)	100% (216)

Question: Some people feel that the government in Washington should see to it that every person has a job and a good standard of living. Others think the government should just let each person get ahead on his own. Where would you place yourself on this scale, or haven't you thought much about this?

Source: ICPSR Archive; CPS 1976 Presidential Election Study.

with the conclusion that attitudes often conflict—and when they do, behavior will often not appear to be produced by them.

SUMMARY

In sum, the relationship between attitudes and behavior is rarely perfect. However, we now have some feel for what causes people to deviate in their behavior from what might be indicated by their attitudes. We all possess a whole set of attitudes, and in a given situation, they may provide contradictory signals as to what we should do. We must also recall the fact that the real world has an effect on behavior, quite apart from any attitude. I may have voted for neither Carter nor Ford, in spite of everything, because I got into an automobile accident on my way to the polls and spent the day in the hospital instead. In spite of these possibilities, the attitudinal approach holds much promise as a technique to bring order to the complicated world of politics. In that spirit, we embark.

NOTES

1. H. T. Reynolds, *Politics and the Common Man: An Introduction to Political Behavior* (Homewood, Ill.: Dorsey, 1974), p. 3.
2. Released by United Artists.
3. Fritz Heider, *The Psychology of Interpersonal Relations* (New York: Wiley, 1958).
4. Richard T. LaPiere, "Attitudes vs. Actions," *Social Forces*, vol. 13, no. 2 (December 1934), 230–237.
5. Allan W. Wicker, "Attitudes versus Actions: The Relationship of Verbal and Overt Behavioral Responses to Attitude Objects," *Journal of Social Issues*, vol. 25, no. 4 (Autumn 1969), 41–78.

Part **II**

The Acquisition of Attitudes: Political Socialization

If you are like most people, you have a feeling of patriotism about the United States. You feel a tingle of pride at a display of national symbols like the flag or a flight of military aircraft passing in review. You may also feel that when we are threatened by a foreign enemy, it is right to take up arms in defense of our country.

Feelings like this do not exist at birth. We acquire them, usually during childhood, through the process called political socialization. This process has been illustrated very well in a study reported by Lawson.[1] Since he could not very well talk to the very young children about their feelings of patriotism, he used a simple substitute: national flags. He asked children from kindergarten through the twelfth grade to choose, from among 20 national flags, the one he or she found to be most attractive. He reasoned that in the youngest children, these choices would be made simply on esthetic grounds; children would choose the prettiest flag (the Siamese merchant flag was a popular one, since it showed a white elephant). As the feeling of patriotism began to grow in these children, however, the purely esthetic choice should shift to one with a more political basis. Specifically, older children should begin to show a greater preference for the flag of the United States as a reflection of their increased feelings of closeness of identification of the United States as "their" country.

What Lawson found was a bit surprising. First, a strong preference for the American flag was shown by children of all grade levels, even those in kindergarten and first grade. Second, the flag of the Soviet Union was rejected by nine out of ten students in every grade level, even though a panel of art experts judged the Soviet flag to be more pleasing on purely esthetic grounds than the American flag. Evidently, the socialization of national preference has already occurred by the age of five in many American children. These individuals know quite clearly that they prefer the United States, and reject the Soviet Union.

The key point is that these young children have no idea *why* they have these preferences. They are certainly not related to any specific knowledge that the Russians were the villains in the cold war, for instance. Nonetheless, these attitudes do exist, and they eventually serve as strong foundations for the attitudes and behaviors of the adult.

This illustration leads to our central question: What *is* political socialization? Of the dozens of definitions available, the following is the one I find most useful:

Political socialization is the process of development of the political self.[2]

For the beginning student, this definition undoubtedly holds a good deal of mystery. I can amplify it slightly by defining the "process of development of the political self" to be the learning of the attitudes, values, manners, and customs of political life in one's country. But even this information fails to push back the frontiers of ignorance any great distance. Accordingly, I shall devote the next four chapters to an attempt to answer two central questions: First, what is learned, or what are the values, attitudes, manners and customs of the American electorate? Second, what is the process of learning like?

NOTES

1. Edwin D. Lawson, "Development of Patriotism in Children: A Second Look," *Journal of Psychology*, vol. 55 (1963), 279–286.
2. Adapted from H. T. Reynolds, *Politics and the Common Man: An Introduction to Political Behavior* (Homewood, Ill.: Dorsey, 1974), p. 53.

4
The Processes of Political Socialization

There is one central problem that we must confront in our discussion of the socialization process: Nobody really knows how it works. At the present time, no single theory can give any adequate explanation to the variety of kinds of learning that political scientists have observed in their research. Consequently, political science has borrowed extensively from other fields, especially psychology and sociology, in order to construct theories of political socialization. The result has been a proliferation of theoretical approaches, each one capable of giving adequate explanation to one area of the field, but often unable to yield any insights in other areas.

This theoretical confusion is inconvenient, to be sure. However, there are good reasons to think that no single explanation could possibly encompass the learning experiences of a single human being from birth to adulthood. People just change too much to be expected to learn things in the same way at every point in their lives. Consequently, in this discussion I shall make no attempt to present a single explanation. Instead I shall discuss three basic approaches to learning that have emerged more or less independently in the literature over the past 20 or 30 years: the psychoanalytic approach, the cognitive-developmental approach, and the social learning approach.

THE PSYCHOANALYTIC APPROACH

Psychoanalytic theory has most often been used in political science to explain such phenomena as the highly emotional reactions experienced by many Americans after the death of a President. Normally, when a person whom we do not know well dies, we experience little if any grief. And yet the deaths of both Roosevelt and Kennedy brought a reaction of extreme grief to many, similar to the grief they might have experienced for the death of a parent or a very close friend. Orlansky[1] reports the following reactions to Roosevelt's death:

> You expect me to say something about what happened. But I cannot speak about Roosevelt's death any more than I could speak about the death of my mother and father. (New York high school teacher to her class)
>
> He was just like a daddy to me always; he always talked to me just that way. (Democratic Representative Lyndon Johnson)

The violent and unexpected death of President Kennedy in 1963 brought much the same sort of reaction. Young teenagers studied by Ginsparg, Moriarty, and Murphey[2] gave the following accounts of their feelings:

> I was completely shaken, it took me several days to get used to the fact that he was no longer alive.
>
> When I heard that the President was dead, I felt a great sense of loss.
>
> There was just a hollow empty pit in the middle of my stomach. I was just numb and stunned.

These examples are suggestive, but in order to see how psychoanalytic theory works, we need to take a rather long step backward in time. This is because the approach has arisen from observation of infants and small children. These observations have revealed that during the early stages of life, children identify themselves wholly in terms of their parents, especially their mothers. Very young children cannot imagine existing without their mother. She exercises complete authority over their life; they can do literally nothing beyond their own bodily functions without her help and consent. Their dependence on her for their every need is total.

At a very early stage, a child recognizes the extent to which he depends on his parents. Since the child remains incapable of survival without the help of his parents throughout early childhood, the possibility that his relationship with his parents might be damaged is extremely threatening. All parents know that withdrawal of affection is a very effective punishment for a child, and it often brings about great distress.

There are two basic ways in which the close parent-child nexus becomes relevant in the political world. First, because of the great importance of his relationship to his mother and father, the child will normally go to great lengths to ensure that this relationship remains strong and healthy. This need to preserve the parents' love generally leads to a very sensitive cue-taking on the part of the child. If the child perceives that his parents expect him to be friendly or aggressive, he will develop these characteristics to please them. The same would be expected if the parents regarded their child as shy, or intelligent, or honest. The point is that traits that become set in an individual's mind during his early youth will remain a part of his personality during adulthood. A child whose parents encouraged him to be aggressive might later become a political activist, while another who was expected to be shy and retiring by his parents might become politically apathetic.[3]

The second way in which the parent-child relationship may influence political behavior in later life involves the effect it has on the child's view of authority. The way the individual behaves with respect to political authority in adulthood depends in some ways on his experiences with parental authority.

Most Americans enjoy successful relationships with their parents. They maintain a relatively high level of affection and respect for each other during childhood. During adolescence, however, children are "generally impelled to demote their parents in their scale of values and to look for other heroes and ideal figures farther from home. This is a time for the displacement of important feelings to admired personages in the world at large."[4]

In theory, if the parental relationship was one of warmth and respect, then the views of other authority figures in the world at large will tend to be the same. Since the major political authority figure for most people is the President, this process of transfer of feelings contributes to the widespread warmth of feeling for the President that exists in the United States. It also helps us understand why the reaction to the death of a President is so much stronger than we might have expected.

Although most Americans have positive feelings about both parental and political authority,[5] a good deal of insight into the political relevance of the parent-child relationship can be gleaned from an examination of unsuccessful relationships. Robert Lane, in his well-known study of New Haven men, studied the question of how a damaged father-son relationship may have political consequences.[6] Lane conducted extensive interviews with 15 men and found four who, unlike most Americans, remembered their fathers either without affection or with outright rejection. These men had endured a childhood of neglect and abuse at the hands of unloving, drunken, and often absent fathers.

From these four case studies, Lane developed a profile of the political consequences of the damaged parental relationship. The first element in the profile is a low level of political information and interest. The lack of a secure parental model forced these men to invest much of their psychological energy into the process of self-discovery and the development of a personal sense of security. Relatively little energy was left with which to explore and keep up with the political world.

The second element of the profile is a high level of authoritarianism. A high authoritarian individual is one who (among other things) is unable to work or live with others "as cooperative equals or at least as trusting partners."[7] Three of Lane's four subjects were highly authoritarian. Once again, the source of this characteristic was traced to the lack of a suitable parental model. Since these individuals had never experienced a trusting or cooperative relationship with their fathers, they had difficulty changing their ways in the relationships they had in adult life.

Closely associated with high authoritarianism is the third element of these four men's profile: the "speak no evil of the political leader" syndrome. All of these men had great difficulty criticizing major political leaders, especially Presidents. Even when a negative comment did slip out during the interviews, the men would quickly retract it or contradict themselves with a compensating positive comment. One set of remarks made about Eisenhower illustrates this point:

> Well, I mean, I thought for being President, I thought he'd (Robert Taft) be a little better in know-how and savvy than Eisenhower, y'know. I ain't got nothing against Eisenhower—he's good, he seems to be honest enough, but I don't . . . I don't . . . I don't think he should have run again because his health is—his health was good enough.[8]

This inability to express negative feelings toward political authority can be traced to the damaged father-son relationship in three ways. First, there is obviously an element of fear, which is carried over from the childhood situation. The abuses suffered at the hands of a drunken, unloving father are not easily forgotten. They remain to color the subsequent relationship with political authority. Second, the child soon realizes that the basis of his father's authority is brute strength. His hatred for the old man fosters a sense of worship and envy of strength, as though he felt that by becoming like his father, the son could escape the abuses in which his father indulged. Finally, the family experience led these four men to the belief that to counter or rebel against authority is not only futile, but dangerous.

The final element of the political profile of Lane's four subjects involves their views on the future of society. A belief in the eventual achievement of the ideal society, according to Lane, is grounded both in "the belief that people are kindly by nature and considerate of one another" and in a view of authority as "strong and directive, yet at the same time solicitous and supportive of the weak in their infirmities. . . ."[9]

Given these definitions, one would naturally expect the four subjects who experienced damaged relationships with their fathers to be much more pessimistic about the future of society than the 11 others, and this is the pattern that emerged from the data. Three of the men who had failed to establish a healthy relationship with their fathers felt that "we are not moving closer to an ideal society," and one said that "we are moving away from an ideal society." References to the decline of religion and the rise of Communism typify this view also. The other subjects saw the future with a good deal more hope. Of the 11, eight said "we are moving closer to an ideal society," three felt "we are not moving closer to an ideal society," and only one responded that "we are moving away from an ideal society." Lane's analysis of course suggests that this image of political authority stems from a healthy ability to trust and deal with political authority, which in turn is based on the early experiences in the family.

THE COGNITIVE-DEVELOPMENTAL APPROACH

The theory proposed initially by Jean Piaget focuses on the individual's cognitive development.[10] He explains the learning process primarily by reference to the child's *ability* to learn, which is in turn governed by the level of development of the structure and organization of his thought processes. Piaget's approach to learning also stresses the unique contribution of the individual and the relevance to the learning process of what goes on in the individual's world. Knowledge is the result of the continuous interaction between the child and his environment. Finally, Piaget has postulated that cognitive development always passes through four stages, each one identified by the set of mental abilities the child manifests.

The process by which learning takes place in Piagetian theory involves three related subprocesses: assimilation, accommodation, and equilibration. Assimilation refers to the process of absorbing new information. Such information, once taken in, becomes organized into patterns of behavior (or schema). For instance, one of the first discoveries made by the infant is that sucking on a nipple produces gratification. At some point in his early development, he will also find that it is possible to suck on his thumb, and that this is also gratifying.[11] Piaget would say that the infant has extended his sucking schema to assimilate a new and slightly different object.

Of course, not all new information fits conveniently into preexisting schemata. The infant may eventually discover that sucking on the wrong end of a lighted cigarette is definitely not gratifying. This new information cannot be assimilated into the existing schema, which tells the infant that sucking on objects brings about gratification. Instead, it forces a reevaluation of the schema. This process is called accommodation.

Although we can distinguish assimilation from accommodation conceptually, in the real world they occur together. Any new discovery will produce a tension in the schema of the individual, until the simultaneous assimilation and accommodation of the discovery is resolved. This set of processes is called equilibration, and it lies at the center of Piaget's developmental process. Once a new idea or object is assimilated/accommodated, the cognitive structure of the individual is changed (or equilibrated), which in turn makes possible further changes. This process eventually makes possible the shift from one stage of cognitive development to the next higher one.

Piaget presents four stages, or plateaus, of cognitive development through which all children are thought to pass. From birth to about two years, the infant is in the sensorimotor stage. During this phase of life, the individual develops his first understanding of space, time, and causality. These structures are derived from a fundamental awareness of the permanence of objects. The child comes to understand that things do not necessarily cease to exist when they disappear. He can look for and find an object he has seen hidden, and he can understand that when his mother walks out of the room she will eventually come back. Finally, the infant becomes aware that he is himself an object that is differentiated from other objects. This last discovery leads to the initial state of egocentrism, the tendency to have only personal motives for behavior.

Clearly, the sensorimotor stage entails primarily the creation of the foundations of thought and has no direct relevance to politics. The second stage, called preoperational, is also prepolitical in the sense that the concepts and cognitive structures necessary to think about common political phenomena are still absent. During the preoperational stage, which lasts from about ages 2 to 7, symbolic thought, abetted by the development of language, becomes evident. The child becomes aware that the name of an object is not a characteristic of the object itself, like its shape or color. Rather, it is a symbol that carries the identity of the object, even though the object itself may be absent.

A second characteristic of the preoperational stage is the tendency to limit reasoning to a single dimension. One of Piaget's well-known experiments touches indirectly on political topics. Piaget interviewed some 200 children between the ages of 4 and 15 about their ideas of homeland. He found that those in the preoperational stage possessed no concept of country. Although the 6- and 7-year-olds knew that they were Genevese (the experiment was conducted in Geneva), they did not understand that they could *also* be Swiss, or that Geneva is located in Switzerland. They considered the two concepts to be distinct and impossible to combine, illustrating the limitation to one-dimensional reasoning.

The child also remains wholly egocentric during this phase. He is incapable of imagining what it would be like to be another person and therefore cannot take a view of a problem other than his own. In short, the preoperational child is incapable of community-oriented thought or behavior.

The third stage of cognitive development involves concrete operations, and is experienced by most children between the ages of 7 and 11. It is at this stage that the child achieves mastery over logical thought. This includes such abilities as addition and subtraction, classification, and ordering. The child also comes to realize that operations are reversible. Piaget found that by age 10 or 11, children are perfectly capable of realizing that they can live *both* in Geneva and Switzerland at the same time. Where in the preoperational stage, children lacked the logical skill to manipulate paired or reciprocal concepts in terms of each other (as a foreigner is someone who is not a countryman), in the concrete operational stage these concepts are mastered.

The acquisition of the reversibility concept also allows the learning of the concept of conservation. The child can now understand that certain characteristics of objects are invariant (conserved), in spite of the fact that other characteristics may change. Needless to say, very little of politics can be understood without this concept. A policeman, for instance, has certain essential functions regardless of whether he rides in a car or on horseback, or walks his beat.

The final stage in Piaget's theory is the formal operational. The typical child passes into this final stage between the ages of 11 and 15. The central characteristic of thought in this stage is the capacity to reason abstractly, without the necessity for referencing concepts to physical objects. The idea of community becomes meaningful and leads to the acquisition of a more sociocentric view of life, as contrasted to the earlier egocentric one. A logical argument may be appreciated independently of its content. The individual is now able to approach problems through the creation of hypotheses and to solve them through the use of deductive logic. Collective concepts that lie at the center of political life, such as Congress or voting, therefore become comprehensible, and the ability to take a sociocentric rather than an egocentric view of events allows the child to move into the role of citizen.

Admittedly, Piaget's experiments relate only remotely to the political behavior of the American electorate. His theoretical discoveries, however, have great relevance, for they allow a much richer understanding of many of the classic findings of political socialization research.

One of the most interesting applications of Piaget to political topics can be found in the work of Adelson on the kinds of political decisions young people make when they are provided with a hypothetical opportunity.[12] To test the relationship between developmental stage and political thinking, Adelson interviewed 120 subjects ranging in age from 11 to 18. Information was gathered after offering these young people the following premise:

> Imagine that a thousand people move to an island in the Pacific, and set about building a community. They are confronted by the tasks of forming a government and of developing laws and other modes of communal regulation.[13]

This premise was then followed by a series of questions of the "what if" variety. For instance, Adelson asked his subjects what would happen if the new government decided not to have any laws, or what the government should do if it needed someone's land for a road and that person refused to sell.

These political dilemmas were discussed by Adelson's young people for many hours. The picture that emerged shows quite clearly that the theories of Piaget have relevance in the area of politics.

The younger children (11 to 13 years old) consistently displayed a view of politics and government that differed in basic ways from that held by the older members of the sample. These differences can generally be grouped into two sets.[14] First, the younger children were egocentric, in Piaget's sense. That is, their view of the world was a purely personal one, in which decisions were based only on their consequences for the individual himself. The older children had achieved the ability to take society's view. Second, the view that the younger children had of government was concrete, even to the literal extent of imagining government to be the buildings in which government is housed. They remained tied to the present, unable to envision long-range social consequences. Abstractions like voting, or even collectivities like Congress were beyond the cognitive capacities of 11-year-olds. In the terminology of Piaget, these young people were generally still in the concrete operational stage.

By the time most children had reached the age of 15, they had developed a solid grasp on formal thought. Dealing with abstractions presented no cognitive problems, although a lack of information or fluency occasionally produced hesitant responses. They had definitely reached the formal operational stage.

The best way to present the changes in political thought that accompany changes in the stage of cognitive development is through illustration. One question in Adelson's study asked: "Another law was suggested which required all children to be vaccinated against smallpox and polio. What was the purpose of that law?"[15] The youngest subjects could not understand political events (like passing a health law) in terms of their collective consequences. The "social order" was an empty phrase to them, and thus the purpose of a vaccination must have been an individual one—the personal protection from disease. Seventy percent of the 11-year-olds took this view. However, health laws clearly have wider purposes, such as the protection of populations from epidemics. Although this does not exclude the personal significance of health care, the interesting fact is that the older children chose the social interpretation nearly unanimously (95 percent of the 15- and 18-year-olds).

A second illustration of the increasing ability of the maturing adolescent to deal with abstractions, and to take society's viewpoint, can be found in a series of questions Adelson asked about the right of eminent domain, the traditional power of government to take possession of private property for the public good.[16] The respondents were told that in the Pacific island community, the government had decided to build a road from one side of the island to the other. For the most part, the government had no trouble acquiring the property, but one man refused to give in. He was offered a fair price for his land, but he replied that he was attached to his land and he didn't want to move. He said the government should buy another piece of land and detour the road. After a long discussion, the government decided to invoke the right of eminent domain and force the landowner to sell his land.

At this point, the young people in Adelson's study were asked whether they thought this decision was fair. Once again, developmental differences emerged that can be understood in terms of Piaget's theories. The patterns of Table 4.1 show the difference age makes in the views of the proposed government action. The younger subjects remained at the side of the individual, refusing to grant any rights to the community. Our earlier discussion suggests, of course, that this is because the youngest of these children have no concept of community and therefore cannot understand that its rights and needs deserve consideration as well. The older respondents, on the other hand, deserted the unfortunate landowner almost entirely. They were willing to take a sociocentric position, and grant rights to the abstract collectivity. Those who did say the government should not force the man off his land generally argued that his sense of social responsibility would lead him to sell—social responsibility being another concept that is foreign to most 11-year-olds.

Another aspect of political life studied by Adelson involved attitudes toward the law.[17] It illustrates how the view of the law matures from the initial, punitive, restrictive, and immutable image (you obey because you

TABLE 4.1. Should the Landowner Be Forced to Sell?

	Age			
	11	13	15	18
Yes, rights of others come first	40%	37%	63%	70%
No, individual rights come first	57	50	33	7
No, social responsibility	3	10	0	23
	100%	97%	96%	100%
N:	(30)	(30)	(30)	(30)

Source: Joseph Adelson and Robert P. O'Neil, "Growth of Political Ideas in Adolescence: The Sense of Community," *Journal of Personality and Social Psychology*, vol. 4, no. 3 (1966), 301. Copyright 1966 by the American Psychological Association. Reprinted by permission.

get punished if you don't) to the more developed concept of the law as beneficial and subject to change.

When asked what the purpose of laws would be in the Pacific island country, Adelson's young people gave a variety of answers. They were scored according to whether they reflected a view of the law as something that restricts, or prevents people from doing things, or as existing to promote the general good or achieve moral or social benefits.

The point made by Table 4.2 should be clear: The restrictive view of the law that dominated the thinking of the younger respondents is replaced by the socially oriented beneficial view among the older individuals. As before, this shift is taken to mean a change in the level of cognitive and moral awareness, which gives these young people the ability to see their world in new ways.

Moving from Adelson's hypothetical Pacific island into the real world, Siegel has applied a cognitive-developmental approach to a much more real political dilemma.[18] In her study of children's reactions to the death of President Kennedy, she also asked what the children thought about the death of Oswald. These answers were compared to those given by a national sample of adults. The youngest children clearly saw the American legal system as existing for the purpose of revenge, often of the medieval kind. Two-thirds of Siegel's fourth-grade respondents and 53 percent of the sixth-graders "hoped the man who killed the President would be shot or beat up." The figure drops to 37 percent by the eighth grade, 24 percent by the tenth grade, and to 17 percent by the twelfth grade. Few adults in the national sample said they had this hope (although 20 percent said they felt glad when it happened). In a similar vein, only 16 percent of the children said they were sorry that Oswald was deprived of a fair trial, but 33 percent of the adults expressed this regret. Evidently, the concept of due process is another of those that does not belong in the cognitive organization of the young child. Perhaps the most instructive part of this bit of evidence, however, is that only one-third of adult Americans gave due process the upper hand in their response to Oswald's death.

TABLE 4.2. View of the Law

	Age			
	11	13	15	18
Restrictive	76%	73%	31%	17%
Restrictive and beneficial	10	17	27	21
Beneficial	14	10	42	62
	100%	100%	100%	100%
N:	(30)	(30)	(30)	(30)

Source: Joseph Adelson, Bernard Green, and Robert P. O'Neil, "Growth of the Idea of Law in Adolescence," *Developmental Psychology*, vol. 1, no 4 (July 1969), 329. Copyright 1969 by the American Psychological Association. Reprinted by permission.

SOCIAL LEARNING THEORY

Social learning theory, of the three approaches to political learning discussed here, has attracted the widest support from both psychologists and political scientists who study socialization.[19] This theory takes the view that a child acquires norms of behavior by imitating or identifying with "models." Models are people with whom the child comes in contact (hence the heavy emphasis on the parents in social learning theory—for the child has few regular contacts with any other adults) and who offer him rewards or other inducements to reinforce his desire to adopt the same norms that he observes in the model.[20] There may also be an added reinforcement which comes from the child himself. The child is motivated to learn because he values identification with the model, and self-esteem is his reward for imitating or behaving like that model.[21]

There are several concepts embedded in social learning theory that need discussion. The best way to approach this task is through an example.[22] You recall that the attitude a person might hold toward President Carter consists of several belief-affect elements: the belief that he is a Democrat, he smiles a lot, he grows peanuts, and he is President, and the affects, positive or negative, attached to each belief. Now suppose the person in question is a young child. How would social learning theory say he had come to possess this attitude?

The following scenario illustrates the process. The night of the first presidential debate, a young boy arrives in the television room only to discover that his father has taken over the television set and is watching the two presidential candidates. The boy, who happens to look at the television set when Jimmy Carter's face is on the screen, says "Ugh, he sure is dumb." His father (who is a Democrat) responds offhandedly, "If you think Carters's dumb, you ought to wait around and listen to Ford." The child, who couldn't care less about politics, is disgusted at not being able to watch his favorite show and wanders out of the room.

Some time later, the boy comes downstairs to the breakfast table to find his father gloating over the newspaper. With obvious pleasure, he reads to no one in particular how President Ford damaged his chances for reelection by his remark during the second debate about the independence of eastern Europe from the influence of the Soviet Union. The boy makes no response, but simply eats his breakfast and goes off to school.

By now, however, the boy has begun to be aware that the presidential campaign is something that interests his father. When he sees Carter's picture in the newspaper a few days later, he ventures the comment, "Gee, he sure looks important." His father says nothing, but looks over at his son with a warm smile.

These three experiences have all contributed to a process in which the boy has learned, step by step, that Mr. Carter is a good man. As time goes along, he will discover, in a similar manner, that he is a good man because (for instance) he is a Democrat, because he is a Southerner, and because he is President.

In theoretical terms, what has happened during the child's three experiences? In the first instance, a *cue situation* arose, the appearance of Jimmy Carter's face on television. The child made a *response*, which happened to be negative, for reasons entirely unrelated to politics. A *model*, his father, then contradicted the response by suggesting that Carter wasn't really the dumb one.

The second instance involved a cue situation again, when the father read the news article about the second debate. This time, however, the child merely observed his father, and made no response.

Finally, a third cue situation occurred with the appearance of Carter's picture. The child was now getting the idea and made a positive response. This time he was rewarded by his father's smile.

Over the course of many trials the boy will eventually fill out his set of attitudes about the presidential race. There may be models other than his parents, such as his teachers or playmates. But from whatever source, the child will progressively discover more and more things about Carter or Ford, and because he seeks rewards, will adopt the positions of his models as his own. Eventually, he will be able to form a response to a cue situation that is new to him without needing the guidance of an immediate reward (or punishment) from any model.

This process of internalizing certain responses depending on whether or not they are rewarded is what the psychologists call instrumental, or operant, conditioning. It lies at the heart of social learning theory, so I will spend a few paragraphs going into some detail with the relevant concepts.

Instrumental Conditioning

Instrumental conditioning centers on the following process: If certain responses to cue situations are rewarded, the individual will tend to make those responses in the future and will cease making responses that are unrewarded or ignored. The boy's eventual arrival at the position that Carter deserved support arose from the fact that he made the connection between taking that position and receiving rewards from his models.

Rewards. We should perhaps speak more correctly of rewarding stimuli to escape the mistaken idea that a reward is limited to material things, like a piece of candy, given to the subject upon satisfactory completion of a task. When a response is made to a cue situation, the person responding may receive some sort of stimulus. We have seen in our example that this stimulus can be positive or negative, and it can be verbal (a remark) or nonverbal (a smile). Regardless of its nature, we know one thing: Humans like to receive positive stimuli—or, in plain language, feeling good is nice.

This really begs the question, however, since it leaves unresolved the problem of defining "feeling good." Some psychologists take the position that people have certain drives or needs (like a need for shelter, security, or affiliation with others), and that any stimulus that satisfies these needs has reward value. This argument certainly reveals why parents are such important models for young children. We assume that a child needs a close and warm relationship with his or her parents. Consequently, any stimulus that tells the child that this relationship in facts exists, such as a smile or an approving remark, will have reward value. The child will do those things that result in this type of reward.

Later in life, of course, the parent loses the position of extreme importance as the child's model. The source of satisfaction of the child's needs passes from the parental family to the peer group during adolescence and then to the marital family and the work group during adulthood. Naturally, we see a parallel decline in modeling on the parent as the child matures. He or she typically passes through a period when the peer group is extremely important as a model, particularly in certain areas like dating. In adulthood, of course, the principal models are the spouse and the important individuals in the occupational group, who often control both psychic and material rewards and with whom a satisfactory relationship is consequently sought.

One further distinction should be made in the discussion of rewards. Some rewards have innate value to the individual and are desired for their own sake. Food satisfies the hunger motive in a direct way. Such rewards are known as primary reinforcers. Other kinds of rewards are secondary reinforcers because they do not satisfy any need directly. Their value as rewards must be learned. The infant does not immediately respond to the mother's smile, because there is no association with any need reduction. However, the infant soon makes the connection between the smile and feeding. Eventually, the smile takes on a reward value, even if it is not always followed by a feeding, because it symbolizes the warm, nurturant relationship the child has experienced with the mother.

In social learning, secondary reinforcement is probably far more important than primary reinforcement. Children are particularly sensitive to small signals, such as a sigh or a grimace, and seem ready to interpret them as messages of importance in the need-fulfillment process.

Finally, when a response goes unrewarded for a long period of time, it becomes less likely to occur. If a behavior ceases to be useful (which is just another way of saying provide a reward), it well be discarded in favor of more productive behaviors. Indeed, some have argued that social and economic progress hinges on the human race's ability to discard old skills and move on to new, more productive ones.

Generalization and Discrimination. We rarely encounter identical cue situations. Even if several cue situations involve the same political candidate, the cue differs with respect to the medium by which the information is conveyed, the situation in which the candidate is depicted, or the particular stage of development of the campaign, to name just a few possible differences. Clearly, the learning that a particular response to a certain cue situation will be rewarded becomes generalized eventually to a broad set of somewhat different cue situations. The child may learn to respond positively to Carter no matter under what conditions he appears. The child may even get to the point where he or she learns that Mr. Carter is just a member of an even larger set, namely Democrats, and that it is appropriate to feel positive toward all Democrats.

Conditions Facilitating Social Learning

At this stage we can reassemble the elements of social learning theory in order to acquire a sense of when such learning is most likely to take place. Two factors seem to arise from our discussion, the characteristics of the environment and the needs of the individual.

The learning environment can be characterized in a number of ways. First, although a stimulus may clearly constitute a reward (or a punishment) in the eyes of an impartial observer, the individual who is actually in the learning situation may see things differently. The first example that I related above, the child's derisive comment about Carter's intelligence because of his disappointment over missing a favorite program, had no direct political content. That response-reward sequence, taken by itself, would almost certainly have not resulted in political learning. Learning is much more likely to take place when the response is to a cue situation that relates to the candidate (as in the third example where the child comments about Carter's picture), and the reward is unambiguously directed at that response.

Learning is also facilitated if the child does not experience contradictory stimuli from different models. If two models, the mother and the father, for instance, reward opposite responses, neither one is likely to be learned. When both parents are Republicans, or both Democrats, the child is more likely to establish his or her own sense of partisanship than is true if the parents support opposing parties.

This idea of contradictory rewards illustrates what the sociologists have called cross-pressure. When a person is exposed to a group of models, the extent to which that group is small, homogeneous, cohesive and in agreement on political subjects will determine its effectiveness in fostering political learning. The family is probably the prototypical small, homogeneous, cohesive group. As we move to larger and less homogeneous groups, such as the peer group or the occupational group, we begin to find contradictory rewards being given to certain responses. The problem is heightened even more when people begin to associate with several different groups. A Catholic may find himself rewarded for speaking well of the Democratic party in a group of his coreligionists, but if his job is in the management of an insurance company, he will likely find that responses friendly to the Democrats are not well received. Rather than be a strong Democrat in one group and a strong Republican in the second, he will probably not consider himself to be a strong partisan at all—or at least he won't talk about it.

The second factor that facilitates social learning focuses on the needs of the individual. If a stimulus fills such a need, the response which elicits the stimulus will be learned. From this we can make two conclusions. First, when an individual's needs in a certain area are already met, he will be less likely to respond to a stimulus that promises a reward in that area. Striving for good grades may be particularly important for a student who needs reassurance that he won't flunk out of school, but a student with a solid B average won't seek that particular reward (a high grade) quite so avidly. His needs have been met. By the same token, a person who moves into a new community may go to a great deal of effort to learn about the new and unfamiliar political situation. A long-time resident, on the other hand, has a basic understanding of how politics in the community operate. Since his need to understand his world is less, the "reward" of increased understanding that comes with the learning of new facts is less central to him.

Imitation.

The student of psychology has probably decided by now that this fancy theory called social learning is really nothing more than operant conditioning. There is one important difference, however. The behavioral psychologists, like Skinner, believe that any response can eventually be learned by an individual through selective reinforcement. All we have to do is wait for the subject to make a response that resembles the one we want. We select that response for a reward and ignore all the others.

The social learning theorists maintain that operant conditioning cannot account for all responses. At some point we find that we want to bring about the learning of a response that is totally unfamiliar to the individual. No matter how long we wait to reward a response that resembles the one we want, it will never come. Language, for example, is composed of a very large set of totally unfamiliar responses and can never be learned through operant conditioning.[23] The acquisition of unfamiliar responses proceeds along the lines laid out in operant conditioning, to be sure, but the observation and imitation of models are the major means by which novel responses are brought into the child's repertory.

SUMMARY

It would indeed be useful if someone were to discover a way to integrate these three theories of learning into a single model for political socialization. There are, after all, certain areas of shared emphasis. Piaget's theory, for instance, deals mainly with the description of cognitive levels and explains behavior from there. However, if we probe deeply enough, we begin to wonder why it is that people bother to go through the process of accommodation and assimilation. It must be bothersome, after all, to have to reequilibrate one's cognitive outlook. The answer to this seems to lie in operant conditioning. People acquire new information because they are rewarded for doing so. That reward may be simply the satisfaction of new understanding, or it may relate to some direct benefit the new information brings. In either case, the social learning approach has some relevance within the context of cognitive-developmental theory.

Psychoanalytic theory overlaps social learning theory because both rely on the concept of need. For the latter the state of need of the individual is one of a number of ideas involved in the overall theory, whereas for the psychoanalytic approach the need felt by the child for his parents' affection is much more central. Nonetheless, we might conceive of psychoanalytic theory as representing a special case of social learning theory, at least in that particular aspect.

Of course, socialization occurs among adults as well as children. Of the three approaches, only social learning theory really applies to adults. Cognitive-developmental theory assumes that the highest level of development is reached by the midteens, and psychoanalytic theory as applied to political socialization focuses on the young child's relationship with his or her parents (although psychoanalytic theory in general encompasses the entire life cycle).

All in all, the best advice I can give is to approach studies in political socialization on a case-by-case basis. The approach most relevant in any given instance must ultimately be the one that enhances understanding the most.

NOTES

1. Harold Orlansky, "Reactions to the Death of President Roosevelt," *Journal of Social Psychology*, 26 (November 1947), 235–266. Quoted from Fred I. Greenstein, *Children and Politics* (New Haven: Yale University Press, 1965), pp. 47–48.
2. Sylvia Ginsparg, Alice Moriarty, and Lois B. Murphey, "Young Teen-Agers' Responses to the Assassination of President Kennedy: Relation to Previous Life Experiences," in Martha Wolfenstein and Gilbert Kliman (Eds.), *Children and the Death of a President* (Garden City, N.Y.: Anchor Books, 1966), chap. 1.
3. For a more extensive discussion of these ideas, see Fred I. Greenstein, *Personality and Politics: Problems of Evidence, Inference, and Conceptualization* (Chicago: Markham, 1969).

4. Martha Wolfenstein, "Death of a Parent and Death of a President: Children's Reactions to two Kinds of Loss," in Wolfenstein and Kliman (Eds.), *op. cit.*, pp. 75–76.

5. Although certain aspects have suffered a marked decline in recent years. See Chapter 5.

6. Robert E. Lane, "Fathers and Sons: Foundations of Political Belief," *American Sociological Review*, vol. 24, no. 4 (August 1959), 502–511.

7. *Ibid.*, p. 507.

8. *Ibid.*, p. 508.

9. *Ibid.*, p. 509.

10. Piaget has produced a nearly endless stream of writings over the past 40 years. Useful here are Jean Piaget, *The Origins of Intelligence in Children* (New York: Norton, 1963), and Jean Piaget, *The Moral Judgment of the Child* (New York: Free Press, 1966).

11. This example and ensuing discussion is drawn from Susan Harter, "Piaget's Theory of Intellectual Development: The Changing World of the Child," in Edward Zigler and Irvin L. Child (Eds.), *Socialization and Personality Development* (Reading, Mass.: Addison–Wesley, 1973), chap. 3.

12. Joseph Adelson and Robert P. O'Neil, "Growth of Political Ideas in Adolescence: The Sense of Community," *Journal of Personality and Social Psychology*, vol. 4, no. 3 (1966), 295–306; Judith Gallatin and Joseph Adelson, "Individual Rights and the Public Good, a Cross-National Study of Adolescence," *Comparative Political Studies*, vol. 3, no. 2 (July 1970), 226–242; Joseph Adelson, Bernard Green, and Robert P. O'Neil, "Growth of the Idea of Law in Adolescence," *Developmental Psychology*, vol. 1, no. 4 (July 1969), 327–332; Joseph Adelson and Lynette Beall, "Adolescent Perspectives on Law and Government," *Law and Society Review*, vol. 4, no. 4 (May 1970), 495–504.

13. Adelson, Green, and O'Neil. *op. cit.*, p. 27.

14. Adelson and O'Neil, *op. cit.*, pp. 297ff.

15. *Ibid.*, p. 298.

16. *Ibid.*

17. Adelson, Green, and O'Neil, *op. cit.*

18. Roberta S. Sigel, "An Exploration into Some Aspects of Political Socialization: School Children's reaction to the Death of a President," in Wolfenstein and Kliman (Eds.), *op. cit.*, chap. 2.

19. For extensive treatments of social learning theory see Albert Bandura and Richard H. Walters, *Social Learning and Personality Development* (New York: Holt, Rinehart and Winston, 1963); Neal Miller and John Dollard, *Social Learning and Imitation* (New Haven: Yale University Press, 1941).

20. Sheilah Koeppen, "Children and Compliance: A Comparative Analysis of Socialization Studies," *Law and Society Review*, vol. 4, no. 4 (May 1970), 545–564.

21. Robert R. Sears, "Identification as a Form of Behavioral Development," in D. Harris (Ed.), *The Concept of Development* (Minneapolis: University of Minnesota Press, 1957), 149–161.

22. This discussion is drawn from H. T. Reynolds, *Politics and the Common Man: An Introduction to Political Behavior* (Homewood, Ill.: Dorsey, 1974), pp. 72ff.

23. Bandura and Walters, *op. cit.*, chap. 1.

5
Political Culture I: Attachments to the Political System

We live in a world of great political instability. In the past few years alone, Lebanon, Nigeria, Angola, Vietnam, and Pakistan have fought civil wars. Two of these resulted in major changes in national boundaries; Vietnam has been reunified and Pakistan has seen its eastern section become the independent nation of Bangladesh. Between the end of World War II and 1968, 17 of the 20 countries in South America experienced successful coups d'état.[1] Canada, our good friend to the north, and long the very symbol of political calm and stability, now finds itself faced with the political violence of a secessionist movement in the French-speaking province of Quebec.

It often seems perplexing that some countries enjoy domestic tranquility, while others are beset with continuous turmoil and occasional revolution. In America we are tempted to think that political stability is the fruit of democracy, and other countries have trouble because of the authoritarian qualities of their regimes. This explanation fails to satisfy, however, when with little difficulty we can find democratic countries that experience turmoil and revolution (Allende's Chile), and authoritarian countries that appear to be quite stable and tranquil (the Soviet Union).

Perhaps this puzzle arises because the assumption that democracy leads to tranquility puts the chicken before the egg. It may be that a certain political consensus must be established first, and then democracy may follow. If this is so, then the study of socialization becomes central to our understanding of politics and the fate of nation states, for it is socialization which underlies consensus. Easton and Dennis, in one of the classic studies in political socialization, explore exactly this sort of question.[2] Their research leads them to the conclusion that the stability of the political system rests heavily on the level of support provided to it by the citizens. This political support can be in concrete form, such as tax revenue, or it can be in very abstract form, such as the willingness to obey the law.

A political system can do much to generate support for itself. All Presidents who are facing reelection know that there are certain things they can do to make the voters feel good about their administration. They can create new jobs, sign education bills, or declare an expansion of the national park system, for example.

But ultimately, a political system cannot buy the support it needs to survive. A war or depression could come along and drain all surplus capital that might have gone for jobs or education. How does a system survive in hard times such as these, when there is no possibility of buying support with favorable policies? The answer lies in the process of socialization and the concept of culture. Through the process of learning about our political world, most of us come to view our political system as *legitimate;* that is, we freely grant it the right to make certain kinds of decisions without regard to whether these decisions benefit us personally. Most of us, for instance, think that the government's requirement that we hand over a large chunk of our paychecks in the form of taxes is legitimate (although the amount is sometimes open to debate). This feeling of legitimacy will sustain mass allegiance to a system of government, even though that system might fail to provide any material benefits over an extended period of time.

THE CONCEPT OF CULTURE

What is this thing I have called political culture? The concept of culture comes to political science from the anthropologists, who have used it to compare social systems by examining the values held by the systems' members.[3] Kluckhohn, for instance, speaks of culture as "the total life way of a people, the social legacy the individual acquires from his group."[4] Others focus more specifically on the psychological component, and speak of the norms, values, myths, and traditions which are shared by a society and which are passed on from generation to generation.[5]

Political culture, then, consists of those particular elements of the total way of life of a people that have political relevance. I define political culture in three parts. First, culture has to do with attitudes that people hold.[6] Whether they are called myths, traditions, or values matters little. I mean basically a person's predisposition to react in a certain way to a stimulus when given the opportunity. Second, these are attitudes that are passed from one generation to the next through the process of socialization. Finally, the attitudes in question have political relevance.

Importance of Political Culture

This system of attitudes that I label political culture has more than academic importance. It is a concept that can explain a great deal about how governments operate and is central even in the explanation of national stability. This is true for two basic reasons. First, culture acts to shape the social process. Second, culture resists change as it is passed from generation to generation.

The Shaping of the Social Process. There can be no doubt that culture, in the broadest sense, influences the modes of behavior that typify a society. Religion, for instance, is a cultural phenomenon having profound influences on behavior. So is language. In the political realm, culture can also be demonstrated to play an important role in influencing the social process. A generally shared feeling of patriotism, for instance, leads to a common sense of threat in wartime, which leads in turn to an extraordinary willingness of individual citizens to accept inconveniences such as rationing, and even sacrifices such as the loss of life, usually without questioning the right of the government to impose rationing or induct young men into the armed forces.

We would be mistaken, however, to see political culture as an overwhelming value force that determines all social responses in the political realm. Political activity can be best understood as the *shared* outcome of an interaction process between the political culture, on the one hand, and the events taking place in the environment, on the other. We should imagine a process in which events provide opportunities for citizens to respond in one way or another. The particular response they choose is *shaped* by their culture. An example of this might be the response made by Americans to the depression of 1929. This national crisis was a severe test of our collective loyalty to our particular political process. Economic hardship was widespread, and yet no major challenge was ever mounted against the way in which political decisions were made. The only important political consequence occurred well within the established rules of the game: The Republicans were voted out of office and the Democrats were voted in.

An interesting contrast to the American experience occurred in Germany. Before World War II, that country was operating under a political system, the Weimar Republic, which had not grown up from German origins but had been imposed by the Allies upon a defeated country at the close of World War I. The political culture of Germany between the wars did not include the idea that the Weimar constitution was necessarily the one that Germany should have. When the depression struck Europe, the stress it placed on Germany proved too great. Hitler was able first to subvert the Weimar constitution and then finally to replace it altogether with the Third Reich. Both America and Germany shared the depression, but differences in the ways the respective political cultures shaped the national responses led ultimately to quite different political outcomes.

The Persistence of Culture. The second characteristic of political culture is that it tends to perpetuate itself from one generation to the next. That is, the basic, consensual attitudes people hold about politics don't change much over time. The explanation for this stability of attitudes arises from the fact that a good many of the basic elements of the political culture are acquired through the process of childhood socialization. Such early learning, particularly if it touches on the psychoanalytic aspect of the parent-child relationship, can be expected to result in some very basic orientations that endure throughout life.

Attitudes learned during the socialization processes of early childhood persist not only because they tend to be linked to basic personality needs but also because they do not have to compete with previously learned attitudes. Children have few, if any, political attitudes. If a young boy begins to sense that his parents favor the Republican party, he will have no problem in adopting that loyalty for his own because he has no previous loyalty to the Democrats. The same thing is true of most other elements of the political culture. Learning is accepted uncritically because there is nothing upon which to base criticism.

In the United States, the central elements of the political culture also persist for a reason that is external to the individual. Our political culture is highly (although not perfectly) consensual. It has the authority of tradition. It has existed in the same basic form from a time well before the memory of any living citizen. This fact makes it quite difficult for Americans even to imagine alternative answers to certain basic political questions. The central elements of the political culture persist in part by default; options are rarely presented.

The consequence of the persistence of culture is that it gives stability to political life in a country. What the political system does and what the mass citizenry does with respect to it become more or less predictable in a country that enjoys a consensual political culture. In our own country there are certain fundamental political actions that take place at predictable times, no matter what. During World War II, when the future of the Western democracies was very much in doubt, the United States continued to hold a presidential election every fourth year, even though the possibility existed that the commander-in-chief would have had to be changed had Roosevelt lost. The very fact that we always accept the elected presidential candidate, no matter how much we dislike him or his policies, is an indication of a deep-seated feeling we have about what is right in politics.

Perhaps these examples seem trivial to you. After all, no one has even proposed not allowing a President to take office.[7] However, when we look to countries in which politics is less predictable, obvious contrasts emerge. For instance, the military has repeatedly intervened to prevent the accession to power of popularly elected heads of state in Latin America on the ground that their ideologies were too leftist.

Political Religion

We have now seen that certain attitudes about politics are held very centrally—and that some of them are so central that they are simply never questioned but are accepted as postulates about the nature of political life. This unquestioning acceptance of certain political attitudes by nearly all Americans has been discussed by Lipsitz and others under the label of political religion.[8] Lipsitz argues that whatever exists politically is the result of choices, decisions either made or unmade (the latter are sometimes called "nondecisions"), of the mass electorate. The existence of a political religion in America means that many, indeed most, basic political decisions are removed from the agenda; that is, most of the possible choices in American politics remain undiscussed. They are nonissues, practices sanctified by nondecisions. We simply accept much of what happens in politics as natural, and therefore beyond serious challenge.[9]

We might take a moment to think of some decisions that could be made by the mass electorate but have instead become nonissues because of the effect of political religion. The decision whether or not our country should be abolished is one which hasn't seriously occurred to any large number of Americans for generations. Deciding elections by a majority vote and even the use of elections at all as the mechanism for making political choices, are two further examples of assumptions we make about our political process without ever imagining that things might be different. The same is true of the idea that elections should be contested freely by opposing candidates. No one seriously proposes that these elements of our system be altered. Yet we need only look at other countries to convince ourselves that our particular choices on these matters are not the only ones possible. The Soviet Union holds popular elections, but the candidates all have the approval of the Communist Party. Greece has an elected government, but that government exists under the constant threat of being disbanded by the army. And why should we have a President at all? There are certainly other solutions. Even among the Western democracies we find prime ministers and kings. We are so inbred with the presidential tradition that we vest enormous trust not only in the office but in the man who holds the office, regardless of how little he may deserve that trust.

It comes as no surprise that political religion, this preemption of many political choices, results from political socialization. There is much in the socialization process that encourages acceptance. Socialization is really a very conservative phenomenon. When your parents discuss partisan politics, they nearly always talk about the Democratic and Republican parties. Each successive generation grows up without any real sense that other options, such as third parties, are possible. Our schools typically teach the basic political dogma about the sanctity of the Constitution and the hero status of various national figures. Not only this, but indirectly, they manage very effectively to get across the idea that obedience to authority is a cardinal virtue.

Is political religion good or bad? It depends upon your perspective. Lipsitz takes a point of view that stresses personal ethics.[10] He recalls that Thoreau grew to be very much concerned with what the state was doing since he believed that because he was a citizen, the actions of the state were carried out in his name. From the perspective of political religion, he refused to allow any political choice to go unexamined. When he discovered that he could not prevent the state from committing acts he considered to be immoral, he attempted to withdraw his membership in the political community. This he did by ceasing to pay his taxes, for which he was unceremoniously jailed.

Thoreau's example illustrates the argument in favor of political religion rather well. This is the pragmatic case, which holds that if all political choices were open for discussion in each ensuing generation, political stability would be impossible. After all, there would really be very little the government could do if the American people ceased paying taxes. It could not very well throw 100 million citizens in jail. Such an event would very likely bring about the end of the system in its present form.

The case against political religion makes reference to one of the underlying themes of this book. The forfeiture of political choices by the mass electorate inevitably increases the power of the political elites. To the extent that the electorate allows the status quo to go unchallenged, those in positions of political authority exercise greater latitude in their own political decision making. Political religion, in other words, leads the mass electorate to default on the sovereignty guaranteed to it under the Constitution.

THE CONTENT OF AMERICAN POLITICAL CULTURE: THE POLITICAL SYSTEM

The time has come to move from the general discussion of political culture into a description of the major elements of the culture in the United States. In order to do this we shall divide the political system into three parts: the political community, the regime, and the government.

The Political Community

One of the most unshakable elements of the American political culture is the sense we have of belonging. Very few people doubt their basic political identity; when you fill out an application for a job or a passport, you just *know* what to put in the box labeled nationality. From an historical perspective, this unquestioned sense of national identity is tied to the fact that, with one major exception, our political experience over the past 200 years has been as a single identifiable political entity.

In contemporary America, attachment to the political community takes a number of forms. Most basically, we can discuss those attitudes that involve identification with the political community and those that involve its symbols.

Identification with the Political Community. One way to assess the feeling of identification with one's country is to ask someone whether, if given a choice, he or she would prefer to live elsewhere. Of several national groups tested, Americans consistently show themselves to be the most partial to their own country. Table 5.1 shows first the fact that Americans are indeed the most ready of these four nationalities to remain at home. Swedes, who reside in another wealthy (and therefore attractive) land, showed comparable levels of preference in both years. The effects of the Second World War are evident in the responses of both the British and the Dutch. The Netherlands in particular was not a very attractive place to be in 1948. The postwar rebuilding and the subsequent economic boom has brought a great change in these people's attitudes about their homeland, a recovery similar to that seen in the United States after the Civil War.

Children tend to be even more positive about their country than are adults. The simple statement "America is the best country in the world" elicited interesting results from Hess and Torney's sample of American youngsters. When their answers are compared with those of a similar

TABLE 5.1. Preference for Native Land

Country	Percent Answering No	
	1948	1971
United States	94%	88%
Sweden	85%	82%
Netherlands	56%	84%
Great Britain	53%	59%

Question: If you were free to do so, would you like to settle in another country?

Sources: *Public Opinion Quarterly*, vol. 12, no. 3 (Fall 1948), 544; *Gallup Opinion Index*, Report No. 71 (May 1971), 25.

group of Colombian children, we discover that between the second and eighth grade American schoolchildren maintain a highly positive attitude toward their country. The feeling that America is the best even increases a little between the younger and the older children. The Colombians, likewise, feel positive about their country at the youngest age level. However, by the eighth grade—about age 13—they have reversed their opinions rather severely.[11] Evidently in the Colombian culture the sense of admiration for the political system is not instilled nearly as effectively as it is in the United States.

Finally, the classic five-nation study of Almond and Verba reveals another aspect of national identity. It sought to find out what adults in five countries were most proud of. In Table 5.2 it is seen that Americans are nearly unanimous in the pride they feel in their nation. Contrast Germany and Italy, two of the losers in World War II, whose inhabitants must have felt considerable confusion about their political systems in the late 1950s when this study was conducted. Not even the British system, with a great political tradition, generates nearly the same level of pride in its inhabitants as is true of the United States.

Symbols of the Political Community. The second main set of attitudes toward the political community involves political symbols. This part of the political culture emphasizes certain artifacts and myths of political importance. These symbols make it easy for citizens to form identifications with the political community. They are easily recognized and universally accepted.

I have already mentioned one of the most obvious of all political symbols, the American flag. Lawson's study illustrated how even very young children not only recognize that the flag "belongs" to them, but they have also learned that it is a "good" flag, while the flag of the Soviet Union is a "bad" flag. Hess and Torney asked a sample of high school teachers

TABLE 5.2. Aspects of the Nation in Which Respondents Report Pride[a]

Percent Who Say They Are Proud of:	U.S.	Great Britain	Germany	Italy	Mexico
Governmental, political institutions	85	46	7	3	30
Economic system	23	10	33	3	24
Physical attributes of country	5	10	17	25	22
Nothing or don't know	4	10	15	27	16

Source: Extracted from Gabriel Almond and Sidney Verba, *The Civic Culture: Political Attitudes and Democracy in Five Nations* (copyright © 1963 by Princeton University Press), p. 102. Percentages do not add to 100 because of multiple responses and because several categories from the original table are omitted here.
[a] Figures are from 1959 except for U.S. figures, which are from 1960.

which they thought was the best flag in the world, and they were even more positive than the children. Fully 92 percent of that group endorsed the American flag.[12]

The Vietnam War provided a graphic example of the emotional attachment that most Americans feel toward the flag. Protesters discovered that they could generate a great deal of attention by burning or otherwise damaging the flag. Indeed, these acts caused so much furor that in 1967 the House of Representatives passed a bill that would have imposed a $1000 fine *and* a year in jail to anyone who defiled the American flag.

Numerous other artifacts provide symbolic links to our sense of belonging to the American political community. Government buildings, such as the Capitol and the White House, are central examples. The Pledge of Allegiance, both in its own right and through its association with the flag, is a symbol of great strength. The Statue of Liberty has special significance for the many immigrants to this country, and it is recognized universally as one of our major political symbols.

Along with these national artifacts, political symbols also include our national heroes. Shortly after World War II, a sample of Americans were asked to name the two or three greatest men who have ever lived. (Franklin D. Roosevelt had died a short time earlier, so his name was dropped from the list.) Of this list of nine individuals, you can easily see that five were former Presidents, and three others were intimately bound up with politics and our national destiny. Only Thomas Edison could be said not to belong to the group of political heroes. The Gallup poll shows the continuing admiration we have for politicians. Every year, seven or eight of the ten most admired men and women are involved in national politics.[13]

TABLE 5.3. Hero Symbols in American History

Choice	Percent Mentioning
Abraham Lincoln	57
George Washington	46
Thomas A. Edison	11
Woodrow Wilson	8
Dwight D. Eisenhower	7
Thomas Jefferson	6
Douglas MacArthur	5
Theodore Roosevelt	5
Benjamin Franklin	4
Other mentions	92
No one	3

Source: *Public Opinion Quarterly*, vol. 9, no. 4 (Winter 1945–1946), 520.

Perhaps no greater place of honor exists in our political culture than that reserved for Abraham Lincoln. Gabriel has gone so far as to compare Americans' reverence for Lincoln to a religious cult.

> A cult requires a sanctuary. That of Lincoln has three—the birthplace in Kentucky, the grave in Illinois, and the great memorial in Washington. Of these the last is most important. . . . It is a Greek temple. Within it is a graven image . . . a romanticized Lincoln. [Certain] devices enhance the religious atmosphere; on the walls in bronze are the words of the hero, and above the brooding figure is an inscription. . . . In such temples and with similar inscriptions the citizens of ancient Greece placed statues of Apollo. By so little is the twentieth century after Christ separated from the fifth before his coming.[14]

Lincoln seems to combine all the best traits of a hero. A common man, raised in humble surroundings, he rose by virtue of his own hard work. He presided during America's greatest period of national crisis, and preserved the nation. And he was martyred just as he was to see the Civil War end. Indeed, there is no wonder that Lincoln is our ultimate political hero, one of the major links between Americans and their political community.

The Regime

When we speak of the regime, we generally refer to the institutions and the structure that define our political system. It represents the "rules of the game." At the heart of the regime is the Constitution and the Bill of Rights. These documents set out how we conduct our political affairs—by elections, through due process, and so forth. They also create the institutions necessary to conduct politics: the executive, legislature, and judiciary.

The Constitution as a Symbol. Let us turn first to a consideration of the attitudes of support for the fundamental political agreements that govern society. Clearly, the most important of these agreements are embodied in the Constitution and the Bill of Rights. These documents form the contract existing between the people and their government, giving that government the right to rule.

What, then, are the attitudes of the American electorate regarding this most central element of our regime? Needless to say, the Constitution and Bill of Rights are generally regarded as something closely akin to holy writ. Any act that might call into question the existence of either of these documents simply does not enter into serious consideration. While other advanced democracies, such as France, feel perfectly comfortable with a shift in constitution every few decades, that prospect does not even exist in the realm of the imagination for most Americans.

A valuable illustration of American's devotion to the Constitution can be had by looking back to the most serious national crisis of this century, the Great Depression. During that period the economy faltered seriously, leaving widespread unemployment, privation, and political discontent. That moment, of all moments, would be the time to expect that Americans might at least have considered changing the political rules of the game. Table 5.4, which reports a 1940 public opinion poll, shows how far such an expectation is from the truth.

We can easily see in this table that Americans, even in a period of great political stress, still gave their unreserved blessings to the Constitution by nearly a two-thirds majority. Only one person in 20 was willing to say that we might eventually have some new form of government.

More recent assessments of support for the Constitution, though phrased in more general terms, send a similar message. In 1973 a national survey asked whether a change in the governmental system should be made. You can see in Table 5.5 some increase in the willingness of Americans to endorse a major change in their form of government between 1940 and 1973, but in part this is because the Constitution is not specifically mentioned. In essence, these data show a continuing majority of the electorate that gives strong support to having our system of government unchanged, and only a small minority (13 percent) firmly committed to making some change.

The Constitutional Rules of the Game. You should not be too anxious, however, to conclude that this show of support means necessarily that the

TABLE 5.4. The Constitution as a Symbol (1940)

1. Our form of government, based upon the Constitution, is as near perfect as it can be and no important changes should be made in it	65%
2. The Constitution has served its purpose well, but it has not kept up with the times and it should be thoroughly revised to make it fit present-day needs	19
3. The system of private capitalism and democracy are breaking down and we might as well accept the fact that sooner or later we shall have to have a new form of government	5
4. Don't know	11
	100%

Question: Which of the following most nearly represents your opinion of the American form of government?

Source: *Public Opinion Quarterly*, vol. 4, no. 2 (June 1940), 349.

TABLE 5.5. Support for a Major Change in Our System of Government (1973)

Strongly agree	37%
Agree, with reservations	26
Disagree, with reservations	17
Strongly disagree	13
Not sure	7
	100%

Question: Although we need better leadership, our government system should not be changed in any major way.

Source: Harris poll, 1973. Reported in *Public Opinion Quarterly*, vol. 40, no. 4 (Winter 1976–77), 551.

great majority of Americans ardently support the political rules of the game as they are set out in the Constitution. These positive attitudes may not arise out of any great respect for the political rules of the game themselves, but rather may merely derive from the Constitution's symbolic value.

Why is this an important distinction? If we are dealing with a symbol-related attitude, we would expect that the person holding that attitude would also feel very positive about other national symbols. Indeed, this is a very common pattern among Americans. On the other hand, if this is a rule-related attitude, then we should also expect endorsement of the various specific rules of the game that the Constitution sets out. This assumption is often made about Americans, but it is worthwhile to probe a little more deeply to discover just how true it actually is.

Prothro and Grigg wondered about some of these same questions some years ago, and they decided to test whether respect for our political rules of the game is really as deep as the feelings of support for the Constitution make it appear. Working in Ann Arbor, Michigan (a relatively liberal city), and Tallahassee, Florida (a relatively conservative city), they explored the acceptance of the rules of the game in two areas: that acts of government should reflect the wishes of the majority and that the minority must be assured of fair treatment.[15]

The first step in their study was to ask whether the people who were interviewed supported a number of basic principles that were logically related to the ideas of majority rule and minority rights. There were five of these basic principles:

Democracy is the best form of government.
Public officials should be chosen by majority vote.
All citizens should have a chance to influence government policy.
The minority should be free to criticize majority decisions.

People in the minority should be free to try to win majority support for their opinions.

As we might expect, Prothro and Grigg found widespread support for these five rules of the game. Between 95 and 98 percent of the people they talked to gave their support.

Prothro and Grigg realized, however, that these five statements of principle are quite abstract and unspecific. As such, they are distant from any particular situation people might actually find themselves in. Endorsing the principle of majority rule is easy, therefore, because it makes no particular demands on anyone's behavior.

The final step in the Ann Arbor–Tallahassee study was designed to put people on the spot. They were asked to apply the principles they had just endorsed to situations with which they could easily imagine coming in contact. Furthermore, some of these situations involved groups or practices that in the past have not been extended the protection of our democratic principles, including blacks, Communists, and atheists. Table 5.6 gives the proportion of the people in the two cities that gave the democratic response to each question—that is, the answer that matched the principles of majority rule or minority rights.

The lesson of Table 5.6 is that Americans' attachment to the political rules of the game is in some measure a symbolic one only. We can see in this table that only one-half to three-quarters of the sample in Prothro and Grigg's study gave democratic responses in specific applications of the very democratic principles they had nearly all endorsed in the same interview. This means that for between one-quarter and one-half of the sample, democratic principles are simply symbols. They may provide a sense of attachment to the regime or to the political community, but this is true only in the abstract. Whenever the observance of the rules is put to the test, these individuals are not able to put these principles into practice.[16]

Another way of measuring Americans' support for the political regime is through their attitudes about the main institution responsible for law enforcement in society: the police. Once again, we find a very strong favorable predisposition among most Americans. The adult sample in the Hess and Torney study rated the policeman right behind their father as the person (or institution) most willing to help with a problem.[17] Almond and Verba found a similar attitude. Eighty-five percent of their American sample said they felt that they could expect to be treated as well as anybody else if they had some trouble with the police. It is interesting to note that not all Western nations share this positive point of view. In Italy only 56 percent of the sample expected equal treatment, and in Mexico the figure dropped to 32 percent.[18]

As was the case in our examination of Americans' devotion to the Constitution, there is also a sinister side to their feelings of support for the police.

TABLE 5.6. Percentage of "Democratic" Responses to Specific Applications of the Basic Principles of Democracy

Majority Rule	
In a city referendum, only people who are well informed about the problem being voted on should be allowed to vote.	49
In a city referendum deciding on tax-supported undertakings, only taxpayers should be allowed to vote.	21
If a Negro were legally elected mayor of this city, the white people should not allow him to take office.	81
If a Communist were legally elected mayor of this city, the people should not allow him to take office.	46
A professional organization like the AMA has a right to try to increase the influence of doctors by getting them to vote as a bloc in elections.	45
Minority Rights	
If a person wanted to make a speech in this city against churches and religion, he should be allowed to speak.	63
If a person wanted to make a speech in this city favoring government ownership of all the railroads and big industries, he should be allowed to speak.	79
If an admitted Communist wanted to make a speech in this city favoring communism, he should be allowed to speak.	44
A Negro should not be allowed to run for mayor of this city.	76
A Communist should not be allowed to run for mayor of the city.	42

Source: James W. Prothro and Charles M. Grigg, "Fundamental Principles of Democracy: Bases of Agreement and Disagreement," *The Journal of Politics*, vol. 22, no. 2 (May 1960), 285.

Gamson and McEvoy placed a national sample of Americans in a situation in which they had to choose between support for the police and support for the rights of the people with whom the police come in contact.[19] The three questions they asked appear in Table 5.7, which indicates the extent to which Americans will support the actions of the police, even if those actions include violence against people who are either innocent or have committed a minor offense (insulting a policeman) and who in any case have not been protected by our system of due process. Nearly one-half of this sample (45 percent) felt that the police are within their rights to "beat up unarmed protestors," and nearly two-thirds felt that the police do not frequently use more force than they need. This response is especially interesting since the data were collected shortly after the well-publicized "police riot" that occurred in Chicago at the time of the 1968 Democratic National Convention. From their summary measure of support for police

TABLE 5.7. Distribution of Responses to Items in Police Violence Index

	Percentages				
	Strongly Agree	Agree	Disagree	Strongly Disagree	Don't Know
The police are wrong to beat up unarmed protestors, even when these people are rude and call them names	12	37	36	9	6
			45		
The police frequently use more force than they need to when carrying out their duties	9	19	46	18	7
			64		
Any man who insults a policeman has no complaint if he gets roughed up in return	13	44	32	7	4
	57				

Source: Reprinted from "Police Violence and Its Public Support" by William A. Gamson and James McEvoy in volume no. 391 of *The Annals of The American Academy of Political and Social Science*. Copyright © 1970 by the American Academy of Political and Social Science.

violence, which combines the three questions in Table 5.7, Gamson and McEvoy conclude that 40 percent of the American public support police violence to some extent, while only 35 percent oppose it.

SUMMARY

Political culture is a complex of attitudes that are generally held by the citizens of a nation, are passed from generation to generation, and have political relevance. The political relevance rests on the influence political culture has on the social process. Especially in times of crisis, a system with a basically supportive political culture may survive while another with a hostile political culture may be overthrown.

The elements of the American political culture can be discussed in terms of attitudes toward the political community and attitudes toward the regime. Americans have a very strong sense of political community. We identify closely with our sense of nationality and with our homeland. We also hold the central symbols of our nation in high reverence.

The aspect of the political culture that relates to the regime, and particularly to respect shown for the political rules of the game, reveals some ambiguity. On the one hand, there is general support for the fundamental rules of free speech, due process, equality under the law, representative government, and the like. We can also see, however, that the devotion of the American electorate to these ideals is at best superficial. They appear to be treated more as symbols of the American system than as rules that actually govern our lives.

NOTES

1. Samuel P. Huntington, *Political Order in Changing Societies* (New Haven: Yale University Press, 1968), pp. 3–4.
2. David Easton and Jack Dennis, *Children in the Political System: Origins of Political Legitimacy* (New York: McGraw-Hill, 1969), chap. 3.
3. For an extended discussion of political cultures in the United States see Donald J. Devine, *The Political Culture of the United States* (Boston: Little, Brown, 1972). The classic work in the area, which compares the American political culture to those of four other nations, is Gabriel A. Almond and Sidney Verba, *The Civic Culture* (Princeton, N.J.: Princeton University Press, 1963).
4. Alfred Kroeber and Clyde Kluckhohn, *Culture: A Critical Review of Concepts and Definitions* (New York: Random House, 1952). These authors discuss 164 separate definitions of culture.
5. Bernard C. Hennessy, *Public Opinion*, 3d ed. (Belmont, Calif.: Wadsworth, 1975), p. 10.
6. Anthropologists would object to this narrow a definition, since it excludes certain obvious cultural characteristics as language or occupational structure. However, for our own purposes, the narrower and simpler definition is preferable.
7. That statement may not be quite true, depending on how 1876 is counted. In that year Tilden won the popular vote, but Hayes was chosen in the electoral college, subsequent to some heavy bargaining about the withdrawal of federal troops from the South.
8. Lewis Lipsitz, "If, as Verba Says, the State Functions as a Religion, What Are We to Do Then to Save Our Souls?," *American Political Science Review*, vol. 62, no. 2 (June 1968), 527–535.
9. Robert Weissberg, *Political Learning, Political Choice and Democratic Citizenship* (Englewood Cliffs, N.J.: Prentice-Hall, 1974).
10. Lipsitz, *op. cit.*
11. Reid Reading, "Political Socialization in Colombia and the U.S.," *Midwest Journal of Political Science*, vol. 12, no. 3 (August 1968), 361. The U.S data were collected by Robert D. Hess and Judith Torney, *The Development of Political Attitudes in Children* (Chicago: Aldine, 1967).
12. Robert D. Hess and Judith V. Torney, *The Development of Basic Attitudes and Values toward Government and Citizenship during the Elementary School Years*, Part I, Cooperative Research Project No. 1078 (Chicago: University of Chicago Press, 1965), p. 80.
13. *The Gallup Opinion Index*, Report No. 115 (January, 1975), pp. 26–27.
14. Ralph Henry Gabriel, *The Course of American Democratic Thought*, 2d ed. (New York: Ronald, 1956), pp. 449–450.
15. James W. Prothro and Charles M. Grigg, "Fundamental Principles of Democracy: Bases of Agreement and Disagreement," *Journal of Politics*, vol. 22, no. 2 (May 1960), 276–294.
16. The one exception to this, involving limiting the electorate in city referenda to taxpayers, simply reflects the actual practice of the two cities in question.
  Incidentally, don't be led to the conclusion that this lack of observance of our basic rules is an isolated thing. About every ten years someone rediscovers the same thing. See, for example, Robert Chandler, *Public Opinion: Changing Attitudes on Contemporary Political and Social Issues* (New York: Bowker, 1972), and *The Sampler* (Princeton, N.J.: Response Analysis), no. 8 (Spring 1977), 4.
17. Hess and Torney, *The Development of Basic Attitudes, op. cit.*, p. 101.
18. Almond and Verba, *op. cit.*, p. 108.
19. William A. Gamson and James McEvoy, "Police Violence and Its Public Support," *Annals of the American Academy of Political and Social Science*, 391 (September 1970), 97–110.

6

Political Culture II: Views of Politicians and Citizens

This chapter continues the discussion of political culture. Here, however, we shift from the concern with the political community and regime, and focus instead on people—specifically two kinds of people. First, I want to discuss the feelings the American electorate holds toward its political leaders. Second, I want to deal with the ways in which we see our role as citizens, participating in the political life of the nation.

THE GOVERNMENT

By government I mean those people who are currently holding the positions of influence in the political structure. Although the presidency is part of the regime, the President belongs to the government. The Congress is regime; congressmen are government.

One of the most enduring findings to emerge from the study of political socialization is that Americans admire their President. Although some of this probably stems from our admiration of the presidency as one of our national symbols and a part of our constitutional structure, there is also no doubt that the person of the President at any given time is vested with considerable respect. Hess and Torney report that among their adult sample the President is seen as "*always* a leader" and "working harder than anyone."

These positive images of the President also appear in the frequent Gallup poll item that reports the percent of the American population which approves of the way the President is handling his job.[1] The *lowest* approval rating ever given to Franklin Roosevelt was 54 percent. Kennedy's lowest rating was 57 percent, and Eisenhower's was 49 percent. Nixon's lowest before Watergate was 48 percent. Ford's lowest rating was 37, and as of the end of 1978 Carter's lowest was 38 percent.

The remarkable thing about Nixon was the willingness of the American public to continue to support him after his troubles with Watergate began. His support did not fall below 48 percent until April 1973. And even at the very end, when he learned that he could not possibly escape impeachment and conviction in the Congress, a full 25 percent of the American electorate still said that they approved of the way he was handling his duties.

How can we possibly explain such steadfast loyalty? Partly, of course, we are tapping support for the regime and even the political community, for, in David Truman's words, the President serves as the "living symbol" of the political system.[2] However, it is also clear that there are characteristics of the man that come into play. Greenstein has made much of the President as father image.[3] Recall that the young child usually develops positive attitudes toward authority as a way of satisfying the basic drive to ensure a satisfactory relationship with his parents. Spurred by his eventual need to break with his parents, he will often seek some alternative authority figure as a substitute for the security he derived from his parents. The President can easily play that role, along with other public officials like mayors and policemen.

We would be mistaken, however, to place total reliance on this psychoanalytic argument as the explanation of Americans' feelings toward their President. It is clear that social learning also plays a major part in creating this image. "Nothing succeeds like success," the saying goes, and the President's popularity among the older generations means that a positive image will be passed along to the younger members of society.

Political Trust and Cynicism

One of the basic ingredients for political legitimacy is the ability of the mass electorate to trust its government. Without a sense that our representatives in Washington are looking out for all the people, that they are honest and know what they are doing, it becomes difficult for the average citizen to continue to believe that he ought to let that government make decisions that intimately affect his life. To be sure, the "religious" underpinnings of the American political culture insulate our political community and regime from any serious challenge. However, in other nations whose political cultures are not so positively oriented, the loss of trust by a government can easily lead to widespread discontent and may even light the fuse of revolutionary change in the political system.

Studies conducted over a period of years affirm that in the early 1960s the United States did indeed have a very trusting culture. Almond and Verba, for example, found the levels of social trust, measured by the extent of agreement with the item "most people can be trusted," to be higher in the United States than in any of the other four countries tested. Fifty-five percent of Americans agreed with that statement in 1960, compared to 7 percent in Italy.[4]

We also find that in the specifically political area, the early 1960s were times when feelings of trust were very strong. Table 6.1 reveals that in four of five questions posed to a sample of the American electorate, only two or three of every ten Americans chose the cynical (nontrusting) response in 1964.

It is clear, however, that since the early 1960s the views of the American people on the subject of political trust have turned sour. For example, the first question in Table 6.1, which summarizes the citizens' feeling of trust for the government in Washington, shows that 22 percent of the electorate felt that the government could be trusted "only some of the time" in 1964, but only 4 years later, the figure had advanced to 37 percent. The 1970s have brought even higher levels of distrust. By 1972, 45 percent extended their trust "only some of the time," and by the post-Watergate year of 1976, the cynical response was given fully 63 percent of the time! Across all five of these items, by 1976 the cynics outnumbered trusting citizens in every case, and in three instances, the trusting responses were outnumbered two or three to one.

How can we explain this remarkable increase in the level of political cynicism in the United States? There are two periods that emerge if we examine Table 6.1 carefully. The first runs from 1964 to 1970 and the second from 1972 to 1976 (and is perhaps still continuing). With respect to the first period, Arthur H. Miller has advanced the hypothesis that the loss of trust during the late 1960s came about from the failure of the political system to provide the policy outputs which were necessary to satisfy the electorate.[5] Not only that, says Miller, but in all probability it is not possible for the government to do much better in achieving satisfactory policy. Opposing groups on the radical and conservative ends of the political spectrum demand different solutions to the problems of poverty and unemployment, abortion, aid to schools, civil rights, and so forth. A shift in policy in favor of one side would simply increase the cynicism of the other.

The second time period (1972–1976) bears eloquent witness to the impact of Watergate on levels of political trust. You can see that by 1972 the increases in cynicism that Miller observed during the 1960s had pretty well run their course. Between 1970 and 1972 the proportion of cynical responses actually declined in two instances and stayed virtually even in a third. The other two items show only small increases in the size of the cynical group. However, between 1972 and 1976 we see a reemergence of the movement toward greater cynicism. The bulk of this change must be attributed to the effect Watergate has had on the public's view of government.

Given my earlier comments about the importance of political trust for the maintenance of political legitimacy and stability, you may well wonder what the declines documented by Miller will mean for the future of our political system. We can at least conclude that the effects will not be good. However, analysis by Citrin suggests that things may not be all that serious.[6] He agrees that the government's image has steadily declined for several years. However, he challenges Miller's conclusion that this decline reflects "a situation of widespread, basic discontent and political alienation" with respect to the regime as a whole. Instead, Citrin maintains that decline in political trust is a measurement of feeling toward the *people in office* and specifically *does not* involve cynicism toward the regime.

Citrin attempts to test this thesis by asking questions that relate directly to our *form* of government, rather than allowing the respondent to interpret the ambiguous word "government" in his own terms. The 1972 data, plus new results collected in 1976, appear in Table 6.2. They contain the strong suggestion that political cynicism for most people does not extend beyond feelings directed at holders of office. There is something more, however. Although this way of looking at political trust reveals a cynical segment of the electorate which amounted to only 20 or 25 percent of the total in 1976 (versus 50 or 75 percent if we use the items in Table 6.1), we can still find that sinister post-Watergate increase, which was so clearly revealed in the previous table. It is especially obvious in the second item, where the proportion of the sample which said that a "big change" was needed in our form of government jumped from 15 to 25 percent between 1972 and 1976. Only time can reveal the meaning of this increase.

The Socialization of Political Trust. The most important fact to remember about the political attitudes of children is that they are almost totally positive. Greenstein reports that in his study of elementary school children, it was virtually impossible to find a response in all the questions he asked that was critical of the political system or a politician.[7]

How can we explain these pervasively positive political images that young children hold about the political system? In part, we have already seen how psychoanalytic theory argues that the close bond between the child and his parent generalizes to a feeling of warmth toward anyone in a position of authority. But there is more. Both cognitive-developmental and social learning theory are necessary for us to arrive at a full understanding of the origins of political trust.

Greenstein does an admirable job of summing up his discoveries about young children. He says that their remarkably positive political outlook

TABLE 6.1. Responses to Cynicism Items, 1964–1976

How much of the time do you think you can *trust* the government in Washington to do what is right—*just about always, most of the time, or only some of the time?*

	1964	1966	1968	1970	1972	1976
Always	14.0%	17.0%	7.5%	6.4%	5.2%	3.5%
Most of the time	62.0	48.0	53.4	47.1	47.9	29.8
Only some of the time[a]	22.0	31.0	37.0	44.2	44.9	63.4
Don't know	2.0	4.0[b]	2.1	2.3	2.0	3.3
Total	100.0%	100.0%	100.0%	100.0%	100.0%	100.0%
(N)[c]	(4658)	(1291)	(1557)	(1514)	(2279)	(2861)

Would you say the government is pretty much run by a *few big interests* looking out for themselves or that it is run for the *benefit of all the people?*

	1964	1966	1968	1970	1972	1976
For benefit of all	64.0%	53.0%	51.8%	40.6%	37.7%	24.0%
Few big interests[a]	29.0	34.0	39.2	49.6	53.3	66.3
Other; depends; both checked	4.0	6.0	4.6	5.0	2.5	2.6
Don't know	3.0	7.0	4.3	4.8	6.5	7.1
Total	100.0%	100.0%	100.0%	100.0%	100.0%	100.0%

Do you think that people in the government waste *a lot* of the money we pay in taxes, waste *some* of it, or *don't waste very much of it?*

	1964	1966	1968	1970	1972	1976
Not much	6.5%	—	4.2%	3.7%	2.3%	2.9%
Some	44.5	—	33.1	26.1	30.0	19.9
A lot[a]	46.3	—	57.4	68.7	65.8	73.8
Don't know; not ascertained	2.7		5.3	1.5	1.9	3.4
Total	100.0%		100.0%	100.0%	100.0%	100.0%

Do you feel that almost all of the people running the government are smart people who usually *know what they are doing*, or do you think that quite a few of them *don't seem to know what they are doing*?[d]

	1964	1966	1968	1970	1972	1976
Know what they're doing	68.2%	—	56.2%	51.2%	54.7%	43.6%
Don't know what they're doing[a]	27.4	—	36.1	44.1	39.9	49.1
Other; depends	1.9	—	1.8	2.3	0.9	1.9
Don't know; not ascertained	2.5	—	5.9	2.4	4.5	5.4
Total	100.0%		100.0%	100.0%	100.0%	100.0%

Do you think that *quite a few* of the people running the government are a little crooked, *not very many* are, or do you think *hardly any* of them are crooked at all?[d]

	1964	1966	1968	1970	1972	1976
Hardly any	18.2%	—	18.4%	15.9%	14.0%	12.6%
Not many	48.4	—	49.3	48.8	45.2	39.6
Quite a lot[a]	28.0	—	24.8	31.0	35.8	41.3
Don't know; not ascertained	5.4	—	7.5	4.3	5.0	6.5
Total	100.0%		100.0%	100.0%	100.0%	100.0%

Source: Arthur H. Miller, "Political Issues and Trust in Government: 1964–1970," *The American Political Science Review*, vol. 68, no. 3 (September 1974), 953; ICPSR Archive: CPS Presidential Election Studies (1972 and 1976).

[a] Indicates response interpreted as "cynical."
[b] Includes 1% coded "It depends."
[c] The sample size for each of the years applies to all five items. For 1964 and 1976, *N* is weighted.
[d] These items were not included in the 1966 election study interview schedule.

TABLE 6.2. Attitudes toward the American Form of Government

	1972	1976
Pride in government		
I am proud of many things about our form of government	86%	80%
I can't find much about our form of government to be proud of	14	20
	100%	100%
Change our form of government?		
Keep our form of government as is	59%	47%
Some change needed	26	28
Big change needed	15	25
	100%	100%
N:	(1016)	(2673)

Questions:

I'm going to read you a pair of statements about our form of government, and I'd like you to tell me which one you agree with more. Would you say, "I am proud of many things about our form of government" or "I can't find much in our form of government to be proud of?"

Some people believe a change in our whole form of government is needed to solve the problems facing our country, whereas others feel no real change is necessary. Do you think a big change is needed in our form of government, or should it be kept pretty much as it is?

Source: 1972 figures adapted from Jack Citrin, "Comment: The Political Relevance of Trust in Government," *American Political Science Review*, vol. 68, no. 3 (September 1974), 975; 1976 figures from ICPSR Archive: CPS 1976 Presidential Election Study.

arises from the "sugarcoating of the political pill" that their parents engage in during their children's early years. In other words, in their discussions with their children, parents shield their children from negative information about the unsavory realities of the political world.[8] This is, of course, an argument which is based on social learning theory. The essential element is that the messages which the child receives from his models are filtered to exclude any which might suggest a negative attitude about politics. The family and the school as well, in effect, indoctrinate the child to believe the best.

The second part of the sugarcoated-pill argument rests on developmental theory. Surely, you might say, the child is not so dumb as to accept all these obviously incorrect messages about the political system, when every day he can see evidence in the media of the nasty side of political reality.

The cognitive-developmental theorist would say in response that it isn't a question of being "dumb." Rather, the youngest children simply do not possess the concepts or frames of reference necessary to understand any but the simplest of political communications. This oversimplification of government can be illustrated by asking young children what the best picture of government is and presenting them with a number of drawings. Some of their answers are summarized in Table 6.3.

The cognitive-developmental position emerges quite clearly in this table. The simplest of political symbols, George Washington (whose picture must hang in nearly every primary school in the country) and the current President (who happened to be Kennedy at the time of the study), were identified most frequently by the youngest children, who were in the preoperational phase of development. Recall that the preoperational phase is characterized by the inability to grasp relationships or to deal with the concept of community or of cooperative behavior. In this light, the lack of references to voting or to Congress among the youngest children becomes perfectly understandable. As the children move into the concrete operational stage (beginning in about the third grade), their perceptions of the government move away from the personalized image (George Washington fades out almost entirely by about grade 4) and begin to focus on the collective aspects of politics. By grades 4 and 5, as the children begin to move more solidly into the concrete operational stage, references to voting and to the Congress begin to predominate. Children in grade 8 have begun to enter the formal operational stage, with its capacity to reason abstractly—that is, without reference to physical objects—and to understand the concept of community and of communal processes. This is illustrated by the similarity of the conception the eighth graders have of government, centered on voting and the Congress, to that of their adult teachers.

TABLE 6.3. Changes by Grade in Choice of "The Best Picture of Government"

Grade	N	George Washington[a]	Voting	Congress	President
2	1619	39.4	4.3	5.9	46.2
3	1662	26.8	8.4	12.9	46.8
4	1726	14.2	10.8	29.0	37.2
5	1789	6.9	19.2	49.0	38.5
6	1740	4.9	28.0	49.7	30.3
7	1714	3.4	39.4	44.2	27.9
8	1689	1.7	46.8	49.1	22.9
Teachers	390	1.3	71.8	71.0	15.1

Source: Robert D. Hess and Judith V. Torney, *The Development of Political Attitudes in Children* (Chicago: Aldine, 1967), p. 34.

[a] Cell entries are percentages of each age group.

The fact that learning about politics begins in the preoperational phase of cognitive development and that political messages are filtered so that the typical child tends to hear only good things about the political system produces a vitally important perspective on early political learning. It occurs almost entirely at the level of affect, with only the simplest of cognitions to accompany it. Since children learn very little about *what* the government is or does; they therefore can easily accept that it is good, or that it does the right things, or that its agents (the President and the policemen, for instance) are good people like their parents who ought to be trusted and obeyed because they will treat them fairly. As children pass through adolescence and into the world of adult life, they gradually lose the very positive political attitudes that are instilled by their earliest socialization experiences. Nonetheless, the centrality of this early learning assures that in each new generation there exists a firm positive foundation upon which the political culture is built.

The loss of political innocence occurs for two reasons. First, as children get older, they advance to higher levels of cognitive ability. They become able to comprehend the idea of a community and of collective action. They begin to understand what the "national interest" is, and therefore can judge when the act of a politician is "good" or "bad" in terms of some perception of that national interest. In other words, cynicism becomes possible.

The second reason that maturing children begin to change their views of government is because they are exposed to a different set of messages. Their original models, their parents, become less careful about giving only positive views of politics. More important, adolescents develop other models as they mature. Their peers, and the media in particular, make little effort to filter the content of the political material they discuss to include only positive references.

Jennings and his colleagues have provided an opportunity to see exactly how young people changed their feelings of political trust over an 8-year period. They first interviewed a national sample of high school seniors in 1965, and then in 1973 they went back and interviewed the same people a second time. Table 6.4 reveals that in 1965, when these young people were seniors in high school, their level of political trust was exceedingly high. Two of every five students (42 percent) felt they could trust the government in Washington "just about always." In 1964, only 14 percent of the adult population gave this response.

Clearly, however, the ensuing 8 years brought about enormous changes in the way these people viewed the government. By 1973 the two in five who felt the government could be trusted "just about always," had declined to one in ten. In 1972, about 7 percent of the adult population was this trusting. Evidently the 7 or 8 years just after high school are critical ones for young Americans. It is during this time that the positive, trusting

TABLE 6.4. Political Trust of Young Adults in 1965 and 1973

	1965	1973	1965 to 1973 shift	Percent
Just about always	42%	11%	Two steps more trusting	1%
Most of the time	50	56	One step more trusting	7
Only some of the time	8	33	Same in both years	39
	100%	100%	One step less trusting	41
			Two steps less trusting	12
				100%
N:	(1058)	(1054)		(1050)

Question: How much of the time do you think you can trust the government in Washington to do what is right?

Source: Paul Beck, Jere W. Bruner, and L. Douglas Dobson, *Political Socialization Across the Generations* (Washington, D.C.: American Political Science Association, 1975), rev. ed., p. 79.

attitudes toward government that remain from childhood confront the hard facts of the real world. The result is a rather shattering change in attitude for a great many people.

Another way of looking at this shift is presented on the right side of Table 6.4. These figures record how many young adults changed two steps in the trusting direction between 1965 and 1973 (that is, said "only some of the time" in 1965 and "just about always" in 1973), how many changed one step, stayed the same, and so forth. We can read from these figures that only 8 percent of young Americans born around 1948 became more trusting between the ages of about 17 and 25. By contrast, fully 53 percent said their trust in government had declined.

ATTITUDES TOWARD THE POLITICAL SELF

Up to this point I have been discussing political culture only in terms of attitudes that have as their object some external entity. From this point on I want to talk about how we view our political selves.

Political Efficacy

One of the most basic political attitudes the citizen possesses about himself has to do with the image he holds about his own political activity. Specifically, the sense of political efficacy may be defined as "the feeling that individual political action does have, or can have, an impact upon the political processes, i.e., that it is worthwhile to perform one's civic duties."[9] The feeling of efficaciousness does not imply that a person will be active in politics. Rather, it simply refers to the idea that "if I do choose to take part in politics, my actions are likely to have some effect."

A close look at American levels of political efficacy is provided by the data collected in the biennial surveys of the University of Michigan. Figure 6.1 shows the levels of response to the four questions generally used to assess feelings of efficacy in the United States. These data are presented for the period from 1952 to 1976.

Figure 6.1 shows that over the past 24 years, Americans have passed through two fairly distinct periods in their feelings of political efficacy.[10] If we set aside the question about voting being the only way to have a say in politics for a moment, we see that these curves tell a similar story. All three show fairly smooth and gradual change in attitude, and all three have one major change in direction. Furthermore, this change occurred in the same year for all, 1960, and in all cases the shift went from increasing efficacy to decreasing.

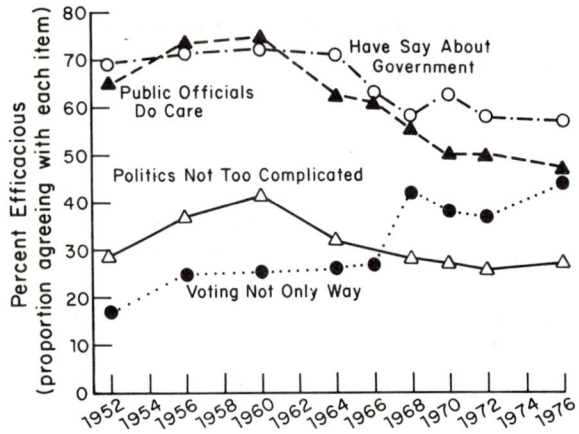

Figure 6.1. Trends in Responses to Political Efficacy Items, 1952–1976.

Question:
  a. I don't think public officials care much what people like me think.
  b. Voting is the only way that people like me can have any say about how the government runs things.
  c. People like me don't have any say about what the government does.
  d. Sometimes politics and government seem so complicated that a person like me can't really understand what's going on.

Sources: Phillip E. Converse, "Changes in the American Electorate," in Angus Campbell and Phillip E. Converse (eds.), *The Human Meaning of Social Change* (New York: Russell Sage Foundation, 1972), p. 328; ICPSR Archive: Survey Research Center, 1970 Congressional Election Study; CPS 1972 and 1976 Presidential Election Studies.

How can these changes be explained? The increase during the 1950s can probably be interpreted as the result of increasing levels of education in the electorate. Education, after all, places the individual in a favored position in society, one in which he can expect to get his way, politically or otherwise.

Since 1960, however, we can see that a decline has begun to occur, and it has continued a steady course through 1976. To interpret this shift, which has occurred in the face of a continuing increase in level of education, we need to consider the events of the past decade and a half. What sorts of things have happened to make the average citizen think that his or her personal input into the political system would be unlikely to have any effect?

The answer to that question is certainly not a difficult one. Virtually all the major political events of the past 15 years have suggested in one way or another that the average citizen has preciously little political power. The tragic assassinations of 1963, 1967, and 1968; the fact that Lyndon Johnson, who was elected by a landslide victory in 1964 against a man perceived to be prowar, wound up escalating that war far beyond what Goldwater ever mentioned; the white backlash and black frustration as the civil rights movement lost steam in the late 1960s; the Watergate scandals and the perception that public officials really don't care—all these things could easily have led many citizens to doubt their own political impact.

The question that we set aside earlier, which asked if voting is the only way to influence government, can also be seen to be a response to political events. The years of civil disobedience that accompanied first the civil rights movement and then the antiwar movement, demonstrated graphically to the participants as well as others, that there *are* ways to get things done other than voting. We see in particular the sudden jump between 1966 and 1968. The latter year was perhaps the peak of activity for anti-Vietnam War protesters.

The Socialization of Political Efficacy. Clearly, in a democratic society, the sense among the citizenry that their input can be effective is one that should be nurtured. It comes as no surprise, therefore, that those who study political socialization have paid rather special attention to this attitude. As we might expect, the major studies[11] have shown that the youngest children, around the age of 8 or 9, do not feel very confident about the prospect of influencing government. Given our earlier discussions of the nature of cognitive development, this is of course quite understandable. Since children lack an understanding of what government is, they cannot perceive themselves as influential political actors in any context. Hess and Torney report that among fourth graders, only one in four believes that "the people rule," and only one in seven believes that "you can say things against the government."[12] By the time children reached the eighth grade, however, three of four and one out of every two students, respectively, agreed with these two statements. These responses by the older students were very much more similar to those given by their teachers than they were to those of the younger students.

This developmental pattern is summarized in Figure 6.2, in which a five-question political efficacy scale is administered to children in all grades from 3 to 8, as well as to their teachers. Contrary to the pattern of development which characterized political trust, the sense of political efficacy *increases* through the school years. In fact, Jennings and Niemi find that by grade 12, the students are markedly *more* efficacious than their parents.[13]

How can the sense of political efficacy increase through childhood, while the sense of political trust decreases through the same period? The answer hinges on the fact that the object of political trust is external (the political system) and the attitude is made up primarily of affect. Children have little concrete information about the political system, and not much is necessary for them to internalize a feeling of political trust. In fact, I have argued that the relatively early stage of cognitive development in which the youngest children find themselves encourages the formation of political trust, since their undeveloped cognitive abilities keeps children at a distance from political reality.

Political efficacy, on the other hand, is an attitude for which the central object is the self. The low level of cognitive development in this instance *prevents*, rather than enhances, the development of the attitude. The

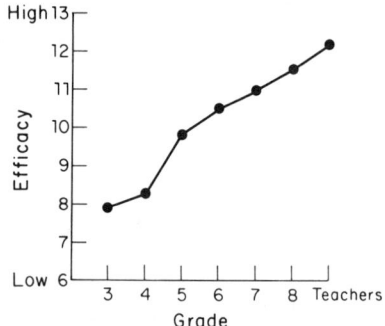

Figure 6.2. Comparison of Means of Grades 3 through 8 in Sense of Political Efficacy.

Questions: The fifth item, in addition to those noted in Figure 6.1, is: The way people vote is the main thing that decides how things are run in this country.

Source: Robert D. Hess and Judith V. Torney, *The Development of Political Attitudes in Children* (Chicago: Aldine, 1967), p. 69.

child remains dependent on his parents and has little conception of what it means to be an independent agent. Add to this his inability to perceive clearly the working of the political world and you have the formula for political inefficacy in the group.

As the child matures, his sense of self-mastery grows as his level of cognitive development advances, and his range of experiences increases. He may begin to attempt to be influential in a school election, for instance, or through participation in class discussions. In the protected environment of the school, these experiences often meet with success. Not until the student leaves high school and encounters the real world does a decline in feelings of efficacy begin to set in.

Partisanship

Perhaps the most common attitude in our political culture is party loyalty. The idea of being a Republican, a Democrat, or an Independent is one that must be familiar to nearly all of us. The first task in describing the content of this aspect of our political culture is to document the existence and distribution of partisans in the American electorate. Partisanship is generally measured in a straightforward manner, by simply asking a person whether he thinks of himself as a Democrat, a Republican, or an Independent.[14] The proportion of the electorate that has fallen into each category over the past half century is presented in Figure 6.3.

This figure describes three major periods that have existed in partisanship since 1920. In terms of presidential politics, the first third of this century was a period of Republican domination. Between 1896 and 1932, only one Democrat occupied the White House; that was Woodrow Wilson, and his victory came as the direct result of the fact that Teddy Roosevelt, denied the Republican nomination, ran as a Progressive in 1912 and split the Republican vote. Wilson was elected with 42 percent of the vote.

Figure 6.3 shows, however, that a period of partisan realignment occurred between 1920 and 1948. The proportion of the electorate that declared a Republican loyalty dropped from 43 percent in 1920 to 39 percent only 8 years later. We generally recognize, however, that it was the stock market crash of 1929 and the Depression of the 1930s that broke the Republicans' hold on the White House. Franklin Roosevelt was elected for the first time in 1932 and the Democrats, who had elected Presidents only four times since the Civil War (Wilson and Cleveland twice each), suddenly won five straight elections.

This Republican failure to capture the White House is mirrored directly in the further decline of Republican strength among the voters between 1932 and 1948. Their share of the electorate dropped to about one-third during this time. The Independents became more numerous, although by 1948 they still constituted only 16 percent of the electorate. Meanwhile,

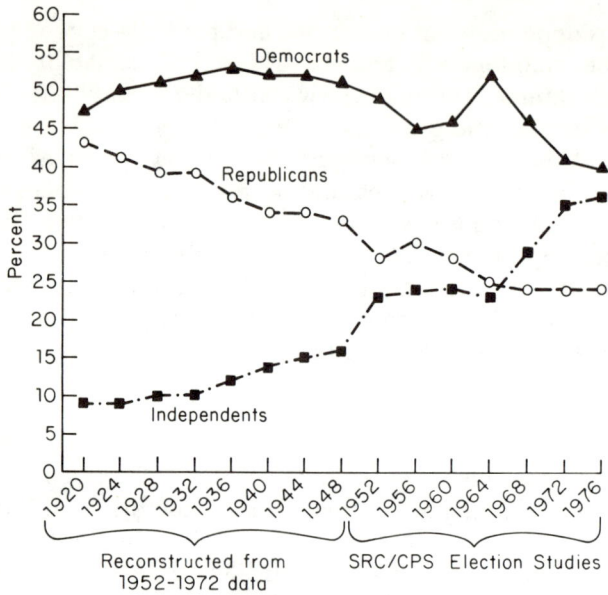

Figure 6.3. Party Identification, 1920–1976.

Source: Kristi Andersen, "Generation, Partisan Shift and Realignment: A Glance Back at the New Deal," in Norman H. Nie, Sidney Verba, and John R. Petrocik, *The Changing American Voter* (Cambridge, Mass.: Harvard University Press, 1976), p. 83, copyright © 1976 by the Twentieth Century Fund. ICPSR Archive: CPS 1976 Presidential Election Study.

the Democrats solidified their position as the majority party, claiming over half the electorate in every election year between 1924 and 1948. This majority bloc has come to be called the New Deal coalition. It united labor, blacks, Catholics, and Southerners, as well as many intellectuals who were sympathetic to the cause of the poor. Forged in the Depression, and bound together by the continuing Democratic support for liberal economic policies, this coalition remained a vital force in American politics well into the 1960s.

The second period in the evolution of American partisanship runs from 1952 through 1964. We might call this the period of unusual elections, since every one of these four presidential contests bears the stamp of abnormality. Eisenhower was elected twice in 1952 and 1956 even though Republican identifiers were greatly outnumbered both times. War heroes have always been popular. The Democrats recognized this in 1948, when they attempted to persuade Ike to run for them.

John Kennedy won a narrow victory in 1960, having to overcome both his Catholicism and the fact that his opponent, Nixon, had been Eisenhower's Vice President. Then, in 1964, Lyndon Johnson benefited both from the fact that Barry Goldwater was perceived by many voters to be an extremist and because the public still mourned the death of Kennedy, the fallen hero, under whom Johnson had served as Vice President.

As you might expect, these unusual events surrounding the presidential elections were accompanied by shifts in the partisan feelings of the voters as well. One important change was the dramatic gain in the number of Independents in 1952, from about one in six to nearly one in every four adults. Since Eisenhower was seen primarily as a war hero, he was not generally identified closely with the Republicans. His support came from all segments of society, and he drew people out of their parties and into an independent, "I'll vote for the man" position. Both the Democrats and Republicans lost strength during the 1950s.

The end of this period is marked by the Johnson-Goldwater contest, which obviously generated a good deal of emotion. The increase in the number of Democratic identifiers, 6 percent, is the largest shift in partisan strength for either party in any single 4-year interval during the entire period. The fact that it vanished again during the ensuing 4 years merely emphasizes the extraordinary nature of this election.

The third phase of partisan identification in America, stretching from 1964 to 1976, is marked by the rise of the Independent. The Republicans, buoyed by Nixon's victories, held their strength at about one-quarter of the electorate. The Democrats lost thousands of supporters, while the Independents scored enormous gains, particularly among young Southerners.

The Democrats have been on a real roller coaster for the past 15 years. The wave of support that brought Johnson to the White House ebbed quickly as Humphrey and then McGovern presented increasingly weak challenges to Nixon. The Democrats have not had a Watergate to worry about, but their problems may be more serious. Their loss of support comes from an increasing sense among some segments of the old New Deal coalition, specifically blue-collar Northerners and white Southerners, that the Democratic party is moving too far in the liberal direction. These two groups are fundamentally conservative, and the support given by the Democratic party to civil rights and social welfare legislation (with the inevitable accompaniment of high taxes and big government) has made them begin to reassess their loyalties.

Overall, the late 1960s and early 1970s have brought about a new look by the electorate at its sense of partisanship. Many people find themselves uncomfortable with either party. In 1968 the Independents outnumbered one of the major parties for the first time, and in 1976 their numbers fell only 4 percent short of making them the largest group in the electorate. Jimmy Carter's election in 1976 seems to have restored some sense of balance. However, it is clear that the days of the New Deal coalition are gone forever, and the party system is currently in a period of transition. Although many Independents will no doubt eventually choose one or the other of the major parties, whether the Democrats or the Republicans will come out on top cannot be predicted.

A final note needs to be added to our review of partisanship in the electorate. Figure 6.3 gives the rather strong impression that *individual* voters are becoming highly unstable in their sense of partisanship, and that the change observed during the past 20 years arises from people shifting from one identity to another. This is not necessarily the case. In fact, over the past 20 years, the number of partisan identifiers who report changing identification during the previous 4 years has remained at a constant level of 3 to 5 percent, which is just a small fraction of the electorate.

If individuals remain this loyal to their parties, how do we explain the undeniable shifts in the aggregate strength of the parties that show up in Figure 6.3? The answer lies in the fact that change in a group can be brought about not only by shifts by individual members but also by additions to and deletions from the membership of the group. Death, for instance, changes the composition of a group by removing its oldest members. Since older Americans tend to be more Republican than the electorate as a whole, their disappearance will increase slightly the proportion of Democrats and Independents.

A far more important factor than death as a mechanism of change, however, is youth. People in their teens and twenties are very numerous in the American population today. Moreover, the 18-year-old vote brought new millions into the electorate in 1972. Much of the change in the third phase of the development of party identification can be explained in terms of this addition of young voters.

DEVIANT SUBGROUPS

I do not want to end this chapter quite yet. If I did, most of you would probably close the book and conclude that there is one immense, homogeneous set of attitudes that makes up the political culture in the United States, and everybody agrees with it. Some of you, I suppose, already know that this isn't so, because you don't agree with the things I have written about. So let me restate: There is a *dominant* set of attitudes about politics in this country, which we call the political culture. However, there are certainly exceptions. So I shall close the chapter not by talking about dominant patterns but by referring to cases in which the dominant attitudes are weaker.

One example I want to present has been called the case of the malevolent leader. We know now that Greenstein and others discovered that the President enjoys the status of a revered national leader in the minds of nearly all children, as well as many adults. He called this discovery the benevolent leader phenomonon. It turns out, however, that the children Greenstein chose to talk to (as well as those interviewed by Easton, Hess, Dennis, and Torney), were mainly white, urban and generally well off financially (that is, not below the poverty line). They do not represent all American children.

Jaros and his colleagues noted this fact and reasoned that something interesting might be discovered if they were to go off to some isolated pocket of America that did not share in the material wealth of the American mainstream.[15] As it turned out, they struck gold.

Jaros conducted his interviews in Knox County, Kentucky, in one of the most depressed sections of rural Appalachia. Unemployment in the coal industry was widespread, and for one reason or another, federal assistance programs for roads, schools, and welfare had not made much impact at the time of the study (1967). No air or rail passenger service was available in the county, and only one U.S. highway crossed it. The annual per capita income was $501, compared to a U.S. average of $2223 for the same time period. In sum, Knox County was isolated, rural, and poor.

Partly because of its depressed condition, no doubt, there is a great deal of antigovernment sentiment in Appalachia. The region has consistently displayed a hostility toward and rejection of political authority, and in particular, of federal authority. Surely, Jaros reasoned, such parents would not be capable of sugarcoating the political pill, as had the parents of Greenstein's children. To the contrary, "the civic instruction which goes on incidental to normal activities in the family," which Greenstein suggested as a source of children's positive affect toward the political system, would in Appalachia be a source of political cynicism.

Table 6.5 reviews the answers given to four of the questions about the President that were originally asked in the so-called Chicago study by Easton and his colleagues of his predominantly white, urban schoolchildren. In addition to the Chicago study and Jaros' sample of Appalachian youth, Hirsch and Gutierrez have added a third study of another isolated out-group: Texas Chicanos. This table illustrates clearly the importance of Jaros' study. There are obviously groups here and there in American society which do not perpetuate a wholly positive political culture. The frequency of positive responses about the President among Texas Chicano and rural Appalachian children are generally about half of the level given by the Chicago respondents. Although other studies have given us enough information to conclude that the *dominant* political culture is in fact a positive and supportive one, nonetheless there are pockets of heterogeneity that remind us that we need to be cautious about drawing any blatant conclusions.

The thrust of Jaros' study, beyond the demonstration that not all Americans admire the President all that much, was primarily to test theories of socialization. His findings lend considerable support to the social learning

TABLE 6.5. Children's Evaluation of the President within Three Subcultures (Grades 5 through 8)

Question	Response	Chicanos	Appalachia	Chicago
1. View of how hard the President works compared with most men	Harder	49%	35%	77%
	As hard	27	24	21
	Less hard	24	41	3
		100%	100%	101%
	N:	(48)	(128)	(214)
2. View of the honesty of the President compared with most men	More honest	*	23%	57%
	As honest	*	50	42
	Less honest	*	27	1
			100%	100%
	N:		(133)	(214)
3. View of the President's knowledge compared to most men	Knows more	41%	45%	82%
	Knows about the same	42	33	16
	Knows less	17	22	2
		100%	100%	100%
	N:	(62)	(124)	(212)
4. View of the President as a person	Best in the world	11%	6%	11%
	A good person	63	68	82
	Not a good person	26	26	8
		100%	100%	101%
	N:	(37)	(139)	(211)

Sources: Appalachian and Chicago data reported in Dean Jaros, Herbert Hirsch, and Frederic J. Fleron, Jr., "The Malevolent Leader: Political Socialization in an American Subculture," *American Political Science Review*, vol. 62, no. 2 (June 1968), 568, reprinted by permission of the authors. The Mexican-American data are reported in Herbert Hirsch and Armand Gutierrez, "The Socialization of Political Aggression and Political Affect: A Subcultural Analysis," an unpublished paper.

*Data not reported.

interpretation of political learning and tend to downplay the importance of psychoanalytic theory. Specifically, the absence of the father from the family led to *more* positive views of the President among the children. This circumstance can only have been produced by social learning. Beyond this, however, there is no effort to interpret these findings from the point of view of the political system. What difference does it make, after all, if some children don't think that the President is the greatest person in the world?

Unfortunately, that question is not easily answered. We are not at all sure exactly what the linkages are between childhood socialization and adult political behavior. We can be fairly sure that linkages exist, but the research done so far has only begun to hint at their nature.

One such study was conducted by Jaros and Kolson, who interviewed a number of old-order Amish children living in Ohio.[16] These children belong to an extremely cohesive religious sect that rejects most aspects of modern culture (including its politics) in favor of the style of seventeenth-century Europe. Although they are not at all hostile toward the American political system (the President is generally admired), they do remain aloof and very isolated.

The significance of this study rests with the fact that Jaros and Kolson attempted to find out what kinds of politically relevant behavior the Amish children expected to engage in as adults. In general, they project a profile that is much more withdrawn from the political world than that of the non-Amish children, as shown in Table 6.6. Their socialization experiences, in other words, have led them away from an expectation that they

TABLE 6.6. Differences between Amish and Non-Amish Children on Selected Variables

	Responses	
	Amish (N = 70)	Non-Amish (N = 194)
Desirability of farming as future occupation	77.1%	36.6%
Desire to serve in armed forces (boys only)	9.1%	68.8%
Makes a difference which side wins an election	48.5%	68.4%
Intention regarding voting at age 21		
Yes	13.0%	47.9%
Don't know	65.2	44.7
No	21.7	7.4
	99.9%	100.0%
Estimation of family say about what government does		
A great deal	18.8%	37.0%
A little	43.5	41.3
None	37.7	21.7
	100.0%	100.0%

Source: Richard Niemi (Ed.), *The Politics of Future Citizens* (San Francisco: Jossey-Bass, 1974). "The Multifarious Leader: Political Socialization of Amish, 'Yanks' Blacks," p. 52.

will ever have any active role in American government. The Amish sects are of course numerically insignificant across the country as a whole. One wonders, nevertheless, what the consequences would be if the dominant pattern of socialization were to shift greatly from positive to negative nationwide.

The final example involves not a deviant subgroup, but a deviant set of events: Watergate. There is no doubt that much negative feeling was generated during Watergate. What we must ask is whether this scandal will have any enduring effect on the political culture. Will the pervasively positive political affect of American children be tarnished by this undeniable blot on the reputation of the presidency?

It is still early to tell for sure what the outcome of Watergate will be for our political culture. However, some data already available suggest that the long-range consequences will not be serious. My own study of Atlanta area youth, for example, as we see in Table 6.7, has determined that the reaction to the affair was very negative, but that these negative feelings were either just emotional expletives ("It just makes me sick!") or were directed at Nixon or other figures or at objects (like the tapes) that were involved directly in the events themselves.[17]

The point to be made here is that the objects of negative affect are nearly all associated with the government as distinct from the regime or the political community. The regime, the process by which politics oper-

TABLE 6.7. Content of Negative Evaluations of Watergate, by Race[a]

	White	Black
Normative or emotional references	29.7%	25.9%
Negative references to Nixon	25.1	43.3
(e.g., "Nixon should be impeached")	3.9	19.1
Negative references to people (other than Nixon) or to the Nixon administration	18.6	14.6
Negative references to objects (e.g., the tapes) or to acts (e.g., the break-in)	10.3	8.0
References to damaging the national image or interfering with the affairs of state	7.1	4.0
Negative references to the political process	9.2	4.1
	100.0%	99.9%
N:	(848)	(725)

Source: This table drawn from "Racial Differences in the Reaction to Watergate: Some Implications for Political Support" by Bruce A. Campbell is reprinted from *Youth and Society*, vol. 7, No. 4 (June 1976), p. 452, by permission of the Publisher, Sage Publications, Inc.

[a] Entries are proportions of total responses. References to impeachment were recorded no more than once per respondent, thus these figures refer to proportion of total respondents.

ates, is not brought into question by most of these respondents, who were high school seniors in 1974. Therefore, when Nixon and his associates left office, the major reasons for disapproval were removed from politics. Respect for the regime seems to have emerged relatively unscathed, and the esteem in which Presidents Ford and Carter have been held has evidently not suffered from the misdeeds of President Nixon. In other words, not even Watergate could do much to shake these young Americans' basic feelings of support for the President and acceptance of the political regime. The rules of the game, the Constitution, and the political community itself seem to be effectively insulated from the unacceptable behavior of politicians, even if such behavior is performed by the President. This fact is tribute enough to the strength of the dominant political culture in America.

SUMMARY

Political culture influences government because it influences the kinds of demands we make on government. Certain sorts of demands are deemed appropriate, while others are not. In the United States, the government is subjected to a very wide range of demands, particularly in the area of social welfare. A government in one of the poorer countries of the world could not possibly afford to meet the sorts of demands that ours routinely does. If the level of demand in a population exceeds the government's ability to provide, however, instability is the result. The so-called "revolution of rising expectations" now going on in much of the Third World concerns precisely such rising levels of demand.

The second way in which the political culture affects the functioning of the political system involves the direct provision of support. That is, does the culture contain the feeling that the political system deserves and ought to be given support? Support comes in many forms. It may be material, as in the payment of taxes. It may be personal, as in the case of the draftees of the Vietnam era who willingly went into the military. In the United States such levels of support are very high, due in part to the religious aspects of the political culture. That we support the system is a "given," in Boorstin's sense.[18] It seems so natural that no other action appears possible.

Finally, the political culture influences the willingness of the citizenry to accept the decisions of government. This willingness is central to the concept of legitimacy; a state whose right to make decisions is unquestioned by the people is highly legitimate. Once again, the "givenness" of the American system means that the acceptance of outputs is exceedingly high. We obey the laws and we accept decisions even if they are not for our personal benefit—mainly because we recognize the right of government to make many decisions.

Now, is all of this good or bad? That question could easily be answered either way; it just depends on what you want. If political stability is the desired goal, then a political culture that has a strong religious element is certainly desirable. The system can function without having to worry much that its policies will be disapproved by the masses, since they would be unlikely to decide that they wanted a different head of state or a different system altogether.

On the other hand, if we seek to maximize democracy, or accountability of those in power to the people, then too much unquestioning acceptance is not a good thing. The idea of givenness, after all, implies that political leaders can do pretty much what they want, whether it is in the public interest or not. The frightening thing about Watergate is that President Nixon, by playing on the American people's devotion both to the presidency and to the idea of national security, almost got away with his subversions of the democratic process.

I suppose that what we want is a system in which the political culture contains enough religious fervor to allow efficient operation in government, but is still vigilant enough to prevent major abuses of the public interest. You may want to reflect about whether that is the sort of political culture we have in America today.

NOTES

1. *The Gallup Opinion Index.* Report No. 111 (September 1974), p. 12; Report No. 138 (January 1977); Report No. 152 (March 1978).
2. David B. Truman, *The Governmental Process,* 2d ed. (New York: Knopf, 1971).
3. Fred I. Greenstein, *Children and Politics* (New Haven: Yale University Press, 1965).
4. Gabriel A. Almond and Sidney Verba, *The Civic Culture* (Princeton, N.J.: Princeton University Press, 1963), p. 267.
5. Arthur H. Miller, "Political Issues and Trust in Government: 1964–1970," *American Political Science Review,* vol. 68, no. 3 (September 1974), 951–972.
6. Jack Citrin, "Comment: The Political Relevance of Trust in Government," *American Political Science Review,* vol. 68, no. 3 (September 1974), 973–988.
7. Greenstein, *op. cit.*
8. Greenstein, *op. cit,* 45–46; David Easton and Robert D. Hess, "The Child's Political World," *Midwest Journal of Political Science,* vol. 6, no. 3 (August 1962), 229–246.
9. Angus Campbell, Gerald Gurin, and Warren E. Miller, *The Voter Decides* (New York: Harper & Row, 1954), pp. 187ff.
10. This discussion follows Philip E. Converse, "Change in the American Electorate," in Angus Campbell and Philip E. Converse (Eds.), *The Human Meaning of Social Change* (New York: Russell Sage, 1972), pp. 327ff.
11. Robert D. Hess and Judith V. Torney, *The Development of Political Attitudes in Children* (Chicago: Aldine, 1967); David Easton and Jack Dennis, *Children in the Political System: Origins of Political Legitimacy* (New York: McGraw-Hill, 1969).
12. Hess and Torney, *op. cit.,* p. 66.
13. M. Kent Jennings and Richard G. Niemi, *The Political Character of Adolescence: The Influence of Families and Schools* (Princeton, N.J.: Princeton University Press, 1974), p. 125.

14. This question is often supplemented by one that separates partisans into weak and strong Republicans or Democrats, and another that separates Independents into "real" Independents and Independents leaning toward the Democrats or the Republicans.

15. Dean Jaros, Herbert Hirsch, and Frederic Fleron, Jr., "The Malevolent Leader: Political Socialization in an American Subculture," *American Political Science Review,* vol. 62, no. 2 (June 1968), 564–575.

16. Dean Jaros and Kenneth L. Kolson, "The Multifarious Leader: Political Socialization of Amish, 'Yanks,' Blacks," in Richard G. Niemi (Ed.), *The Politics of Future Citizens* (San Francisco: Jossey-Bass, 1974), chap. 3.

17. Bruce A. Campbell, "Racial Differences in the Reaction to Watergate: Some Implications for System Support," *Youth and Society,* vol. 7, no. 4 (June 1976), 439–460.

18. Daniel J. Boorstin, *The Genius of American Politics* (Chicago: University of Chicago Press, 1953).

7

The Sources of Political Learning

You now have a fairly clear idea of the processes by which attitudes are learned, and you know a good deal about what those attitudes are. Now it is time to discuss their *origins*. There are two ways to approach this question. From the social learning theory perspective, the source of learning is the model. The three models, or "agents" of socialization, that we shall discuss below are the parents, the school, and the peer group. In this consideration of the sources of political learning, I do not want to neglect sociological factors, however. One of the most profound influences on a person's eventual political attitudes is the group he is born into, identified by race and socioeconomic status. This "social nexus" forms the second major part of this chapter.

THE AGENTS OF POLITICAL SOCIALIZATION

The Family

From the theoretical perspective, the family must be the first agent to which we turn in our search for the origins of political learning. Psychoanalytic theory is quite explicit in linking the child to his parents in early life because of the child's need to maintain security and establish a coherent identity for himself. Cognitive-developmental theory is less explicit in its focus on the parents and in fact holds that in order to reach the highest levels of development, the individual must break away from the parents' influence. At the earlier stages of development, however, the parents have great significance simply because they are the only individuals of significance in the child's life. This same fact underlies the great reliance that social learning theory places on the parent. These models, since they occupy a unique place of respect and authority in their children's lives, are obviously in the best position to offer rewards or punishments when the child adopts or rejects the modeled behavior.

From whichever theoretical perspective we approach the process of political socialization in young children (say, before the age of 10), the parents emerge as the most important agents. The problem becomes very clouded, however, when we begin to try to find evidence of these relationships. Two factors obscure the parent-child relationship. First, the young child can hold no political attitudes that have complex or abstract objects of reference. He has no attitudes about Congress, for instance, because he has no understanding of what Congress is. Because there is a lack of cognitive structure, political thinking in the young is affective. That is, most of what the child learns from his parents about politics relates to feelings, which tend to be vague and without specific reference. Although we assume that these feelings lay the foundation for the later attitudes adults hold toward the political system, when we attempt to measure parent-child relationships we generally find rather little.

The second difficulty we face in trying to demonstrate the effect the parent has on an offspring's political attitudes is that by the time the child reaches high school, he or she is already under the influence of other agents. It becomes very difficult to tell whether a certain attitude has been acquired from the parent, or whether it has come from the school, the peer group, the media, or from the adolescent's own increasing personal experience with the political world.

Parent-Child Attitude Similarities

We are all familiar with the phrase "like father, like son." Is this true in the political realm? I shall answer that question by examining three political attitude areas, to see whether parents' attitudes are like those of their children.

Partisanship. As it turns out, partisanship is the one attitude that is consistently and clearly passed on from parent to child. Consider the data from the Jennings and Niemi study. As Table 7.1 shows, there is a clear tendency for the offspring (who were high school seniors) of Democratic parents to think of themselves as Democrats and the offspring of Republican parents to think of themselves as Republicans. Jennings and Niemi studied a wide range of political attitudes and discovered that this tend-

TABLE 7.1. Party Identification of Parents and Their Children

Children	Parents		
	Democrat	Independent	Republican
Democrat	66%	29%	13%
Independent	27	53	36
Republican	7	17	51
	100%	99%	100%
N:	(915)	(443)	(495)

Source: M. Kent Jennings and Richard G. Niemi, *The Political Character of Adolescence: The Influence of Families and Schools* (copyright © 1974 by Princeton University Press), Table 2.2, p. 41. Reprinted by permission of Princeton University Press.

ency for children to be like their parents was far stronger in the case of party loyalty than it was in any other respect.

Even this strong a relationship between parent and child is not perfect, however. There are many instances in which the child has failed to acquire the partisanship of his parents. A close look at Table 7.1 reveals that it is the Democratic party that reaps the benefit of this failure of socialization. You can see, for example, that nearly two-thirds of the children of Democratic parents called themselves Democrats, while only about one-half of the children of Republicans remain loyal to that identification. This indicates that there are other agents of socialization that push these young people toward a Democratic identification no matter what party their parents belong to. This shows up most clearly among the children whose parents are Independents. Presumably, in these families there are no cues given that favor either party. The children of such parents therefore acquire their partisan attitudes elsewhere. These other sources of cues obviously must favor the Democrats, because nearly 30 percent of the children of Independents call themselves Democrats, while a Republican identity has attracted only 17 percent.

There is one final aspect of the parent-child relationship for which we must look beyond Table 7.1. There is a much stronger tendency among the parents to be partisans, while their children are more likely to call themselves Independents. Specifically, about 24 percent of the parents in Table 7.1 are Independents, but 36 percent of the children chose this category. Beyond the direct socialization from parent to child, then, there are clearly generational differences that must be taken into account.

The reasons that parents are so successful in communicating their party loyalties to their children are not difficult to understand. First, partisanship is a simple concept. There are only two parties worth discussing and they have both been in continuous existence in the United States for over a century. Second, the sense of identity of most adults does not change often. The cues a parent sends to his children will very likely be consistent throughout the time they are growing up. Third, party loyalty is an important attitude; virtually all political debate in the American electorate eventually gets boiled down to identifying the Democratic and Republican positions. You can understand that if any political conversation at all goes on in the typical American family, it will almost certainly give the child cues about which party is the approved one. Finally, party loyalty is socialized with such success because both our major parties (and most of the minor ones) accept and support the system. Neither major party advocates overthrow of the government, or any similar illegal action. Therefore, there is no reason to conceal one's partisanship. The same is not true in France or Italy, for instance, both with large Communist parties. In those cultures, partisanship is often linked with opposition to the *form* of government, and people are much less willing to discuss their loyalties, even within their families.

Political Knowledge. These arguments illustrate, I trust, not only why partisanship is successfully socialized in the United States, but also why items of political knowledge are not so successfully transmitted from one generation to the next. Unlike the simple concept of party, political knowledge—that is, knowledge of the facts about politics—is hopelessly diffuse. A child might hear his or her parents mention that there are nine justices on the Supreme Court, but the subject is certainly not frequently discussed. Cues involving political information that the child can imitate are simply not consistently given in the family environment.

These initial observations tend to suggest that the child should have lower levels of political information than the parents. Furthermore, since the parent presumably does not communicate this sort of information very effectively in the process of socialization, the relationship between the parents' level of political knowledge and that of the child also should be low.

The test of the question of whether parents know more about politics than their children (who are high school seniors in these examples) can be answered quite simply by asking a series of common political facts that members of the electorate might be expected to know. Six such facts appear in Table 7.2.

Perhaps the most surprising thing about this table is the shockingly low levels of information which people possess. The fact that fewer than three adult Americans in ten know that a Senator serves a term of six years or that there are nine justices on the Supreme Court is a disturbing finding indeed. When we compare the levels of information possessed by these parents and their children, we find that in three cases of the six, the parents' level of knowledge is higher, just as we suspected. These members of the older generation have, after all, had a lifetime of experience

TABLE 7.2. Child and Parent Responses to Information Questions

Question	Percentage Giving Correct Answer			
	Children		Parents	
Governor of their state	88%	(2062)[a]	93%	(1920)
Country with WW II concentration camps	83	(2062)	83	(1916)
Was Franklin Roosevelt a Democrat or a Republican?	64	(2063)	93	(1923)
Length of Senator's term	50	(2048)	29	(1916)
Number of justices on Supreme Court	38	(2062)	23	(1918)
Country Tito is leader of	27	(2059)	43	(1914)

Source: M. Kent Jennings and Richard G. Niemi, *The Political Character of Adolescence: The Influence of Families and Schools* (copyright © 1974 by Princeton University Press), Table 4.1, p. 94. Reprinted by permission of Princeton University Press.

[a] Sample sizes given in parentheses.

with politics. They lived through FDR's administration, and remember he was a Democrat from personal experience. They have been reading the newspapers for thirty years, and have doubtlessly heard that Tito is the leader of Yugoslavia more than once during that period. The inexperience of youth, on the other hand, denies to the student the same access to information, resulting in the higher levels of ignorance shown in the table.

There are two instances, however, in which the parents are not more informed than their children. These involve the length of the Senator's term and the size of the Supreme Court. A little thought solves the riddle easily. These are two of the basic facts which a young person learns in high school civics. This alternate agent of socialization has provided these two facts much more directly and recently to the students than it has to their parents, hence the greater level of knowledge.

The question is, to what extent are the parents responsible for the levels of political information possessed by their children? One way of getting at this is to look at the relationship between the level of knowledge of the parent and the level of knowledge of that parent's child. I don't mean to suggest that a high degree of association between those two levels proves that the parent is necessarily teaching specific information. Rather, we can assume that a positive association is based on the fact that in homes where parents are politically informed there will be an atmosphere that is conducive to the socialization of political knowledge by the children. This concept of atmosphere goes beyond direct parent-child communication, of course. It includes such things as the sort of newspapers, magazines, and books found in the house, the television viewing habits of various members of the household, and the sorts of things the parents may discuss with friends who are invited to the home and might be overheard by the child. It also includes the kinds of communication patterns that exist between parent and child—critical or supportive; rigid or flexible.

Table 7.3 shows a relationship between child and parent level of political information that, though not nearly as impressive as that of party identification, nonetheless does reveal some parental influence.[1] When parental knowledge is high (the right-hand column), 45 percent of the children also had the highest score and none had the lowest score. On the other hand, 26 percent of the children of the most ignorant parents (the left-hand column) also have the lowest possible political knowledge scores, whereas only 5 percent manage to score in the highest category.

In general, then, there is some tendency for parental levels of information to match those of their children. The deviations from this pattern are also significant, however. For instance, nearly a third of the children of the most ill-informed parents have high levels of knowledge (scores of 5, 6, and 7). Influences outside the family obviously also contribute to the socialization of political knowledge.

3 *Citizenship Roles.* There is a good deal of consensus between the parent and child generation on the subject of what it means to be a good citizen. Both groups report that active participation, including voting and maintaining high levels of interest in politics, characterize good citizenship. There is also a general consensus on loyalty and obedience to laws. Good citizens are also expected to be tolerant and helping toward others and to espouse moral values and behavior such as honesty and religiousness.[2]

Although Americans of every age tend to agree that all these things are true of the good citizen, we can detect certain distinct differences in emphasis between the generation of the parent and that of the teenage child. Most clearly, the older generation focuses more heavily on the social

TABLE 7.3. Relationship between Child and Parent Political Knowledge

Children's Knowledge	Parent Knowledge[a]					
	Low 1	2	3	4	5	High 6
Low 1	26%	23%	8%	5%	2%	0%
2	28	16	17	6	3	1
3	9	10	13	17	14	8
4	5	14	29	25	27	22
5	17	22	14	17	17	8
6	10	8	13	12	11	14
High 7	5	7	6	17	25	45
	100%	100%	100%	99%	99%	98%
N:	(34)	(41)	(237)	(782)	(492)	(337)

Source: M. Kent Jennings and Richard G. Niemi, *The Political Character of Adolescence: The Influence of Families and Schools* (copyright © 1974 by Princeton University Press), Table 4.2, p. 97. Reprinted by permission of Princeton University Press.

[a] Knowledge is a combined measure (Guttman scale) based on five of the six items appearing in Table 7.2 (excluding the length of a Senator's term).

and moral aspects of citizenship. In Jennings and Niemi's study, for instance, 14 percent of the parents defined a good citizen as one who "helps other people," and 12 percent mentioned "getting along with other people." The comparable fractions of the children's group were 9 percent and 4 percent, respectively. Almost 17 percent of the parents mentioned religiousness as part of good citizenship, compared to 5 percent of the children.[3]

The younger group, on the other hand, stressed the participation aspects of citizenship. While 27 percent of the parents felt voting was important, and 12 percent mentioned being interested in politics, the comparable figures for the children were 38 percent and 22 percent, respectively. This difference is one that reappears continually when the generations are compared along political lines. The younger generation usually appears to be more optimistic, more eager to get involved in politics, and more expectant that their involvement will make a difference.

Since parents are not terribly forthright in the messages they send to their children concerning politics, and since the political experiences of the older generation differ so markedly from those of the young, we would not expect there to be great continuity in the socialization of attitudes that are bound up in political experience—specifically, the feelings of political efficacy and political trust. This expectation is reinforced by the relatively abstract nature of these two attitudes; cues that relate to them will nearly always be indirect.

Table 7.4 displays the association between parents and children in the area of political efficacy. Parents appear to have some influence on their children, but it is quite weak. On the whole, many children feel at least moderately efficacious regardless of their parents' feelings. The only effect the parents seem to have is to reinforce a tendency toward efficacy that is already present in their children and does not depend on their own attitude.

TABLE 7.4. Relationship between Child and Parent Scores on Political Efficacy

Children		Parents				
		Low Efficacy 1	2	3	4	High Efficacy 5
Low efficacy	1	32%	27%	26%	18%	16%
	2	37	35	34	41	35
	3	31	38	40	41	49
		100%	100%	100%	100%	100%
	N:	(261)	(302)	(415)	(416)	(491)

Source: M. Kent Jennings and Richard G. Niemi, *The Political Character of Adolescence: The Influence of Families and Schools* (Princeton, N.J.: Princeton University Press, 1974), p. 128.

The impact parents have on their offsprings' feelings of political trust resembles the above pattern very closely. There is a modest relationship; that is, trusting parents make it somewhat more likely that the children will be trusting.

From Table 7.5 you can easily see that there are very few children in the low-trust categories at all. The parental level of trust has some slight effect nonetheless. The least trusting parents have the least trusting children; 12 percent of the latter are in the two most cynical categories, while 34 percent are in the two most trusting categories. When the parents are very trusting, the size of the least trusting group of offspring shrinks to 3 percent, while the most trusting group expands to 52 percent. As was the case with political efficacy, we can see once again that parental socialization has only a marginal effect on these attitudes of the children. Most of the cues relating to political trust come from outside the family.

In conclusion, while we feel intuitively that the family is central in the process of political socialization, and while our theories of learning give the family a most prominent place, we run into considerable trouble when we try to measure the family's influence in the real world. The preceding paragraphs have illustrated this point nicely: Only the rather special attitude of party loyalty is passed on with impressive regularity.

Should we therefore abandon the idea that the family is an important agent of political socialization? I think not. Instead, we should turn our attention to the role the family plays in inculcating consensual attributes. Much of what I have placed in the category of political religion—the acceptance of our political community, the legitimacy of government, and the filling of political posts by election, to cite a few examples—is passed

TABLE 7.5. Relationship between Child and Parent Scores on Political Trust

Children		Parents					
		Least Trust 1	2	3	4	5	Most Trust 6
Least trust	1	8%	9%	4%	4%	5%	2%
	2	4	3	3	3	1	1
	3	17	19	13	11	9	12
	4	36	35	40	36	36	33
	5	22	20	24	29	29	27
Most trust	6	12	15	16	18	19	25
Total		99%	101%	100%	101%	99%	100%
	N:	(95)	(52)	(246)	(685)	(479)	(321)

Source: M. Kent Jennings and Richard G. Niemi, *The Policital Character of Adolescence: The Influence of Families and Schools* (copyright © 1974 by Princeton University Press), Table 5.6, p. 146. Reprinted by permission of Princeton University Press.

on by the family in such a consensual way that these basic political rules of the game are effectively established beyond any challenge by the time the individual reaches adulthood.[4]

The School

The school differs from the family as an agent of political socialization in two basic ways. First, in addition to socializing in the indirect and often incidental manner of the family, the school is also responsible for direct political socialization. Under the name "civics" or "citizenship training," American public schools are supposed to provide their students with a broad range of specific knowledge and attitudes about our political system.

The second difference between the family and the school involves the fact that the school does not occupy the place of primal importance for the child that is typically held by the parents. The child does not usually enter school until the age of 6, when he has already resolved a good many of his initial identity problems. Instead of a single authoritative individual or two, as is the case in the family, the school is filled with authority figures. Although one teacher may become extremely important to a particular student, the typical pattern is that the student experiences relationships with a wide range of authority figures. The messages they send will tend naturally to be contradictory to some extent, thus reducing the impact from that possessed by the parents, who are far more likely to be consistent.

Direct Socialization in the School. By direct socialization I simply mean that certain values and specific beliefs are taught intentionally. Intentional teaching is obviously the primary purpose of the school, but the process occurs in a surprisingly varied number of ways and with varying degrees of success.

The basic element of the direct socialization effort of the school is lodged within the curriculum. The importance of the school curriculum in instilling "correct" political thinking in the children of a nation is well illustrated by the great lengths to which revolutionary systems go to take over the schools and bend them to their own uses. The Soviet Union is perhaps the leading example of a nation that has used its schools for political indoctrination. Soviet principles of pedagogy have as their aim "the formation of behavior, character, and traits of personality necessary to the Soviet state."[5]

How are these goals accomplished through the schools' curricula? An example from an arithmetic textbook used in another revolutionary society, Cuba, answers the question rather clearly.

Between January 3 and June 10 in 1961, North American military airplanes violated Cuban airspace 3 times in the month of January, 15 in February, 17 in March, 9 in April, 8 in May, and 10 in June. What was the average monthly number of violations of Cuban airspace by North American military airplanes?[6]

In revolutionary societies this manipulation of the educational curricula is necessary because the very essence of a revolution is the replacement of one political culture with another. This is a task that cannot be accomplished by military force. The kinds of socialization that continue to take place, particularly within the family, often do not change, and they continue to instill values favorable to the defeated regime. The educational system is one agent of socialization that is easily controlled by the government and therefore has the utmost importance in presenting the values of the new culture.

In the United States, of course, there are no great differences between the socialization that goes on within the family and the sorts of values the government would consider acceptable. We live in a consensual political culture. Does this mean, then, that no indoctrination takes place in American schools? It does not. It means only that the process of indoctrination is less obtrusive than it is in revolutionary societies.

Edgar Litt investigated the indoctrination carried out in American schools by examining the textbooks used in three different types of schools (referred to as Alpha, Beta, and Gamma) that he found in the Boston area.[7] Alpha was an upper-middle-class school in a community in which there was a good deal of political activity; Beta was a lower-middle-class school in a community with moderate political activity; and Gamma was a working-class school in a community with little political activity.

Litt sought to discover whether the content of the teaching of civics varied from one type of school to the other. He did this by reading the textbooks used in the schools and by recording how often each of five subjects was mentioned. These included (1) emphasis on citizen political participation; (2) political chauvinism, the glorification of American political institutions, procedures, and public figures; (3) the democratic creed, or references to the rights of citizens to attempt to influence government; (4) emphasis on the political process, or references to politics as an arena involving people and the use of power, as contrasted with a mechanistic set of institutions that carry out their functions automatically; and (5) emphasis on politics as the resolution of group conflict, especially including the idea of an agreed-upon framework of political rules of the game.

We can see in Table 7.6 that there was one area of basic agreement in all three of these schools, and that is the stress put on the democratic creed. All the textbooks made frequent mention of the rights of citizens

TABLE 7.6. References on Salient Political Dimensions in Civics Textbooks

Political Dimension	Alpha	Beta	Gamma
Emphasis on democratic creed	56%	52%	47%
Chauvinistic references to American political institutions	3	6	2
Emphasis on political activity, the citizen's duty, efficacy	17	13	5
Emphasis on political process, politicians, and power	11	2	1
Emphasis on group conflict-resolving political function	10	1	2
Other	3	26	43
Totals	100%	100%	100%
Number of paragraphs	(501)	(367)	(467)

Source: Edgar Litt, "Civic Education, Community Norms and Political Indoctrination," *American Sociological Review*, vol. 28, no. 1 (February 1963), p. 72.

to petition their government. Another area of agreement involved the number of chauvinistic references. None of the civics curricula put much emphasis on an isolationist or jingoistic view that American government is the best in the world.

In the other three areas studied by Litt, certain regular differences did emerge. Only in Alpha was there much attempt to communicate a "real" image of government—that is, an image of people engaged in power struggles, of groups in conflict, and of ordinary citizens taking an active part. In Gamma especially, an unusually bland picture of government was presented. The books in that school contained a large number of simple descriptive references (names, date of events, charts of political processes, etc., labeled "other" in Table 7.6), instead of the descriptions of the real political world that appeared in Alpha's textbooks.

It appears that the students in these three schools were being trained to assume three very different types of political roles. The working-class school trained its students in the mechanics of democratic procedure, but did very little to suggest that those students would ever have a real place in the political process. Politics was portrayed as being conducted by various anonymous governmental institutions working in harmony for the benefit of all the citizens.

The training in Beta, the lower-middle-class school, differed from Gamma in that the responsibilities of citizenship received some stress. The idea that everyone has a voice in politics and should exercise his citizen's duty, was included in the textbooks. However, the image of politics remained one of harmony in the context of smoothly running political institutions.

Only in Alpha, located in an affluent and politically active community, do we find that a true picture of politics emerged in the textbooks. The democratic creed was stressed as before, and the principle of citizen involvement was also present. In Alpha, however, we also find images of the real world of politics, with its competition for power and group conflict. Only these students, of those in all three schools, were being trained in political roles that match the political world into which they will move as they reach adulthood.

There is something more sinister in this study: the apparent relationship between the wealth of the school district and the content of the curriculum. The students from the wealthy school were being trained to fill the activist roles into which their socioeconomic status will very likely lead them as they take over positions of prominence in the world of work. But what of those children who by chance were born into a less privileged social class? They face a handicap for future political involvement in the socialization they receive. They absorbed the consensus values of American political life but were not taught the skills they will need to be anything but passive participants in politics.

So far we have discovered that high school civics textbooks differ, and that the differences appear to relate to the types of communities in which the schools are located. However, we have assumed that because there is a difference in curricula, there will also be a difference in the attitudes of the students who take those courses. The question is, how effective are high school civics courses in teaching material about politics?

Fortunately, Langton and Jennings, using the national sample of high school seniors that I have already presented, investigated precisely this question.[8] They split their sample into two parts, one consisting of students who had taken no civics courses during grades 10 to 12 and the other of students who had taken one or more civics courses. (About one-third of the students had not taken any civics, and most of the others had taken just one course.) These two groups were then tested in eight areas: (1) political knowledge and sophistication, centered on a knowledge of political facts; (2) political interest; (3) spectator politicization, that is, the amount of attention paid to the political reporting of the mass media; (4) political discourse, that is, the amount of political discussion engaged in by the student; (5) political efficacy, or the feeling that individual political action makes a difference; (6) political cynicism, or the lack of trust in politics and politicians; (7) civic tolerance, relating to support for civil liberties; and (8) participative orientation, that is, a view that the "good citizen" is one who takes an active part in politics.

Clearly, we ought to expect that certain kinds of differences should emerge in these eight areas between those who have taken civics and those who have not. Political knowledge, interest, attention to the media, political discourse, and political efficacy should all increase. Political cynicism should decrease, and civic tolerance and a participative orientation should both increase. What Langton and Jennings found was therefore rather startling. In the sample as a whole they "found not one single case

... in which the civics curriculum was significantly associated with students' political orientations."⁹

Langton and Jennings' work represents a strong indictment against the ability of American schools to perform specific training tasks, but it does not necessarily mean that the schools are unimportant in the process of political socialization. In the first place, the curriculum is only one aspect of the total school experience. Second, a major reason why the high school civics course appears to have such little impact involves the redundancy effect. That is, the typical student receives so many cues about the eight subjects involved in this study, from so many sources, that it is impossible to trace the origin of an attitude to any one specific source. This redundancy of cues means that, from a given course, a student will be exposed to very little that is new. Rather, what he or she has already learned will be reinforced. It is significant to note, by the way, that the one area in which a civics course would likely present new information, factual knowledge of politics, is also the one area in which the largest differences were found between the students who had taken civics and those who had not.

While Langton and Jennings' findings apply to their total sample, there is one subgroup of students for whom civics courses did have an important role to play. Black students, especially those from deprived backgrounds, were significantly affected in their political attitudes by taking civics. This finding fits very well with the redundancy hypothesis, of course. Poor blacks, for a wide variety of reasons, are precisely those individuals who would have the least opportunity to pick up political messages in other places. For them, the civics course is in fact saying new things, and it does have an effect.

There is another aspect of the school experience that involves direct socialization. This is classroom ritual. A significant amount of time is spent in the schools extolling the virtues of the American system and reinforcing the students' feelings of devotion to that system. In many states, American flags are displayed in every classroom, and the daily pledge of allegiance is a familiar experience to most of us. The national anthem is also commonly sung at school gatherings. The child seldom questions these feelings of respect for the pledge and the national anthem, which receive daily reinforcement. After all, the teacher, who is the child's primary authority figure in the school environment, leads the pledge, and every other child in the group participates. It would be an unusual child indeed who could ever conclude that there was anything wrong with the sentiments expressed in such a context. The consensual atmosphere in which the patriotic values are learned, coupled with the virtual absence of any contradictory messages from other sources, goes far to explain why such elements of the political culture as support for the political community are accepted religiously. The underpinning of the political religion concept, after all, is the total absence of any sense that these values might even possibly be different.

Indirect Socialization in the School. The school is generally considered to be an important agent of socialization because it is the single agent in society that is organized expressly for the purpose of socializing the young in a direct fashion. I believe, however, that there is good reason to think that the impact of the school as an agent of socialization is greater in the realm of indirect, or unintended, socialization. There are two ways in which indirect socialization in the schools can be examined: by looking at the influence teachers have outside the curriculum, and by looking at the general school environment.

By virtue of his or her position as a substitute parent in the school environment, we can readily understand why the teacher possesses such great authority in the eyes of the students, particularly those in the elementary grades. The teacher also has immense opportunity to influence students. By one estimate, in the typical school day the elementary school teacher will interact more than 10,000 times with his or her students.[10] But only a fraction of those interactions involve the teaching of the curriculum itself. Many are devoted to the informal, but very important "lesson of obedience." In the elementary grades especially, the formal content of the curriculum such as reading and arithmetic, is often considered by the teachers to be less important than an emphasis on compliance to rules and authority.[11] The lesson does not involve *what* is taught in the school, but involves *the way* things are taught. Children learn how to keep quiet and how to sit still for long periods. They learn to follow certain rules of organization such as asking permission from the teacher to perform virtually every act. They learn docility, to accept the demands of the teacher-authority figure before all else.[12]

I do not, of course, mean to suggest that every classroom in America is a lockstep jail in which students are taught to be robots and the child's natural excitement about learning for its own sake is slowly suffocated. I would be surprised, however, if any reader cannot recall these kinds of experiences occurring at some time or another during his or her elementary or secondary school career.

The question we need to face is, does the atmosphere of strict or permissive authority in the school classroom make a difference in later political behavior? The problem has never been studied well enough to give a definitive answer, but Almond and Verba do allow me to make some statement.[13]

Table 7.7 shows us two things. First, you can figure out (if you are willing to do a little calculating) that the typical American does not really experience a totally authoritarian school environment. Only 38 percent of the American sample recalled being allowed no formal school participation (that is, had no ability to participate in formal classroom discussions). American schools have an authoritarian streak, but are nothing like those of other Western nations.

TABLE 7.7. Percent Who Scored Highest in Subjective Competence[a] among Respondents Who Report Varying Degrees of Formal School Participation, by Nation and Education

	Total					
	Could and Did Participate in Discussions		Could Participate and Did Not		Could Not Participate	
Nation	%	N	%	N	%	N
United States	76	(387)[b]	53	(144)	63	(329)
Great Britain	78	(139)	46	(75)	61	(651)
Germany	70	(109)	43	(49)	47	(650)
Italy	63	(81)	46	(26)	45	(415)
Mexico	59	(111)	39	(176)	39	(491)

Source: Gabriel Almond and Sidney Verba, *The Civic Culture: Political Attitudes and Democracy in Five Nations* (copyright © 1963 by Princeton University Press), Table 22, p. 359. Reprinted by permission of Princeton University Press.

[a] That is, those who received the three highest scores on the subjective competence scale.
[b] Numbers in parentheses refer to the bases upon which percentages are calculated.

The more interesting part of Table 7.7 from our present point of view lies in the effects that both the ability to participate in classroom discussion and the actual participation have on adult political attitudes (here measured by "subjective competence," or the feeling that one can appeal to a set of regular and orderly rules in one's dealings with administrative officials). This effect is present in all countries. In the United States the feeling of subjective competence characterizes fewer than two-thirds of those who had no opportunity to participate in class discussion, but more than three-quarters of those who had the chance and took advantage of it.

The second major type of indirect socialization in the school comes from the school environment. The school, after all, is a society just like any other. It has leaders and followers, rules and procedures, and discipline and punishment for transgressors. Much of this exists independently of the teachers and the curriculum. We are all aware, for example, that most American high schools devote tremendous resources to extracurricular activities. To be sure, this has always been justified in terms of educational goals. Perhaps you can recall the high school football coach's lectures to local groups that "athletics is the crucible of democracy because it teaches fair play and teamwork."[14] The informal side of high school has also been extolled in the following way:

> Students who participate in [extracurricular activities] have a clearer image of what is conventionally regarded as good citizenship. . . . In school, they are

giving socially appropriate responses and have a better idea of what responses are socially appropriate.[15]

It turns out, however, that participation in extracurricular activities has more political meaning than the teaching about "democracy" or good citizenship. Ziblatt has proposed that extracurricular activities serve as laboratories where young people can practice real-world political skills and where they can earn rewards in the form of status from their peers.[16] He hypothesizes therefore that students who are "insiders," who occupy positions of status in a school's system of extracurricular activities, will view politics positively, whereas "outsiders" will take a more negative view.

Ziblatt summarizes his findings as follows: First, the more frequently a student participates in extracurricular activities, the greater is his feeling of integration into the school status system. Second, the greater the student's feeling of integration into the school's status system, the greater his feeling of social trust. Finally, the greater the feelings of social trust, the more positive is the student's attitude about politics.

An interesting sidelight to this study reminds us of some results that have emerged before. Those from the working class, who are most likely to benefit from the experience of joining an extracurricular group because of the lack of opportunity to learn political skills elsewhere, are the least likely to do so. Once again, the opportunity to acquire attitudes that would lead to political activity in adult life seems to have an economic bias.

To sum up, it would be most accurate to say that the major role the school plays in the political socialization process involves the formation of consensual values and the development of the norm of compliance. Consensual values are the basic, unchallenged ideas we hold about the political system, which we discussed earlier under the name political religion. They include the feeling of belongingness as a member of the American political community, the belief in the legitimacy of the political system, and the uncritical acceptance of the democratic creed.

The norm of compliance is the feeling that authority is benevolent and should be obeyed. It also contains an element of passivity. In the political realm, this is translated into the belief in the citizen's duty to vote, coupled with the belief that politicians are usually right and that their decisions should not be challenged.

Surprisingly, the schools do not seem to teach much in the way of factual information about politics. Nor are they very successful in encouraging students to acquire attitudes like political trust or efficacy. We concluded that this finding probably reflected the phenomenon of redundancy. That is, by the time a person reaches the age of 16 or 17, he is exposed to a great many sources of politically relevant cues. It becomes very difficult under such circumstances to say that one single agent is responsible for any specific part of the individual's socialization. Only in the case of the most isolated students, the lower-socioeconomic-level blacks, was the high school curriculum not redundant.

Last, but perhaps most important, we have seen that wealth has a good deal to do with the sorts of socialization one experiences in the school. Wealthy schools give different, and more useful, depictions of politics to their students. And within a school, the children of wealthy parents are better able to take advantage of extracurricular activities, which provide practice and a positive orientation toward later political activity.

The Peer Group

Few Americans who have reached high school age need to be told that the peer group is important. These primary groups, composed of members sharing relatively equal status and intimate ties, often dominate the informal social environment. They may set standards of conduct in both nonacademic and academic areas. They may give enormous status to certain individuals, and condemn others to the painful fate of being ignored. James Coleman, in his study of peer groups in ten Illinois high schools, described how the school's "leading crowd" set a premium on athletic ability and good looks and hypothesized that the leading crowd was able to discourage academic achievement among the bulk of the students so that standards of achievement would not be set uncomfortably high.[17]

Why is the peer group so important? The findings of study after study, that primary group members tend to think and act alike, have been explained in fairly simple terms by Cartwright and Zander.[18] They give three general reasons which underlie the group's influence: (1) "Membership in a group determines to a great extent many of the things a person will learn, see, experience, or think about." (2) "An individual may act like other members of a group because they are attractive to him and he wants to be like them." (3) "A person may act like the other members of a group because he fears punishment, ridicule or rejection by the rest of the group if he does not."

To these three conditions I would add a fourth. The group will be influential in those areas that its members feel are important. It will not affect attitudes and behavior in areas of no concern to the members. Brittain, for instance, found that the adolescent peer group was authoritative in the area of dating, but had very little to say about the choice of courses to take in school.[19]

There is a good deal of disagreement over the extent to which the adolescent peer group influences the political attitudes of its members. If we consult the only two studies in which the peer attitudes were measured directly, we find that certain political values are fairly closely related to the peer group's view, while others seem to come mostly from the parents.[20]

The entries in Table 7.8 fit reasonably well with some of the things we have discussed previously. You will recall that the one political attitude that the parents seem to socialize in their children is party identification. When the parents' influence is compared with that of the peers in this table, we still find that the parents' influence dominates. The partisanship of the student's peers has relatively little impact on the student's own sense of loyalty.[21] Another measure of partisanship, the preference for

TABLE 7.8. The Impact of Parents and Peers on Student Political Attitudes

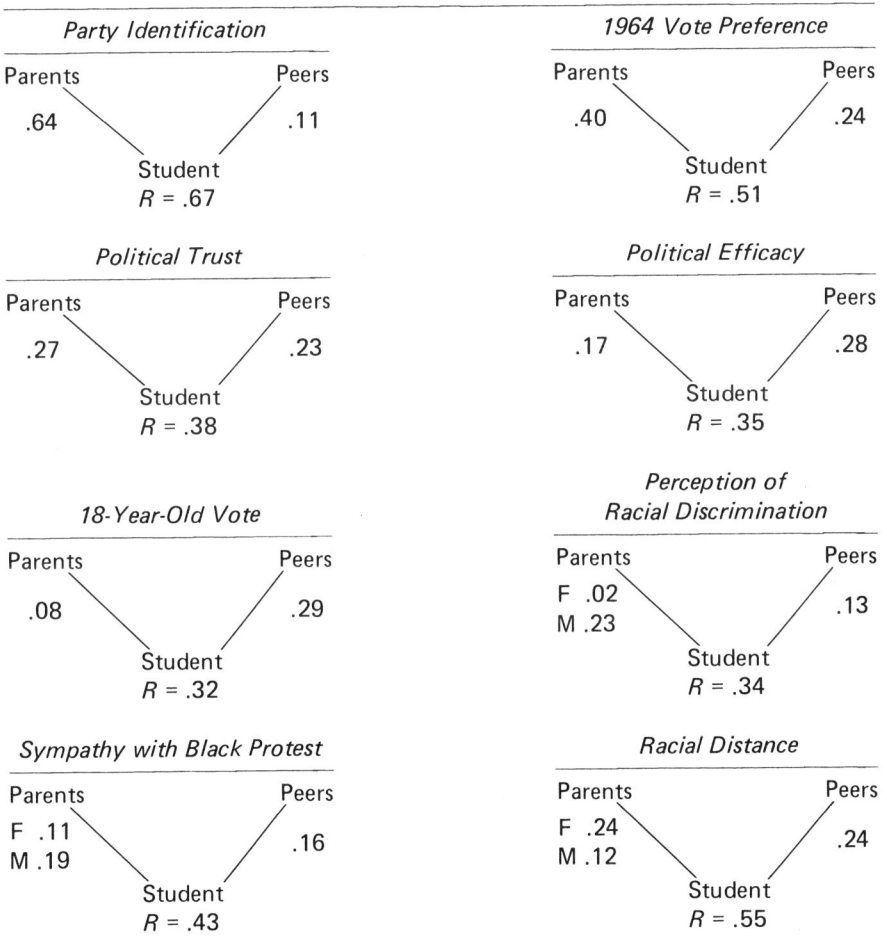

Sources: M. Kent Jennings and Richard G. Niemi, *The Political Character of Adolescence: The Influence of Families and Schools* (copyright © 1974 by Princeton University Press), Figure 9.3, p. 243, first five entries (with amendments and additions). Reprinted by permission of Princeton University Press. Bruce A. Campbell, Atlanta Student Study, last three entries (racial attitudes).

Johnson or Goldwater in the 1964 presidential race, shows a similar pattern. The voice of the parents remains quite strong in influencing their children's preference. The peers are still less important, although the association between the student's choice and that of his peers is stronger in this case than it was previously.

Once we move beyond these measures of partisanship, the pattern of strong parental influence and weak peer influence disappears. In the case of both political efficacy and the 18-year-old vote, the peers seem to be significantly more influential than the parents in determining the student's position. In the four remaining instances, the peer-student associations have approximately the same strength as the parent-student associations.[22]

The overall lesson of Table 7.8 is that although peer attitudes do have a measurable association with student political feelings, in no case could we claim that student attitude or behavior is dominated by this factor. For the most part, the adolescent peer group probably does not exercise a great or lasting influence on the patterns of political socialization of the typical American teenager.

Summary

To conclude this section, I want to present an illustration (Figure 7.1) that lays out in simplified form the relative importance of the different agents of socialization throughout the life cycle. We see the initially dominant position of the parents from birth to junior high school or so. After graduation from high school, the parents' input to the socialization process declines to a low level. The school has no influence at all before age 6, of

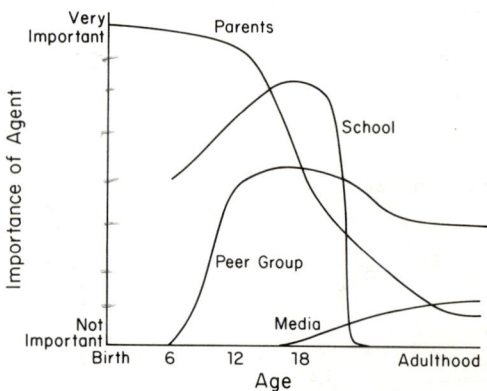

Figure 7.1. The Importance of Different Agents of Socialization through the Life Cycle.

course. However, once the child enters school, that institution has a steady and important influence on socialization experiences. This begins to decline after age 18, when many youngsters leave school. However, the majority of young Americans attend college now, so the influence of the school may persist into the early twenties, and it is more important than that of the parents during this period. The peer group begins to exercise some effect on socialization when the child enters school, but its influence really doesn't reach its peak until junior high school. Its effect declines as the individual passes into adulthood. However, of the childhood agents, the peer group is the only one to retain an active role in socialization during adulthood, when high school friends are replaced by spouse, neighbors, and co-workers. Finally, the influence of the media is the last to be felt, but like the peer group, the media continue to have an effect on political learning throughout life.

GROUP DIFFERENCES IN POLITICAL SOCIALIZATION

For the most part, this section of the book has presented a fairly conventional view of political socialization. I have depicted a process that is essentially conservative, serving to perpetuate a variety of positive, passive, or accepting attitudes about politics in the United States. The basic impact of that process is to produce a political climate in which the mass citizenry is accepting rather than vigilant, and in which politicians operate within relatively wide constraints. This closing section is intended to counter the image that the socialization of the American electorate is a monolithic and positive thing.[23] Two factors which generate much heterogeneity are discussed here: social class and race.

Social Class

The way people view politics is undoubtedly affected by the amount of money they have. Karl Marx, after all, based his entire political philosophy on the inevitability of class struggle. For Marx, the only political question of any importance was the conflict between the owners of the means of production and those who provide the labor.

Obviously, the American experience has not followed Marx's predictions very well. We have not experienced total class polarization and antagonism. We do find cooperation among the classes, as evidenced by the fact that Jimmy Carter received 58 percent of the working-class vote *and* 37 percent of the middle-class vote in 1976.

But to say that Marx failed to predict the second American revolution does not deny that there are differences between the social classes in the United States. We know, for instance, that those who belong to the poorer classes are more generally favorable toward liberal economic policies such as government health insurance, unemployment insurance, old-age pensions, and so forth.[24] On the other hand, the wealthier classes support less government participation in the economy and more tax incentives for business. Class differences can also be seen in the extent to which Americans are willing to tolerate dissent and nonconformity. The Vietnam protestors of the 1960s found their most ardent opponents among the hardhats. Despite their liberal economic views, many poorer Americans are much more ready to deny constitutionally guaranteed freedoms of speech and assembly to Communists, Nazis, atheists, or other unpopular groups.[25]

Given these differences in the political attitudes of the middle and working class, we are led to wonder whether they are produced by the class differences in childhood socialization.

Relationship to the Political System. You will recall that we stressed how most young Americans acquire a very positive view of the political system, a "sugarcoated" kind of paternalism in which the political leader—whether President, mayor, or policeman—could do no wrong. We also noted certain developmental trends suggesting that as the child grows older, he begins to conceive his world in more advanced and abstract terms. At each stage, however, lower-class children lag behind their middle-class peers. The consequence is that "as a middle-class child begins depersonalizing and de-idealizing political authority, the lower-class child persists in his more naive and benevolent imagery."[26] Lower-class children also retain their view of the law as unchanging and punitive longer than middle-class children, who move more quickly to the view that laws can be unjust, can be changed, and exist not for punishment but for the general good. The overall effect of these class differences is to give the middle-class child the advantage in understanding the way politics really works and consequently to prepare him better for his own political activity as an adult.

Political Information and Participatory Skills. A real-world view of politics is a useful basis on which to build political activity. However, it must be accompanied by information and skills in order to translate into influence. Are middle-class children better prepared by their socialization experiences than lower-class children in these areas as well?

Since all students are required by law to take courses in school that teach the facts of government, it is not surprising to find no class differences in this area among younger children. However, higher-status children seem to have a better grasp of the informal aspects of politics and also seem more able to see what is important in political life. Sigel reports, for instance, that middle-class children in Detroit were better able to remember John Kennedy for his political achievements, the policies he had adopted. Lower-class children mentioned Kennedy's personal characteristics when they were asked to say what they remembered about him.[27] Greenstein suggests that it is the lower-class parents' unwillingness to discuss controversial political topics in the home that keep their offspring from going beyond the conventional facts they learn in school. These parents also have less to say because of their generally lower levels of political information. The upper-class family is much freer in its discussions, which impart to the child a much more sophisticated view of politics.[28]

As the child matures into adolescence, even the earlier equality in the level of factual knowledge about government disappears. While no group of high school seniors is really very well informed about government, upper-class children do respond more accurately when asked how many justices sit on the Supreme Court or what Franklin Roosevelt's party was. Since we know already that taking civics courses has relatively little effect on increasing the political knowledge of upper-class students, we can conclude that there are basic motivational differences leading these individuals to acquire political knowledge and skills that lower-class children do not have. In all likelihood these differences in motivation center around the family, where the upper-class child's political learning is reinforced and the lower-class child's is not.[29]

There is also evidence to suggest that there is a difference in the abilities of lower- and upper-class children to view partisan politics from an abstract, ideological point of view. Upper-class children are more likely, for instance, to defend their choice of candidates in terms of their underlying party loyalties. The lower-class child, while no less likely to *have* a party loyalty, has greater problems connecting the general feeling of partisanship with specific political decisions.[30] He or she often (43 percent of the time) cannot think of any difference at all between the Republican or Democratic parties. The middle-class child is unable to do so only 31 percent of the time. The middle-class child, on the other hand, is able to accurately associate the parties with the broad ideological perspective of "liberal" and "conservative" in nearly 30 percent of the cases, compared to only 17 percent of the lower-class children.[31]

In addition to the cognitive advantages of middle-class living, the middle-class families' treatment of the child's individuality has political relevance. The child's opinions tend to be taken more seriously, leading to a greater feeling of self-confidence and personal efficacy.[32] The middle-class child acquires a greater confidence in his own judgments and standards. For example, Greenstein reports that upper-class children more frequently say that they made their *own* choice of a candidate to vote for, rather than consulting others.[33]

While social class differences are rooted primarily in the family, the school has its own effect. We have previously discussed how the school curricula in lower-class schools stress obedience and passivity, while upper-class curricula give more encouragement for activism as well as a more realistic view of the political process. Extracurricular activities also have a class bias. Their effects in the inculcation of positive feelings toward politics tend to be concentrated in the upper-class children who are the ones who most often rise to positions of leadership in that environment.

I do not want to conclude by suggesting that American society practices a premeditated program of subtle repression of the lower classes through the mechanism of political socialization. This is simply not the case. Nor are the social class differences we have discussed usually all that large. Once again, the truth lies in the fact that no single agent can be responsible for more than a fraction of a child's political learning. In a variety of ways, children of the upper class are presented with more opportunities to acquire useful political knowledge than are their lower-class peers. Wealth does produce a biasing effect in the socialization process, and you may want to form some judgment about that on your own. However, the effects tend to be small, and opportunities for lower-class children to acquire political skills emerge on numerous occasions later in life.

Race

While I may maintain that differences by social class tend to be small, and opportunities to bridge the gap are numerous, this is a much more difficult argument to make when it comes to racial differences. Political differences between blacks and whites in the United States are larger than between any other major groups, and have proved to be extremely enduring as well.

Conflict between the races in the United States has a centuries-old tradition. Blacks have differed from whites in such areas as voting rights, schooling and public accommodations, political representation, and economic status, to mention just a few. Perhaps more damaging than these manifestations of black disadvantage, however, is the legacy of white supremacists' efforts to "depoliticize black citizens and to socialize them to accept their inferior status as just and unchangeable...."[34] Are blacks still being socialized to accept their inferior position and remain politically passive, or is there evidence that political activism is a norm to which blacks now subscribe to the same extent as whites?

Relationship to the Political System. Like lower-class white children, black children tend to personalize the political system.[35] Weissberg suggests that this reflects the images of government that blacks have traditionally been encouraged by whites to have: that "good treatment would flow from the benign and knowledgeable white folk (provided, naturally, that blacks kept out of trouble and accepted their place). Government was akin to a big, benevolent father whose goodness and generosity were not subject to direct political pressure."[36]

However, research shows that as blacks grow into late adolescence, the personalization of government fades away. Blacks are not more likely to idealize specific political figures, such as the President or the policeman, than are whites. Nor are they less likely to perceive that government matters to them personally than are whites.[37] In both racial groups, positive feelings are initially very strong and then slowly decline.

In the area of political trust, however, feelings do differ enormously by race. Although both races became less trusting during the late 1960s, Miller found that the shift toward political cynicism that occurred among blacks between 1966 and 1970 was nearly three times as great as the white shift.[38] In 1976, 76 percent of American blacks felt that they could "trust the government in Washington to do what is right" only some of the time or none of the time. Among whites, 64 percent gave this response.

There is another aspect of blacks' relationship to the political system that has attracted particular attention. Curiously, it is a phenomenon that has arisen at the opposite end of the political spectrum from the image of blacks as subservient to a paternalistic, white-dominated government. I refer to black nationalism. In a study done in 15 cities (some of which had experienced disorder during the middle 1960s, others of which had not), Campbell and Schuman found that about 6 percent of blacks interviewed advocated the formation of a separate black nation.[39] While 6 percent seems to be a fairly small number, remember what we have said about the religious nature of most Americans' attachment to their political community (their sense of being American). The great majority still hold to the traditional norm, but for even this small percentage to break away from the consensual belief must require a great deal of conviction. This conviction must also exist in other blacks who do not necessarily favor a separate national identity. As an illustration of this, the Campbell and Schuman investigation also found that 43 percent of their sample agreed that "Negro schoolchildren should study an African language."

Participation-Related Norms and Attitudes. If we cast a careless glance at the data on the norms of political participation and involvement, we find that few racial differences exist in America today. Black youths are at least as oriented toward voting, for instance, as white. If we delve a little more carefully, however, we soon discover that the attitudes that lie at a deeper level do differ by race. A good example is the conception young people have of what makes a good citizen. Jennings' national sample of high school seniors provides the information contained in Table 7.9. Here we can see racial differences with considerably clarity. Blacks defined the good citizen in passive terms, as one who supports the system. That is, he accepts and obeys political leadership. The whites, on the other hand, saw

TABLE 7.9. High School Seniors' Conception of "Good Citizen," by Race

Attribute	Race	
	White	Black
Supports the political system	29.0%	42.8%
Politically active	40.3	19.5
Participates in community affairs	10.6	8.7
Interpersonal and social behavior (helps others, is considerate, neighborly)	7.9	16.9
Moral and ethical traits (honest, religious, fair)	7.3	6.7
Other personal attributes (concerned about family and job, works hard)	4.1	5.4
Miscellaneous, don't know	.8	0.0
	100.0%	100.0%

Source: ICPSR Archive: Jennings-Neimi Student Socialization Study.

political activism as the dominant trait of the good citizen. Over twice as many whites (40.3 percent) as blacks (19.5 percent) valued action over support.

Preadult Political Activity. When we consult the reports by whites and blacks about the sorts of political involvement they engage in, we continue to get an image of a white group that is on its way toward integration into the political system and a black group that is not. Preadult political activity constitutes important training for adult participation in the real world of politics. Table 7.10 indicates a generally broader base of experience among whites. For the most part, this table shows that whites engage in political activity more frequently than blacks. Younger whites were more active in six of the nine categories listed. When we move over to the older group, we find that racial differences in activity levels do not diminish. In several cases, such as talking politics with parents, the older group has a larger black-white difference (24 points) than the younger group (19 points).

Summary

Overall, the message of Tables 7.9 and 7.10 is that blacks are socialized at a very young age—as early as age 8—to regard active political participation as inappropriate. Furthermore, as these children grow older, racial differences become larger, not smaller. The racial gap in exposure to norms and situations that lead to the development of political skills increases.

TABLE 7.10. Preadult Political Activity, by Race and Age

| | Young (8-11) | | Older (12-15) | |
Political Activity	White	Black	White	Black
Written letter to President	6[a]	7	6	9
Helped a candidate campaign	10	12	18	14
Wore a campaign button	22	23	40	29
Talked with parent about candidate	49	30	65	41
Talked with friend about candidate	51	31	64	46
Talked with parents about our country's problems	57	47	69	47
Read about candidate in newspaper or magazine	54	43	70	52
Talked with parents or friend about Vietnam War	73	55	77	59
Watched the President on TV	80	70	74	65
N:	(404)	(100)	(396)	(60)

Source: Joan E. Laurence, "White Socialization: Black Reality," *Psychiatry*, vol. 23, no. 2 (May 1970), 180.

[a] Entries are percentage of group engaging in each activity.

How can these racial differences be explained? Perhaps the most obvious explanation lies in the unfortunate fact that a larger proportion of blacks come from the lower class. Hence, the sorts of arguments made in the preceding section can be applied to the explanation of racial differences as well. However, differences in socioeconomic status can tell only part of the story. The black experience in America, while in large part an experience in poverty, has also been an experience with discrimination and a closed political system. I would argue that a good deal of the disinterest that blacks seem to show in conventional politics stems from a perception of political reality. Participation is not valued simply because experience has shown attempts at participation to be futile or even dangerous. This political-reality argument succeeds in reconciling the contradiction between the passive image of black political thinking shown in these pages and the great outpouring of political activity on the part of blacks as a part of the civil rights movement of the past two decades. Conventional participation may be seen as a futile waste of time, but this does not mean that blacks are politically uninterested or apathetic. An outlet that is new and promises to produce results, such as civil disobedience, can recruit many activists to the cause.

NOTES

1. The correlation between parent and student party identification was tau-beta = .47, compared to tau-beta = .25 in Table 7.3. Suffice it to say that tau-beta is a measure which reflects the tendency for students and their parents to have similar scores on the variables in question. Further elucidation can be obtained from a statistics text such as Hubert Blalock, *Social Statistics,* 2d ed. (New York: McGraw-Hill, 1972).

2. See M. Kent Jennings and Richard G. Niemi, *The Political Character of Adolescence: The Influence of Families and Schools* (Princeton, N.J.: Princeton University Press, 1974), p. 121.

3. *Ibid.* p. 121.

4. M. Kent Jennings and Richard G. Niemi, "The Transmission of Political Values from Parent to Child," *American Political Science Review*, vol. 62, no. 1 (March 1968), 169–184

5. Frederic C. Barghoorn, *Politics in the USSR* (Boston: Little, Brown, 1966), p. 85.

6. Richard R. Fagen, *Cuba: The Political Content of Adult Education* (Stanford, Calif.: The Hoover Institution of War and Peace, 1964), p. 68.

7. Edgar Litt, "Civic Education, Community Norms and Political Indoctrination," *American Sociological Review*, vol. 28, no. 1 (February 1963), 69–75.

8. Kenneth P. Langton and M. Kent Jennings, "Political Socialization and the High School Civics Curriculum in the United States," *American Political Science Review*, vol. 62, no. 3 (September 1968), 852–867.

9. *Ibid.* p. 866.

10. Richard E. Dawson and Kenneth Prewitt, *Political Socialization* (Boston: Little, Brown, 1969), p. 162.

11. Robert D. Hess and Judith V. Torney, *The Development of Political Attitudes in Children* (Chicago: Aldine, 1967), p. 110.

12. Jules Henry, "Docility, or Giving the Teacher What She Wants," *Journal of Social Issues*, vol. 2, no. 2 (1955), 33–41.

13. Gabriel A. Almond and Sidney Verba, *The Civic Culture* (Princeton, N.J.: Princeton University Press, 1963), p. 354.

14. David Ziblatt, "High School Extracurricular Activities and Political Socialization," *Annals of the American Academy of Political and Social Science*, vol. 361 (September 1965), 21.

15. Helen Lewis, "The Teen-age Joiner and His Orientation toward Public Affairs" (unpublished Ph.D. dissertation, Department of Political Science, Michigan State University, 1962), pp. 171–172.

16. Ziblatt, *op. cit.*

17. James S. Coleman, *The Adolescent Society* (New York: Free Press, 1961).

18. Dorwin Cartwright and Alvin Zander, "Group Pressures and Group Standards: Introduction," in D. Cartwright and A. Zander (Eds.), *Group Dynamics: Research and Theory*, 2nd ed. (New York: Harper & Row, 1960), chap. 9.

19. Clay V. Brittain, "Adolescent Choices and Parent-Peer Cross-Pressures," *American Sociological Review*, vol. 28, no. 3 (June 1963), 385–391.

20. Suzanne Koprince Sebert, "The Political Texture of Peer Groups," in M. K. Jennings and R. G. Niemi, *The Political Character of Adolescence, op. cit.*, chap. 9; Bruce A. Campbell, "Peer Influence in Political Socialization," paper presented at the annual meeting of the Southern Political Science Association, Nashville, Tenn., November 6–8, 1975.

21. These entries are Pearsonian product-moment correlation coefficients. The parent-student and peer-student measures are *partial* correlations, showing the effect of each of the former variables on student attitudes, assuming that they are unrelated to each other. The multiple *R* reported below each entry is the extent to which the given student attitude is associated with both parents' and peers' attitudes.

22. The three measures of racial feeling were presented by Angus Campbell in *White Attitudes toward Black People* (Ann Arbor, Mich.: Institute for Social Research, 1971). They are designed to capture the major elements of the more complex overall attitude about race. The cognitive element is measured by asking the extent to which people perceive discrimination to exist. The affective element is measured by asking feeling of warmth or sympathy toward the blacks' civil rights activities of recent years. The cognitive element, or action-

orientation, is measured by determining what the respondent says he would do when put in a variety of circumstances of contact with members of the opposite race.

23. The following discussion is inspired by Robert Weissberg, *Political Learning, Political Choice, and Democratic Citizenship* (Englewood Cliffs, N.J.: Prentice-Hall, 1974), pp. 94ff.

24. Lloyd A. Free and Hadley Cantril, *The Political Beliefs of Americans* (New Brunswick, N.J.: Rutgers University Press, 1967), chap. II.

25. See, among others, John P. Robinson, "Public Reaction to Political Protest: Chicago, 1968," *Public Opinion Quarterly*, vol. 24, no. 1 (Spring 1970), 1–9.

26. Weissberg, *op. cit.*, p. 97.

27. Roberta S. Sigel, "Image of a President: Some Insights into the Political Views of School Children," *American Political Science Review*, vol. 62, no. 1 (March 1968), 216–226.

28. Fred I. Greenstein, *Children and Politics* (New Haven: Yale University Press, 1965), pp. 98–100.

29. Hess and Torney, *op. cit.*, pp. 174–176.

30. Greenstein, *op. cit.*

31. Weissberg, *op. cit.*, p. 102.

32. Melvin L. Kohn, "Social Class and Parent-Child Relationships: An Interpretation," *American Journal of Sociology*, vol. 68, no. 4 (January 1963), 471–480; George Psathas, "Ethnicity, Social Class and Adolescent Independence from Parental Control," *American Sociological Review*, vol. 22, no. 4 (August 1957), 415–423.

33. Greenstein, *op. cit.*, p. 103.

34. Weissberg, *op. cit.*, p. 106.

35. Edward S. Greenberg, "Political Socialization and Support of the System" (unpublished Ph.D. dissertation, Department of Political Science, University of Wisconsin, 1969), p. 121.

36. Weissberg, *op. cit.*, pp. 106–107.

37. Greenberg, *op. cit.*, pp. 290–292.

38. Arthur H. Miller, "Political Issues and Trust in Government: 1964–1970," *American Political Science Review*, vol. 68, no. 3 (September 1974), 951–972.

39. Angus Campbell and Howard Schuman, *Racial Attitudes in Fifteen American Cities* (Ann Arbor, Mich.: Institute for Social Research, 1968).

Part **III**

The Expression of Attitudes: Public Opinion

On the evening of October 29, 1884, James G. Blaine, the Republican candidate for President, sat on a New York City rostrum before a large gathering of Protestant ministers and divinity students. The Reverend Dr. Samuel D. Burchard introduced Blaine with a biting attack on the Democratic party, "whose antecedents," Burchard said, "have been rum, Romanism, and rebellion."[1] Blaine later reported that the remark stunned and amazed him. Yet, when he rose to speak, *he failed to repudiate Burchard.* His judgment, made literally on the spot, was that to make any comment would simply draw attention to the issue. He supposed that few persons had actually heard the remark, and that if left unmentioned, its offensive potential would die.

Unfortunately for Blaine, reporters present did not let the slur on the Democratic Party die. The newspapers gave it loving attention, and by election day, had identified the insult so closely with Blaine that in the public's eye, the remark had become an expression of Blaine's own political feelings. In Catholic New York State, Blaine lost by 1149 votes. The reason this anecdote is interesting is because had he carried New York State, he would have become President. Blaine himself later attributed his defeat to the impact on public opinion of this single event.

Of course, presidential elections are rarely this close, and thus we rarely have the opportunity to identify any such finite act as pivotal to the outcome. You may even want to argue that to isolate such an incident is ridiculous on its face, because the election's outcome could equally well be attributed to any other one of the tens of thousands of discrete events that made up voters' minds. Nonetheless, this illustration brings out a point: No government, and certainly not a democratic government, can afford to neglect the political opinions of the mass electorate. These opinions serve notice; that is, they say, "If such a policy is made, or if such a position is taken, we will take action." Action may mean the vote, as the unfortunate Blaine discovered; it may include political violence, or it may be manifested in more complex ways. The threatened impeachment of President Nixon could not move from dead center until the members of Congress had made certain that the opinions of their constituents were sufficiently aroused to support such a radical act. Few congressmen were willing to proceed with impeachment until they were convinced that to do so would not spell defeat for themselves in the next election. The moral? Public opinion is of vital importance in American government because it sets boundaries beyond which political elites may not stray.

V. O. Key once wrote that "to speak with precision of public opinion is a task not unlike coming to grips with the Holy Ghost."[2] He devoted years to the task, however, so perhaps there is some hope. The first issue before us is the matter of definition. One of the most useful is the following:

> Public opinion is the complex of preferences expressed by a significant number of persons on an issue of general importance.[3]

We can flesh out this definition by discussing the concepts one at a time.

Presence of an Issue

The most basic idea in the study of public opinion is that it gathers around an issue. While "public opinion" or "the wisdom of public opinion" is sometimes cited as if it were an independent political or social force, it is really much more accurate to view public opinion with reference to some actual question. Implicit in this view is also the idea of disagreement. To speak about the opinion that the sun rises in the East seems a little silly. Opinion on an issue implies disagreement.

The Complex of Preferences in the Public

It is really incorrect to speak of public opinion as if there were one simple position about which the public agrees—or even two positions, each having its adherents. Public opinion is usually extremely diffuse. The complex of preferences includes people who don't care or those who have a neutral opinion, as well as those who have intense opinions favoring different alternatives.

V. O. Key captured the essence of these distinctions in his concept of the "attentive" public. He felt that "unless the public becomes aware of actions or events, whatever latent attitudes exist will not be converted into conscious opinion with a potential bearing on behavior through voting or otherwise."[4] On most issues the number of people whose latent attitudes have been mobilized into conscious opinion is extremely small. Watergate provides a good example. Most of us hold a latent attitude that values honesty and obedience to the law. Nevertheless, in spite of the fact that the break-in of the Democratic headquarters at Watergate was publicly known in 1972 and some of Nixon's closest aides were implicated, this event was not an issue in the 1972 elections. Watergate's attentive public did not grow much in size until nearly two years later, when the weight of evidence and of national media exposure grew overwhelming.

There are two conclusions to be drawn. First, the electorate allows its government to commit and then get away with wrongful acts primarily because it doesn't care enough about politics. Becoming aware of actions and events, the hallmark of the attentive public, costs us something in terms of time and intellectual effort. For most of us, it isn't worth it. The second conclusion is that a good deal of what is done in government is influenced not by the direct expression of opinion but by the political leadership's expectation that if they did a certain thing, public opinion *would be* extremely hostile. Politicians are careful not to arouse certain of the latent attitudes that exist in the electorate. The imposition of a one-dollar per gallon federal gasoline tax might be favored by many congressmen as of this writing. However, these leaders know that the public would be outraged should such a policy be instituted. They are, therefore, unwilling to risk supporting that policy at this stage, even though they may feel that it is needed and that it may very likely come about within a few years in any event.

Number of Persons Involved

Scholars have sometimes argued about how many people have to be involved before opinion becomes public opinion. Since this book is about the American electorate, I tend to focus on the whole population and on its collective opinions on the issues. This is not necessary, of course. There are many publics, defined differently according to the issue in question. Federally supported health care for the elderly will generate strong opinions among the elderly, and the Vietnam draft coalesced the opinions of young men eligible for the draft (along with many others).

Clearly, all else being equal, political scientists should be more interested in opinions involving many people rather than those involving only a few. However, the importance of an opinion depends on factors other than the number of people holding it. The opinions of the American

Medical Association on Medicare, of the American Bar Association on appointments to the Supreme Court, or of the National Rifle Association on gun control are generally very influential in government. This is true in spite of the fact that none of these organizations has a membership that exceeds a tiny fraction of a percent of the American population. What they do have is status, good organization, and money. With these resources they are able to reach the ears of congressmen in ways that tend to be more influential than those open to other groups that may be larger in terms of membership.

NOTES

1. Reported by Bernard C. Hennessy, in *Public Opinion* (North Scituate, Mass.: Duxbury Press, 1975), 3d ed., pp. 48–49.
2. V. O. Key, Jr., *Public Opinion and American Democracy* (New York: Knopf, 1961), p. 8.
3. Hennessy, *op. cit.*, p. 5.
4. Key, *op. cit.*, p. 282.

8
The Acquisition of Opinion: Intrapersonal Processes

In the 1976 presidential election study conducted by the University of Michigan, a strange result emerged. When asked whether Jimmy Carter was a liberal, a "middle-of-the-roader," or a conservative, 62 percent replied liberal, but 20 percent said middle-of-the-roader, and 18 percent replied conservative. Without doubt, you can easily think of reasons to explain how Carter could have been seen as both liberal and conservative simultaneously. The media may have portrayed Carter differently in different parts of the country. Carter may have said different things in different places. Or, since politics are so terribly complicated, a candidate may actually *be* both liberal and conservative, depending on the issue.

In 1976 all of these things were true. But in this chapter I want to take another approach. Because of differences that exist in people's surroundings and in their thought processes and attitudes, the very same stimuli may result in very different opinions in two different people. In order to understand this fact, I want first to present a model of the opinion formation process.

A MODEL OF OPINION FORMATION

At the most superficial level an opinion is nothing more than the expression of an attitude. To understand the ways in which opinions come into being, and then change, we must therefore turn once again to a consideration of attitudes and the forces which produce them.

144 THE EXPRESSION OF ATTITUDES: PUBLIC OPINION

The model in Figure 8.1 displays two processes.[1] The simpler one is the opinion elicitation process. It begins with a stimulus that gives the individual the chance to voice an opinion. In this case, he has been asked how he feels about Jimmy Carter. This is a passive stimulus. It does nothing to challenge the attitudes the individual already holds; it simply asks for a readout of those attitudes. When this response is provided, we call it an opinion: Either Carter is doing well, or he isn't, depending on what attitudes we hold, and which of them happen to have been elicited by the question.

This model makes it plain, however, that there is much more going on in the opinion formation process. In fact, there is a whole second, much more complex, process that we must take into account before we can claim to understand public opinion. This process begins again with a stimulus, and ends with an attitude, or attitude set. This time, however, we are dealing with an active stimulus, one that *does* affect the attitudes held by an individual. Such a stimulus takes the form of new information.

Figure 8.1 shows that three factors operate on a stimulus before the new information has its final impact on attitudes. First the incoming stimulus is filtered through a perceptual screen. How this occurs depends on the personality of the individual and on the attitudes he already possesses. Second, the personality, in addition to its influence on the perceptual screen, has its own direct impact on attitudes. Finally, social reality influences the process through its connection with personality and with the individual's preexisting attitudes.

As we go into greater detail with regard to these concepts and their interrelationships, I want to divide the material along an intrapersonal-

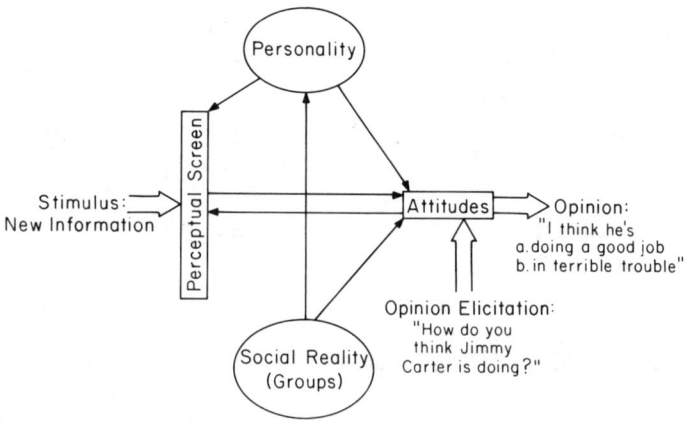

Figure 8.1. A Model of the Opinion-Formation Process.

interpersonal dimension. Events that occur *within* the individual, intrapersonal events, will occupy our attention for the remainder of this chapter. Events that occur *between* individuals, interpersonal events, are the subject of Chapter 9.

THE DYNAMICS OF ATTITUDE FORMATION AND CHANGE

In order to achieve a solid grasp of the process of opinion formation, we need to understand the forces that lead to changes in attitudes. How is it that new information might lead a person to alter the way he views the world? To answer this question, I want to consider two concepts: the concept of function and the concept of rationality in American public opinion.

The Concept of Function

The noted psychologist, Daniel Katz, has developed the concept of function to explain how attitudes are determined. His idea is a very simple one. We hold attitudes because it is *useful* for us to do so. In Katz's words: "The basic assumption . . . is that both attitude formation and . . . change must be understood in terms of the needs they serve. . . ."[2] There are four basic ways in which attitudes can be useful for the individual. They can perform the adjustment function, the ego-defensive function, the value-expressive function, or the knowledge function.

The Adjustment Function. Holding a certain attitude may help us get something we want, or it may help us avoid something we dislike. During the depression years, Katz points out, many blue-collar workers discovered that the Democratic Party was more effective in meeting their economic needs than was the Republican Party. This led, naturally enough, to a very strong favorable attitude among the working class toward the Democrats. The dynamic was so strong, in fact, that much of the working class retains a basic Democratic loyalty even though economic conditions have been altered practically beyond recognition over the past three decades.

Another example of the adjustment function of attitudes arises from the interaction among people in groups. If you think for a moment about the groups you belong to, you will probably realize that there are few deep divisions of opinion within them. This harmony does not exist just by chance. People realize that if they disagree with other members of their group, they may make themselves unpopular, lose status, or even be forced from the group. Therefore, in order to gain the desired place of respect in a group, we either adjust our attitudes to conform with those held by others or we carefully avoid conversations that might reveal such disagreements.

The Ego-Defense Function. Another way in which an attitude serves our needs may be by allowing us to live more easily with ourselves and with our world. These attitudes, says Katz, "include the devices by which the individual avoids facing either the inner reality of the kind of person he is, or the outer reality of the dangers the world holds for him."

Ego-defensive attitudes are generally divided into two classes: The first encompasses denial and avoidance, and the second includes rationalization, projection and displacement. Denial is the sort of attitude that may be acquired by an individual whose world is too fraught with danger to allow him to cope with it in more rational ways. In Nazi Germany, many Jews remained in their homes and attempted to lead as normal a life as possible, even though it was abundantly clear to those on the outside that their lives were threatened. They denied reality, holding the attitude that Hitler wasn't really serious, often to the very moment when they, too, were taken off to the concentration camps.

The second part of the ego-defense mechanism, rationalization, projection and displacement, involves deceptions that, though less extreme than the preceding example, are very much more common. Instead of attitudes taken to relieve the threat of an external reality, we find attitudes that people adopt to insulate themselves from some unacceptable aspect of their own character. Racial prejudice has often been discussed as an ego-defensive attitude. A person who is affected with a deep sense of personal inferiority may be unable to accept himself in those terms. He avoids that necessity by projecting his weakness onto another individual or group. Since blacks in America have traditionally occupied the bottom rung of the socioeconomic ladder, they are often selected as the recipients of projected inferiority. This projection allows the individual to feel superior to this group and thus escape the necessity of confronting his own inferiority.

The Value-Expressive Function. One of the major psychological tasks that we all face is the formation of a sense of self and the consequent need to declare to the world who we are. This need arises initially in adolescents, who must break away from their parents and establish themselves as individuals. The subservience and extreme conformity often found in high school peer groups may be manifestations of the adolescent's slightly defiant declaration that he is no longer tied to his mother's apron strings.

Later in life, certain political attitudes may also be understood as serving the value-expressive function. Many individuals have taken a position in favor of the legalization of marijuana, for instance, without the slightest knowledge of the medical evidence regarding the effects of its use and without any appreciation of the legal and constitutional issues involved. Instead, this attitude may reflect the belief that support of marijuana legalization is the "liberal" position and, as such, demonstrates to the world how liberal a person is.[3]

The Knowledge Function. Finally, Katz points out that certain attitudes are held because they help us make sense of our world. The world is a terribly complicated place, far beyond the capacities of any individual to figure out. Nonetheless, we crave order, and we feel distinctly threatened if there is a part of our world that cannot be pinned down, defined, and understood. In order to achieve a sense of order amid the world's chaos, we adopt frames of reference, or stereotypes, to aid us in classifying the welter of bits of information that come our way every day.

A stereotype works in the following way. We are ceaselessly confronted by situations that, on the one hand, must be judged and evaluated but, on the other hand, are so complicated that the typical person cannot judge and evaluate them. In such a situation, the individual makes use of a stereotype. That is, he will search out one single element of the situation that he *is* able to judge and evaluate and will then substitute that judgment for a judgment of the whole. Now, this process has obvious costs. For instance, we may choose an aspect of a situation that is irrelevant to our purposes. Suppose we set out to buy an automobile. Most of us do not have the time to examine the engineering reports or the frequency-of-repair records of any particular model of car that interests us. Instead, we may purchase a Ford because Fords have performed well in the past or because we have seen some effective television advertising, and we have developed a stereotype that says that Fords are superior automobiles. By doing this we neglect the possibility that another make may be more economical to operate and thus might be the better choice.

Although the risk of an incorrect judgment always accompanies the use of stereotypes, they also have undisputed benefits. Most basically, they allow us to deal with the overly complex and often ambiguous information that bombards us constantly. Without stereotypes, we would simply be unable to make any sense out of our world. It has become too complicated.

Beyond this, stereotypes are extremely efficient. The effort necessary to understand politics (or anything else) entails a certain cost. There are costs of time and money in the purchasing and reading of newspapers. There are also psychological costs. For instance, if by examining the issues we discover that the candidate we favor has voted against legislation that we also favor, we are faced with an inconsistency that must either be tolerated or resolved by sacrificing one of our attitudes. Reliance on stereotypes helps to reduce these costs.

As a matter of fact, the political world provides one of the best examples of the use of stereotypes, in the concept of party identification. The attitude of partisan loyalty means that the individual need make only one simple judgment about most political issues. If he is a Democrat, he knows that when a bill is supported by Democrats, he is for it as well. In the case of the Ford-Carter debates, he need not have understood the issues being discussed. He could choose the winner on the basis of party. Reinforcing this point, an analysis done by the Harris poll immediately after the first debate in September 1976, found that the major effect was to strengthen the choice of those who were already committed to one or the other of the candidates.[4]

From this discussion we can see that new information will act to change attitudes and opinions because it creates changes in the way old attitudes serve the individual's needs. In the case of the adjustment function, for example, a traditionally Democratic union worker may shift to the Republicans because he now values social order and defense of the public morality more than he values continuing wage increases, and feels that the Republicans will get him what he wants. Or, where the value-expressive function was once served by voicing opinions favorable to white supremacy in the South, that value has passed out of fashion, and racial attitudes have become much more conciliatory. In general, the concept of function links our attitudes with what is happening around us.

The "Rationality" of American Public Opinion

H. L. Mencken once referred to the human race as "homo boobiens," and declared that no one would ever go broke underestimating the tastes of the American people. In politics, similar portrayals exist. The voter has been pictured as a dullard who knows little or nothing about politics, can't understand the issues, and, if he votes, just pulls the party lever.

Let me say right away that I believe this picture has been greatly exaggerated. Nonetheless, there is enough truth in the accusation that it merits our attention. I want therefore to discuss three aspects of public opinion that reveal something about its rationality: the level of information which accompanies opinion; the amount of belief system constraint in the American electorate; and the extent of interopinion consistency.[5]

Levels of Information and Public Opinion. It is a fact that levels of political knowledge are surprisingly low in the American electorate. This leads us to wonder to what extent the opinions that people have on political issues rest on a solid foundation of factual knowledge. Can it be true that the typical voter's information level is so low and so full of errors that the opinions themselves are meaningless?

Two examples illustrate this possibility. In 1961 the Soviets began to build the wall which now separates East and West Berlin. Of course, at first the border was simply closed, and barbed wire was strung up. It was only over a period of months that the masonry wall was actually built. During this initial period, a great public outcry arose in the United States, as you can well imagine. A public opinion poll taken at the time revealed the existence of a group which advocated aggressive military countermeasures. Specifically, many people felt that the U.S. forces in West Berlin should intervene to prevent the construction of the wall. That same survey went a little deeper, however, to discover what other information the respondents possessed about the Berlin situation. It found that nearly one-half of them, "including a large number of those who felt that vigorous military retaliation was the appropriate response, did not happen to know that Berlin was encircled in depth by hostile military troops."[6] Perhaps the knowledge of this fact would not have changed many minds, but at least we would expect such a vital bit of data would be necessary for the formation of opinion on the subject.

A second example of how opinion and background information can sometimes fail to mesh occurred in New Hampshire in 1968. Eugene McCarthy entered the presidential primary in that state, opposing Lyndon Johnson, the incumbent President. McCarthy's campaign up to the time of the primary vote had been single-mindedly focused on the peace issue. McCarthy advocated a rapid disengagement from Vietnam and his challenge to Johnson was based on the latter's failure to follow a policy of withdrawal.

McCarthy received 42 percent of the New Hampshire vote, against 48 percent for Johnson. This was seen as a stunning "victory" for McCarthy and was generally interpreted by the press and probably by the President as well, as a sign of a strong and growing opposition to the administration's Vietnam policies. It may even have been central to Johnson's later decision not to seek reelection.

Survey analyses of the New Hampshire vote show these results in a rather different light, however. It was true that a large portion of McCarthy's support came from Democrats who were upset with the administration on any number of issues, Vietnam among them. To be sure, there was a hard-core group of doves among his supporters. However, "the bulk of McCarthy support came not from doves but from 'hawks' disgusted that the Johnson administration was not pursuing the war with greater bellicosity."[7] Evidently the electorate knew that McCarthy opposed Johnson, and that was enough. They failed totally to look deeply enough to see that their preferences were not at all represented by McCarthy. Indeed, evidence of this came later when many McCarthy voters of the primaries ended up voting for Wallace in the general election.

Constraint of American Political Belief Systems. These examples, which indicate that public opinion may really be based on the sands of ignorance, suggest that we explore the problem more deeply. One idea we encounter repeatedly as we move through this book is that politics is not terribly important to the bulk of the electorate. People pay relatively little attention to what is going on in the political world. In consequence, we find situations like the two mentioned above. Can it be, though, that ignorance and inattention have eroded the very bases of political thought in the American electorate? In order to answer that question, I want to present some information about how well (or poorly) Americans organize their political thinking.

Table 8.1 illustrates the fact that political thinking tends to be disorganized and incorrect in the United States. In this table the electorate has been classified according to its "level of conceptualization" of politics. This is the extent to which a person could give correct and meaningful reasons for liking or disliking the two major parties.[8]

A short description of each of the levels included in Table 8.1 illustrates their content. Looking first at level A, the ideologue is the person who uses some kind of ordering dimension in his comments about the parties, and both the parties and the reasons cited for liking or disliking them are located among that dimension. The most common ordering of this kind is the liberal-conservative distinction. In other words, only 3 percent of the

TABLE 8.1   Levels of Conceptualization in the American Electorate

	1956	1968
A. Ideology		
I. Ideology	3%	6%
II. Near-ideology	10	17
B. Group benefits		
I. Perception of conflict	15	9
Single-group interest	18	19
II. Shallow group benefit responses	11	5
C. Nature of the times	25	25
D. No issue content		
I. Party orientation	4	8
II. Candidate orientation	9	7
III. No content	5	5
	100%	101%
Not classified	4.5%	12%

Source: Philip E. Converse, "Public Opinion and Voting Behavior," in Nelson W. Polsby and Fred I. Greenstein (Eds.), *The Handbook of Political Science*, Vol. 4, © 1975, Addison-Wesley,

1956 electorate and 6 percent of the 1968 electorate viewed the parties as liberal or conservative and could attach some sort of meaning to those labels in terms of policies that liberals or conservatives support.

The near-ideologue is the individual who knows the words "liberal" and "conservative" and uses them to describe the parties but gives no evidence of understanding what the terms mean or what they imply for party performance.

Level B in Table 8.1 is labeled "group benefits." Here we find people who view the parties and political competition in terms of groups of people in the population. The typical ideas that the Democrats are for the working man or the Republicans are for big business would qualify a person for this level of conceptualization. Such a view of politics is a good deal narrower than what is demanded of the ideologue. The group benefit response cannot be generalized to situations in which the group's interest is not at stake. A person who favors the Democrats because it is the party of the working man will have no immediate way to evaluate where his party should stand on the construction of a new atomic submarine.

At level C is the "nature of the times" classification. This view of politics is even less structured than the group benefits belief system. People were classified here when they evaluated the candidates and parties according to whether times were "good" or "bad." An issue or two might emerge occasionally in one of these interviews, but if it did, it remained clearly isolated in the respondent's mind, not tied in to any more general view of politics. Comments about the "horrors of war," the morality of the other party, or the condition of the stock market are typical of this type of response.

At the lower end of Table 8.1 are those who provided no issue content whatsoever. Many of these confined their comments to remarks about the personal characteristics of the candidates (Eisenhower's smile was a common reference in 1956). Other responses contained obvious errors or crashing irrelevancies. One man "was pleased with Eisenhower because he was the first American President who had ever gone to church." Another respondent was perplexed by the Republican convention of 1956. Even though she had watched the proceedings in their entirety on television, she still couldn't understand how the Republicans could nominate Richard Nixon for Vice-President, since he was a foreigner.[9]

Table 8.1 does reveal some reason to be encouraged, however. While only 13 percent of the American electorate could be classified as ideologues in 1956, by 1968 the figure had expanded to 23 percent. A reanalysis done in 1972 found another jump to 27 percent located in the ideologue category.[10] In other words, over one-quarter of the electorate was able to view political competition with some degree of structure in the latter year. In terms of our earlier vocabulary, these people possessed belief systems that could be characterized by some degree of constraint and could generalize to take account of a relatively wide range of political issues.

I would like to think that the level of political conceptualization of the American electorate has continued to rise since 1972. Although the figures have not been recalculated since then, there are reasons to believe that this should be true. Most particularly, we know that the more highly educated individual tends to have a more highly constrained belief system. In 1956 about one-third of all college-educated people were classified as ideologues, whereas only about five percent of those with a grade school education viewed politics in that way.[11] Since the average level of education is rising continuously in the United States, this should mean that more and more people will qualify as ideologues as time passes.

The relevance of these findings to the problem of understanding attitude change should be fairly clear. The more highly constrained the belief system, the more difficult it is for new information to have any effect. What this means, of course, is that political attitudes in the American electorate are potentially rather fluid. Since most people's thoughts do not have underpinnings in a structured system of attitudes, major changes can come about with relatively little resistance. In fact, the last few years have witnessed two such changes: the enormous swing of opinion on Vietnam and on the issue of Nixon's impeachment.

Consistency of Opinions. The material in the preceding section poses a fairly strong indictment against the quality of political thought in the mass electorate. In order to explore this further, we can also evaluate the rationality of public opinion by examining the extent to which opinions are logically interrelated. In the following paragraphs we will explore some of the interrelationships which existed in the American electorate at the time of the 1976 election.

Let us begin with two issues which ought, on the face of it, to be related. These are the issues dealing with marijuana and abortion. Both of these problems belong to what I call the domestic non-economic category. Both involve the so-called social issue, and both are viewed by some as threats to the moral fabric of society, by others as signs of great social progress. Thus, we might expect a person who felt permissive about marijuana to feel the same way about abortion, and a person who opposed one should oppose the other.

As we expected, Table 8.2 shows considerable consistency of opinion. The shaded areas indicate those individuals who either took a liberal position on both issues, or else took a conservative position on both. Over 59 percent of the total sample falls into these areas. We might conclude that many people are giving their political views sufficient thought at least to be consistent on these two closely related issues. Even so, we cannot

TABLE 8.2. Relationship of Opinion on Marijuana and Abortion[a]

		Opinion on Abortion	
		Against Abortion	In Favor of Abortion
Opinion on Marijuana Legalization	Legalize	7.7%	19.4
	Neutral	7.8	8.4
	Increase Penalties	39.9	16.8

100.0%
N: (2005)

Questions:

"Still on the subject of women's rights, there has been some discussion about abortion during recent years. Which one of the opinions on this page best agrees with your view? (Abortion should never be permitted; abortion should be permitted only if the life and health of the woman is in danger; abortion should be permitted if, due to personal reasons, the woman would have difficulty in caring for the child; abortion should never be forbidden, since one should not require a woman to have a child she doesn't want.)"

"Some people think that the use of marijuana should be made legal. Others think that the penalties for using marijuana should be set higher than they are now. Where would you place yourself on this scale, or haven't you thought much about this?"

Source: ICPSR Archive: CPS 1976 Presidential Election Study.
[a] Entries are percentages of the total sample.

neglect the fact that one-quarter of the sample had contradictory opinions.

But what about issues that have a logical but more distant interrelationship? For instance, we might consider whether the electorate takes any consistent position on civil rights, on the one hand, and government health insurance, on the other. Abortion and marijuana have a kind of gut-level relationship; it doesn't take much analysis just to "know" that you are either for or against them both. In the case of civil rights and government health insurance a relationship exists, but it exists at a more remote ideological and intellectual level. We have to argue, for instance, about the correct role of government in society. Should it be interventionist or laissez-faire? If you support the interventionist position, then you should subscribe both to government action in civil rights *and* in the health care field. If you believe that government should keep its hands off, then that means *both* in the area of civil rights and health care.

154   THE EXPRESSION OF ATTITUDES: PUBLIC OPINION

You can see in Table 8.3 that these two issues are somewhat less consistently related in the minds of the electorate than were the first pair. Only about 52 percent of the sample took positions that were both either interventionist (the government should take action) or laissez-faire (the government should stay out). In addition, over 35 percent held opinions that, by using my definition, are contradictory. Evidently what we are seeing is the effect of the higher level of abstraction at which these issues are related. Fewer voters are able to evaluate politics in a way sophisticated enough to grasp the relationship between these two issues.

Our final investigation of interopinion consistency puts the national sample to its most severe test. How do people structure their views when one opinion belongs to the domestic scene and another involves an issue of foreign affairs? You might want to argue that there is no reason to expect any consistency, since the two areas are so different. However, there is no reason, in theory, that we should have one view of domestic politics and

TABLE 8.3. Relationship of Opinion on Government Role in School Integration and Government Role in Health Care[a]

		Opinion on Government Help in Health Insurance		
		Support Government Insurance Plan	Neutral	Support Private Insurance Plan
Opinion on Government Role in School Integration	Government Should Intervene	21.8%	3.9	12.3
	Government Should Not Intervene	23.4	8.4	30.2

100.0%
N: (1474)

Questions:

"There is much concern about the rapid rise in medical and hospital costs. Some feel that there should be a government insurance plan that would cover all medical and hospital expenses. Others feel that medical expenses should be paid by individuals, and through private insurance like Blue Cross. Where would you place yourself on this scale, or haven't you thought much about this?"

"Do you think the government in Washington should see to it that white and black children go to the same schools or stay out of this area as it is not its business?"

Source: ICPSR Archive: CPS 1976 Presidential Election Study.
[a]Entries are percentages of the total sample.

a separate one for foreign politics. The problem is just that the connections are a good deal more abstract. For example, the two issues I have chosen to illustrate this point are the government's guarantee of jobs and a good standard of living, and a measure of isolationism on the international level. As before, the issue is: Does the federal government get involved, or doesn't it? Table 8.4 presents this relationship.

You can easily see that the electorate sees no relationship between these two issues at all. Only 24 percent of the sample held positions that could be defined as consistent on an interventionist–laissez-faire dimension. Nearly half the sample held inconsistent opinions, including 41 percent who believed that the United States should be involved in problems in other parts of the world but should not be involved in securing jobs and a good standard of living at home.

In sum, when we try to find solid evidence of rational thinking in the mass electorate on the subject of politics, our search often proves disap-

TABLE 8.4. Relationship between Opinion on Government Guarantee of Good Jobs and Standard of Living and on Foreign Isolationism[a]

		Foreign Isolationism	
		Stay Home	Do Not Stay Home
Government Guarantee of Good Jobs and Standard of Living	Government Should Guarantee	8.1%	13.5
	Neutral	6.2	21.1
	Government Should Not Guarantee	10.1	41.0
			100.0% N: (1803)

Questions:
"Some people feel that the government in Washington should see to it that every person has a good standard of living.... Others think that the government should just let each person get ahead on his own.... And of course, some people have opinions somewhere in between. Where would you place yourself on this scale, or haven't you thought much about this?"

"This country would be better off if we just stayed home and did not concern ourselves with problems in other parts of the world."

Source: ICPSR Archive: CPS 1976 Presidential Election Study.
[a]Entries are percentages of the total sample.

pointing. In cases where two issues are closely related, perhaps two-thirds of the population take a consistent position on both. As the levels of abstraction required to understand the interrelationship rise, the extent of consistency in the electorate falls. Generally when we look at the way in which people relate their views on domestic issues to their views on foreign affairs, the level of consistency is nearly random.

The problem that these facts illuminate is that misinformation and the inability to relate issues in terms of abstract concepts may lead to a flawed image in the public's eye of what the consequences of political decisions might be. One wonders, for instance, how many Californians would have supported the recently successful Jarvis-Gann referendum, which reduced property taxes by 60 percent, had they known in advance that of the $7 billion tax reduction, nearly $5 billion will go not to individual homeowners but to businesses and agriculture. Moreover, hundreds of millions will be lost to California entirely as out-of-state property owners claim their reductions, and additional hundreds of millions will go to the federal government in higher income taxes as a result of reduced property tax exemptions.

These facts bring up a most awkward point. I have argued in this book that the American electorate should seize opportunities like the Jarvis-Gann referendum to bring government under popular control. And yet I am indeed guilty of suggesting that this very same electorate may be incompetent to make these sorts of decisions. The way out, it seems to me, is through civic education. At the very least, any move toward a national referendum program must be accompanied by an equally far-reaching program of public information on the issues in question.

THE PERCEPTUAL SCREEN

I now want to move away from our discussion of the dynamics of attitude formation and change, and take up the second major element in Figure 8.1. This is the perceptual screen, the personality's defense mechanism. When new information is received, the individual engages in a subconscious "preprocessing" before attempting to integrate the new information into his belief system. If the new information is too disruptive —if, for example, it contradicts a central attitude—the perceptual screen will deny it entry. This is accomplished either by screening out the stimulus altogether or by perceiving it in some way that allows it to fit in more easily with preexisting attitudes.

Two basic sets of characteristics, one relating to the individual and the other relating to the incoming message, need to be taken into account in order to understand the perceptual screen.[12]

Individual Characteristics

Selective Exposure. The most basic way in which a person controls the information he receives is by choosing to expose himself to it. Suppose, for instance, that you are a very strong Republican and you admired Nixon very much. It is very likely that, as the summer of 1974 wore on, you were less and less inclined to view the House Watergate Committee hearings, to read the reporting of Watergate in the papers, or view the evening news. You simply wanted to shut out information that you strongly suspected would upset your view of the political world. If you were a strong Democrat, on the other hand, the chances are that you sought out these programs. They spoke to your prejudices, and we all like to see our beliefs confirmed by those in authority.

Clearly, selective exposure conforms to the expectations we would derive from consistency theory. If we know new information is going to throw our belief system out of balance, we will strive to avoid it. A deeper explanation may be found in Katz's functional approach. Those individuals who are fearful of the disorder of the world (it may appear as crime, for instance) may have a personal need to believe in the goodness of the nation's leadership. This is what Katz would call an ego-defensive attitude. To forsake that belief would knock a prop out from under the adjustment this type of individual had made to a threatening environment. Such a person will resist changing his or her attitude by refusing to listen to any stimulus that might be upsetting.

Selective Perception and Retention. Selective exposure can explain some differences in opinion in the American electorate, but certainly not all. There are, after all, many stimuli that we find difficult to avoid. You can turn the channel from a favorite TV show to avoid a 30-second political spot, but unless the message is especially threatening, you won't bother. Besides, you may not know ahead of time that a stimulus will run counter to your previous beliefs until it is too late.

The individual personality has a second line of defense to combat these possibilities; we frequently read our own meanings into the messages we receive. Reynolds cites a fascinating study of Allport and Passman to illustrate this point.[13] These researchers presented a white subject with a picture of a white man threatening a black man with a razor. This person was then instructed to describe the picture to a second white subject, without showing him the picture. The second then described the picture to a third, and so on through a group, all of whom were white. This experiment was run several times. In more than half the cases, by the time the description had reached the last member of the group, it was the black who was seen threatening the white. Allport and Passman contend that this reversal occurred because the new description gave a better fit to some whites' preconceptions: in this case, that blacks threaten whites with razors, and not the other way around.

A contemporary example of selective perception, and perhaps of selective exposure as well, involves the energy crisis. We are simply too accustomed to a high-energy-consumption life-style, based on the availability of cheap energy, to take very seriously the growing number of reports of an impending disaster. At the current rate of production of oil by the Arab states, we may face a permanent shortage within a very few years. Even if the Arabs allow production to increase to meet demand, demand will outpace available supplies before the year 2000. And clearly, should the Arabs choose to cut production, a logical step to ensure income from oil beyond the year 2000, we could be faced with the onset of a permanent energy shortage at any time.

The reason the public refuses to take the energy crisis seriously is precisely because it is so serious. Our entire society runs on cheap energy. No person who has worked overtime for five years to buy a new van likes to contemplate the thought that he won't have enough money to buy the gas to run it. But the luxuries will be only the first sacrifices. The private automobile may eventually go the way of the dinosaur. We may be faced with rationing of energy to heat our homes; we may have to do without air conditioning entirely. We may have to give up things like processed food, or fresh vegetables like tomatoes that are grown indoors year round. I could go on, but I trust I make my point. These thoughts are just plain *upsetting*. It is so much easier not to think about it or to believe that a breakthrough in solar or atomic technology will solve all our problems.

Characteristics of the Message

Another way to understand the origins of public opinion is to consider the types of messages that are most likely to penetrate the typical individual's perceptual screen. It turns out that certain kinds of messages can slip more easily through the perceptual screen, a fact well known to skilled politicians.

Fear-Arousing Communications. One of the functions of attitudes described by Katz, you recall, is the adjustment function. We adopt attitudes to obtain rewards and avoid punishments. A technique often used by propagandists, therefore, is to take the position that by adopting a proposal, a negative consequence like social disapproval, physical danger, or deprivation can be avoided.[14] A common political technique over the years has been to arouse anxiety in the audience by posing the threat of some internal enemy. Hitler used this technique with great success in the 1930s by presenting the Jews as the enemy of German society. Once levels of anxiety are high, the politican then presents himself as the vehicle by which disaster may be avoided. Such techniques undoubtedly contributed to the electoral success of the Nazi Party in 1933. In the United States, such right-wing groups as the John Birch Society and the Ku Klux Klan use similar techniques to maintain enthusiasm in their memberships.

Amount of Change Advocated. Both experimental and practical evidence support the common sense idea that the greater the change from previous attitudes or behaviors advocated by a message, the less likely it is that the message will be passed through the perceptual screen. Campaigns, for example, act to get out the loyal vote, and perhaps to convince some Independents to choose one party over the other. However, a strong Republican is almost never convinced to vote for a Democrat on the strength of a political campaign.

This principle can be easily understood in the context of the concept of balance. Messages advocating little change are by definition those that do not disrupt a person's belief system. If I am a strong Democrat, I can readily accept a message exhorting me to vote for Jimmy Carter. It doesn't cause me to change any attitudes. But consider the situation if I receive a message encouraging a vote for Gerald Ford. In order to act on that, I must overcome my positive feelings toward Carter and ignore all the attitudes that backed that up. Such a decision generally produces too much dissonance. Far more likely is the decision to perceive the contradictory message as "less fair, less informed, less logical, less grammatical, and less interesting...."[15]

Organization of the Message. There are at least two ways a politician (or anyone) can organize his or her message in order to make it more convincing. The first is to state the conclusion. Although logic may indicate that a message is more effective if the receiver arrives at the intended conclusion by himself, thus achieving a feeling of accomplishment and a positive orientation toward the message, in practice a much more likely outcome is that a message without a conclusion is simply not understood by many people. One Democratic television spot some years ago showed nothing but an elephant, walking backwards, getting smaller and smaller until it finally disappeared. Now, for those who got the message, that was a memorable piece of campaigning. But how many people saw nothing more than an elephant walking backwards? A lot. Overall, then, a message in which the conclusion is stated tends to be more effective.[16]

The second way in which a message can be organized involves what the psychologists call "primacy effects" and "recency effects."[17] That is, things said first or last have more impact than what is said in the middle. Joseph Napolitan, a prominent campaign consultant, described a technique he used in the 1950 campaign of Endicott Peabody for governor of Massachusetts.[18] He ran a 5-minute spot just before the evening news, which was set up to resemble a news program rather than an ordinary partisan commercial (disclaimers were shown both before and after the spot). During the 5 minutes, the campaign was "reported," which meant presenting two or three of the other candidates (in the seven-man primary race), taking potshots at the front-runner, and making room for "some comments highly favorable to Endicott Peabody, including, according to our plan, the *final item* of each program."[19] The intent was obviously to leave the audience with only one message: Vote for Peabody.

Nature of the Communicator. Some years ago Hovland and Weiss conducted a fascinating experiment in which they attempted to discover what influenced the credibility of messages. Their hypothesis was that if the receiver of the message thought highly of the source, he would be more likely to believe the message than he would be to believe *the same* message from a source he mistrusted.[20] In the experiment, an article on atomic submarines was given to 16 people. Twenty-five of these were told that the article was written by Robert Oppenheimer, a noted American atomic physicist. Thirty-six were told that the article had appeared in the Russian newspaper, *Pravda*. The outcome was as you would expect. Some 95 percent of those who thought Oppenheimer wrote the report found it "fair," and about 80 percent felt the author's conclusions were "justified by the facts." The corresponding figures for those who thought *Pravda* had published the article were: 70 percent thought it fair and 45 percent thought the conclusions were justified. These differences in perception led directly to the concluding result. Twenty-six percent of the group who thought Oppenheimer wrote the article reported changing their opinion about atomic submarines in the direction advocated by the article. None of those who thought the article had come from *Pravda* did the same.

THE PERSONALITY

The third of the major elements of Figure 8.1 that I want to discuss is the personality. This is a terribly broad concept; let me therefore limit my definition, for present purposes, to one that is a good deal narrower than that used by most psychologists. I have in mind two basic aspects of personality: intelligence and personality traits.

Intelligence

Intelligence relates to the process of acquiring opinions in a number of ways. Most directly, intelligence is linked to literacy. Although, in theory, nearly the entire American population is literate enough to read simple material, the phenomenon known as "functional illiteracy" may exist among millions of people. Functional illiteracy means that a person can read if it is necessary. However, his skill is so poor that reading requires considerable effort. So in spite of his ability, which shows up in the statistics, he almost never reads anything in his day-to-day life. In the political sphere, one person for whom reading is a tedious chore may simply read the headline of a long news article and get a very different view of a political issue from that of a person who reads the entire article—particularly considering how misleading headlines often are.

The second effect of intelligence has to do with the ability to engage in abstract reasoning. A person at a lower level of intellectual development is less able to comprehend difficult or abstract arguments. This may act either to inhibit or enhance opinion change, however. An intelligent person may refuse to accept an argument because he is able to spot an error of reasoning within it.[21] A person of lesser intelligence may be persuaded because he remains unaware of these problems.

On the other hand, if we cannot understand an argument, we tend to be suspicious of it and therefore unwilling to go along. A person of high intelligence can grasp the details of something like the strategic arms limitation treaty and can see, for instance, that the Soviets have more missiles, but the United States has more warheads *per missile*. This argument may escape another person for whom "warheads per missile" is not a meaningful concept. If the Soviets have more missiles, it must be a sellout of U.S. interests, period.

Why is it important for an understanding of public opinion to know about the role of intellectual ability? This insight may, at least, make understandable the extreme simplification of the issues (or even the absence of issues) during political campaigns. As Napolitan asks, would you rather see a politician's face while he outlines his position on pollution, or would you rather see a polluted stream and find out how it got that way? Perhaps most people who read this book would prefer to hear the candidate's position, but you have to admit that the polluted stream is going to have more impact. It is just more simple, more graphic, and more understandable for the average citizen.

Personality Traits

You have probably heard, at one time or another, of the authoritarian personality.[22] Authoritarianism is known as a personality "trait," that is, an element of the personality which is "relatively stable, highly consistent, and which exerts widely generalized causal effects on behavior."[23] The authoritarian trait, among other things, is thought to emerge as a mistrust of the unfamiliar and as an inability to tolerate ambiguity. Since liberal causes so often involve changing the way things are done, they tend to involve high levels of ambiguity and unfamiliarity. Authoritarians, for these reasons, tend to favor conservative causes. At a more extreme level, the so-called conspiracy theory of politics gives evidence of the presence of authoritarian thought processes on the radical right. There is a certain seductive simplicity to the argument that the Communists are responsible for all that is wrong in society. And if no one finds evidence of Communist activity? Well, that's just what's so dangerous about them, they stay out of sight. If you can't find any evidence of their influence, that just proves they have been at work. It's a nice, simple, closed system, but it is not very satisfying intellectually.

Another personality trait that has received some attention recently is social desirability, sometimes known as "influenceability."[24] Perhaps because of a feeling of personal inadequacy, some people tend to look for ways to gain social approval. Yielding to what they perceive to be majority opinion is one way to accomplish this. Making oneself like others is one way to gain acceptance and to achieve some sense of personal worth.

SUMMARY

This chapter has presented a model that describes the opinion formation process. Since opinions are simply the expression of attitudes, the material we have discussed has dealt mainly with attitudes and the intrapersonal factors that influence attitude formation and change.

Three major concepts occupied our attention: the dynamics of attitude formation and change, the perceptual screen, and the personality. In the case of the dynamics of attitude formation and change, we first dealt with the idea that attitudes exist because they serve functions for the individual. Then we moved to a discussion of the rationality of attitudes and found that political thinking in the American electorate is generally unstructured and often mistaken. This fact relates to the concept of function in a fascinating way. Clearly, since political thinking has been allowed to fall into such a dilapidated state by so many Americans, political attitudes must not serve any very important functions for most of us. This in turn presents a key to understanding why the electorate has chosen to give our political elite such free rein over decisions that influence all of us. We are simply complacent about politics. We apparently believe that we cannot fulfill any of Katz's functions any better by having a highly structured and ideological political belief system than we can by neglecting this entire area. Since the latter takes far less time and effort, there is no wonder that the state of political thinking in the electorate has reached its present low level.

What then can be done to raise the level of political thinking in America so that the electorate can reassert control? Since the problem lies with the relationship of attitudes to the functions they serve, this relationship is where we will find the solution as well. To encourage an improvement in the quality of political thinking, the functions served by such thought must be made clear. The notion that rewards, in the form of more responsive government and more desirable policies, may follow if we pay greater attention to our political world could persuade citizens to invest time and effort to become more informed and active.

NOTES

1. This model is drawn from the one presented by James J. Best, *Public Opinion: Micro and Macro* (Homewood, Ill.: Dorsey, 1973), p. 39. It also owes a great deal to Lester W. Milbrath, *Political Participation* (Chicago: Rand McNally, 1965) and to M. Brewster Smith, "A Map for the Analysis of Personality and Politics," *Journal of Social Issues*, vol. 24, no. 3 (July 1968), 15–28.
2. Daniel Katz, "The Functional Approach to the Study of Attitudes," *Public Opinion Quarterly*, vol. 24, no. 2 (Summer 1960), 163–204.
3. H. T. Reynolds, *Politics and the Common Man: An Introduction to Political Behavior* (Homewood, Ill.: Dorsey, 1974), p. 28.
4. As reported in the *Atlanta Journal-Constitution*, September 26, 1976, p. 20A.
5. The use of the word "rational" has been roundly criticized in political science, primarily because it defies definition. I am not too worried about that here. I simply have a conversational meaning in mind; opinions are "rational" if they make some kind of logical sense.
6. Philip E. Converse, "Public Opinion and Voting Behavior," in N. W. Polsby and F. I. Greenstein, *Handbook of Political Science*, Vol. 4 (Reading, Mass.: Addison-Wesley, 1975), p. 80.
7. *Ibid.*, p. 81.
8. Angus Campbell, Philip E. Converse, Warren E. Miller, and Donald E. Stokes, *The American Voter* (New York: Wiley, 1960), chap. 10.
9. *Ibid*, p. 245.
10. Taken from the unpublished work of Arthur H. Miller of the University of Michigan, as quoted in Warren E. Miller and Teresa F. Levitin, *Leadership and Change: The New Politics and the American Electorate* (Cambridge, Mass.: Winthrop Publishers, 1976), p. 15.
11. A. Campbell, et al., *op. cit.*, p. 250.
12. The organization of this section is drawn from Reynolds, *op. cit.*, pp. 92ff.
13. *Ibid.*, p. 93.
14. Carl I. Hovland, Irving L. Janis, and Harold H. Kelley, *Communication and Persuasion* (New Haven: Yale University Press, 1953), p. 60.
15. William J. McGuire, "The Nature of Attitudes and Attitude Change," in G. Lindzey and E. Aronson (Eds.), *The Handbook of Social Psychology*, 2d ed., Vol. 3 (Reading, Mass.: Addison-Wesley, 1969), p. 221.
16. *Ibid.*, pp. 208–209.
17. Carl I. Hovland (Ed.), *The Order of Presentation in Persuasion* (New Haven: Yale University Press, 1957).
18. Joseph Napolitan, *The Election Game and How to Win It* (New York: Doubleday, 1972), pp. 73–74.

19. *Ibid.*, p. 74.
20. Carl I. Hovland and Walter Weiss, "The Influence of Source Credibility on Communication Effectiveness," *Public Opinion Quarterly*, vol. 15, no. 4 (Winter 1951–52), 635–650.
21. Reynolds, *op. cit.*, p. 94.
22. T. W. Adorno, Else Frenkel-Brunswik, Daniel J. Levinson, and R. Nevitt Sanford, *The Authoritarian Personality* (New York: Harper & Row, 1950).
23. Walter Mischel, "Toward a Cognitive Social Learning Reconceptualization of Personality," *Psychological Review*, vol. 80, no. 4 (July 1973), 252–283.
24. D. Crowne and D. Marlowe, "A New Scale of Social Desirability Independent of Psychopathology," *Journal of Consulting Psychology*, vol. 24, no. 4 (1960), 349–354.

9
The Acquisition of Opinion: Interpersonal Processes

This chapter completes our discussion of the opinion acquisition process. The focus will be on the interpersonal processes that shape attitude and opinion. They are grouped under the two remaining headings of Figure 8.1: social reality and new information.

In discussing the influence of social reality we shall look at the differences in political opinions that have arisen between people who have had different experiences in life. Specifically, I mean the group-based differences of socioeconomic status, race, and age. Their influence is indirect; none of them can exert any direct effect on attitudes. We shall also consider, therefore, the mechanisms by which these factors ultimately produce differences in attitudes and opinions.

The second interpersonal process to be discussed here has a much more direct effect on attitudes and opinion. This is the provision of new information by the media. By definition, our model describes the source of attitude change as new information. The media represent only a narrow range of the sources from which individuals acquire new information, but they are among the most important in the area of politics.

SOCIAL REALITY

Socioeconomic Status

No one is really quite sure how to measure socioeconomic status. People with college degrees may earn relatively little money; wealthy people sometimes have no education at all; and what are generally regarded as high-status occupations sometimes cannot support the same standard of living as a so-called lower status occupation (a college professor, for instance, may earn less than a bricklayer). We confront this confusion by considering education and income separately, knowing that neither one will give a completely accurate picture of socioeconomic status, but that both together will give a useful approximation.

In spite of the possible exceptions, it is obvious that a person's position on the ladder of success has a profound influence on the way he or she views politics. In general, the pattern that emerges is "Karl Marx upside down," in the words of Louis Harris.[1] That is, in most areas of public opinion it is the higher-status groups who take the more liberal positions, rather than the Marxian formula of working-class liberalism (or radicalism). I can demonstrate this by showing you two sorts of opinion: those involving noneconomic domestic issues (what Harris has called "change issues" and what Scammon and Wattenberg[2] have called "the social issue") and foreign policy issues.

Table 9.1 presents a range of noneconomic domestic issues. The list of items illustrates that across a broad range, those who are wealthy are consistently more liberal. On civil rights and integration, abortion, consumerism, pollution control, women's lib, and freedom of the press, a majority of those with incomes of $15,000 and over take the liberal side *in every case,* while a majority of those with incomes of $5,000 or less takes the conservative position in every case.

In the general area of foreign policy, this same pattern emerges again. Those at the lower end of the socioeconomic scale more readily take the "isolationist" positions, while those at the upper end take a more "interna-

TABLE 9.1. Contrast between the under-$5000 and $15,000-and-Over Income Groups on Noneconomic Domestic Issues

	Percent Giving Indicated Response	
	Under $5000	$15,000 and Over
Pro–Ralph Nader efforts	37	67
Willing to raise taxes to curb pollution	42	71
Pro–women's lib efforts	48	59
Against student demonstrations	54	38
Pro–U.S. Supreme Court school desegregation orders	48	69
Believe blacks asking for more than are ready for	56	41
Believe blacks have less native intelligence than whites	59	21
Favor legalized abortions	27	62
Support newspapers on publishing Pentagon Papers	42	56
Favor easing penalties for use of marijuana	30	43

Source: Selected from Louis Harris, *The Anguish of Change* (New York: Norton, 1973), pp. 36–37. Copyright © 1973 by W. W. Norton & Company, Inc.

tionally minded" position. These differences are captured in Table 9.2 using a composite scale of foreign policy. You can easily pick out the fact that people in high-income groups and the college educated are generally about twice as likely to be "completely internationalist" as people who fall at the opposite end of these scales. People at the lower ends of these scales, by contrast, are two or three times as likely to be isolationist.

There is one specific issue, however, where socioeconomic groups display very little difference. Opinions on Vietnam are about the same across educational and occupational groups. About 65 percent of the unskilled workers took a dovish position on our involvement in Vietnam in late 1968, while about 62 percent of professionals did the same. Looking at differences in education, 39 percent of those white adults who lacked a high school education in 1968 favored an expansion of the war, while 41 percent of those with some college favored the same option.[3]

When we turn to the area of economic issues, however, the pattern of middle- and upper-class liberalism disappears. In Table 9.3 we see that those with the least education and income are the most likely to take positions that endorse a variety of federal interventions in the economy,

TABLE 9.2. International Patterns[a] and Social Status

	Completely Internationalist	Predominantly Internationalist	Mixed	Predominantly or Completely Isolationist	Total
Income					
$10,000 & over	45%	32	18	5	100%
$5000–$9999	32%	35	27	6	100%
Under $5000	23%	36	29	12	100%
Education					
College	47%	30	19	4	100%
High school	30%	38	26	6	100%
Grade school	19%	34	34	13	101%
Percent of					
total sample	30%	35	27	8	100%
					N: 2941

Source: Lloyd A. Free and Hadley Cantril, *The Political Beliefs of Americans: A Study of Public Opinion* Copyright © 1967 by Rutgers, The State University. Reprinted by permission of The Rutgers University Press.

[a] Internationalism/isolationism scale based on agreement/disagreement with the following statements: (1) "The U.S. should cooperate fully with the United Nations"; (2) "In deciding its foreign policies, the U.S. should take into account the views of its allies in order to keep our alliances strong"; (3) "Since the U.S. is the most powerful nation in the world, we can go our own way in international matters, not worrying too much about whether other countries agree with us or not"; (4) "The U.S. should mind its own business internationally and let other countries get along as best they can on their own"; (5) "We shouldn't think so much in international terms but should concentrate more on our national problems and building up our strength and prosperity here at home."

whereas the ones most likely to oppose these measures stand at the upper end of the socioeconomic scale.

Overall the picture of the influence of socioeconomic status on public opinion indicates a rather surprising feeling of liberalism at the upper end of the status hierarchy. Only in the case of social welfare policies does the liberalism of the working class emerge. These differences are summed up in Table 9.4.

The question I want to confront now is: Why do these status differences in opinion exist? There seem to be three answers to that question, each related to the others and none providing more than a partial explanation. They are the educational explanation, the psychological explanation, and the economic self-interest explanation.

The effect of education, and especially higher education, is twofold. It widens our intellectual horizons and increases our ability to reason abstractly. These two aspects of a high socioeconomic status have two liberalizing effects. First, a broadened value system means that the individual is less likely to adhere to a value system that focuses exclusively on making money. A well-educated person, who is generally assured of an adequate income in any event, has the intellectual ability to consider alternate values. Second, the ability to reason abstractly is conducive to the support of certain civil libertarian causes, since the defense of such causes is generally made on abstract grounds. The fact that the American Civil Liberties Union can take the side of George Wallace or the American Nazi party along with its more customary liberal clients cannot be understood without a solid grasp of its underlying principles of justice and equality.

In addition to these intellectual arguments, education has a very practical effect on opinion. People who are well educated are generally insulated, by virtue of where they live and work, from the threats of racial violence, crime, or unemployment. Those at the lower end of the socioeconomic scale are precisely the ones who have to deal with these issues, and who will therefore take a rather dim view of the protection of the civil liberties of accused lawbreakers, for instance.

The second way to look at the impact of socioeconomic status on opinion has psychological roots. If you go back to the tables presented earlier, you will notice that those on the lower end of the socioeconomic scale generally hesitate to take positions favoring the imposition of equality where inequality presently exists, as in the area of race, and tend to oppose radical changes in established morality, as with abortion or marijuana. These positions may arise from the need that most people have to feel superior to someone.[4] Those at the lower end of the socioeconomic scale feel this need more acutely because—in material terms, at least—they are superior to almost nobody. Since this is true, it becomes more important to feel *morally* superior, hence the tendency toward a condemnation of the life-styles of upper-status groups such as college students and the rigid opposition to changes that appear to threaten the morality of society.

TABLE 9.3. Economic Liberalism[a] and Social Status

	Completely Liberal	Predominantly Liberal	Middle of the Road	Predominantly Conservative	Completely Conservative	Total
Income						
$10,000 & over	32%	21	25	10	12	100%
$5000–$9999	41%	21	24	7	7	100%
Under $5000	52%	21	16	6	5	100%
Education						
College	32%	21	25	10	12	100%
High school	42%	23	22	6	7	100%
Grade school	54%	21	16	6	3	100%
Percent of total sample $N = 3041$	44%	21	21	7	7	100%

Source: Lloyd A. Free and Hadley Cantril, *The Political Beliefs of Americans: A Study of Public Opinion.* Copyright © 1967 by Rutgers, The State University. Reprinted by permission of The Rutgers University Press.

[a] Operational liberalism scale based upon responses to the following items dealing with approval/disapproval for (1) "Federal grants to help pay teachers' salaries"; (2) "Medicare program financed out of Social Security taxes"; (3) "Federal government making grants to help build low-rent public housing"; (4) "Federal government making grants to help rebuild rundown sections of our cities"; and (5) "The federal government has a responsibility to try to reduce unemployment."

TABLE 9.4. Typical Relationships between Socioeconomic Status and Opinions

Type of Issue	Lower Status (Low Income, Education, and Occupational Status)	Higher Status (High Income, Education, and Occupational Status)
Social welfare (Medicare, guaranteed job)	More liberal	More conservative
Civil rights (racial integration[a])	More conservative	More liberal
"Social issues" (dissent, civil liberties, etc.)	More conservative	More liberal
Foreign policy: general	More isolationist (conservative)	More internationalist (liberal)
Foreign policy: Vietnam, war and peace	Little difference[b]	

Source: Robert S. Erikson and Norman R. Luttbeg, *American Public Opinion: Its Origins, Content, and Impact* (New York: Wiley, 1973), p. 179. Copyright © 1973 by John Wiley & Sons, Inc. Reprinted by permission of John Wiley & Sons, Inc.

[a] Tendency shown is greater in the South than in the North.
[b] If anything, upper-status people are more "hawkish" or conservative.

The economic self-interest argument naturally lends itself best to the explanation of the greater liberalism of the lower socioeconomic group in the area of economic policy. This is an obvious conclusion inasmuch as those in the socioeconomically disadvantaged group stand to gain the most from federal action in the area of jobs, welfare, housing, health insurance, and so forth. These people are able to take the side on which their material interest lies, in spite of the fact that it goes against what might be expected if we were to follow only the educational or psychological explanation.

To conclude, it is instructive to consider for a moment the shifts over time in the tendency of different socioeconomic groups to call themselves liberal. In Table 9.5 we find the percentage of three educational groups that took the liberal identification rather than the conservative one in three different years. The first was 1964, the year that civil rights was just beginning to be a national issue. Vietnam had not yet emerged and marijuana and abortion were "nonissues"; they were there, but nice people didn't talk about them. By 1972, all that had changed. We had had Vietnam, George Wallace, race riots, student riots, abortion, and the drug explosion. Between 1972 and 1977 we survived the resignation of a Vice-President and a President, and we continue to confront the issues of abortion, drugs, and corruption in government. Consider, then, the changes in citizens' sympathy with the liberal and conservative positions that are revealed in this table. As you can see, in 1964 lower-status people were more liberal than upper-status people. Over time, however, this pattern has been reversed drastically. Although college-educated people

TABLE 9.5. Education and Self-Identification as a Liberal or a Conservative

	Percent Who Call Themselves Liberals[a]				
Education	1964	1972	1977	1964–1972 Change	1964–1977 Change
Grade school	51	30	28	–21	–23
High school	46	41	31	– 5	–15
College	45	51	45	+ 6	0

Sources: Lloyd A. Free and Hadley Cantril, *The Political Beliefs of Americans: A Study of Public Opinion.* Copyright © 1967 by Rutgers, The State University. Reprinted by permission of The Rutgers University Press. *Gallup Opinion Index*, Report No. 83 (May 1972), p. 10; *Gallup Opinion Index*, Report No. 149 (December 1977), pp. 28–29.

[a] Don't know, middle of the road excluded.

maintained about the same level of sympathy for the liberal side, those with less education shifted radically. Identification with the liberal side dropped by about a third from 1964 to 1977, among those with a high school education, and by half among those with a grade school education.

How can we explain this? Consider the nature of the times. In 1964 domestic economic issues dominated the scene. The recession of the late 1950s was over and the lower socioeconomic group was benefiting from a tidal wave of government spending in the social area. People were not very worried about society's moral fabric or the Vietnam War. Eight years later, however, the world had been transformed. Economic issues were pushed aside, and as the lower socioeconomic group confronted the issues of the seventies, they found they didn't like what was going on very much. Those in the middle range of the educational scale maintained their feelings of liberalism fairly well until 1972, but over the next five years they too became much more conservative. Only the group with college experience failed to become more conservative. More than likely, this is because theirs was a more ideological liberalism to begin with, and therefore was not tied nearly as closely to the state of the economy and the society.

Race

The gap between the races in the area of public opinion is broader than that between any other two groups in American society. And nowhere is it manifested more clearly than in the area of civil rights. While whites show a great deal of ambivalence even now in their feelings about desegregation, blacks know their minds very well. They do not like segregation, period.

Table 9.6 shows some narrowing in the racial differences in attitudes toward segregation over the past eight years. Nonetheless, disturbing disagreements remain. In 1976 three-quarters of all blacks wanted desegregation, compared to only one-third of the whites. Two blacks in five wanted civil rights to move faster, a position taken by only 1 white in 20. At the same time, only 1 black in 20 believed civil rights to be moving too fast, but nearly half of all whites felt this way.

Of course, we would fully expect to find such differences in opinion in an area so intimately related to race itself. However, racial differences in political opinions extend far beyond this area. As shown in Table 9.7, blacks are generally more likely to take the liberal position on a wide range of issues than are whites. In the areas of economic policy, power of the federal government, and Vietnam, blacks who have an opinion are between 17 and 55 percentage points more liberal than whites. Even in areas that do not touch them directly, such as reducing the penalty for the use of marijuana or women's rights, blacks remain somewhat more on the liberal side.

Two explanations come immediately to mind when we seek to understand these differences. First, of course, there is the economic self-interest argument. Blacks are often found at the lower end of the socioeconomic ladder. Their support of federal activity in the economic area can therefore be understood in terms of arguments made in the previous section.

The second explanation is a psychological one. Blacks have been subjected to discrimination and humiliation at the hands of white society for hundreds of years in the United States. Harris discusses the results this experience has had on the psychology of blacks, and especially black men. By 48 percent to 41 percent, a national sample of blacks reported in mid-1971 that "white society has treated blacks so badly that it is hard for black men to have any real authority." Harris feels that this suggestion that blacks are inferior "is widely viewed as a challenge to the basic manhood of black males."[5]

Given these intense emotional states, it is hardly surprising that black opinion on many issues has been polarized. The civil rights movement has been able to channel these feelings in a productive direction, for a sense of identity and racial pride has emerged in this group as a way of combating the psychological and emotional damage of discrimination. Blacks are very conscious not only of being the underdog but of seeing this as an unnecessary and unacceptable position. From this rises their support for a broad range of liberal policies, since liberalism is seen as the haven for racial justice and social change in general.

Age

With all the talk about the "generation gap" and "you can't trust anyone over 30," you might expect that American public opinion has been strongly polarized on the basis of age, with younger people taking extremely liberal positions and older people defending conservative posi-

TABLE 9.6. Race and Opinion on Desegregation and Civil Rights

Question: Do you favor "strict segregation" of the races, "desegregation," or "something in between"?

	1968		1972		1976	
	Whites	Blacks	Whites	Blacks	Whites	Blacks
Desegregation	33%	78%	39%	68%	36%	73%
Something in between	50	19	47	30	53	25
Strict segregation	17	3	14	2	10	2
	100%	100%	100%	100%	99%	100%
N:	(2636)	(271)	(2357)	(263)	(2431)	(283)

Question: Do you think that civil rights leaders are trying to "push too fast," "too slowly," or "at about the right speed"?

	1968		1972		1976	
	Whites	Blacks	Whites	Blacks	Whites	Blacks
Too slowly	5%	29%	5%	31%	6%	38%
About right	24	63	42	59	49	56
Too fast	71	8	52	10	46	6
	100%	100%	100%	100%	100%	100%
N:	(2638)	(273)	(2293)	(259)	(2361)	(279)

Source: ICPSR Archive: SRC and CPS Presidential Election Studies.

TABLE 9.7. Race and Opinion on Selected Noncivil-Rights Issues

	Percent Support among Opinion Holders		
	White	Black	Difference (Black–White)
The government should see to it that every person has a job and a good standard of living	30	85	55
Penalties for the use of marijuana should be reduced	26	38	12
Oppose a stronger stand in Vietnam that might mean invading North Vietnam (1968)	60	81	21
The federal government is not getting too powerful	27	55	28
The tax rate on high incomes should be increased	39	56	17
Women and men should have an equal role in running business, industry, and government	54	63	9

Sources: ICPSR Archive: CPS 1976 Presidential Election Study and SRC 1968 Presidential Election Study.

tions. We do find differences between the old and the young, it is true. However, these differences are rarely as extreme as conventional wisdom might suggest.

For the most part, survey data reveal that young people take more liberal positions on the issues than do older people. The extent to which this occurs can be seen in the selection of opinions presented in Table 9.8.

TABLE 9.8. Age and Opinion on Selected Political Issues

Belief	Percent of Opinion Holders Supporting Belief		
	21–29 Years Old	50 Years or Older	Difference (Young–Old)
Red China should be admitted to the United Nations (1970)	60	34	26
Do not disapprove all protest meetings or marches that are permitted by the local authorities (1972)	80	42	38
Penalties for the use of marijuana should be less strict (1972)	44	20	24
The government should support the right of blacks to go to any hotel or restaurant they can afford (1972)	82	63	19
The United States should give aid to other countries if they need help (1968)	64	50	14
The government in Washington should see to it that white and black children go to the same schools (1976)	45	35	10
Believe their local courts deal too harshly with criminals (1969)	23	12	11
The government in Washington should help towns and cities provide education for grade school and high school children (1968)	40	31	9
The government should see to it that every person has a good job and a good standard of living (1976)	38	40	−2
The government in Washington should help people get doctors and medical care at low cost (1968)	61	69	−8

Sources: The first, third, and seventh questions are recalculated from the *Gallup Opinion Index* for 1970, 1972, and 1969, respectively, omitting those with no opinion. The remaining questions come from the SRC/CPS Presidential Election Studies for the years cited.

Over a wide range of issues, dealing with economic and domestic noneconomic matters as well as foreign policy, the young are more likely to take a liberal position. Only in the instances involving health care, jobs, and standard of living are the older respondents more in favor of government action.

One of the key reasons for the greater liberalism of the young relates to the unique historical experiences of the current younger generation: the so-called generational effect. Just as blacks have had experiences that set them psychologically apart from whites, the younger generation of today has grown up during a time that differs greatly from preceding generations. Those of you who are under 30 today have experienced civil rights and Vietnam, the crisis of corruption in government, and the consequent questioning of widely held values during your formative years. Those above the age of 50 had already passed through their period of socialization by 1960. They adjusted to the way things were before Selma and Woodstock and thus have been less able to change. The young, on the other hand, not being locked in on a previously determined value system, have been able to respond more readily to these events.

Gallup poll data show just this. People under 30 were about as liberal in 1977 as they were in 1964. Those over 30, on the other hand, have become much more favorably inclined toward the conservative side.[6]

Another argument offered to explain the liberalism of the young has to do with their place in the life cycle. This approach argues that *every* generation starts out taking liberal positions and then becomes more conservative as time passes. There is undoubtedly some truth in this idea. Unfortunately, to test whether this is the case would require information that we currently do not possess. We would like to know, for instance, what the political opinions of the current retired group (65 and over) were when they were in their twenties. This would require them to have been interviewed during the 1930s—and, of course, this was not done.

The question of the political consequences of aging can also be answered by looking at old people. The greater conservatism of the elderly, which is documented in Table 9.8, can be explained in three ways. The first is the same generational effect that we just applied to the explanation of the liberalism of youth. Being raised during different historical periods certainly contributes to differences in political outlook.

The second explanation is a psychological one. Glamser argues that "increasing conservatism is part of the aging process. Personality changes related to psychological changes may make adaptive behavior more difficult. New ideas may be confusing and are therefore resisted by the older person. . . ."

Finally, a social explanation would suggest that as people grow older they become adjusted to their social situation. In their day-to-day activities people develop commitments to certain behavior patterns. They will resist changing partly because to change is more difficult than to remain the same. Also as we age, we tend to acquire prestige and material goods. "[These] give the individual a vested interest in the status quo which is likely to render him less receptive to innovation."[7]

Although the elderly have traditionally been conservative, they have not generally agitated for policies favorable to themselves *as* old people. The recent activities of groups like the Gray Panthers, as well as the passage and renewal of the Older Americans Act, have led political scientists to wonder whether the elderly are going to develop into a group that pursues common political goals. This is a possibility to be reckoned with. There are about 23 million Americans 65 and over today, around 10 percent of the population. By the year 2030, when the postwar baby boom of 1947–1957 has reached retirement age, there will be about 52 million. This enormous group of voters will also be more likely to be politically active than are old people today. In 1972, about 19 percent of those over 65 had a high school education and 81 percent did not. In 2016, these figures will have shifted to the point where 86 percent of the elderly group will have at least a high school education and only 14 percent will not. If you recall our earlier section on social group differences, you will doubtlessly conclude that this change will have profound effects on the political profile of the old.

Summary

The social realities a person has experienced—his or her socioeconomic status, race, and age—have no direct effect on political attitudes. The year I was born or the number of dollars in my savings account are not psychological concepts; they do not have any direct relationship to attitude or to opinion. Their influence lies in the fact that they give me a distinct place in society and a distinct view of my political world. Social realities will therefore influence the kinds of experiences a person has and the kinds of interpretations he or she derives from them. These experiences and interpretations, in turn, do have a direct effect on attitudes and opinions.

Although the influence of social reality on opinion is indirect, we can still understand its nature without too much difficulty. In part, people simply respond rationally to the situation in which they find themselves. Poor people favor liberal economic policies, old people favor free health care, and blacks favor desegregation. A second theme is that the downtrodden seem to favor change and the rights of other downtrodden groups. Blacks, in particular, are more liberal than whites on a wide range of social issues, including, for instance, drug reform and women's rights. Finally, the marginal groups in society, the elderly and the poor, tend to take a conservative stand on issues that involve the maintenance of traditional social or moral standards. Drug reform, civil rights, abortion, women's lib, all these things threaten people whose grip on their position in life is uncertain. They want to avoid losing status and feel that change can only undermine the positions they hold—whether they are workers struggling to keep their house in the suburbs or old people struggling to stay off welfare.

THE IMPACT OF THE MEDIA

It is obvious that to form opinions about political issues, people must obtain information from somewhere. We may know perfectly well that we are going to vote for the Democrat on election day, but we at least have to know his or her name before we go into the voting booth. And if we are truly undecided about an issue, we would like to gather considerable information about it before we vote for or against. Where does that information come from? Almost by definition, the mass media make it available to us. It is theoretically possible, of course, to observe sessions of Congress or to read government publications and to talk to bureaucrats in order to find out about an issue. But about the only people who do that are news reporters. Most of us must rely on what those reporters tell us in turn of their experiences—on the radio or television or in print.

The first step in assessing the impact the mass media have on American public opinion is to look at the amount of use made of them. After all, unless a medium actually achieves exposure in the electorate, its effect will be minimal. It comes as no surprise that television is most frequently reported as the source of information about politics and current events. Approximately 81 percent of the 1976 Michigan sample reported that they relied on television the most for this information. Radio was named by only 36 percent. Over the years newspapers have been mentioned by about half of the electorate as the source of most of its information.[8] All in all, the public's contact with the media is quite widespread; only about 1 person in 20 failed to mention at least one medium when asked about his sources of information.

The Image of Politics

The media, no matter how hard they try, cannot ever transmit a perfectly accurate picture of the world. They must content themselves with transmitting an image of that world—a selection of times, places, and events that represents what they are trying to portray. Clearly, the world can have many images; even an event as clear-cut as a sports contest can be viewed from very different perspectives. One sportswriter might stress the glory of the winning team, whereas another might focus on how well the losers played and how they really exceeded all expectations since they weren't expected to win anyway—and what a great year they're going to have next year.

Political events, unlike sports, tend to be enormously diffuse, complicated, and confusing. Thus the likelihood that different images of political events will be extracted by different people is extremely great. Consider an example. It involves the portrayal that the Durham (N.C.) *Morning Herald* chose to publicize of the weekly meetings of the Durham city council during a period in 1969–1970. In spite of the reporters' honest attempts to portray the meetings accurately, a study by Paletz and his colleagues concluded that a stereotyped image was being projected.[9] Specifically, the newspaper pictured the meetings as orderly, rational, fair, and professionally carried out. Paletz's own observation, to the contrary, was that the ordinances passed by the council were the "product of bickering, bargaining, compromise, and expediency."

You may have the feeling right now that this is a trivial quibble with the way the press reports news. I would like to suggest, at least, that this reporting may have had an important effect on public opinion and on subsequent political action. The image of a city council proceeding in its deliberations in an orderly, fair, and rational manner vests its ultimate decisions with a certain authority. If ordinances are the outcome of careful and judicious deliberation, then the public is much more likely to accept them as legitimate. Had the public been made aware of the true nature of the city council's decision process, it might have been much more willing to voice opposition.

Another way in which the media may project only a limited image of an event involves political campaigns. Joe McGiniss wrote a book in 1968 called *The Selling of the President*, in which he quoted Leonard Hall, a former Republican national chairman, as saying "You sell your candidates and your programs the way a business sells its products."[10] That is to say, a campaign exists to put forward that aspect of a candidate which will get the most votes. That may sound perfectly sound and rational. However, McGinnis and others have concluded that the aspects which most campaigns choose to project have relatively little to do with political issues. You may have been struck, as you encountered campaign advertising in 1976, by how difficult it was to learn anything about the actual issues. We were much more likely to hear general statements extolling the virtues of one party or condemning the other. We may hear that a candidate is horrified by the increase in the crime rate that has occurred under the other party's administration and promises solemnly to take direct action to confront the problem. He does not, if he can avoid it, commit himself to, or even discuss, a point-by-point program to achieve that end. Perhaps the most extreme example of the general promise made without any specifics was Nixon's "secret plan" to end the war, which became a campaign issue in 1968. When asked for details of this plan, Nixon replied that to divulge them would threaten the Paris peace conference then in progress. George McGovern, on the other hand, was very explicit about his proposed "Demogrants," cash payments from the federal treasury that he proposed to make to every American. The Republicans immediately calculated how much this would cost and had a field day pointing out that McGovern would bankrupt the government.

I do not want to suggest that political campaigns can use the media to sell any candidate for office to the American electorate. This is not the case, as the section on the impact of the media will illustrate. It is clear, however, that the image politicians choose to project in the media (and which the media themselves choose) is not a very helpful one for the voter who is trying to gather information in order to make up his mind how to vote. Kissing babies and shaking hands at the factory gate remain better media events than a discussion of the SALT negotiations.

Bias in the Media

You must have wondered by this time: If the media can choose certain images of the world to project, can't they consistently choose certain kinds of images that consistently distort the world in a given way? The answer is: Of course they can, and of course they do. This sort of distortion, which regularly gives the same slanted interpretation to events, is called bias.

Since newspapers are traditionally the most political of the mass media, it is clear that American newspapers take a conservative view of politics. Nor should we wonder about the reasons for this. A major newspaper, in Hennessy's words, is a "large business enterprise, having most of the characteristics of all large business enterprises."[11]

> To put an honest man in charge of $10 million or $20 million or $50 million worth of highly perishable property belonging to other people and then expect him to lash out boldly in defense of what is right but unpopular is to subject human nature to an unbearable strain.[12]

It may be easy for us to understand why newspapers tend to be conservative; we would also like to know how conservative they are and how this is manifested politically. To begin with, most newspapers support Republican policies and candidates as a matter of editorial policy. The best indicator of this bias is probably the endorsements issued by American newspapers during the quadrennial presidential campaigns. Table 9.9 gives the scorecard since 1952, and these figures reveal the expected result. Eight or nine of every ten papers that issue endorsements for President back the Republican. Only in 1964, when Goldwater presented an extremely conservative profile, was there any change in this pattern. Carter did rather poorly in 1976, winning the endorsement of only 16

TABLE 9.9. Endorsements for President of American Newspapers: 1952–1976

Endorsements	Percent of Papers Endorsing:			N	Percent Endorsing
	Republican	Democratic			
1952	82%	18	100%	(1135)	82%
1956	80%	20	100%	(929)	77%
1960	78%	22	100%	(939)	74%
1964	45%	55	100%	(799)	77%
1968	80%	18	98%	(792)	76%
1972	93%	7	100%	(809)	76%
1976	84%	16	100%	(491)	74%

Sources: *Editor and Publisher* for the following dates: November 1, 1952, p. 9; November 3, 1956, p. 11; November 5, 1960, p. 9; October 31, 1964, p. 9; November 2, 1968, p. 9; November 4, 1972, p. 9; October 30, 1976, p. 5.

percent of those newspapers polled. Only George McGovern, with a mere 7 percent of the newspapers on his side, had less support in this medium.

The influence that newspaper endorsements have on the actual vote has proven difficult to determine. The most recent studies suggest, however, that their impact is a good deal stronger than was earlier supposed. Robinson, in his analysis of the 1968 and 1972 elections, discovered that there was a six- or seven-point difference in the vote nation-wide, depending on whether the local newspaper endorsed the Republican or the Democrat. In 1972, for example, if McGovern was endorsed, the vote for McGovern was 40 percent, compared to a 33 percent Democratic vote in places where Nixon was endorsed.[13]

Coombs' study of the national electorate in 1976 shows that in certain cases the effect can be even greater. Among the 60 percent of the population that reads a newspaper, the endorsement by that paper, if it ran contrary to the reader's own party identification, produced a defection rate to the party endorsed that was between 16 and 21 percentage points higher than it would otherwise have been. Among nonreaders, an endorsement contrary to party identification produced a 10-point increase in the defection rate. Given what we discovered about newspaper endorsements in Table 9.9, these results indicate that the nation's press gives a substantial advantage to Republicans across the country.[14]

Editorial policies of newspapers give one indication of partisanship. Newspapers can also favor parties or candidates in other ways, of course. Bias can appear in news articles, headlines, letters to the editor and even in pictures. Numerous analyses have been done on these other sources of possible bias, with contradictory results. It does seem clear, however, that present day newspapers are a good deal more fair and equal in their presentation of political subjects than they were at the turn of the century.[15] Analyses of the 1952, 1960, and 1964 campaigns, using a variety of different newspapers, have revealed a good deal of evenhandedness. In fact, one examination of the two latter years concluded that news coverage (as distinct from editorial endorsement) was so equal that the editors must have been making a conscious effort to achieve a 50-50 split.[16]

On the whole, then, we can conclude that in their editorial policies newspapers favor the Republicans heavily. In their treatment of the news, however, partisanship is much less obvious. The Republicans have in the past received a more favorable treatment than Democrats, but the Democratic claim that America has a "one-party press" seems to be greatly exaggerated.

The television industry has not come under quite the same scrutiny as have the nation's newspapers in the area of political bias, in spite of the attacks of Vice-President Agnew in the late 1960s. Agnew accused the networks of misusing their "vast power" by indulging in "querulous criticism" of the Nixon administration. "Perhaps it is time," he suggested, "that the networks were made more responsive to the views of the nation."[17] Agnew's threats stemmed from the perception of the Republican leadership that the TV evening news had not treated Nixon fairly during the 1968 campaign. Exactly what "treated fairly" means is difficult to determine. However, Edith Efron has conducted a controversial study of the network news which does support the charge of liberal bias.[18] By analyzing every word spoken on the three network news programs during the fall of 1968, Efron found *ten times* as much "anti-Nixon" comment as there was "pro-Nixon" comment. The balance for Wallace and Humphrey was about even. She also found favorable treatment given to liberals generally, Vietnam war opponents, and black militants. A similar, though smaller scale, analysis carried out in 1972 showed again a bias in favor of the Democrat, George McGovern.[19]

On the other side, work by Cirino suggests that during the Vietnam period, the evening news programs went out of their way to present events in a manner that would be seen favorably by the Pentagon and the White House.[20] The coverage of Moratorium Day, October 15, 1969, exemplifies his contention. Huntley and Brinkley on NBC devoted 3:20 minutes to speeches and interviews. Four dissenters received 1:37 minutes, but only Senator McGovern's 20-second statement presented a clear position against the war. The remaining 1:43 minutes were given to supporters of the war, all of whom expressed their views clearly. The longest interview of the entire segment was given by South Vietnamese President Thieu.

Three weeks later, Huntley and Brinkley covered a pro-Vietnam demonstration on Veteran's Day. Three persons were interviewed. All spoke in favor of the administration's policies. There were no anti-Vietnam interviews.

182 THE EXPRESSION OF ATTITUDES: PUBLIC OPINION

And how does the public feel about bias in the network news? Is this a phenomenon noticed only by Spiro Agnew and a few scholars toiling away in universities? A 1971 Roper poll attempted to measure whether people thought "television is fair or is not fair about showing different points of view." The result may surprise you. In spite of Nixon's poor relationship with television journalists, in spite of their negative treatment of him in the 1968 campaign, and in spite of Agnew's attacks, only 7 percent of the American public felt that television was biased toward the left. Fully 69 percent saw no bias at all, and judged TV to be "fair" in showing different points of view.

These statistics serve as a fitting introduction to our next section. They suggest that the American public does not judge bias in the media very harshly. Does this mean that the media are not absorbed as intended, or not understood at all? What, exactly, is the political impact of the media?

The Political Impact of the Media

There must be an article of faith among politicians that media advertising wins elections, because they spend an incredible amount of money on it. Total spending in presidential campaigns tripled between 1952 and 1972, with the final bill in 1972 coming to around $138 million.[21] All candidates for public office spent $59.6 million on radio and television in 1972, and the presidential candidates alone spent $10.5 million. As large as this latter figure was, it would have been considerably larger had not the Federal Election Campaign Act of 1971 set limits on spending. Presidential expenditures on radio and television were $18.7 million in 1968 and would have gone well over $20 million in 1972 without the legal limits.[22]

The 1976 election was the first in which federal funding was given to qualifying candidates. Both Carter and Ford chose to accept this money, a decision that limited their campaign expenditures to a relatively modest $21.8 million apiece. In addition, about $2.2 million was made available to each party to arrange and run the nominating conventions, and the parties were authorized to spend two cents per voting-age citizen, or about $3.2 million in 1976, on behalf of their presidential candidates. Thus, the expenditures by the two major parties and their candidates from the time of the conventions through election day in 1976 totaled about $55 million. (This does not include expenditures "not controlled by the parties or candidates.")[23]

The ten-million-dollar question is: Do people who spend more money win? The answer is reasonably clear: not necessarily. There are a number of ways that question can be treated, however. The most obvious is to compare total expenditures to the won-lost record. In 1970, for instance, of the 32 candidates for the Senate, the candidate (excluding Independents) who spent the most money won only 56 percent of the time. And in 1976, the score was even closer. In only 52 percent of the 31 contested races did the winner outspend the loser. Among the 34 governor's races in 1970, the wealthier candidate won in 59 percent of the contests. Finally, if we look at the 1970 performance of the nine most prominent (and expensive) political campaign consulting agencies, the record is positively dismal. Even excluding those races where two of the nine competed against each other, the score was 8 wins and 12 losses.[24]

When we look at contests for the House, the question of the importance of money becomes considerably more complex. At the most superficial level, winners outspent losers in House races by about 70 percent in 1976. However, this statistic hides the fact that incumbents almost always win, and incumbents usually enjoy not only widespread name recognition and access to the media but have campaign funds easily available as well.

A recent analysis by Jacobson of the effects of campaign spending in congressional elections suggests that when we remove the advantages that accrue to the incumbent, we find that the dollars spent by the challenger have a much greater effect on the outcome than do dollars spent by the incumbent. In fact, the more the incumbents spend, the worse they do. Jacobson explains that "the reason is that [the incumbents] raise and spend money in direct proportion to the magnitude of the electoral threat posed by the challenger, but this reactive spending fails to offset the progress made by the challenger that inspired it in the first place."[25] The reason campaign expenditures are more useful for challengers is that they buy what is potentially most valuable in a House race: recognition. This explains why spending is so much more important to the challenger. The challenger can obtain something he does not have, while the incumbent is usually well recognized, and his spending can buy relatively little more.

If we turn to another measure of media importance, we find additional reason to think that the media have a fairly weak impact on public opinion during political campaigns, in spite of the huge sums spent. This indication is the voters' report of when they make up their minds as to how they intend to vote for President. Table 9.10 reports two elections: In 1972 there was a Republican landslide in which there was scarcely any doubt that Nixon would win. In 1976 Carter started with a big lead in the polls, but the outcome became more and more dubious as the campaign went along.

In both of these years we can see that huge numbers of voters made up their minds how to vote before the campaigns even began. In 1972 some 63 percent of the voters had made up their minds once they knew who the nominees would be. In 1976 this number dropped to 54 percent, reflecting the electorate's hesitation over the choice between an unknown Democrat on the one hand and a weak Republican on the other. Even in the latter year, however, less than half of the electorate was even available

TABLE 9.10. The Times When Voters Made Up Their Minds during the 1972 and 1976 Presidential Campaigns

Time of Decision	1972	1976
Respondent knew all along how he would vote	34%	25%
Before the conventions	11	8
At the time of the conventions	18	21
During the campaign	23	22
Within two weeks of the election	8	17
On election day	6	7
	100%	100%
N:	(1464)	(1641)

*Question: How long before the election did you decide that you were going to vote the way you did?

Source: ICPSR Archive: CPS 1972 and 1976 American National Election Studies.

to be influenced by the campaign. During the final 2 weeks, when the media blitz was most intense, only 14 percent of the 1972 voters and 24 percent of the 1976 voters reported making their decisions.

With relatively few voters available to be influenced by the campaigns, the primary effect of all the preelection hoopla falls in the area known as reinforcement.[26] That is, the messages provided by the media tend to have the effect of strengthening the opinions of people who have already made up their minds. This is true because it is the people who take the greatest interest in politics and who have the strongest political opinions to begin with who are the most likely to pay attention to what the media are saying during a political campaign. People who have weak preferences, or no preferences at all, precisely those whom the campaigns try to reach, are the least likely to be paying attention. Much of the effort to persuade the voters, for which candidates pay millions of dollars, thus "falls only upon the eyes and ears of those who have already been persuaded."[27]

An illustration of this idea can be seen in the studies which were done following the Kennedy-Nixon debates of 1960. Roper found in a nationwide poll taken after the fourth debate that 44 percent of his respondents had been "influenced" by them. Only 5 percent, however, said that the debates had been decisive in their decision to vote for Kennedy or Nixon.[28] The main effect of the 1960 debates was not that they convinced people to choose one candidate over the other. Instead, they rallied the party faithful behind their respective leaders. To an extent this may have helped Kennedy more than Nixon. Two of Kennedy's major drawbacks during the campaign were his inexperience and the fact that he was not well known. The debates demonstrated to the electorate, and to Democrats in particular, that Kennedy was a serious, legitimate candidate for whom they could vote without hesitation.[29]

THE ACQUISITION OF OPINION: INTERPERSONAL PROCESSES   185

The effect of the Carter-Ford debates in 1976 was encouragingly different. While the 1960 event mainly brought out personality factors, with little or no information gain on the part of the viewers, in 1976 those who witnessed the debates learned a good deal about the issues involved (as well as about the personalities of the two candidates). Whether the knowledge gained by the viewers of the debates changed many votes remains unclear. As was true in 1960, the major effect seems to lie in the reinforcement of the party faithfuls' original intentions to vote for their man. If anything, the debates probably contributed to President Ford's impressive achievement in cutting Carter's 30-point August lead to just 3 points in November. However, we cannot say for sure how much of that shift would have occurred without the debates.[30]

Why, then, if the impact of the media exists only at the volatile fringes of the electorate, is so much money spent year after year? How do the politicians justify their faith in this expensive style of media-oriented campaigning? In part, the answer has to do with state and local contests, which I have not mentioned here. Clearly, in a small constituency a campaign can be directly tailored to the needs and interests of the people, and has a greater potential for influence than in the heterogeneous national constituency. Second, media-oriented campaigns work best in certain kinds of situations where name recognition is important. A constituency that is represented by a man who has no particular popularity can be effectively "blitzed" by a campaign intended only to make the challenger's name known. If the constituency is ready for a change, this sort of campaign can have the dramatic effect of making an unknown into a winner.[31]

The final reason for the popularity of media-oriented campaigns arises from the fact that presidential elections are often surprisingly close. Kennedy in 1960, Nixon in 1968, and Carter in 1976 were all elected by a whisker, well below the 5 percent who said they made up their minds after viewing the 1960 debates or the 11 percent who decided for whom they would vote after seeing the 1976 debates. Although the effects of a campaign are difficult to pin down with any precision, it is clear that in many cases a shift of only a few percentage points will swing an election. The potential for accomplishing this exists during a campaign.

Summary

The kinds of political attitudes and opinions we hold depend largely on the sorts of new information we receive from the media. We have seen that this information is necessarily incomplete and may also be biased. Yet the media do not control political thinking in America, by any means. For one reason, there are too many alternative sources of information. For another, the most successful reporters these days are those who specialize in "investigative journalism." The premium is placed not on covering up but on uncovering stories.

A third reason that the media's control of public opinion is weaker than we might expect is that while most political information comes from the media, we often do not receive it directly. Instead, what appears in print or on television is filtered by a personal or group process, often several times rather than just once. An excellent illustration of this is the way in which the news of Kennedy's death was spread. About half the population reported hearing the news from the media, and half said they heard it from another person.

The importance of this "two-step flow" hypothesis rests with the fact that the information contained in the media is obviously not transmitted through the social communication network in verbatim fashion. The opinions of the opinion leaders are fastened on; facts are changed, added, or forgotten. In short, whatever the original message may have been, it is homogenized, its rough edges polished until it can be fit into an individual's preconceptions of his political world without disrupting the balance too greatly. What may have been a radical message in its original form can lose a great deal of its impact by this social processing. The population is insulated in this way from direct influence by the media.

So although the media's *direct* impact on political thinking is blunted in a number of ways, I want to suggest that their *indirect* influence on public opinion may be many times greater. The media do not usually tell us what to think, but they are very effective in telling us *what to think about.* Through the choice of what to print or include in the network news the media define what is news. This control of what the public sees and hears is probably the most important area of media influence.

I don't mean to say that the editors of major newspapers and the major network news programs carefully go through the news every day, removing all items that have been previously blacklisted. However, selection is a necessity in presenting the news. Consider the comments of Lester Markel, a former *New York Times* editor.

> The reporter, the most objective reporter, collects fifty facts. Out of the fifty he selects twelve to include in his story. Thus he discards thirty-eight.
> Then the reporter ... decides which of the facts shall be the first paragraph of the story, thus emphasizing one fact above the other eleven.[32]

Now you can easily imagine that if the reporter or the newspaper has any ideological position at all, it is virtually inevitable that his broad latitude in selecting facts and even whole stories will lead to a certain bias. An editor with a particular ax to grind will have no trouble at all making a political candidate look bad. Let me recall, for instance, George Romney's ill-fated campaign for the presidency in 1968. At one point, he stated that the war in Vietnam would be the number one issue in the election. The CBS radio outlet in Honolulu introduced the story as follows: "Romney is the only candidate to put the Negro in second place."³³ This incredible headline was followed by a story that made no mention of Romney's stand on the racial issue and failed even to mention the word "Negro." Perhaps we can assume that this sort of skulduggery made little impression on the voters. It is true, however, that Romney's statement that he was "brainwashed" by the generals he talked to during his trip to Vietnam was ridiculed in the media to such an extent that he was virtually laughed out of contention for the presidential nomination.

Sadly, one of the most effective uses of the media in recent years has been made by terrorist groups. Who can forget the agony of Aldo Moro, the former Prime Minister of Italy, who faced threats of death many times as his Red Brigade captors repeatedly sought to extort concessions from the Italian government by releasing Moro's letters to the media? They counted on this massive publicity both to mobilize public opinion for the release of their comrades from Italian jails and to publicize their own political beliefs.

In short, terrorism has become a kind of lurid media event. Terrorists assume that the more vicious and inhumane their behavior, the more publicity they will receive. Viciousness and inhumanity therefore become a part of their strategy. By their mere existence, then, the media encourage incidents of international terrorism. This puts a heavy mantle of responsibility on the shoulders of those who decide what the media will report. The indirect nature of the media's influence means that doing nothing at all could be far more beneficial to the public interest than the most strongly worded editorial condemning terrorism.

NOTES

1. Louis Harris, *The Anguish of Change* (New York: Norton, 1973), p. 52.
2. Richard M. Scammon and Ben J. Wattenberg, *The Real Majority* (New York: Coward-McCann, Inc., 1970).
3. All data are from the SRC national election study of 1968.
4. On this point, see Alan D. Monroe, *Public Opinion in America* (New York: Dodd, Mead, 1975), p. 91.
5. Harris, *op. cit.*, p. 232.
6. Lloyd A. Free and Hadley Cantril, *The Political Beliefs of Americans* (New York: Simon and Schuster, 1968), p. 223; *Gallup Opinion Index*, Report No. 83 (May, 1972); *Gallup Opinion Index*, Report No. 149 (December 1977), pp. 28-29.
7. Francis D. Glamser, "The Importance of Age to Conservative Opinions: A Multivariate Analysis," *Journal of Gerontology*, vol. 29, no. 5 (September 1974), 549-594.
8. ICPSR Archive: CPS 1976 Presidential Election Study; *What People Think of Television and Other Mass Media 1959-1972: A Report by the Roper Organization, Inc.* (New York: Television Information Office, 1973).
9. David L. Paletz, Peggy Reichert, and Barbara McIntyre, "How the Media Support Local Governmental Authority," *Public Opinion Quarterly*, vol. 35, no. 1 (Spring 1971), 80-92.

10. Joe McGinniss, *The Selling of the President 1968* (New York: Trident Press, 1969).
11. Bernard C. Hennessy, *Public Opinion*, 3d ed. (New York: Duxbury, 1975), p. 274.
12. Gerald W. Johnson, "The Superficial Aspect," *New Republic* (May 2, 1955), p. 6.
13. The following information is drawn from Hennessy, *op. cit.*, pp. 277ff.
14. Robert S. Erikson, "The Influence of Newspaper Endorsements in Presidential Elections: The Case of 1964," *American Journal of Political Science*, vol. 20, no. 2 (May 1976), 207–233.
15. Robert Batlin, "San Francisco Newspapers' Campaign Coverage: 1896, 1952," *Journalism Quarterly*, vol. 31 (Summer 1954), 297–303.
16. Sidney Kobre, "How Florida Dailies Handled the 1952 Presidential Campaign," *Journalism Quarterly*, vol. 30 (Spring 1953), 163–169; Charles E. Higbie, "Wisconsin Dailies in the 1952 Campaign: Space vs. Display," *Journalism Quarterly*, vol. 31 (Winter 1952), 56–60; Guido Stempel, III, "The Prestige Press Covers the 1960 Presidential Campaign," *Journalism Quarterly*, vol. 38 (Spring 1961), 157–163; and "The Prestige Press in Two Presidential Elections," *Journalism Quarterly*, vol. 42 (Winter 1965), 15–21.
17. Quoted in Robert S. Erikson and Norman R. Luttbeg, *American Public Opinion: Its Origins, Content, and Impact* (New York: Wiley, 1973), p. 148.
18. Edith Efron, *The News Twisters* (Los Angeles: Nash Publishing, 1971). It should be noted that Efron's methodology and her conclusions have received a great deal of criticism as inaccurate and misleading.
19. *"Liberal Bias" as a Factor in Network Television News Reporting* (Washington: The American Institute for Political Communications, 1972).
20. The following examples are drawn from Robert Cirino, *Don't Blame the People* (New York: Vintage, 1971), pp. 148ff.
21. Herbert E. Alexander, *Financing Politics* (Washington, D.C.: Congressional Quarterly Press, 1976), p. 16.
22. Hennessy, *op. cit.*, pp. 259–260.
23. Alexander, *op. cit.*, pp. 243–244.
24. Erikson and Luttbeg, *op. cit.*, pp. 151–152.
25. Gary C. Jacobson, "The Effects of Campaign Spending in Congressional Elections," *American Political Science Review*, vol. 72, no. 2 (June 1978), 469–491.
26. The classic study in this area is Paul Lazarsfeld, Bernard Berelson, and Hazel Gaudet, *The People's Choice*, 3d ed. (New York: Columbia University Press, 1968). See especially the table on p. 102.
27. Monroe, *op. cit.*, p. 131.
28. Richard S. Salant, "The Television Debates: A Revolution That Deserves A Future," *Public Opinion Quarterly*, vol. 26, no. 3 (Fall 1962), 335–350.
29. Elihu Katz and Jacob J. Feldman, "The Debates in the Light of Research: A Survey of Surveys," in Sidney Kraus (Ed.), *The Great Debates* (Bloomington: Indiana University Press, 1962).
30. I am grateful to Jack Dennis, Arthur H. Miller and Sidney Kraus for their personal communications regarding their research on the 1976 debates. This information will be published in Sidney Kraus (Ed.), *Great Debates, Carter vs. Ford, 1976* (Bloomington: Indiana University Press, forthcoming).
31. See Joseph Napolitan, *The Election Game and How to Win It* (New York: Doubleday, 1972).
32. As quoted by Robert Cirino, *Power to Persuade: Mass Media and the News* (New York: Bantam, 1974), p. 50.
33. KHVH, February 24, 1968.

10
The Distribution of Opinion in the Electorate

You now have a sense of the factors that influence attitudes and opinions at the individual level. In this chapter, I should like to step back and take a look at the electorate as a whole and to describe the content of American public opinion.

THE CONCEPT OF DISTRIBUTION

If we want to talk about the opinions of the American electorate, we obviously cannot deal with people one at a time. We must have some way to summarize information so that we can understand the essential profile of opinion and still avoid being buried in a mass of numbers. The tool we use to do this is called a distribution, by which I simply mean the record of the number or proportion of people who hold each of several different positions on an issue.

The Dichotomy

The simplest kind of distribution is the dichotomy, which has only two positions (also called categories). These categories are often "yes-no" or "agree-disagree." Dichotomies such as these have one great virtue; they are simple. They are easy to administer in a questionnaire, and they are easy to present in a report. However, virtue may conceal vice and in this case it probably does. Most political opinions are far too complex to be captured in only two categories. People sometimes feel that they can neither agree or disagree on a question but want a third option. Often we find people insisting that "it all depends" when they are asked dichotomous questions in national surveys.

This shortcoming can be remedied by the obvious step of including a range of several answers from which the survey respondent can choose. However, even this improvement still enables the individual to reveal only one part of his or her opinion. Opinions, like the attitudes they reflect, have two parts. They have direction and intensity. In the case of opinions on pollution, for example, I am either for industry over pollution or I am against it. That is the direction of my opinion. However, it is also very important to know *how strongly* I hold that opinion. If I am against pollution but am not very concerned about it, I will probably accept everything that happens in this particular area without getting very disturbed. However, if my feelings about pollution are very intense, then I will be likely to take some action to back them up. I may boycott products, disrupt construction of power plants, write letters to my Congressman, or contribute money to groups who seek antipollution legislation.

The Likert Scale

A common type of distribution, which was designed to capture *both* direction and intensity of opinion at the same time is known as the Likert scale.[1] The respondent in a survey is asked whether he agrees or disagrees with a statement, *and* how strong his feelings are. The result is coded into one of seven categories:

Strongly Agree	Agree Somewhat	Agree a Little	Neutral	Disagree a Little	Disagree Somewhat	Disagree Strongly

An example of the Likert scale in use can be found in the study that I carried out in six Atlanta-area high schools in 1974. About 1000 high school seniors were asked to react to the following statement:

"In general, it is all right for black and white people to date each other."

Their answers were coded in the form of a Likert scale, and the result is shown on Table 10.1. This table tells us, for instance, that of the 934 students who answered the question, 271 agreed strongly, and they constituted 29 percent of the total group. A similar statement can be made for each category. No neutral category was used in this particular study to prevent people from avoiding what may have been a difficult question by claiming they neither agreed nor disagreed.

THE DISTRIBUTION OF OPINION IN THE ELECTORATE   191

TABLE 10.1. Distribution of Opinion on Interracial Dating

	N	Percent
Agree strongly	(271)	29.0%
Agree somewhat	(171)	18.3
Agree a little	(118)	12.6
Disagree a little	(79)	8.5
Disagree somewhat	(86)	9.2
Disagree strongly	(209)	22.4
	(934)	100.0%

Question: In general, is it all right for black and white people to date each other?

Source: 1974 Atlanta Student Study.

Frequency Polygons

While this table is a totally accurate way of describing the information which was produced by the question, we often find it more convenient to express that information in a chart, rather than a table. A chart conveys the shape of the distribution more forcefully, and also allows us to superimpose a second distribution for purposes of comparison.

The chart equivalent to the information contained in Table 10.1 is shown in Figure 10.1. Here we can clearly see that the question has tapped a source of disagreement among these high school seniors. While the bulk of these people said they favored interracial dating (about 60 percent fall in one of the three "agree" categories), a large minority took the opposite view, including over one-fifth of the total in the "disagree strongly" category.

Comparison of Distributions

Often we find it instructive to look at two opinion distributions side by side. This may be simply to compare which of two groups is the more liberal, or it may represent an attempt to figure out whether the opinions of one group may have been modeled upon those of another group. To illustrate the latter possibility, we might consider the opinions of our high school seniors' mothers on the issue of interracial dating. Figure 10.2 presents both the students' and the mothers' distributions. The key piece of information contained in these data, that the mothers are considerably more conservative on the issue of interracial dating than their children, comes through very clearly in this chart. The preponderance of "disagree somewhat" and "disagree strongly" among the mothers stands in stark

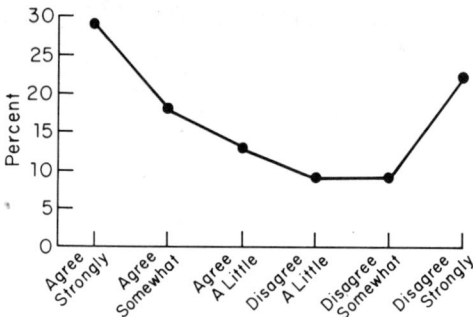

Figure 10.1. Frequency Polygon of Opinions on Interracial Dating.

Question: In general, is it all right for black and white people to date each other?

Source: 1974 Atlanta Student Study.

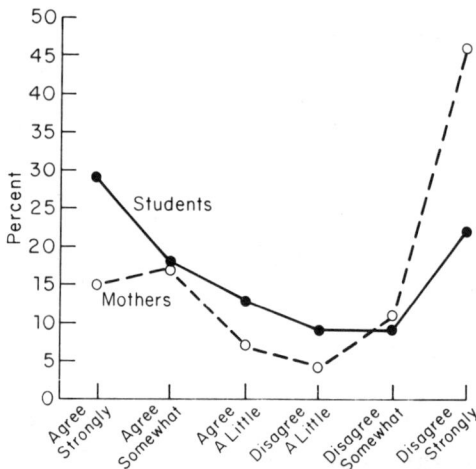

Figure 10.2. Frequency Polygons of Students' and Mothers' Opinions on Interracial Dating.

Question: In general, is it all right for black and white people to date each other?

Source: 1974 Atlanta Student Study.

comparison with the much lower levels found among the students. We might be willing to conclude from this that some of the opinions of the students come from the mother, but that some force, unaccounted for in this table, has produced more liberal attitudes among the students.

TYPES OF DISTRIBUTION AND PUBLIC POLICY

Although opinion may be distributed in any mumber of ways in the electorate, there are certain basic types of distribution that are often observed. These distributions are useful to consider because of their implications for public policy.[2]

Unimodal Distributions

One frequently encountered type of distribution has a single hump, or mode, in the middle, which tails off in either direction; in other contexts it is known as the normal distribution.[3] This distribution is important in politics because it means that a consensus exists in the electorate. Since most people cluster in a single central category or a group of contiguous categories, it means that essential agreement on the issue in question exists, and that this consensus is middle-of-the-road.

A fair example of a consensual distribution can be found in the 1976 CPS Presidential Election Study, in which the respondents were asked how they felt about the government "seeing to it that everyone has a job and a good standard of living." The distribution of opinion appears in Figure 10.3.

This distribution reveals a rather wide range of attitudes on the question. The electorate tends toward the conservative side, but relatively few

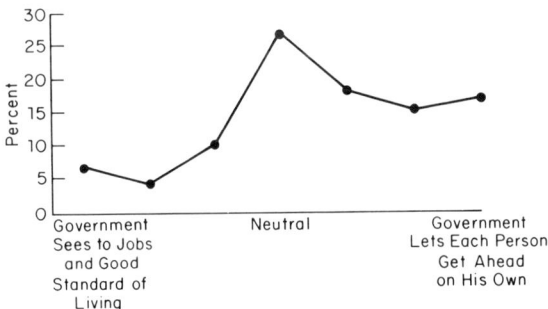

Figure 10.3. Frequency Polygon of Opinions on Government Guarantee of Jobs and Standard of Living.

Question: Some people feel that the government in Washington should see to it that every person has a job and a good standard of living. Others think that the government should just let each person get ahead on his own. And, of course, some people have opinions somewhere in between. How would you place yourself on this scale, or haven't you thought much about this?

Source: ICPSR Archive: CPS 1976 Presidential Election Study.

people (24 percent) take the extreme positions. Over 55 percent chose one of the three central positions. Such a consensus allows policymakers a wide latitude. Most people do not have strong opinions on this topic and therefore will not be upset by any policy decision made within fairly wide limits.

Other types of distributions share with the one pictured above the single mode. They differ in the location of the consensus. Such distributions are said to be "skewed." One good example can be found in the area of school busing. There has never been much doubt that busing is opposed by many Americans. Figure 10.4 shows just where the consensus on this issue lies.

The fact that the mode of this distribution is on the one hand so large (containing nearly seven of every ten respondents in this national sample), and on the other hand is located at the extreme end of the opinion scale, has profound implications for government. Even though the *Brown* decision of the Supreme Court struck down segregated schooling more than 25 years ago, it is clear that public opinion does not view favorably the use of busing to redress racial imbalance in the schools. Policymakers know

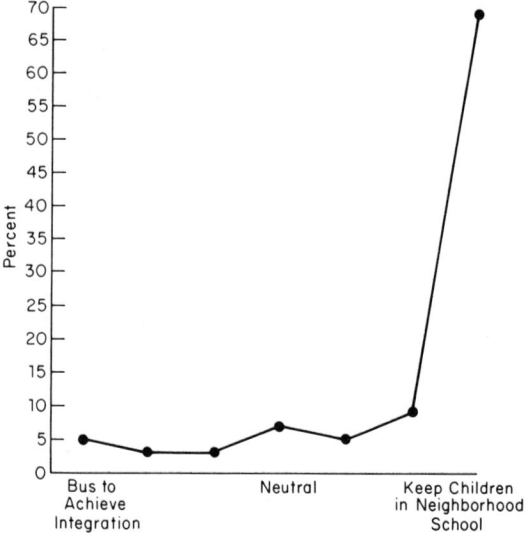

Figure 10.4. Frequency Polygon of Opinions on School Busing.

Question: There is much discussion about the best way to deal with racial problems. Some people think that achieving racial integration of schools is so important that it justifies busing children to schools out of their own neighborhoods. Others think that letting children go to their neighborhood schools is so important that they oppose busing. Where would you place yourself on this scale, or haven't you thought about it?

Source: ICPSR Archive: CPS 1976 Presidential Election Study.

Multimodal Distributions

Often opinion does not form any consensus on an issue at all. There may be several concentrations of opinion, each one containing a minority of the citizenry, and none large enough to give policymakers a clear indication of the public will. Such a distribution occurs when opinions about the contemporary roles of men and women are assessed. The Michigan study asked the 1976 national sample the following question: "Recently there has been a lot of talk about women's rights. Some people feel that women should have an equal role with men in running business, industry, and government. Others feel that women's place is in the home. Where would you place yourself on this scale?"

This particular opinion distribution has three concentrations. While the group favoring the sharing of roles is the largest, with about one-third of the sample, there is an additional fifth at the neutral position, as well as a smaller group that takes the extreme conservative position of believing that the woman's place is in the home. Numerical superiority is clearly not the deciding factor as far as influence is concerned, however. Even though

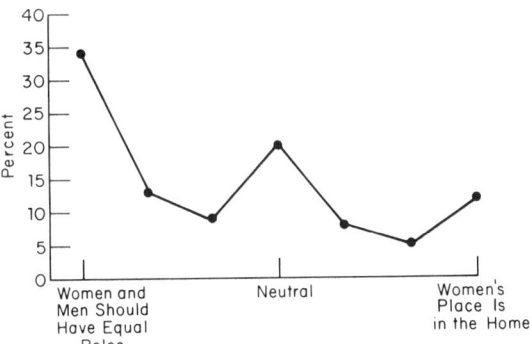

Figure 10.5. Frequency Polygon of Opinion on Women's Role.

Question: Recently there has been a lot of talk about women's rights. Some people feel that women should have an equal role with men in running business, industry, and government. Others feel that women's place is in the home. Where would you place yourself on this scale?

Source: ICPSR Archive: CPS 1976 Presidential Election Study.

the conservative group is badly outnumbered by the group at the opposite extreme, it appears to be having considerable success in the ratification battle over the Equal Rights Amendment. (An interesting footnote is that although ERA remains stalled, the size of the extremely conservative group decreased by almost half since 1972, when 20 percent of the sample chose this position.)

Multimodal distributions pose serious problems for government policymakers. No matter what course is taken, a major group in the electorate ends up being dissatisfied. Arthur H. Miller identifies this as the major cause of the decline of political trust that has occurred over the past 20 years in the United States.[4] His analysis locates two groups: one, largely black, has "an unfilled desire for social change"; the other "is an even larger group of alienated individuals who are fearful of change." No set of policy alternatives that government might pursue can possibly satisfy both groups. Miller predicts a continued decline in political trust and the possible development among blacks of a separatist movement.

THE MAJOR DIMENSIONS OF POLITICAL OPINION IN THE ELECTORATE

Over the years public opinion polls have measured literally thousands of opinions in the electorate. Choosing a few of those opinions to present in this chapter is an act of courage in itself. Fortunately, we have a few criteria for guidance. First, I prefer to present the opinions of the national electorate, so a nationwide sample is required. Second, I want to present change in opinion over time, so we need to look for studies that have asked the same questions over a period of years. Third, I would like to be as current as possible.

These criteria are all met by the Michigan presidential election studies, which have been carried out on national samples at every presidential election from 1952 through 1976. Unfortunately, even focusing on one set of studies, we are still confronted with by far too much information. Therefore, I have divided opinions into three major groups: domestic economic, domestic noneconomic, and foreign affairs. Within each of these major groups, I have chosen a few examples of American public opinion. The data allow an examination of how opinion has changed over time and also provide an estimate of how many people actually have an opinion in each area.

Domestic Economic Issues

One of the basic debates in domestic economic policy over the years has been whether the federal government should concern itself with the standard of living of individual citizens. Should the government be in the business of providing jobs, or should it let people get ahead on their own? We can see in Table 10.2 how the Michigan studies demonstrate how opinion in the area has evolved over the past 20 years.

Wording and format changes complicate the reading of this table. In particular, the abrupt shift in the conservative direction, from about 65 percent favorable to government action in 1960 to only about 36 percent favorable in 1964 must be largely attributed to the change in wording. In 1964 and thereafter, "a good standard of living" was added to "a job" as something the government should provide. While Goldwater's campaign also moved people in the conservative direction, the question asked in the later years is clearly a more "difficult" one to endorse, thus reducing the number of liberal answers.

TABLE 10.2. · Distribution of Opinions on Federal Support of Jobs and Standard of Living over 20 Years

	1956	1960	1964	1968	1972	1976	
Agree strongly	48%	53%			16%	7%	See to job and good standard of living
			36%	35%	7	5	
Agree somewhat	15	12			9	10	
Neutral	8	9	13	12	23	27	
Disagree somewhat	11	8			15	18	Let each person get ahead on his own
			51	53	8	16	
Disagree strongly	18	18			22	17	
	100%	100%	100%	100%	100%	100%	
N:	(1568)	(1740)	(1335)	(1386)	(1172)	(1914)	
No opinion; haven't thought much about it	10%	10%	15%	11%	14%	19%	

Question:
1956–1960: The government in Washington ought to see to it that everybody who wants to work can find a job.

1964–1976: In general some people feel that the government in Washington should see to it that every person has a job and a good standard of living. Others think the government should let each person get ahead on his own. Where would you place yourself on this scale?

In 1972 and 1976 the phrase "or haven't you thought much about this?" was added

Source: ICPSR Archive: ISR/CPS Presidential Election Studies.

If we set aside this difference, however, we see that there has been a creeping movement toward favoring less government action since 1964. Between 1956 and 1960, the favorable group grew by about 2 percent. From 1964 to 1976, however, the movement has been in the opposite direction. The total of "agree" or positive responses was 36 percent in 1964, 35 percent in 1968, and 32 percent in 1972. Between 1972 and 1976, the conservative creep became a gallop, with the proportion approving government activity dropping 10 points to 22 percent.

The second issue in the area of domestic economic concerns for which we have data involves the extent to which the government should be involved in health care. This issue has attracted some attention recently because of President Carter's proposal to institute national health care. However, the federal government has taken an active role in the health field for years, particularly since the passage of Medicare in 1965. Table 10.3 indicates the extent to which this sort of policy meets with the approval of the electorate.

Once again, there have been changes in wording over the years that make direct comparisons difficult. This is particularly important in 1972, when the question called for approval of government support of *all* medical and hospital costs, instead of the earlier provision of low-cost doctors and hospital care. Clearly, we would expect a decline in the percent agreeing with the statement in 1972 and 1976 simply because of this change. The 1972 and 1976 question is a "harder" one in the sense that it presents a more extreme position.

The data in Table 10.3 show that Americans are a good deal more supportive of free health care than they are of a guaranteed job and standard of living. There was a strong approval for government action in 1956 and 1960, moving from 61 to 66 percent. This trend reverses slightly in 1964, with a leveling off in the proportion approving, but with a large increase in the proportion disapproving government action. The 1968 distribution remains virtually unchanged.

The change in question wording that took place in 1972 had a less drastic effect than we might have expected. Free medical care is endorsed, at least to some degree, by 46 percent of the sample in 1972, although it is opposed by 41 percent. Once again, between 1972 and 1976 opinion remained highly stable on this issue. The proportion endorsing free health care as well as the proportion advocating private health insurance in 1976 (both 44 percent) show no significant differences from the 1972 figures.

The fact that opinion on health care did not become significantly more conservative in 1975, as did opinion on federal support of jobs and the standard of living, poses some interesting questions. These are both domestic economic issues, yet in one case the electorate is about evenly divided and in the other it is conservative and becoming more so. I can

TABLE 10.3. Opinions on Government Help for Health Care, 1956–1972

	1956	1960	1964	1968	1972	1976	
Agree strongly	44%	54%			31%	28%	Government
			60%	62%	7	9	Insurance
Agree somewhat	17	12			8	7	Plan
Neutral	9	12	7	7	14	12	
Disagree somewhat	9	6			7	9	Private
			33	31	6	10	Insurance
Disagree strongly	21	16			28	25	Plan
	100%	100%	100%	100%	100%	100%	
N:	(1554)	(1752)	(1312)	(1308)	(1112)	(2248)	
No opinion	12%	9%	17%	16%	18%	21%	

Questions:

1956–1960: The government ought to help people get doctors and hospital care at low cost. (5-point scale)

1964–1968: Some say the government in Washington ought to help people get doctors at low cost. Others say the government should not get into this. Have you been interested enough in this to favor one side over the other? If yes, what is your position? (3-point scale)

1972–1976: There is much concern about the rapid rise in medical and hospital costs. Some feel there should be a government insurance plan which would cover all medical and hospital expenses. Others feel that medical expenses should be paid by individuals and through private insurance like Blue Cross. Where would you place yourself on this scale, or haven't you thought much about this? (7-point scale)

Source: ICPSR Archive: ISR/CPS Presidential Election Studies.

only propose an explanation. It is that the question of federal support of jobs and the standard of living evokes much more than feelings about economic policy. There is an important moral element, which is bound up with traditional American beliefs in independence and self-sufficiency. How easy it is to condemn those who accept welfare, especially since there seems to be so much fraud, "welfare chiselers," "welfare Cadillacs," and the like, to provoke moral outrage among those who do not receive public assistance. On the other hand, people can't help getting sick, so health care escapes the stigma that welfare possesses in the minds of many citizens.

Domestic Noneconomic Issues

The 1960s were turbulent years for American society. Two great events, the Vietnam War and the civil rights movement, unrolled simultaneously and brought the American electorate to a sudden awareness of the problems it had managed to ignore through the 1950s. The social fabric seemed to come unraveled, as Americans confronted not only difficult moral questions but also other symptoms of discontent that struck much closer to home. Drugs, urban unrest, hippies, civil disobedience, and crime all contributed to a concentrated period of unrest that lasted for about a decade, from the early 1960s to the early 1970s. This complex of events is gathered together in what Scammon and Wattenberg call the "social issue."[5] I have chosen three: opinions on the civil rights movement, abortion, and marijuana.

The 1960s saw enormous activity in the area of civil rights as the last vestiges of legal segregation were finally demolished, and the slow and agonizing process of attacking *de facto* segregation was begun. One of the many ways of measuring opinion in this area over the years has been to ask people how they felt about the speed of the civil rights movement.

The trend in the area of civil rights shows considerable change over the 12 years from 1964 to 1976, a period during which we find a clear shift in the liberal direction. In each 4-year interval, the number of people who felt that the movement was pushing too fast declined, from two out of every three in 1964 to only about two out of five in 1976. Since 1972, more than half of the population has felt that the civil rights movement was moving "about right" or "too slowly."

It is probably fair to say that two questions which lie at the very core of the social issue involve abortion and marijuana. Prior to the 1960s these were taboo subjects for most of society: People were unwilling even to discuss abortion, and the media avoided reference to it. Drugs had not yet come out of the ghetto into middle-class suburban schools. All in all, the attentive public in this area remained very small until the past decade and a half.

TABLE 10.4. Opinion on the Speed of the Civil Rights Movement

	1964	1968	1972	1976
Too fast	68%	65%	48%	42%
About right	27	28	44	50
Too slowly	5	7	8	8
	100%	100%	100%	100%
N:	(1540)	(1479)	(2543)	(2674)
No opinion	6%	3%	5%	5%

Question: Some say that the civil rights people have been trying to push too fast. Others feel they haven't pushed fast enough. How about you? Do you think that civil rights leaders are trying to push too fast, are going too slowly, or are they moving at about the right speed?

Source: ICPSR Archive: ISR/CPS Presidential Election Studies.

The upheavals of the 1960s meant that the American public was suddenly confronted not only with discussion of abortion and drugs, but in some cases with changes in the legal structure sanctioning practices that had been unthinkable only a few years earlier.

In January 1973 the Supreme Court ruled that a state may not prohibit a woman from obtaining an abortion during the first three months of pregnancy. Table 10.5 reveals how public opinion has shifted on this issue

TABLE 10.5. Opinions on Abortion

Date	Proabortion Response			Antiabortion Response		Don't Know
November 1969	44			56		10
November 1972	25	17	47	11		2
December 1973	51			49		9
March 1974	52			48		9
October 1974	51			49		NA
March 1976	48			52		6
November 1976	27	17	45	11		2
August 1977	57			43		7

Questions:

1969 (November), 1973 (December): Do you favor or oppose a law which would permit a woman to go to a doctor to end a pregnancy at any time during the first three months?

1972 (November), 1976 (November): Still on the subject of women's rights, there has been some discussion about abortion during recent years. Which one of these opinions best agrees with your view: abortion should never be permitted; abortion should be permitted only if the life and health of the woman is in danger; abortion should be permitted if, due to personal reasons, the woman would have difficulty in caring for the child; abortion should never be forbidden, since one should not require a woman to have a child she doesn't want? (CPS)

1974 (March), 1977 (August): The U.S. Supreme Court has ruled that a woman may go to a doctor to end pregnancy any time during the first three months of pregnancy. Do you favor or oppose this ruling?

1974 (October): Abortions throughout the third month of pregnancy should continue to be legal.

1976 (March): A constitutional amendment has been proposed which would prohibit abortions except when a pregnant woman's life is in danger. Do you favor this amendment, which would prohibit abortions, or do you oppose it? (*Gallup Opinion Index*, March 1976)

Sources: November 1972 and November 1976, ICPSR Archive: CPS Presidential Election Studies; all others, *Gallup Opinion Index* for the dates indicated, except August 1977, which is a Harris poll quoted in *Public Opinion Quarterly*, vol. 41, no. 4 (Winter 1977–78), p. 555. The text of the 1977 question is somewhat involved, but is basically the same as that of March 1974.

both before and after that decision. Although a number of different questions have been used to elicit opinion on this subject, a remarkable stability of opinion emerges from this table. Before the decision of the Supreme Court, about four of every nine Americans took a proabortion position. After January 1973, just over half have supported the woman's right to terminate a pregnancy in a variety of questions asked by the Gallup poll. In November 1976, the Michigan presidential election study repeated the question it had asked in November 1972. It showed 44 percent of the American electorate in favor of abortion, about 2 percent more than four years earlier. The most recent poll, taken in August 1977, found 57 percent of the American public in support of the 1973 Supreme Court decision, 5 points more than had supported it three years earlier.

Given the variety of questions reported here, I conclude that opinion on abortion has changed relatively little over the past eight years. Whatever change there has been has gone in the liberal direction, but opinion remains almost exactly split between those who favor and those who oppose.

Opinions on marijuana use show a curious contrast to those on abortion. In 1969, the proabortion group was already quite large, claiming 44 percent of those holding an opinion. Opinion on marijuana, on the other hand, was much less favorable (see Table 10.6). The public has had a good deal more trouble accepting the legalization of marijuana than it has in accepting the legalization of abortions. Perhaps this has to do with people's inability to see marijuana as any different from the so-called "hard" drugs. In 1977, for example, the Gallup poll asked its national sample what the effects of marijuana are. It was found that 55 percent felt that "for most people the use of marijuana is physically harmful," 59 percent also believed marijuana to be "addictive or habit forming."

With these kinds of beliefs, it is no wonder that so few of the public have supported the legalization of marijuana. However, time has brought rapid changes, perhaps reflecting the increasing use of marijuana. The number over the age of 17 who have tried this drug at least once doubled between 1973 and 1977 to about one-quarter of the population. Not surprisingly, by 1977 nearly one-third of the adult population felt that marijuana should be made legal.

In summary, what can we say about the reaction of public opinion to the social issues of the 1960s and the 1970s? Some writers, especially those in the popular press, have depicted an electorate in a state of near hysteria, fearing the changes in morality and the social structure embodied in the civil rights movement and in the demands for abortion and the legalization of marijuana. Some commentators have predicted radical shifts in public policy as large groups of people gather at the conservative end of the spectrum to defend the familiar and the status quo.

When we look at national opinion data, however, no such picture emerges. Instead, we come away with the feeling that opinion in the domestic noneconomic area is really very diffuse, with different divisions of opinion and different trends over time, depending on the issue. In the area of civil rights, the trend runs toward the emergence of a new liberal majority. In the area of marijuana, the trend indicates greater and greater acceptance, but the solid majority of opinion remains conservative. Finally, opinion on abortion appears to be split down the middle, with no significant trend in either direction. We must conclude that opinion in the domestic noneconomic area remains heterogeneous and cannot be understood with any single explanation.

Foreign Policy Issues

Perhaps the greatest transformation in public opinion in the past dozen years has occurred in the context of the Vietnam War. In the mid-1960s, when President Johnson first sent massive numbers of troops to Vietnam, there was very little dissent in American public opinion. In August of 1965, when American strength had mounted to several hundred thousand troops, only 24 percent of the electorate felt that the United States had made a mistake in sending these men to fight in Vietnam.

Figure 10.6 shows the way this opinion changed as casualties mounted and the American public became more and more war weary. By 1971, three out of five felt a mistake had been made, and the same proportion was still in opposition when the peace accord was finally signed. Since

TABLE 10.6. Opinion on Legalization of Marijuana

Date	Marijuana Should Be Made Legal				Marijuana Should Not Be Made Legal			Don't Know; Haven't Thought Much About It
October 1969	13				87			4
March 1972	16				84			4
November 1972	11	5	6	11	6	7	54	6
October 1974	27				73			6
November 1976	14	6	7	17	8	9	39	14
April 1977	30				70			6

Questions:
1969, 1972 (March), 1973, 1977: Do you think the use of marijuana should be made legal, or not? (*Gallup Opinion Index*)

1972 (November), 1976: Some people think that the use of marijuana should be made legal. Others think that the penalties for using marijuana should be higher than they are now. Where would you place yourself on this scale, or haven't you thought much about this? (CPS)

Sources: November 1972 and 1976: ICPSR Archive: CPS Presidential Election Studies; all others: *Gallup Opinion Index* for the dates indicated.

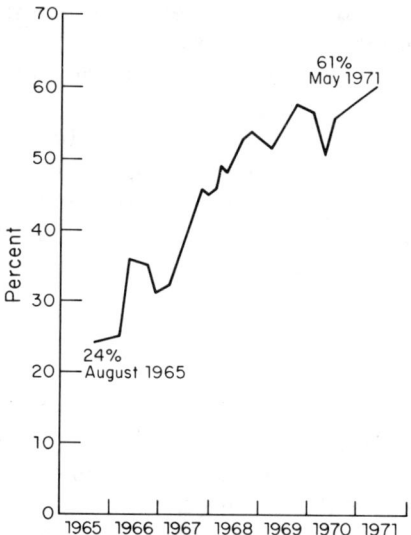

Figure 10.6. War Opposition.

Question: In view of the developments since we entered the fighting in Vietnam, do you think the United States made a mistake in sending troops to fight in Vietnam? (Entries are percent yes.)

Source: *Gallup Opinion Index*, No. 73 (June 1971), p. 2.

Vietnam has so completely dominated public opinion in the foreign affairs area over the past 10 years, it is very difficult to project what positions the American electorate will take in the future as the memory of Vietnam fades. For the moment, its influence seems to be somewhat contradictory. On the one hand, our experiences there have undoubtedly contributed to an uneasiness about America's position in world affairs. This has been manifested lately in the hard-line stand that many Americans now advocate in the arms limitation talks with the Russians. On the other hand, Vietnam has produced great hostility toward any renewed military activity abroad. Knowing the state of public opinion, no one should have been surprised, for instance, when the United States refused to become involved in the Angolan civil war.

PUBLIC OPINION POLLING

Every year we see more and more public opinion polls reported in newspapers or mentioned on television. Candidates for public office depend heavily on polls to tell them the mood of the electorate. Undoubtedly, policymakers are increasing the attention they pay to public opinion. These facts make it important for us to know how public opinion is measured, because only if the measurement is done according to certain rules can we be sure that opinion has been accurately portrayed.

Perhaps you have already noticed that no poll of public opinion measures every person in the electorate. Only the monumental decennial census attempts to do this. Much more typically, the studies I have used in this book have questioned between 1000 and 2000 people. Now, theoretically, it is possible for a sample as small as this to represent a population of 215 million. That is, what these 1000 or 2000 people tell us can be a representation of what the entire population thinks—within a range of 2 or 3 percent. However, this will happen only if the people who answer the questions, the respondents, are chosen in a certain way. They must be selected according to random procedures, which means that every person in the population must have an equal chance of being drawn.

Most of the major polls use variations of random procedures; certainly the CPS and Gallup studies that I have presented are among those that do. Unfortunately, this type of selection is very expensive, and thus many pollsters cut corners. Among the most typical techniques to reduce sampling costs is the quota sample. An interviewer may be instructed to obtain interviews from an equal number of men and women, and from young and old people. These quotas will assure that the sample will be representative with respect to age and sex, but often, other important characteristics will be seriously under- or overrepresented. I can remember once falling into a quota sample in the lobby of the Prudential Building in Chicago. I asked the interviewer whether she worried whether her study would be representative. She said, "Oh no, everybody comes here." Well, it may have seemed like it to her, but I immediately noticed that there were no black faces in the crowd. If we remember the enormous differences in political opinions that exist between the races, that study probably produced biased results.

Even if a sample is set up according to random procedures, we are not assured that its results will be representative. A second pitfall in the polling process is the response rate. Unless we receive responses from the bulk of those we want to talk to, we must assume that the people who did respond are somehow unusual. For example, some years ago, the state of Michigan attempted to estimate the number of deer killed by hunters by mailing a returnable postcard to all who had purchased hunting licenses. They received about 15 percent of these cards back, and the replies indicated an unusually large kill that year. Clearly, however, this study was not to be trusted. A hunter who had gotten his deer would probably be proud of the fact and would therefore be likely to return the card in order to tell others of his success. The hunter who failed to bag a deer, on the other hand, would be much more likely to throw the card in the wastebasket. The proportion of hunters who killed a deer, *among those who returned the cards,* therefore was higher than the proportion in the entire sample.

Finally, even if we solve all sampling problems and manage to collect information from a perfect sample, we still must be careful to interpret its meaning. The reason is that unless we are very careful in wording our questions, we may fall victim to instrument bias. For example, some years ago, a legislator from northern Michigan sent out a questionnaire that he intended to use to measure the opinions of his constituents. In this questionnaire was the following question: "Do you approve of violating the laws of God and man, and allowing murder by abortion?"

It is obvious, I hope, that this is an extremely poorly worded question. But can you say why? Most basically, it is poor because instead of assessing opinion on just one subject, abortion, there are three subjects to which the person receiving this questionnaire must respond. In addition to abortion, we also find murder and the laws of God and man.

Now imagine what kind of response this question will produce. I may be moderately favorable on the subject of abortion, but I am definitely opposed both to violating the law and to murder. Since this question asks about all three, I might just take the average. I would then answer "No, I do not approve." The point is, there is no way to disentangle these three attitudes once I have provided my answer. The only way to solve this problem is to make very sure beforehand that the questions in a questionnaire contain only one subject each. If you look back over some of the tables in this chapter, you will find numerous examples of correctly constructed questions.

You will be able to judge fairly accurately the quality of any poll results you may run across in the future if you keep these simple questions in mind: What kind of sample was used? What was the response rate? Were the questions unbiased?

SUMMARY

The bulk of this chapter has been set aside to describe the opinions of the American electorate on economic, domestic noneconomic, and foreign policy issues. But I have tried to introduce analytic elements as well. The idea that public policy is affected by the shape of the distribution of public opinion is not a new one, but is no less true today than it was 20 years ago.

In the United States most important issues are consensus issues, with most people grouped loosely around a central, neutral position. Even Vietnam, which had the potential to be extremely divisive, was eventually resolved with a reasonably broad consensus of support for American withdrawal.

This consensus of public opinion has two sources and two results. First, the issues of the day tend to reflect the political culture. The homogeneity of these basic beliefs constitutes a powerful source of consensus of opinion on the issues of the day. The second source of consensus, related to the first, is the general lack of interest Americans show in politics. Low levels of interest produce weak attitudes, and such attitudes are rarely extreme.

The result of consensus is twofold. First, since opinions do not reflect deep divisions in the political culture, they cannot evoke the kind of crisis that is possible in Canada, where issues often involve the problem of French-speaking Canadians, and hence, of separatism. Second, consensus allows the maximum freedom to policymakers, who know that if most people don't care about an issue, their range of possible decisions will be extremely broad.

NOTES

1. Rensis Likert, "A Technique for the Measurement of Attitudes," *Archives of Psychology*, no. 140 (June 1932), 1–55.
2. Cf. V. O. Key, Jr. *Public Opinion and American Democracy* (New York: Knopf, 1965), chap. 2–4.
3. Those of you who know a little about statistics will realize that, strictly speaking, the normal curve is a continuous distribution, that is, one with infinitely many categories, rather than just the seven of the Likert scale. This is not a distinction that we need go into here.
4. Arthur H. Miller, "Political Issues and Trust in Government: 1964–1970," *American Political Science Review*, vol. 68, no. 3 (September 1974) 951–972.
5. Richard M. Scammon and Ben J. Wattenberg, *The Real Majority* (New York: Coward-McCann, 1970), chap. 3.

Part **IV**

Attitudes in Action: Political Participation

What is political participation? Such an obvious question scarcely seems worth asking—until we try to answer it. Participation is certainly behavior of one sort or another, so let us think in terms of specific behavior types. In the first place, political participation is behavior that has political relevance. That is, by engaging in a behavior an individual (perhaps in company with many others) has some impact on governmental policy. There are two basic kinds of such behavior. One type is of a ceremonial or symbolic kind. It involves demonstrating allegiance by marching in parades, or by voting in ceremonial elections (such as those in the USSR, which have only Communist party candidates). It may also involve low-visibility behaviors, which include obeying the law or avoiding participation in a demonstration or riot.

The second sort of participation has the goal of influencing governmental policy decisions, either directly by influencing the selection of decision makers or indirectly by influencing the decisions made by governmental personnel. We might call this *active* participation. Here we find voting and writing letters to the editor on the mass level, as well as the activity of interest groups and lobbies. We might also include under the label of direct participation acts of disruption and violence, including the most violent act of all, assassination.

There is a second way we can classify political behavior, which cuts across the active-symbolic distinction. Certain behaviors are "within the system," or conventional, by which I mean behaviors generally recognized as legal and legitimate. Other behaviors fall into the nonconventional category. Here I would put much of the political protest which we have all witnessed in the United States over the past 12 or 15 years.

These different types of behaviors can be organized most conveniently into a fourfold figure. I have filled in a few examples to clarify the categories. They appear in Figure IV.1.

The following chapters make no attempt to encompass all of these categories. Instead, my main concern will be with the upper-left-hand cell: direct, conventional participation. More than this, I have chosen only one type of such participation: voting in presidential elections, because it is arguably the most important kind of participation engaged in by large sectors of the American electorate. Nonetheless, it is only one of many types. Therefore I shall spend a few pages describing the other major types of active, conventional political participation.

MODES OF ACTIVE CONVENTIONAL POLITICAL PARTICIPATION

Scholars have often talked about a "scale" of political participation. A scale is something like a ruler: It lets us "measure" people and find out that one participates in politics "a lot," while another participates "a little" or "not at all." How does this scale work? Originally, political scientists like Milbrath used a simple three-step process.[1] First, they sat down and thought of all the different ways a person might participate in politics. The list in Table IV.1 presents a dozen examples of different direct, conventional ways that ordinary people can participate in politics.

The next step was to ask each person in a study how many of the 12 acts he or she engaged in. The percentages in Table IV.1 indicate the proportion of a national sample of the electorate engaged in each activity in 1967. It is clear that political activity is not something to which Americans devote a great deal of time. No more than one-third of the electorate does

	Active	Symbolic
Conventional	Voting Writing Letters to Congressmen	Fourth of July Parades
Nonconventional	Sit-ins[a]	Riots

Figure IV.1. A Typology of Political Behaviors.

[a]The difference between active and symbolic nonconventional participation is less in the content of the behavior than in its intent. A demonstration may have a specific policy goal—opening a segregated lunch counter to blacks, for instance; or it may simply be a process of blowing off steam, where the participants have no particular policy desires, but just want to show somebody they're angry.

anything of a political nature other than vote, and no activity that requires any significant investment of time or energy is performed by more than 30 percent of the electorate.

The final step in measuring political activity is to count up the number of activities a person engages in. It stands to reason that someone who does all 12 of the things listed in Table IV.1 participates more than someone with a score of 10, and so on.

TABLE IV.1. Percentage Engaging in Twelve Different Acts of Active-Conventional Participation

Types of Political Participation	Percentage
1. Report regularly voting in presidential elections[a]	72
2. Report always voting in local elections	47
3. Active in at least one organization involved in community problems[b]	32
4. Have worked with others in trying to solve some community problems	30
5. Have attempted to persuade others to vote as they did	28
6. Have ever actively worked for a party or candidate during an election	26
7. Have ever contacted a local government official about some issue or problem	20
8. Have attended at least one political meeting or rally in last three years	19
9. Have ever contacted a state or national government official about some issue or problem	18
10. Have ever formed a group or organization to attempt to solve some local community problem	14
11. Have ever given money to a party or candidate during an election campaign	13
12. Presently a member of a political club or organization	8
N: 3095 (weighted)	
2549 (unweighted)	

Source: From *Participation in America; Political Democracy and Social Equality* by Sidney Verba and Norman H. Nie: Table 2-1, p. 31. Copyright ©1972 by Sidney Verba and Norman H. Nie. Reprinted by permission of Harper & Row, Publishers, Inc. See especially their Appendix B.1.

[a] Composite variable created from reports of voting in 1960 and 1964 presidential elections. Percentage is equal to those who report they have voted in both elections.
[b] This variable is a composite index where the proportion presented above is equal to the proportion of those in the sample who are active in at least one voluntary association that, they report, takes an active role in attempting to solve community problems. The procedure utilized was as follows: Each respondent was asked whether he was a member of fifteen types of voluntary associations. For each affirmative answer he was then asked whether he regularly attended meetings or otherwise took a leadership role in the organizations. If yes, he was considered an active member. If he was an active member and if he reported that the organizations regularly attempted to solve community problems, he was considered to have performed this type of political act.

The problem with this procedure is that participation is not unidimensional. That is, the scaling procedure I just described assumes that the 12 items in the table are like rungs on a single ladder, and all we have to do to measure participation is count how far up the ladder the person climbs. It turns out, however, that a much more realistic way of viewing participation is as a set of several short ladders. People tend to specialize. An individual can be extremely active in politics but do only one of the things listed in the table: work in a campaign, for instance. That person has climbed to the very top of a certain type of participation ladder, but he may not even step on the bottom rung of the ladder that involves voting.

Verba and Nie have used this view of voting as a multidimensional phenomenon to develop a new measure of participation.[2] They reasoned that participatory behavior could be classified in four ways: It could be electoral or nonelectoral; it could involve conflict or not; the outcome could be collective or particularized (that is, individual); and it could involve little initiative or a lot of initiative.

Using these criteria, Verba and Nie discovered that instead of one single type of participation, there are in fact four in the American electorate. Figure IV.2 describes them. The two types of activity that involve elections are self-explanatory: Voters vote and campaigners campaign. These kinds of participation are both conflictual and both include collective outcomes. They differ only with respect to the initiative required. Campaigning obviously requires a more sustained level of activity than voting.

The two types of nonelectoral activity require a bit more explanation.

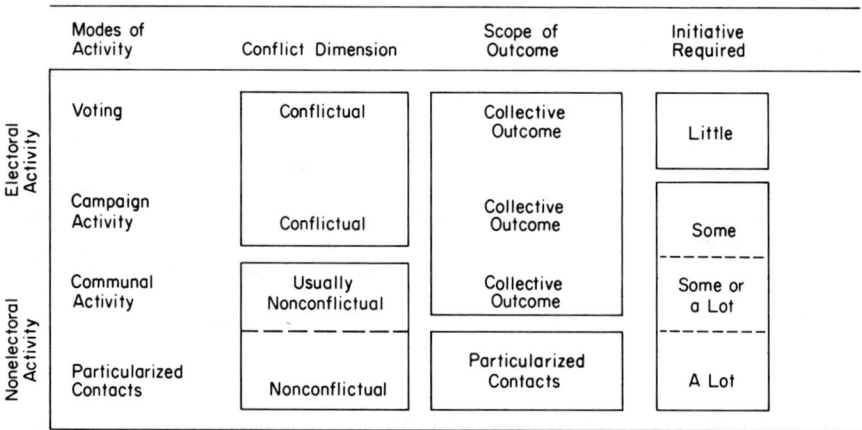

Figure IV.2. The Four Modes of Participation and the Dimensions of Participation.

Source: From *Participation in America: Political Democracy and Social Equality* by Sidney Verba and Norman H. Nie: Table 4–6, p. 73. Copyright © 1972 by Sidney Verba and Norman H. Nie. Reprinted by permission of Harper & Row, Publishers, Inc.

Communal activity refers generally to work with others on local problems, or membership in local problem-solving organizations. Such activity is usually nonconflictual, has a collective outcome, and requires a moderate amount of initiative.

The final type of activity involves making particularized contacts. This includes contacting local, state, or national leaders (for instance, by writing letters to Congressmen) for some personal reason. These contacts tend to be nonconflictual but require a great deal of initiative.

The final step in Verba and Nie's analysis is to move from types of participation to types of participators. We cannot assume that there are just four groups in the population, each one specializing in only one of these four types of participation. There could be any number of combinations, with some people engaging in several different types at the same time.

It turns out that in the American electorate, there are six major types of participators. By referring to Table IV.2, we can get a very rich sense of what this political participation is like.

About one-fifth of all Americans are politically inactive (or were in 1967). They make no effort to contact government officials, and take virtually no role in communal affairs or in political campaigns. Most don't vote at all, and those who do vote do so only occasionally.

The second group, the voting specialists, also make up about a fifth of the electorate. They differ from the inactives in only one respect; they all reported voting in presidential elections and they either always or almost always vote in local elections. While this group is a large one, it is a good deal smaller than many experts would have guessed. It is just not typical of Americans to vote and do nothing else.

The smallest of the six groups, the parochial participants, accounts for 4 percent of the total. These people are distinguished by their very high levels of particularized contacts. They *all* report engaging in such activity. They have no interest in communal or campaign work and are about average as voters. Evidently these individuals are very deeply interested in politics, but this interest is limited to the ways that politics affects their personal lives.

Another fifth of the electorate are the communalists. Here we find people who are very heavily engaged in work in community problem-solving groups, who vote fairly regularly, but who do very little campaigning. About one American in five, in other words, is quite willing to take an active part in political affairs, but is unwilling to engage in the conflictual realm of the political campaign.

The mirror image to the communalist group is the campaigner group, which contains about one American in six. Again, these people vote regularly and are also quite willing to go beyond voting to invest their time and energy in more demanding activities. Evidently, they prefer the battle and excitement of the campaign and don't mind taking the partisan positions necessitated by campaign work.

214 ATTITUDES IN ACTION: POLITICAL PARTICIPATION

TABLE IV.2. Participatory Profiles of the American Citizenry[a]

Groups Produced by Cluster Analysis	Voting	Campaign Activity	Communal Activity	Particularized Contacting	Percent of Sample in Type
1. Inactive	37	9	3	0	22%
2. Voting specialists	94	5	3	0	21
3. Parochial participants	73	13	3	100	4
4. Communalists	92	16	69	12	20
5. Campaigners	95	70	16	13	15
6. Complete activists	98	93	92	15	11
					93
Unclassified					7
					100%
Population means on the participation scales	76	29	28	14	

Source: From *Participation in America: Political Democracy and Social Equality* by Sidney Verba and Norman H. Nie: Table 4-9, p. 79. Copyright © 1972 by Sidney Verba and Norman H. Nie. Reprinted by permission of Harper & Row, Publishers, Inc.

[a] Scores in this table are means on standardized scales of activity. See Verba and Nie, Appendix F, for further explanation.

Finally, a fairly hefty piece of the electorate, 11 percent, are complete activists. They are highly involved in voting, campaign, *and* communal activities. In short, they engage in all types of activities that involve collective rather than particularized outcomes.

This portrait of conventional participation in the electorate is undeniably more complicated than the old single-dimension concept developed by Milbrath. In this book, unfortunately I can only pause briefly to mention these different types of participation. The rest of this section is devoted to a single participatory act: the vote. Nonetheless, I hope you will remain aware of the other sorts of activities that attract the efforts of many people.

NOTES

1. Lester W. Milbrath, *Political Participation* (Chicago: Rand McNally, 1965).
2. Sidney Verba and Norman H. Nie, *Participation in America* (New York: Harper & Row, 1972).

11
The Demographic Bases of the Vote

The first step in this three-chapter discussion is to integrate the act of voting into the structure that we have erected to this point. This summary model appears in Figure 11.1.

Four major factors influence voting behavior. The one closest to the vote in the psychological sense is attitudes. The first step in understanding the vote is the determination of the voters' atttitudes about the political parties, the issues, and the candidates. If these three sets of attitudes are consistent, that is, if they all point to one candidate, the voter will usually choose that person.

The second factor includes social and economic determinants of the vote, which can be expressed as membership in various groups. As Figure 11.1 should make clear, there are in fact no *direct* effects of group membership on voting behavior. We could not logically say that being a businessman, or a black, or a Catholic, or any other kind of group member, has any direct effect on behavior. Instead, I would argue that there are *attitudinal consequences of group membership* that *do* influence behavior. The density of skin pigmentation cells cannot make a person vote in a certain way. However, the experience of being black in American society tends to produce attitudes that are very favorable to the Democratic party. The attitudes, *not* the group membership, produce the vote.

Why, then, bother with the voting behavior of groups at all? The reason has to do with measurement. We can measure group membership much more easily and more accurately than we can measure attitudes. More-

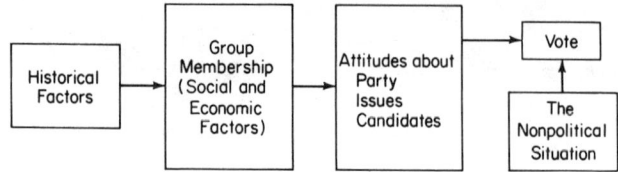

Figure 11.1. A Basic Model of Voting Behavior

over, attitudes cannot, at the present time, give us a complete understanding of behavior. Knowledge of group differences therefore continues to push back the boundaries of ignorance—and as long as that is true, their study will be useful.

Another reason to pay attention to groups is that politicians think in group terms. Campaigns are designed to appeal to groups in the electorate: blacks, Catholics, the working class, and the South all figure prominently in contemporary politics. As students of politics we cannot neglect this focus.

To the left of group membership factors in Figure 11.1, we find historical factors. Here we may include national crises like the Great Depression or the Civil War, as well as individual characteristics like whether one's parents immigrated to the United States or were native-born. While such factors are obviously remote in time, traces of their effects can still be found in the political behavior of the American electorate today.

Sometimes, of course, no matter how well we understand attitudes, social and economic factors and history, we still fail to predict the vote. A person may feel close to the Republican Party, he may admire Gerald Ford and mistrust Jimmy Carter, and he may prefer Ford's positions on the issues. Yet he votes for Carter. In order to understand this, we must take into account the nonpolitical situation. If we looked closely enough, we might discover that the morning of election day this voter's wife told him she would divorce him if he voted for Ford. In another instance, a person might favor Carter on political grounds but vote for Ford because he knows that all the boys at the office are Ford supporters. He also knows that he will be questioned by his friends the day after the election and if he votes for Carter, he will face the unpleasant choice of lying to them or telling them the truth and suffering their displeasure. This situation may have nothing to do with politics, but it still can determine a person's vote.

Unfortunately, social scientists find it extremely difficult to discover when a person has had a fight with his wife, or when he has buckled under to pressure from his co-workers. Therefore, the major tools with which we shall analyze voting behavior are group memberships, which reflect the social and economic situation, and the attitudes the voter holds about parties, candidates, and issues.

PRIMARY GROUPS

Primary groups are those groups with which we have continuous face-to-face contact. It stands to reason that since these are the people with whom we communicate the most, their influence on a variety of political behaviors should be reasonably strong. In fact, you should be able to make a fairly strong theoretical case for such a hypothesis, drawing from social learning theory or from consistency theory, for example.

In order to test whether primary groups are important in our political behavior, Kovenock and his colleagues asked a large sample of Americans not only how they voted in 1968, but also how their spouses, co-workers and friends voted. The results of this study appear in the Table 11.1. Apparently there is a healthy relationship between what the primary

TABLE 11.1. Relationships between Group Memberships and Voting

Respondent Voted for	Number of Respondent's Friends Who Voted for Humphrey				
	All	Most	Some	A Few	None
Humphrey	92%	87%	42%	21%	7%
Nixon or Wallace	8	13	58	79	93
	100%	100%	100%	100%	100%
N:	(279)	(1080)	(1685)	(1120)	(477)

Respondent Voted for	Number of Respondent's Coworkers Who Voted for Humphrey				
	All	Most	Some	A Few	None
Humphrey	85%	76%	43%	23%	17%
Nixon or Wallace	15	24	57	77	83
	100%	100%	100%	100%	100%
N:	(78)	(423)	(747)	(374)	(194)

Respondent Voted for	Respondent's Spouse Voted for		
	Nixon	Humphrey	Wallace
Nixon	92%	7%	11%
Humphrey	6	92	9
Wallace	2	1	80
	100%	100%	100%
N:	(1724)	(1674)	(449)

Source: ICPSR Archive: Comparative State Election Project, quoted in H. T. Reynolds, *Politics and the Common Man: An Introduction to Political Behavior* (Homewood, Ill.: Dorsey, 1974), pp. 154–155.

group did in the 1968 election and what these individuals did. And since one person cannot often impose his own views on his entire group of friends or co-workers, it seems sensible to conclude that a causal relationship exists in the opposite direction: The group has influenced the individual. The case is not so clear where married couples are concerned. While much agreement is reported, we have no way of knowing which member of the couple dominates when disagreement exists.

In any event, we can see that when the cue from the primary group is unambiguous (that is, *all* or *none* of them voted for Humphrey), there is a nearly unanimous agreement of behavior on the part of the respondents. There is one rather significant fly in the ointment, however. Kovenock and his colleagues relied on their respondents' reports of the behavior of their spouses, friends, or co-workers. It turns out that, to an amazing extent, we tend to be ignorant of the political preferences of these people. This means that a good deal of guesswork has infiltrated the results that appear in these tables. If you recall what consistency theory has to say, you can easily understand why I would warn you that the agreement documented here is likely to be greatly overstated. By how much we unfortunately cannot say.

SECONDARY GROUPS

The study of group bases of the vote has not lingered for long at the primary level, however. The classical work in this field focuses on the effect of membership in secondary groups. Such groups tend to be very large, their members do not necessarily ever meet each other, and membership is generally involuntary. We typically include here such groups as social class, age, sex, and race, among others.

The Index of Political Predisposition

One of the most important works in the area of voting behavior is a study of the electorate of Erie County (Sandusky), Ohio, that was undertaken in 1940.[1] For our purposes, the importance of the study arises from the relationship these scholars established between social characteristics of the individual, and his vote for President. They summarize their findings as follows: ". . . a person thinks, politically, as he is, socially. Social characteristics determine political preferences."[2]

What led Lazarsfeld and his colleagues to make such a sweeping conclusion? The simple fact is that in Erie County in 1940 certain sociological, or group, characteristics did an amazing job of distinguishing Democratic voters from Republican voters. To be specific, the authors found that a high socioeconomic status, affiliation with Protestantism, and rural residence tended to define Republican voters. Democrats tended to be poor, Catholic, and city dwellers. These three factors made up what the authors called the "Index of Political Predisposition."

The extent to which membership in these three groups predisposed a person to vote in a certain way can be seen in Figure 11.2. This figure tells us that of the voters who had all three of the critical memberships (rich, Protestant, rural—labeled "strongly Republican" in the table) nearly three-quarters voted Republican. Five out of six of those lacking all three (who were poor, Catholic, and urban, the "strongly Democratic" group), voted for the Democrat. I might mention in passing that a good deal more weight should be given to these results than to those of Kovenock because there is virtually no measurement error when it comes to social group membership. People may lie a bit about their incomes, but even here the extent of falsification is not serious.

Considerable time has passed since 1940 and the data that Lazarsfeld collected should be brought up to date. We therefore turn to the Michigan

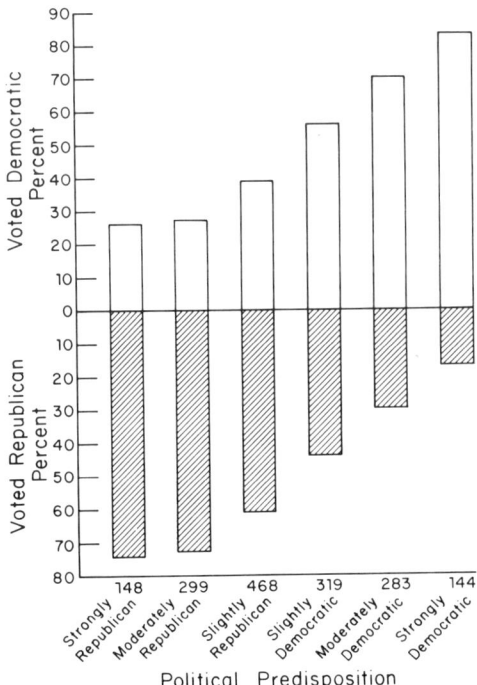

Figure 11.2. The Relationship between the Index of Political Predisposition and the Intended Vote for President in 1940.

Source: Paul Lazarsfeld, Bernard Berelson, and Hazel Gaudet, *The People's Choice*, 3rd ed. (New York: Columbia University Press, 1968), p. 26.

studies in order to follow the participation records of a variety of major groups in the American electorate from 1952 through 1976. In all cases we shall look at two indicators of participation: the proportion that turns out to vote in each presidential election and the proportion voting for the Democratic candidate.

Religion

Historically both Catholics and Jews have been much more inclined toward the Democrats than have Protestants. In the Catholic case, this preference can probably be traced to the period of massive emigration out of Europe, first from Ireland and then from eastern and southern Europe, which took place in the last century. Great numbers of these individuals took up residence in the cities of the Northeast and Midwest, cities that happened at the time to be under the control of Democratic political machines. Without any sense of partisanship initially, these new Americans had what the political bosses wanted: their votes. So in exchange for their political support, these immigrants received jobs, patronage, protection, and a place in the American political system.

Jews have had a vastly different experience in America than Catholics, but if anything they are today more faithfully Democratic. Unlike Catholics, the predepression vote of the Jewish community tended to be Republican, perhaps reflecting the affinity between Republicans and business. However, Jews know what it means to be the underdog and thus identified closely with Roosevelt's efforts on behalf of the downtrodden during the 1930s. The experience of the Second World War also had a profound influence on American Jews. The importance of Roosevelt's early leadership in the battle against Nazism and Hitler's treatment of European Jews had a critical effect in crystallizing Jewish loyalty to the Democratic Party.

The data in Figure 11.3 show that the historical patterns noted by Lazarsfeld have persisted to the present, although they are not consistently strong. In terms of turnout, Protestants have always voted less than Catholics, who in turn have always trailed behind the Jews. This pattern may make no sense at first, but it can be deciphered if we give a bit of thought to the other groups to which these people belong. Protestants, while heavily represented among wealthy, highly educated, and very politically active people, also make up the bulk of the southern electorate, which is known for its low levels of participation. Jews, on the other hand, have high average levels of education and wealth, both of which are indicators of high voting turnout.

The partisanship of these groups also follows predicted patterns. Protestants are consistently most Republican, Jews are the most Democratic, with Catholics in between. These patterns vary somewhat with the individual election. In 1960, the Catholic Kennedy brought a great many of

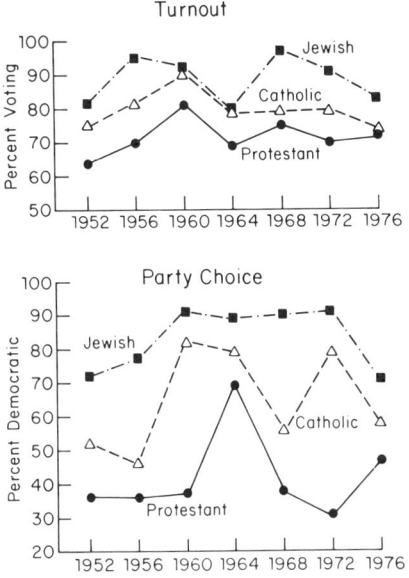

Figure 11.3. Turnout and Party Choice by Religion, 1952–1976.

Source: ICPSR Archive: SRC/CPS Presidential Election Studies.

his coreligionists over to the Democratic party from their Republican votes of 1952 and 1956. And in 1976 the Baptist Carter lost a good deal of support among Jews and Catholics, but did very well among Protestants (better than any Democrat except Johnson during this entire period), even though he failed to win a majority of the Protestant vote. What effect Carter's recent gestures toward the Arab states of the Middle East, or the Camp David summit, will have on the Jewish vote remains to be seen.

Social Class

Social class was another of the distinctions that Lazarsfeld included in his Index of Political Predispositions. Social class differences have been a vital part of American politics since Colonial times, when the vote was allocated according to the amount and type of property owned. Throughout our history, with some temporary deviations, the "haves" have been represented by one party, and the "have-nots" by another. And at least since the election of Andrew Jackson in 1828, the Democratic Party has been seen as the party of the common man.

In the contemporary period, the class bases of the two parties are rooted in the Great Depression and the New Deal. The poor Catholic immigrants whom I mentioned above merely shared in the consolidation of the working class under the banner of the Democratic Party during the 1930s. The Republicans, whose image centered on their role as the patron of big business and who were unfortunate enough to be in control of the White House when the stock market crashed, could not make a successful appeal to the working class. Franklin Roosevelt's crusade to get things moving again, specifically with massive infusions of federal aid to the working class, had a catalytic effect. His New Deal coalition, which united Catholics with labor, the South, and blacks on the basis of economic self-interest, was formed during these years between the Depression and the Second World War.

In Figure 11.4 we find that the working class turns out to vote at a level that is consistently some 10 to 15 points below that of the middle class. This difference reflects the extent to which the two groups are involved in politics. The working class has relatively fewer links with the political world. Its members lack the wealth that would generate interest in tax legislation, for instance, and they are unlikely to be personally acquainted with political leaders. Both characteristics are much more common among members of the middle class. In addition, the lower average levels of education in the working class make politics more remote than it is for the middle class.

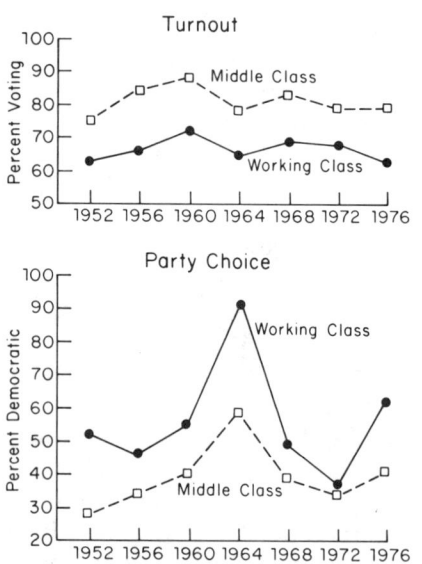

Figure 11.4. Turnout and Party Choice by Social Class, 1952–1976.

Source: ICPSR Archive: SRC/CPS Presidential Election Studies.

The data on percent Democratic of the presidential vote show a similar pattern, with one variation. Through the 1968 and 1972 elections, the partisan differences between the classes diminished to a point of near extinction. Looking ahead from 1972, we might have been tempted to predict that the partisan differences in social class were about to disappear. However, the Carter-Ford contest rekindled class feelings. The difference in support for the Democratic candidate in 1976—the working class was 21 points more Democratic than the middle class—is comparable to the large differences found in 1952 and 1956. This pattern reflects a basic shift in the nature of political issues, which I shall discuss at greater length in the next chapter. In brief, class differences in partisanship arise from an economic foundation. In 1968 and 1972, economic concerns were overshadowed by certain new noneconomic issues on the domestic front and by Vietnam. However, the reemergence of the dual problems of inflation and unemployment in the mid-1970s has repolarized the classes along the old party lines. We therefore cannot predict that class differences are about to disappear from American politics.

Race

Here is where Lazarsfeld's work leads us seriously astray, for he interviewed no blacks. But political differences between the races are enormous and must be taken into account if we are to reach a satisfactory understanding of mass political behavior.

The patterns that appear in Figure 11.5 clearly show how distinct the political experiences of the two major races have been since 1952. In the case of turnout, whites—except for a modest spurt in 1956 and 1960—have voted at a fairly constant rate over this entire 24-year period. Black turnout, on the other hand, shows a radically different pattern, more than doubling between 1952 and 1968. Of course, the low rates of participation among blacks in the 1950s present no mystery. They stem directly from discrimination. Blacks were simply kept away from the polls with techniques varying from legal prohibition to violence. Another product of discrimination, the relatively low average level of education that exists among blacks, also lowers turnout.

Turning to racial differences in partisanship, the picture we find is considerably more complex. After the Civil War, during the Reconstruction and Redemption periods, when blacks in the South took part in politics, the party that supported their cause—often by force of arms—was the Republican Party. Lincoln, a Republican, was generally considered a sort of messiah by blacks of that period. This sense of loyalty was strengthened around the turn of the century when southern whites used the Democratic party as the instrument not only to deprive blacks of their

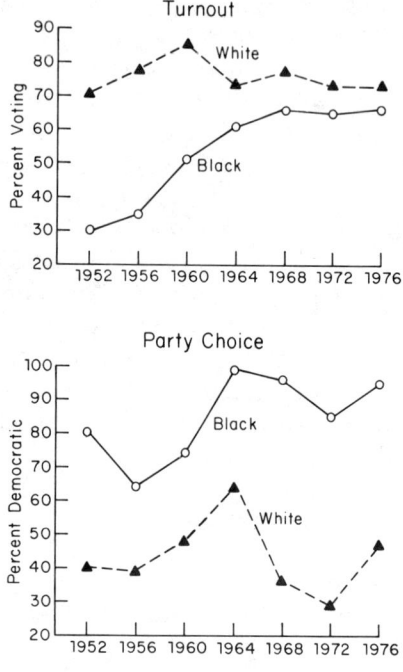

Figure 11.5. Turnout and Party Choice by Race, 1952–1976.

Source: ICPSR Archive: SRC/CPS Presidential Election Studies.

political rights but generally to impose on them a white supremacist culture. Down through the 1940s, southern one-partyism was founded on the dominance of the Democratic Party and specifically on its opposition to any attempt by the black population to change its status.

Blacks first began to question their loyalty to the Republican Party during the New Deal. They shared their poverty with many whites who came into the Democratic Party during the 1930s. But unlike poor whites, black retained strong ties to their Republican loyalties. Not until the 1940s, when the Democrats began their first timid rustlings in the area of civil rights, did a major shift in partisanship begin to gather momentum. This momentum gathered speed through the 1950s and in 1964, received its final boost. The campaign of Barry Goldwater, rightly or wrongly, was widely perceived by blacks as antiblack, and Lyndon Johnson was the first President to take an agressive position on civil rights legislation. The result was a dramatic shift in black presidential voting, to a point where today blacks are nearly unanimous in their preferences for Democratic presidential candidates.

When we compare black and white partisanship, the first thing we notice is the size of the differences. Even in the years when the two lines are closest, 1956 and 1960, blacks preferred the Democratic candidate by some 25 points more than whites. And in other years, the size of the disagreement is simply astounding. The election of 1968, with all its acrimony and the racially oriented campaign of George Wallace, produced a split of 60 points between these two groups in their vote for Hubert Humphrey! While Jimmy Carter achieved a significant recovery among whites, the near unanimity of the support given to Democrats by the black population in America virtually assures that a racial split will continue to be a dominant factor in the voting behavior of the electorate.

Education

Education has traditionally been one of the most consistent predictors of electoral behavior. We rarely go wrong in assuming that those with more education will participate in politics more than those with little or no education. There are numerous reasons why this is true. Consider the differences in day-to-day life between one person with a college degree and another person who dropped out of school after the sixth grade. To begin with, the college graduate reads more newspapers, more books, more everything. He therefore exposes himself to far more political material than the dropout. The graduate will also make better use of the information he takes in. His education has exposed him to many of the ideas that exist in the political world, and he therefore can understand political debate better than the dropout. In a broader sense, the graduate has a stronger feeling for the importance of government. He can see how a decision in Congress will eventually affect his interests, often even if the effect is only indirect. The dropout will probably not anticipate such relationships and can only react when something actually happens to him that he doesn't like. By that time it is often too late to change policy, and the dropout discovers his powerlessness to change the system. Thus participation is further discouraged.

There are other, external differences in the levels of participation. The graduate is more likely to be wealthy and to engage in business practices, while the dropout is more likely to be poor and to work as an employee, often as an unskilled laborer. The graduate will be motivated to participate because he sees his economic interest at stake. Tax laws may make a huge difference for a businessman, but are rarely even noticed by someone who works on the assembly line at GM. The graduate will also have more spare time to devote to politics, while the dropout may work two jobs just to make ends meet.

The data from 1952 to 1976 in Figure 11.6 confirm that the level of education influences the rate of voting turnout. College graduates consis-

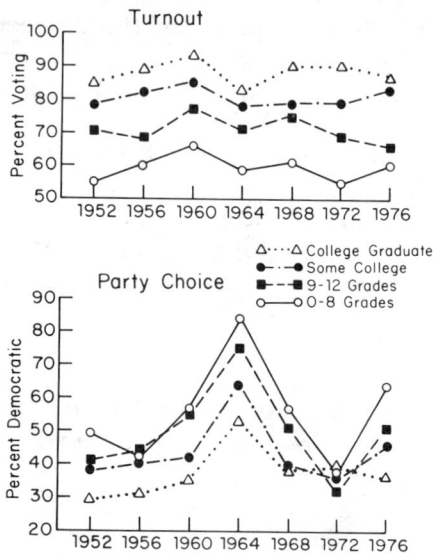

Figure 11.6. Turnout and Presidential Choice by Education, 1952-1976.

Source: ICPSR Archive: SRC/CPS Presidential Studies.

tently vote at levels 10 to 20 points higher than those with high school educations, whose turnout is 5 to 15 points greater than those with grade school or no education at all. Turnout rises and falls over the years and, in nearly every case, every educational group rises or falls in identical fashion. These overall fluctuations can therefore not be understood in terms of educational differences.

On the question of partisanship, the Depression and the New Deal, which forged the Democratic majority in the electorate, divided people according to education because of the relationship between education and wealth. The poor generally lack education and therefore supported the Democratic policies that led the country out of the Depression. Those who were well educated, generally wealthy, and engaged in business or the professions retained their traditional loyalties to the Republican party.

The data show that of the 1952-1976 time period, those with less education have been more likely to vote Democratic, while the Republicans have done better among the well educated. However, there is a small part of this figure between 1968 and 1972, which suddenly presents a striking exception. McGovern, who did so terribly poorly in the electorate as a whole, managed to do best among the college educated, the group that in the five previous elections has been the most Republican! This trend also appeared among those with some college background, who were more strongly for McGovern than might have been predicted from earlier elections. When the dust had settled, Nixon had scored his greatest success among those with high school educations, usually the second most pro-Democratic group.

How can we possibly explain that? Most probably, McGovern's success among the college educated is simply an artifact of his lack of success among other educational groups. The vote of people with a college degree was about the same for McGovern as it was for Carter and Humphrey. It sticks out in 1972 only because McGovern did 15 or 20 points worse among those with a high school education or less than did Carter or Humphrey.

There is one process of change that involves educational groups, which does not emerge in Figure 11.6. A moment's thought should convince you that nearly all Americans with less than a high school education are old. The waves of immigrants who came to this country with little or no schooling are now in their eighties. Native Americans of rural background whose major occupation in childhood was helping on the farm and who attended school casually, if at all, are now in their fifties and sixties (or older). What this means is that as time removes these older members of the electorate, the average level of education will rise. Indeed, the Census Bureau informs us that this process is well along already. The political consequences of this change should be obvious. A more educated electorate will participate more regularly and, in general, a more informed and vigilant electorate should emerge.

Region

My earlier remarks about economic and racial differences fairly well summarize what can be said about regional differences in electoral participation. The South is poorer, and has a much larger black population than the rest of the country. In addition, the long-time dominance of the Democratic Party in this region has reduced turnout in the November elections because the winner for many years had already been chosen in the Democratic primary.

During the 1950s, turnout in presidential elections ran 20 or 30 points lower in the South than in the rest of the country. The recruitment of both blacks and whites into the active electorate has raised southern turnout to a level that since 1960 has stayed around 10 or 15 points lower than that of the non-South. The other regions of the country, the Northeast, the Midwest, and the West, do not differ in turnout rate in any major ways. We do notice, however, that the average turnout outside the South has declined by about 5 points since 1952.

A vital change involving regional differences in the partisanship of the vote has been that since 1952 the old "solid South"—the one region that would automatically support the Democratic presidential candidate—has

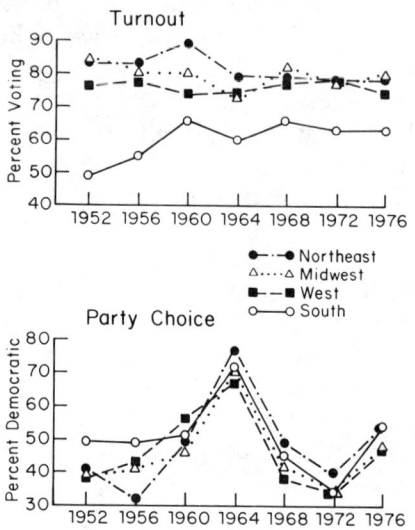

Figure 11.7. Turnout and Presidential Vote by Region, 1952–1976.

Source: ICPSR Archive: SRC/CPS Presidential Election Studies.

disappeared. Stevenson fared rather well in the South when he ran against Eisenhower, outpacing his performance elsewhere by about 10 points each time. Since 1956, however, the South has turned away from the Democratic presidential candidates. Not even Jimmy Carter could win much more support in the region of his birth than elsewhere.

Age

One of the intriguing things about voting in America today is the mystery of the youth vote. Here we have an enormous number of voters, less bound by party loyalty than any other group, and less hampered by the infirmities of old age or the responsibilities of position and family. You could justifiably expect this to be the most important bloc of votes in the entire electorate.

In truth, young people are the least important age group among all voters. Young people have an abysmal turnout record, usually about 15 points lower than the older electorate. Not even citizens over the age of 70 vote less than people between 18 and 30 (except in 1972).

The explanation for this behavior is simple. Many young people see no reason to think that politics is important. They have had little experience in the political world and have not developed party loyalties or economic status, all of which tend to encourage participation. Young people's atten-

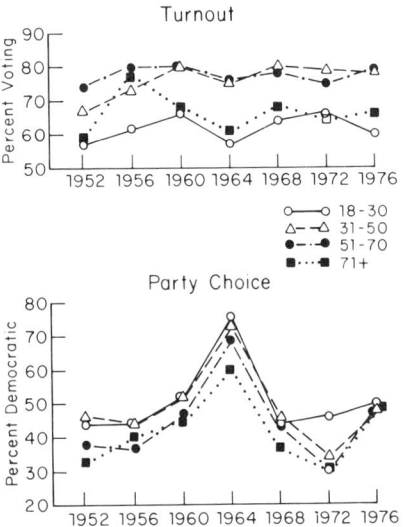

Figure 11.8. Turnout and Presidential Vote by Age, 1952–1976.

Source: ICPSR Archive: SRC/CPS Presidential Election Studies.

tion is focused on school, courting and marriage, or doing well in their first jobs. They are also highly mobile and therefore often run afoul of local registration requirements. So politics is simply postponed.

Not only do young people fail to turn out to vote, but when they do vote they fail to deviate much from the rest of the electorate in their choices for President. McGovern did a bit better among the young in 1972 than among older voters, but it is really more accurate to say that he did less poorly among the young. In every other election during the 1952–1976 period, the only distinguishable difference between age groups is that older voters tend to be a few points more Republican than younger voters. This difference can be explained by the fact that these older folks were already confirmed Republicans by the time the Depression and the New Deal came along. They were therefore less susceptible to the forces of that period that created so many new Democrats.

SUMMARY

One basic shortcoming plagues the group approach as an explanation of behavior. Most of us belong to many groups simultaneously. If all of them share the same partisanship, then the vote is generally predictable and understandable. But what of voters for whom group memberships conflict? They could be wealthy, rural Catholics, or poor, urban Protestants. In these cases, some group memberships indicate a Republican vote, while others speak for the Democratic candidate. Such a voter experiences cross-pressure. When cross-pressure exists, the group approach breaks down, for we have no way to predict which of the conflicting voices the individual will choose to follow.

In the top and bottom boxes of Figure 11.9 are those voters who feel no cross-pressure. (I have used Lazarsfeld's groups here. Perhaps you can suggest which groups would be most relevant today for the electorate or which groups have the most impact on your own behavior.) All the political forces of group membership push in the same direction. The result is a high proportion of either Democratic or Republican votes.

The groups in the middle suffer from cross-pressure. In those cases, the political forces push in opposite directions; some favor the Republicans, while others favor the Democrats. The result is indeterminate. We simply do not know how members of these groups will vote.

There are other, more direct, indications that the prediction of the vote from knowledge of group membership doesn't always work. For example, there is simply no way to explain the landslide that elected Lyndon Johnson by looking at group differences. In order for that approach to work, we need to find certain groups in the electorate that shifted heavily from Republican to Democratic between 1960 and 1964 relative to others that did not. The trouble is that very few groups failed to support Johnson more than they had supported Kennedy four years earlier. If you glance back at some of the figures given earlier in this chapter, you will find that *all* social classes, *both* races, *all* educational groups, and *all* regions became more Democratic in 1964 than they were in 1960. (Catholics and Jews did

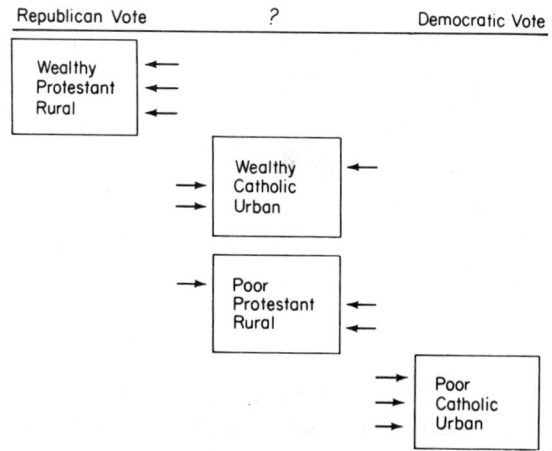

Figure 11.9. The Effect of Cross-Pressure on Voting.

not, because of their extremely heavy Democratic votes in 1960. They were still much more Democratic in 1964 than were the Protestants, however.)

Given these patterns, it is clear that we must continue our search for an adequate explanation of political behavior. The obvious alternative is to consider the attitudinal bases of the vote.

NOTES

1. Paul F. Lazarsfeld, Bernard Berelson, and Hazel Gaudet, *The People's Choice: How the Voter Makes Up His Mind in a Presidential Election*, 3d ed. (New York: Columbia University Press, 1968).

2. *Ibid.*, p. 27.

12
The Attitudinal Bases of the Vote

Group differences in the vote have undeniable importance. They are the grist of journalistic accounts of electoral behavior, and they are crucial to the candidate attempting to win office. But they leave the political scientists unsatisfied. We may be able to understand why blacks are more Democratic than whites by looking at group characteristics, but this information gives no clue as to why *both* blacks and whites supported Carter in 1976 more than they supported McGovern in 1972.

Such questions must be answered by the factor that lies closest to voting behavior: the voter's attitudes about the parties, candidates, and issues. The discussion in this chapter will be divided into two parts. The first deals with the attitudes that lead to turnout, and the second looks at the attitudes that influence whether a voter pulls the Republican or the Democratic lever.

TURNOUT

Historical Trends

People fail to vote in great numbers in the United States. It is usually true that presidential elections attract the largest numbers of people to the polls, but even then, only 53 percent of all eligible Americans voted for President in November 1976. And turnout has dropped over the years, not increased. Figure 12.1 gives the turnout for President and Congress in each election since the Civil War.

THE ATTITUDINAL BASES OF THE VOTE   233

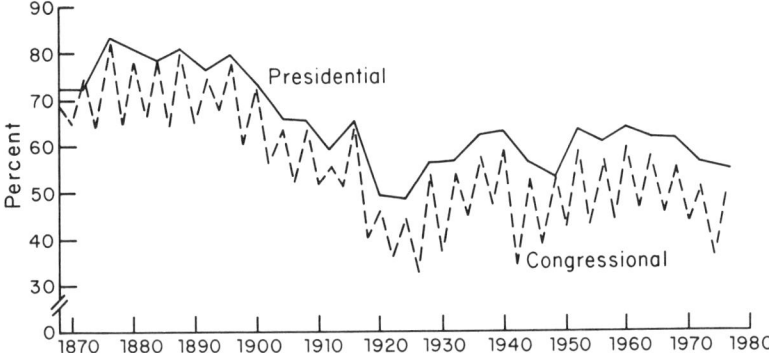

Figure 12.1. Turnout of Eligible Voters in Presidential and Congressional Elections, 1868–1976.

Source: Years 1868–1928 quoted from William H. Flanagan and Nancy H. Zingale, *Political Behavior of the American Electorate*, 3d ed. (Boston: Allyn and Bacon, 1975), p. 20. 1930 to 1976: U.S. Bureau of the Census, *Statistical Abstract of the United States: 1976* (97th ed.), (Washington, D.C.: Government Printing Office, 1976), Table 813, p. 508.

You can easily see that a relatively clear pattern of turnout exists for presidential elections over the past 100 years. In the years from the end of Reconstruction (1876) to about 1892, Americans exercised their right of franchise in extremely large numbers. About 80 percent of the eligible electorate voted during that period. Then came an enormous decline in turnout rates. Between 1896 and 1920, turnout dropped from 80 percent to less than 50 percent. This low point, reached in the 1920s, was followed by a slow rise that, interrupted by 1944 and 1948, peaked again at about 62 percent in the 1950s. While it is really too early to tell for sure, it appears that another period of decline began after 1960 and continues today.

To be sure, not all of these changes can be attributed to attitudes. Every few years, the U.S. Census samples the electorate to find out why people do not vote in our national elections. Table 12.1 gives the results that were obtained in the survey of November 1974.[1]

Some of these reasons obviously have nothing to do with attitudes. If you look at those who were registered but did not vote in 1974, you can see that poor health, lack of transportation, or being called out of town kept large numbers of voters from the polls. About half of this group, in fact, reported reasons for not voting that are more structural than attitudinal. (That is, their reasons involve conditions beyond their control.)

The failure to register, reported by 32 percent of the electorate as its reason for not voting, can likewise be the product of either attitudinal or structural forces. A voter may not register simply because he doesn't care enough about voting to do it. On the other hand, registration has been

TABLE 12.1. Reasons Given for Not Voting and for Not Registering in November 1974

	Number	Percentage
Total electorate	141,299,000	100.0%
Registered and voting	63,164,000	44.4
Did not vote	78,135,000	55.3
Registered but did not vote	24,725,000	17.5

Reasons for Not Voting among Those Registered	Percent of Registered but Not Voting	Percent of Total
Illness, disability, or family emergency	17.5%	3.1%
Could not leave work, could not get to polls	13.6	2.4
Machines not working, lines too long	.5	.1
Out of town or away from home	13.3	2.3
Did not know of election	.9	.2
Not interested	18.6	3.2
Dislikes politics	2.5	.4
Did not prefer any candidate	8.7	1.5
Believed vote would not matter	1.5	.3
Other reason	13.8	2.4
Missing data	9.1	1.6
	100.0%	17.5%

Reasons Not Registered	Percent of Not Registered	Percent of Total
Not a citizen	8.9%	2.8%
Residency requirement not satisfied	4.3	1.4
Recently moved, have not registered	10.7	3.4
No transportation	1.0	.3
Registration inconvenient	3.0	1.0
Did not know how or where to register	4.4	1.4
Physical disability or illness	3.6	1.2
Not interested	37.4	11.9
General dislike of politics	4.8	1.5
Did not prefer any candidate	2.7	.9
Believed vote would not matter	1.5	.5
Other reason	12.0	3.8
Missing data	5.7	1.8
	100.0%	31.9%
Did not know and not reported on registration		5.9
		37.8%

Source: U.S. Department of Commerce, Bureau of the Census. *Current Population Reports, Population Characteristics*, "Voting and Registration in the Election of November 1974," Series P-20, no. 293 (April 1976).

denied to many citizens in the past for discriminatory reasons, as we have seen. Even today, the fact that Americans move so much means that, at any given moment, hundreds of thousands of people will not have lived long enough in a place to be eligible to register.

The question of whether low registration is produced by attitudinal or structural factors has given rise to a most interesting debate about the reasons underlying the remarkable drop in voter turnout that we have already noticed between 1896 and 1924. Walter Dean Burnham has examined a wide array of data from this period, and concludes that the decrease was produced by the "theft" of the electoral system by the Republican industrialist-capitalist elite in 1896.[2] That is, the Republicans managed to put together a combination of wealthy urban and rural electoral support that effectively isolated the urban working class. The depression of 1893 had alienated the workers from the Democratic Party, and William Jennings Bryan had taken the party even further from their interests in his attempts to capture the rural and western electorates.

The Republicans won a crushing victory in 1896, and the workers, according to Burnhm, were left without a political home. No matter how they voted, power and policy would continue to be controlled by the business-Republican elite. In Burnham's view, the workers simply gave up in the face of these reverses. The electoral system lost its relevance as a place where grievances might be resolved. The result was the sharp decline in participation, which we can see in Figure 12.1.

Philip Converse presents another interpretation of this decline in turnout.[3] History shows that during the period of high turnout from 1876 to 1896, there were few registration laws in use to control voting. Converse's thesis is that those high turnout rates were merely the product of enormous corruption and fraud that typified elections in this country before 1900. The vote was inflated, sometimes beyond a 100 percent turnout rate, by illegal additions of votes to the final tally. Although this interpretation of the data may seem at least as farfetched as Burnham's "theft of the electoral system" hypothesis, Converse cites numerous studies which document the way elections were run in this country during the nineteenth century. The following quote will give you the flavor of the situation that Converse uncovered.

> The variety of mechanisms employed to swell the vote of a candidate artificially compel admiration. Within the cities, the most common method, however, involved the use of "repeaters," or swarms of men recruited for a day's drink or pay either from the transient districts of the city center or from surrounding towns in the rural hinterland, who walked or were carted from one polling place to another, casting and recasting the appropriate votes from dawn till dusk. There was often little or no attempt to disguise the nature of the operation. Men moving along recognizable trails between polling stations

"in droves of 50 or more" were part of the familiar carnival of Election Day in some areas and, in a degree hard to comprehend by modern standards, the bystander reaction emerging in contemporary accounts was often as much amusement as indignation. Nor were such incursions on honest voting limited to the polling stations of large cities. Instances of rural authorities reporting vote tallies for their jurisdictions exceeding the number of adult males shown by the census appear on the public historical record. Cases were even reported of unknown men riding up to hinterland polling places and admixing wads of votes at gunpoint.[4]

In Converse's view, then, the drop-off in turnout came not from attitudinal sources, but was purely a result of the institutions of effective registration laws and the consequent drop in fraudulent voting.

Attitudinal Bases of Turnout in the Contemporary Electorate

When we seek to answer the question, "Why do so few Americans vote today?" we can look to a number of different psychological factors for an explanation. The first I will discuss is the stimulus level of the election. This is not an attitude, but it is a factor that acts directly upon the attitudes of the voters. The other factors are all attitudinal: sense of political efficacy, sense of citizen duty, and strength of partisanship.

Stimulus Level of the Election. In Figure 12.1, when we compare the turnout rates for presidential elections with those of congressional elections, or the rates of presidential and congressional voting in presidential years, we can see two things. First, the congressional vote is nearly always lower than the presidential vote. Second, in the off years when there is no presidential contest, the turnout rate drops markedly, often by 10 or 15 points.

These differences reflect the differences in the levels of stimulation produced by each election. That is, during a campaign, certain things happen that attract the voters' attention. Most notably, the parties and candidates buy television and radio time, as well as space in the printed media. The campaign, in presidential years especially, is all around us. We can scarcely escape the feeling that a lot of people think that voting for one party or the other is really important. Since by far the most time and money flows in the presidential campaigns, these are the elections that are surrounded by the highest levels of stimulation. The excitement of the campaign alone is enough to pull some voters to the polls who would not bother to vote in the more lackluster off-year congressional elections.

The presidential campaign possesses a second type of stimulus. The fact that they are voting for the most important office in the country motivates some people who, two years later, would not bother to go to the polls to vote for their Congressman. This factor extends even to the congressional vote in presidential years. Figure 12.1 shows that about one voter in 12 will pull the presidential lever but will leave the Congress lever untouched.

Sense of Political Efficacy.[5] It makes a good deal of sense to believe that people who think they can get something done by participating in politics are a lot more likely to vote (or participate in other ways) than those who are convinced that nothing they can do will make any difference.[6] It is but a short step to demonstrate that this feeling of efficacy, the feeling that political involvement can bring results, actually does relate to the decision to vote. If this is true, then we have discovered at least one of the reasons that turnout in presidential elections has been declining since 1960, since levels of political efficacy in the American electorate have fallen consistently during that time.

We see in Table 12.2 that voter turnout is fairly strongly related to feelings of political efficacy, especially at the higher levels; that is, those individuals who felt very efficacious turned out in virtual unanimity. Some 91 percent in 1956 and 92 percent in 1976 reported that they had voted.

TABLE 12.2. The Relationship between Political Efficacy and Turnout in 1956 and 1972

		Sense of Political Efficacy[a]				
		Low				High
1956	Voted	52%	60%	75%	84%	91%
	Did Not Vote	48	40	25	16	9
		100%	100%	100%	100%	100%
	N:	(263)	(343)	(461)	(501)	(196)
1976	Voted	60%	65%	65%	83%	92%
	Did Not Vote	40	35	35	17	8
		100%	100%	100%	100%	100%
	N:	(502)	(493)	(73)	(502)	(252)

Sources: 1956: Angus Campbell, Philip E. Converse, Warren E. Miller, and Donald E. Stokes, *The American Voter.* Copyright © 1960 by John Wiley & Sons, Inc. Reprinted by permission of John Wiley & Sons, Inc. 1976: ICPSR Archive: CPS Presidential Election Study.

[a] Sense of political efficacy was scored according to the responses to the following questions:
1. I don't think public officials care much what people like me think.
2. Voting is the only way that people like me can have any say about how the government runs things.
3. People like me don't have any say about what the government does.
4. Sometimes politics and government seem so complicated that a person like me can't really understand what's going on.

Why, if highly efficacious people vote so regularly, do those with low efficacy vote at all? We might expect, working from simple logic, that this left-hand group in Table 12.2 would hardly ever vote. The answer, of course, is that there are reasons other than efficacy that lead people to vote. Feeling efficacious virtually guarantees a vote; the lack of efficacy is made up in half the cases by other factors.

Sense of Citizen Duty.[7] One such factor is the sense of citizen duty. This attitude is a direct result of childhood socialization, when the child learns a sense of belonging to society and the consequent obligations of that membership. Many of you can doubtlessly identify within yourselves a feeling that voting is the "right thing to do" or something that good citizens should do, in spite of the fact that you know perfectly well that you will never cast the decisive vote in a presidential election.

Here again, we find in Table 12.3 that the attitude in question relates strongly to the decision to vote. In 1956, five of six voters with a strong sense of citizen duty voted. Of those without any such sense, only one in eight made it to the polls. In 1976 the same turnout rate prevailed for those whose sense of citizen duty was strong (five of six). Of those with a weak sense of citizen duty, about one in five voted.

TABLE 12.3. The Relationship between Sense of Citizen Duty and Turnout in 1956 and 1976

		Sense of Citizen Duty[a]				
		Weak				Strong
1956	Voted	13%	42%	52%	74%	85%
	Did Not Vote	87	58	48	26	15
		100%	100%	100%	100%	100%
	N:	(89)	(78)	(146)	(639)	(812)
1976	Voted	21%	38%	23%	71%	84%
	Did Not Vote	79	62	77	29	16
		100%	100%	100%	100%	100%
	N:	(53)	(79)	(47)	(843)	(1105)

Sources: 1956: Angus Campbell et al., *The American Voter*. Copyright © 1960 by John Wiley and Sons, Inc. Reprinted by permission of John Wiley & Sons, Inc. 1976: ICPSR Archive: CPS 1976 Presidential Election Study.

[a] Sense of citizen duty was scored according to the responses of the following questions:
1. It isn't so important to vote when you know your party doesn't have a good chance to win.
2. A good many local elections aren't important enough to bother with.
3. So many other people vote in national elections that it doesn't matter much to me whether I vote or not.
4. If a person doesn't care how an election comes out he shouldn't vote in it.

The obvious difference between this measure and the previous one comes at the lower end of the scale. Without a sense of citizen duty, very few people bother to vote; no other attitude can make up for this lack. Fortunately, the effect on turnout of a weak sense of citizen duty is muted considerably by the fact that there are relatively few people who have that attitude. In fact, in 1976, only about 2½ percent of the sample gave the lowest score on the citizen duty scale.

Political Partisanship. The most important role of political partisanship comes in the area of party choice: Once the voter gets into the booth, which lever does he or she pull? However, the sense of partisanship also has something to do with getting that voter into the booth in the first place. After all, a person who is a strong partisan presumably has some reasons for that attitude. Most likely, he or she identifies with the loyalties of his or her parents. Beyond that, there are probably other reasons that act to reinforce his choice. His economic interests may be served better by his chosen party than by the other party (in his perception, at least). His ethnic, racial, or religious identity may also find a more comfortable home in one of the two major parties. For these reasons, the strong partisan is more likely to see his party as the defender of his interests than the weak partisan or the Independent. A motive exists to get to the polls on election day and cast that vote for the cause. The Independent, by definition, has no such motive. He sees neither party as his ally, except perhaps in specific instances. We would not, therefore, expect the Independent to vote as frequently as the strong identifier from either party.

Once again, we find our hypothesis confirmed. Table 12.4 shows that the stronger the attachment to a party, the more likely is the individual to vote. This effect remains approximately as strong in 1976 as it was in 1956. The one exception occurs among Independents in 1956, who turned out in unexpectedly large numbers to vote for Eisenhower. We can explain this by a combination of Eisenhower's personal magnetism, which attracted large numbers of habitual nonvoters, and of a dispiritedness among the Democrats, who must have known that their man, Adlai Stevenson, was going to be beaten soundly—as indeed he was.

Anticipating the flow of my argument a bit, there are some very interesting aspects of Table 12.4 that bear on the question of who wins presidential elections. These data show that the least reliable voters are the Independents, in the sense that they are least likely to vote. The strong identifiers are most reliable, but there is a difference. Of all the partisan groups in the electorate, strong Republicans are the most highly motivated to get out and vote. You can probably make a pretty strong argument why this should be true, based on the socioeconomic profile of the partisan groups. The strong Democrats, while they are the next highest in

240   ATTITUDES IN ACTION: POLITICAL PARTICIPATION

TABLE 12.4. The Relationship between Strength of Partisanship and Turnout in 1956 and 1976

		Partisanship				
		Strong Republican	Weak Republican	Independent	Weak Democrat	Strong Democrat
1956	Voted	81%	79%	75%	68%	79%
	Did Not Vote	19	21	25	32	21
		100%	100%	100%	100%	100%
	N:	(262)	(250)	(412)	(402)	(364)
1976	Voted	92%	74%	66%	68%	81%
	Did Not Vote	8	27	33	32	19
		100%	100%	100%	100%	100%
	N:	(222)	(354)	(866)	(583)	(422)

Sources: 1956: ICPSR Archive: SRC 1956 Presidential Election Study; 1976: ICPSR Archive: CPS 1976 Presidential Election Study.

their turnout record, are not nearly as faithful as their Republican counterparts.

By this time, you have no doubt begun to ask yourself "if all of these things taken one at a time affect the vote, then someone who scores high on all of them must spend all his time participating in politics." Well, that isn't quite true, of course, but the idea is not a mistaken one. Working from the 1956 data, Campbell and his colleagues identified each member of their sample according to his or her score on all of the attitudes discussed above (plus two others), giving each person a score from one to nine.[8] Of those who were least involved, 22 percent voted in that year; of those who were most involved, fully 96 percent went to the polls.

PARTY CHOICE

Once the citizen has made the decision to vote and has entered the voting booth, he faces the second decision: which candidate to choose. The identification of the attitudes that underlie this choice has attracted the interest of scholars for years. Their research has led to the following image of the vote. There are two sets of attitudes that determine party choice. One set, called the "standing commitment," contains attitudes acquired over a long period of time, often beginning in childhood. They therefore tend to be stable; that is, all else being equal, the individual's standing commitment will lead him to vote for the same party in election after election. In the United States the dominant attitude that makes up the standing commitment of most Americans is party identification. However, if you stop to think about it, there are certainly other possibilities. In many parts of the world, religion and politics are much more closely intertwined than they are in the United States. Parties that receive support from the Catholic church in Europe benefit from a standing commitment of many Catholics to support them. And in the Third World, tribal loyalties have much political relevance: They form the basis of standing commitments to support one governing faction or another and may even give rise to secessionist movements, as occurred in the Biafran region of Nigeria.

I repeat, all else being equal, the standing commitment determines the vote. Clearly enough, however, "all else" is rarely equal. Attitudes acquired during childhood socialization may form the basis for adult behavior, but that behavior is also heavily influenced by what is happening in the world of today. Today's events generate the second set of politically relevant attitudes, called "short-term forces." These forces are produced by the candidates on the one hand, and the issues on the other. Clearly, in any given election there will be a unique combination of short-term forces. In 1976, Jimmy Carter happened to be a Southerner, and this short-term force led to a relatively strong showing for the Democrats in the South. In the 1974 congressional election, Watergate weighed on the minds of the voters, and that short-term force led to the defeat of many Republican Congressmen.

Once you understand the nature of the standing commitment and of the short-term forces, the key to unlock the mysteries of the behavior of the electorate is in how the two sets of attitudes are combined. Standing commitment and short-term forces exist in what the physicists called a "dynamic equilibrium." In an election where the short-term forces are weak, the standing commitment (that is, party identification in the American electorate) will determine the greater part of the vote. In another year, when short-term forces are very strong, their effect will dominate, washing out to some extent the influence of the standing commitment.

Party Identification

In the words of Flanagan and Zingale, "partisanship is the most important single influence on political opinions and voting behavior. Many other influences are at work on voters in our society, but none compare[s] in significance with partisanship."[9] I have already reviewed the nature of the origins of partisanship, its distribution in the electorate, and its effect on turnout. Now is the time to consider its relationship to party choice. This information appears in Table 12.5, which sends us a clear message. Even though I have chosen three quite different elections (a Republican landslide in 1956, a Democratic landslide in 1964, and a fairly close Democratic victory in 1976), the relationship of party loyalty to party choice retains its basic shape. In all three cases we find the expected increases in

TABLE 12.5. The Relationship between Party Identification and Party Choice: 1956, 1964, and 1976

		Party Identification				
		Strong Republican	Weak Republican	Independent	Weak Democrat	Strong Democrat
Voted for in 1956:	Democrats	1%	7%	36%	63%	85%
	Republicans	99	93	64	37	15
		100%	100%	100%	100%	100%
	N:	(210)	(193)	(223)	(269)	(285)
Voted for in 1964:	Democrats	11%	45%	68%	84%	96%
	Republicans	89	55	32	16	4
		100%	100%	100%	100%	100%
	N:	(148)	(157)	(234)	(303)	(416)
Voted for in 1976:	Democrats	3%	22%	54%	75%	91%
	Republicans	97	78	46	25	9
		100%	100%	100%	100%	100%
	N:	(401)	(492)	(1056)	(742)	(534)

Source: ICPSR Archive: The SRC/CPS Presidential Election Studies of 1956, 1964, and 1976.

loyalty as we move from the Independent group outward to the strong identifiers. Consider first the strong Republicans. These are consistently the most loyal voters in the electorate. Even in 1964, when Goldwater suffered such a crushing defeat at the hands of Johnson, only 11 percent of this group deserted to the Democrats. In better years, the strong Republicans support their party's candidate in near unanimity. Eisenhower was of couse a very easy man to vote for in 1956, but even in 1976, when many strong Republicans had fought hard for Ronald Reagan in the primaries, there was still a phenomenal loyalty displayed for Gerald Ford on election day.

On the other end of the spectrum, strong Democrats display characteristics similar to those of their Republican counterparts. The only difference is a somewhat weaker loyalty felt for their party. While Eisenhower lost only 1 percent of his most loyal supporters in the Republican landslide of 1956, Johnson failed to get the vote of 4 percent of the strong Democrats in the Democratic landslide of 1964. And in the relatively evenly balanced year of 1976, there were three times as many desertions among the strong Democrats, where 9 percent voted for Ford, as among the strong Republicans, where only 3 percent voted for Carter.

The Independents give us valuable insights about the role of party identification in voting behavior because they illustrate what happens when party loyalty is absent. Compared to the relative stability of party choice among the strong identifiers, the Independents flow first one way and then the other. Although 64 percent of their vote went to Eisenhower in 1956, 68 percent went to Johnson only eight years later. And in 1976 their vote split nearly in half. In other words, without the stabilizing influence of a standing commitment, party choice in the American electorate becomes extremely volatile.

Why Third Parties Fail. There is another message to be read from Table 12.5. Since party identification plays such a dominant role in the vote choice, there is a virtual guarantee that no "third" party—that is, no party other than the Democrats or the Republicans—stands much chance of winning the presidency. History has borne this fact out. Since the birth of the modern party system after the Civil War, no President has belonged to other than the Democratic or Republican party. Only three third-party candidates have received more than 6 percent of the vote in all that time: Wallace in 1968, LaFollette in 1924, and Teddy Roosevelt in 1912.

The limits of third-party fortunes are probably best illustrated in the 1912 election. Teddy Roosevelt had already been President for nearly two terms as a Republican, from 1901 to 1909. He left office, only to return in 1912 in a bid to capture the Republican nomination once again. In this he failed, defeated by William H. Taft. Roosevelt wasn't one to quit, however, and entered the race as a Progressive (for obscure reasons, he called his group the Bull Moose Party). The Bull Moosers recorded the greatest success of any third party since the Civil War. They received about 28 percent of the vote, and outpolled the Republicans, who received 23 percent. But even the presence of a highly charismatic former President at the head of the ticket failed to win the election. Wilson, the Democrat, took the White House with 42 percent of the vote.

The moral of this story is that over the past 100 years, at least, it has simply been too difficult to uproot partisans from their traditional loyalties for a third party to have any sort of chance. Teddy Roosevelt obviously received the vote of millions of Republican loyalists who felt that they were really voting for a Republican in spite of the party label. George Wallace's success can be attributed in part to the same phenomenon: He was a lifelong Democrat, a fact that allowed many of his supporters to feel that they weren't really deserting their party to vote for him in 1968. Even so, the pull of party loyalty was sufficiently strong to ensure that the bulk of the electorate cast its vote for one of the traditional parties.

Short-Term Forces

In any given election the personalities of the candidates and the issues that happen to be important will exercise an influence on the vote. The voter perceives a candidate, let us say, in his various television appearances. These perceptions are incorporated into the voter's belief system, where they are assessed in terms of the attitudes that are already present. If, for instance, the voter has a very strong feeling that "what America needs is a strong, aggressive leader who can deal with the Communists" and if a particular candidate comes across as strong and aggressive, then we would obviously predict from our knowledge of consistency theory that the voter would form a very positive attitude about that candidate. Since an attitude constitutes "a predisposition to react in a certain way to an object," this attitude will be carried into the voting booth, where it will emerge as a motive to pull the strong, aggressive candidate's lever. This motive, or force, exists only in the short term because at the next election there will probably be a different candidate and another set of perceptions.

Naturally, in a typical election a voter will be confronted with hundreds of stimuli about the issues and the candidates. This diversity can be distilled into six basic categories into which all short-term forces can be classified. They are:

Attitudes toward the Democratic and Republican candidates for President
Attitudes toward the issues of domestic and foreign policy
Attitudes toward the political parties as managers of government
Attitudes toward the various groups involved in politics.

Candidate Attitudes. Over the period from 1952 to 1976, the short-term forces produced by the presidential candidates have shown more variability than any other. Figure 12.2 gives a graphic interpretation of the impact of the candidates on the vote.

In this figure, the fact emerges that over the years, the Republicans have fared considerably better than the Democrats in their selection of candidates. General Eisenhower, as we have already seen, brought the image of a conquering general into the contest against Stevenson in 1952. While Stevenson's image declined a bit in 1956, public confidence in Eisenhower reached a zenith, leading to an 8-point advantage for the Republicans in that year. Stokes and his colleagues conclude:

> It was the response to personal qualities—to his sincerity, his integrity and sense of duty, his virtue as a family man, his religious devotion, and his sheer likeableness—which rose sharply in the second campaign. These frequencies leave the strong impression that Eisenhower was honored not so much for his performance as President as the quality of his person....[10]

With one important exception, both of the candidates who contested the 1960 election were viewed favorably by the electorate. Richard Nixon was seen as a personable individual who was clearly qualified and experienced enough to be President. Kennedy entered the contest amid suspi-

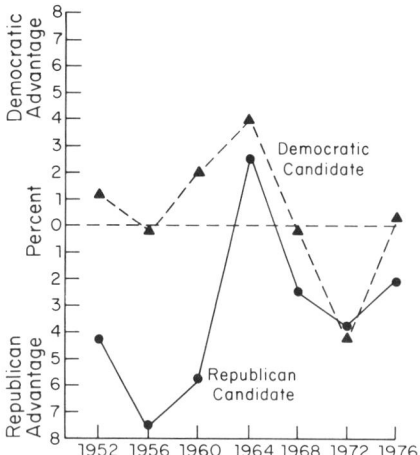

Figure 12.2. The Electoral Impact of the Democratic and Republican Candidates, 1952–1976.

*In this figure and Figures 12.3 and 12.4 what is being measured is the effect on the two-party vote attributable to the attitudinal component in question. For example, the 1956 entry in the above figure for Republican candidates should be interpreted as indicating that the GOP received an advantage of about 8 percent in the popular vote due to attitudes toward Eisenhower.

Source: Reprinted by permission of the publisher, from Michael Kagay and Greg Caldeira, "A 'Reformed' Electorate? Well, At Least, a Changed Electorate, 1952–1976." In the forthcoming book by William J. Crotty. (ed.), *Paths to Political Reform*, to be published by Lexington Books, Lexington, Mass. Copyright © 1979, D. C. Heath and Company.

cions that he lacked the qualifications to be President. The campaign, and in particular the televised debates, dispelled this image. In the end Kennedy's strongest characteristics were his education and his informedness.[11]

The one exception to this generally positive picture involved Kennedy's religion. A Catholic had never been President, and the only other Catholic candidate, Al Smith, had suffered a crushing defeat in 1928. Ironically, the issue of Kennedy's Catholicism was much more important to Protestants than it was to Catholics. Only about 11 percent of all Catholics said they liked Kennedy because he was a Catholic, but fully one-third of all Protestants made negative references to Kennedy for reasons of religion.[12]

We can safely conclude that Kennedy's religion damaged his candidacy seriously. Converse has estimated that this issue alone cost Kennedy some 2.2 percent of the vote, or about 1.5 million votes.[13] Fortunately for the Democrats, most of the loss came in the fundamentalist Protestant South, where the traditional Democratic lead more than overcame the disadvantage. Outside the South, where Catholics are more numerous, Kennedy gained slightly on the religious issue. This regional bias shows up in the electoral vote, where one estimate shows Kennedy *gaining* a net 22 electoral votes on the basis of his Catholicism, in spite of the loss in the popular vote.[14]

The year 1964 was one the Republicans would obviously like to forget. In part, Goldwater ran poorly because in his campaign he focused explicitly on a number of unpopular issues. On a more personal level, however, the public's image of Goldwater was heavily negative; he was nearly as much of an asset to the Democrats as was Johnson himself! Goldwater was depicted, fairly or not, as a trigger-happy, impulsive arch-conservative, a man who believed that "extremism in the defense of liberty is no vice."[15] To his slogan "In your heart you know he's right," disillusioned Republican moderates added, "Yes, far right."

Lyndon Johnson was no knight in shining armor, but he did have two powerful qualities. He was obviously experienced, and he bore the mantle of the nation's fallen hero, John Kennedy. No one who saw the "Camelot" film presented at the 1964 Democratic national convention in memory of Kennedy could doubt the influence of martyrdom on the electorate. These advantages made him the most powerful candidate the Democrats nominated during the entire 1952–1976 period.

The 1968 election was complicated considerably by the presence of a powerful third-party movement: the American Independents of George Wallace. I have reserved discussion of Wallace for a later section; for the moment let us concentrate on Humphrey and Nixon.

Eight years after his defeat at the hands of John Kennedy, and six years after his last try for public office, Richard Nixon still possessed considerable popularity. (He ran for governor of California in 1962. When he lost, he delivered his famous "you won't have Dick Nixon to kick around anymore" comment to the press.) His experience was undeniable, and he had earned the loyalty of Republican party leaders with his untiring work for his party during his years out of office. He began the campaign with a large lead, in spite of a definitely lukewarm reaction by the public to his vice-presidential choice, Spiro Agnew. He ran a cautious campaign, a strategy that in the end nearly let the Democrats slip in as he began to be perceived as "ducking the issues."[16] Even so, his candidacy meant a more than 2-percentage-point edge for the Republicans.

Hubert Humphrey, a man who had been a candidate for something nearly all his life, never really got his campaign off the ground. The Democrats had expected to nominate Lyndon Johnson and to win the election going away. They therefore scheduled their convention in late August, leaving only two months for the campaign. Vietnam changed their plans. Humphrey became the Democrats' standard-bearer after Johnson had withdrawn, the man who might have won—Robert Kennedy—had been killed, and Gene McCarthy had led the antiwar forces in a bitter struggle to prevent Humphrey from getting the nomination. Humphrey could never establish himself in the public's eye as a positive force. The net effect of this warm and capable human being on the vote was almost zero.

The 1972 election should remind us all how short our memories are. It seems impossible that as recently as this, Richard Nixon would have been seen as a strong and popular leader. Yet we have the fact that his candidacy represented about a 4 percent advantage for his party in that year. Most of this undoubtedly came from the edge enjoyed by any incumbent. The person who sits in the White House has a certain attractiveness simply because he's *been* President for four years. And, of course, Nixon had scored telling victories during his first administration, particularly his visit to Peking.

The Republican task in 1972 was aided considerably by the fact that the Democrats nominated a candidate who turned out to be very weak. The style of McGovern's campaign, while motivated by a desire for reform, gave the candidate a very bad image in the public's eye. Because McGovern and his closest aides made themselves completely accessible to the press, all the disputes, disagreements, and quarrels that inevitably crop up in a campaign were aired in public. Timothy Crouse, a newspaperman covering the campaign, viewed the situation in the following way:

> It is one thing for a candidate to see the press frequently and answer their questions honestly, which McGovern tried to do, thereby providing an admirable contrast to the reclusive Nixon. However, it is another thing for a campaign staff to talk openly about its problems, feuds, and discontents. That is the political equivalent of indecent exposure, and the McGovern staffers indulged in it with a relish that bordered on wantonness. While the Nixon people, by keeping their mouths tightly shut, managed to keep the lid on the largest political scandal in American history, the McGovern people, by blabbing, succeeded in making their campaign look hopelessly disorganized and irresponsible.[17]

In addition to projecting an image of disorganization and irresponsibility, an event during the campaign caused serious damage to the Democratic cause. This was the discovery that McGovern's running mate, Thomas Eagleton, had been treated on a number of occasions for mental exhaustion. McGovern first defended Eagleton, giving him his "1000 percent support," but within days dropped him from the ticket. This turnaround lowered McGovern's credibility considerably and sowed doubts in the minds of the voters about his ability to lead the nation. By election time, McGovern's candidacy had become almost as strong a pro-Republican force as was Nixon's.

The picture in 1976 returned much closer to normal. Even though he was the incumbent, Ford suffered from the fact that he had never been elected to a national office, and in the early part of the campaign he was widely depicted as clumsy and slow-witted by the media. The campaign itself featured the challenge from Ronald Reagan, spokesman for the conservative wing of the Republican party. Conservatives are outnumbered by moderates and liberals about two to one among Republican identifiers. However, crossover voting by conservative Democrats and Independents brought Reagan a number of critical primary victories in mid-campaign. The result was that when the Republican convention opened in August, neither Ford nor Reagan was sure of victory. Although Ford did manage to secure the nomination, the cost was high. His close brush with defeat in the convention damaged his image as a winner. He became vulnerable in the voters' eyes, no longer assured of reelection simply because he was the sitting President.

On the Democratic side, Carter's early anonymity was both his greatest strength and his greatest weakness. In January 1976, only 4 percent of all Democratic identifiers preferred him. However, this early position allowed Carter to run as a candidate who had no ties to the "mess in Washington." He could not be the target of the voters' frustrations about governmental mismanagement, corruption, or interference. Carter took full advantage of his position, stressing in his campaign his patriotism, his love of country and his intention to bring honesty and pride into government once more. By May, his early competition began to drop away, and he emerged as the clear favorite, with the support of over 40 percent of Democratic identifiers.

State caucuses and primaries had virtually assured Carter of the nomination more than a month before the convention, and the former governor of Georgia made good use of the time. He managed to iron out virtually all of the party's platform battles before the convention. This assured that the public would witness a party united behind a consensually endorsed candidate at its convention, in marked contrast to the two previous experiences.

Once the campaign against Ford began, Carter faced the task of proving he was "presidential timber." He faltered seriously in the early going with his *Playboy* interview, in which he admitted that he had "committed adultery in my heart many times." Later on, however, Carter made up some lost ground when Ford declared that the countries of eastern Europe were "independent, autonomous ... [and] ... are not under the domination of the Soviet Union," during the second televised debate. The result was to make Carter appear competent in the area of foreign affairs, which is typically where an incumbent President should have his greatest strength.

In the end, Carter influenced the popular vote less than 0.5 percent in the Democrats' favor in 1976. He was, however, perceived as a trustworthy, well-organized candidate and picked up much critical support from his home region, being the first southern major-party candidate for President since the Civil War. Ford's influence for his party's cause was stronger, giving about a 2 percent advantage to the Republicans. In spite of all else, he was the incumbent, and this fact outweighed his weaknesses.

Domestic Policy. With one or two exceptions, the impact of the electorate's attitudes on foreign and domestic policy reflects the old adage: "The Democrats are the party of prosperity and the Republicans are the party of peace." Or, put in another way, the Democrats always seem to be in office during wars, and the Republicans always seem to bring economic hard times.

Whatever the truth of this folk wisdom, we can see in Figure 12.3 that in the area of domestic policy, voters' attitudes generally favor the Democrats; that is, a Democratic candidate tends to be favored when social welfare issues are at stake.

In 1952 relatively little attention was paid to domestic policy. The Democrats had achieved notable success with the New Deal under Roosevelt and with Truman's Fair Deal in the late 1940s. The economic good times of that period carried into the election of 1952. The Democrats were generally credited by the voters for their domestic policies, as the nearly 4-point Democratic advantage in this area indicates.

Upon the election of Eisenhower, however, the perception of the electorate shifted, as the Republican administration had the good fortune to preside over a continuation of postwar prosperity. Times were good in 1956. The impact of the Democrats' claim to defend the interests of the little man was considerably muted by the fact that the little man had done rather well during Eisenhower's first term. The Democrats enjoyed only a slender advantage in the area of domestic policy in 1956.

The domestic debate in 1960 can best be described as foggy. Kennedy was fond of accusing the Republicans and Nixon of standing for the past, while proclaiming that he stood for the future. If there was any substance to the argument at all, it was the emphasis on a word, an optimism, and a willingness to sacrifice rather than on any specific domestic policies. Not surprisingly, the Democratic advantage in the domestic policy area was marginal in 1960.

The election of 1964 represents an important turning point in the role of issues, and particularly of domestic policy, in presidential elections. Goldwater's campaign stood out because it set out a number of explicit conservative positions on both domestic and foreign issues. Goldwater's willingness to take these stands appears foolhardy in the light of his defeat, but in fact the strategy fit in with Goldwater's view of the electorate. He believed that there existed in the electorate an invisible "army on the right." Through his reading of newspaper editorials and letters to the editor, he concluded that there were actually millions of conservatives

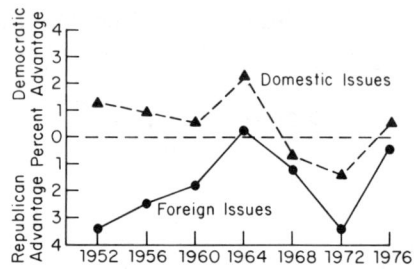

Figure 12.3. The Electoral Impact of Domestic and Foreign Policy Issue Attitudes, 1952–1976.

Source: Reprinted by permission of the publisher, from Michael Kagay and Greg Caldeira, "A 'Reformed' Electorate? Well, At Least, a Changed Electorate, 1952–1976." In the forthcoming book by William Crotty (ed.), *Paths to Political Reform*, to be published by Lexington Books, Lexington, Mass. Copyright © 1979, D. C. Heath and Company.

who had never voted before because *both* the major parties had always been too liberal.[18]

The silent majority to which Goldwater pitched his campaign never materialized, of course. The candidate was unsuccessful in convincing the electorate to accept his domestic policy. His speeches suggesting the sale of the TVA or the placing of Social Security on a private basis seemed frighteningly radical to many people. Lyndon Johnson countered this image with the Great Society, a sort of super New Deal centered on enormously expensive programs like the war on poverty. On balance, the Great Society idea persuaded many voters that the Democrats were more to be trusted in the domestic area.

The real significance of 1964 lies not in Goldwater's failure to get on the right side of the issues. Instead, 1964 turned out to be the last time the Democrats could successfully sell the New Deal. The economic interests of the working class, which had bound them to the Democratic Party since 1932, had begun to wane as many blue-collar workers began to find a degree of financial security and even prosperity. By 1964, the bread-and-butter economic planks in the Democratic platform were overshadowed by new forces on the domestic scene. The most fundamental of these was the "social issue." As discussed earlier, this combination of domestic concerns includes the racial question, the hippie movement, the decay of public morality, and the Vietnam protest movement.[19] Its central element, however, is fear, such as the fear of the white, middle-aged housewife in the suburbs of Dayton that she might be victimized by crime, or that a black family might move in next door, or that her children might follow the example of hippies in their school and start using drugs.

In 1964 the social issue emerged as the most important problem facing the nation, as reported by the Michigan survey of voters. In that year, such problems were on people's minds because of the buildup of activity in the area of civil rights. The social issue remained the most important domestic problem perceived by the voters until 1976. However, the composition of the concerns that are grouped under this label changed in important ways. By 1968 the major concern of Americans on the domestic front was public disorder, as well it might have been in the wake of the urban riots of the mid-1960s. On the scale of major problems, public disorder ranked after Vietnam and ahead of civil rights and poverty. Inflation and unemployment, the two traditional concerns in the economic area, were cited by fewer than 5 percent of the electorate.[20]

Perhaps the best illustration of the emerging importance of the social issue in 1968 was the American Independent party. The candidacy of George Wallace can be explained almost entirely in such terms.[21] Without it, Wallace could never have reached national prominence. Wallace's whole message was that there wasn't "a dime's worth of difference" between the two major parties. He offered the chance to "send them a message" by staking out a hard-line stance on different aspects of the social issue. For instance, his stand on protestors and demonstrators emerged in his statement: "The first anarchist who lies down in front of my automobile when I become President, that's the last automobile he'll ever want to lie down in front of."[22]

The hypothesis that Wallace's support came mainly from people who were worried about the social issue can be seen in the positions taken by those who voted for him. Among white supporters of Nixon and Humphrey, only 10 percent favored "strict segregation" as opposed to integration or something in between; among Wallace voters, nearly 40 percent chose strict segregation. In the area of law and order, the distinctive nature of the Wallace vote can be seen in its reaction to the rioting that took place at the Democratic convention in Chicago. Many people felt that Mayor Daley's police had used "about the right amount" of force in putting down the disturbance. Among the remainder, those who voted for Humphrey or Nixon split about 50–50 between the view that the police used too much force, and the view that they used too little force. When we look at Wallace voters, however, this remainder split 87–13 in favor of the tougher policy (87 percent said the police did not use enough force). On Vietnam, about 36 percent of the white voters for the two major candidates favored "taking a stronger stand even if it means invading North Vietnam." Fully two-thirds of Wallace's voters took that position. Finally, the idea that Wallace was an issue candidate is supported by the fact that a vote for Wallace was totally unrelated to party identification. Wallace drew as easily from among Republicans as Democrats.

However interesting the Wallace campaign may have been, it remains a sidelight in 1968. Richard Nixon won the election partly because he, as well as Wallace, was able to capitalize on the social issue. Nixon's wisdom lay in his ability to reassure the fearful that he would do something about crime, busing, drugs, and the rest. But just exactly what he would do he left unclear. He didn't talk about running over protestors as Wallace had. He therefore avoided frightening one part of the electorate by proposing extreme solutions, while leaving enough doubt in the minds of those who wanted extreme solutions to enable them to vote for him. Figure 12.3 illustrates the importance of the social issue quite nicely. It meant that, for the first time, the Democrats lost their traditional edge in the area of domestic policy.

The role of the electorate's attitudes on domestic policy in 1972 can be summed up rather briefly. Nixon and his people managed to tag McGovern as a domestic radical, the candidate of "acid, amnesty and abortion." McGovern didn't help himself much by making such ill-conceived proposals as the $1,000 grant to every American, and then waffling when the Republicans pointed out how much it would cost.

There was, however, a cloud on the 1972 horizon. The economy, which had failed to attract the concern of more than about 17 percent of the voters since 1960, slowly began to reappear. About as many people cited the economy as mentioned an aspect of the social issue (public order, social welfare, or race relations) in naming the most important problem facing the nation in 1972. Since the economy had not done badly during Nixon's first term, however, the Republicans continued to reap the benefit of good times. As a result of these various factors, for the second election in a row the Republicans' positions on domestic issues were more popular in the electorate than those of the Democrats.

As Figure 12.3 makes clear, 1976 restored the earlier pattern, in which the Democrats have benefited in the domestic issue area. The social issue, which had given the Republicans an unaccustomed advantage in 1968 and 1972, weakened greatly in 1976. Only about 12 percent of the electorate cited public order, race relations, or social welfare as "most important problems" in 1976, compared to 36 percent in 1968 and 28 percent in 1972. In addition to this, Ford and Carter took nearly identical positions on the potentially explosive issues of abortion and school busing. Such other issues as women's rights, the urban crisis, and marijuana were largely ignored.

The major reason for this lack of interest in social issues in 1976 was of course the recession of 1973-1974. Economic issues dominated the domestic scene in 1976, being cited by over 70 percent of the electorate as the nation's most critical problem. Income was eaten way by double-digit inflation while increasing unemployment swelled the relief rolls.

In this crisis the two parties fell back onto their traditional positions. The Republicans stressed the evils of inflation. Inflation, they claimed, destroys jobs and therefore the proper response for government is to eliminate the federal deficit by reducing the budget. Reductions are accomplished by tax cuts as well as the elimination of deficit spending. Tax cuts put more money into the hands of the producers, either directly or indirectly through the stimulating effect they have on purchases. These producers will then automatically solve the unemployment problem by hiring more workers to meet the increased demand for their products. At the same time, the elimination of deficit spending helps solve the inflation problem by limiting the total number of dollars in the economy. As the availability of goods increases and the dollars available to buy them become fewer, the pressure to increase prices is eliminated. Ford's consistent position throughout the campaign was to reduce federal spending and to ease regulations on business.

Carter and the Democrats also took a traditional position. Their central concern was with employment, harking back to the days of the New Deal when 25 percent of the work force was unemployed. The Democratic view of economics stated that by increasing employment, demand for products will increase, which will lead to the expansion of business to meet that demand. Putting people to work is the proper way to reduce federal spending and eliminate inflation. The Democrats were fond of pointing out that in 1976 unemployment cost $103 billion in expenditures and lost revenues. Each percent of the work force out of work, they argued in the party platform, costs $3 billion in unemployment compensation, $2 billion in welfare and related costs and $14 billion in potential taxes. Their position was that full employment should come first. Carter eventually endorsed the Humphrey-Hawkins full-employment bill, which proposed that the federal government guarantee each citizen the right to a job, provided that job is necessary.

Thus, the positions of the two parties on the most important issue of 1976 were quite distinct. And, reflecting the fact that there are more workers than producers in the United States, the advantage in the domestic area passed back to the Democrats after an eight-year lapse.

Foreign Policy. The dominant foreign policy issue of 1952 was Korea. The Truman administration was saddled with a war that, like Vietnam 15 years later, appeared to be a stalemate. Truman's disagreements with the extremely popular General MacArthur over the conduct of the war, which led to MacArthur's dismissal, did nothing to inspire public confidence in the Democrats' ability to conduct foreign policy. The Republicans on the other hand, struck gold with the nomination of General Eisenhower. He had been the supreme allied commander of the victorious allied armies in Europe only a few years earlier, and when he said he would "go to

Korea," the public's confidence that the end of the war would come with a Republican victory grew enormously. The Republican advantage of about 3½ percentage points in the foreign policy area was the largest margin observed during this entire 24-year period.

By 1956 the Republican position of strength in the area of foreign policy was well entrenched. The drama that Korea had generated in 1952 had subsided, since Eisenhower had concluded the hostilities. This explains the slightly reduced, but still solid, Republican advantage in this area. This success is reflected by a 35 to 1 GOP advantage in citizen comments on the issue of war and peace in 1956.[23]

Foreign policy concerns played a relatively small role in the 1960 election. When a sample of voters was asked to cite the most important problem facing the United States, no one issue was mentioned by more than 8½ percent of the electorate (that issue involved keeping the peace).[24] In general, the campaign centered around the rather meaningless argument about who would be tougher on the Russians. The Democrats came up with the "missile gap" to show that the Eisenhower administration had let America's position in the world deteriorate; after the election the missile gap mysteriously vanished.[25]

Goldwater's positions on foreign policy issues attracted no more support from the electorate than did his domestic platform in 1964. Vietnam had just begun to appear on the horizon, but Goldwater failed to capitalize on the traditional preference of the voters for Republican foreign policy, perhaps because of some careless remarks he made about putting control of nuclear weapons in the hands of field commanders. His image as trigger-happy and unstable led the voters to believe Johnson when he said he would keep American boys out of Vietnam. In 1964 we have the only instance in this whole series of elections in which foreign policy favored the Democrats.

Foreign policy in the two elections following 1964 meant just one thing: Vietnam. In 1968, 43 percent of the electorate thought Vietnam was our most important national problem and 25 percent still felt that way in 1972. Lyndon Johnson *had* sent troops to Vietnam, in spite of his 1964 promises. The United States was embroiled in an increasingly unpopular war.

In 1968 the candidates took similar positions on Vietnam during the campaign. They amounted to "advocacy of war as usual, with a rather gradual de-escalation of American effort if and when certain conditions were met."[26] Nonetheless, the party in power usually gets the blame when things go wrong. President Johnson halted the bombing of North Vietnam on October 31, 1968, about a week before the election. His goal was to get the Paris peace talks off the ground and give the Humphrey campaign a boost. Unfortunately, the South Vietnamese refused to go along. This demonstration that peace was not at hand may have cost Humphrey the election.[27]

The 1972 contest saw quite a different position taken on Vietnam by Nixon and McGovern. Nixon "defended his policy of extended negotiations and continued military intervention," and McGovern called for immediate withdrawal from Southeast Asia.[28] While public enthusiasm for the war was never very great, Nixon's position on the war was nonetheless closer to the bulk of public opinion.[29] With Henry Kissinger's dramatic, if somewhat premature, "peace is at hand" announcement before the 1972 election, the Republican edge in foreign policy climbed past 3 percent.

It comes as something of a surprise that the Republicans gained so little advantage from the foreign policy issue in 1976. The Nixon-Ford administrations had achieved remarkable success in this area, opening relations with the People's Republic of China, undertaking détente with the Soviet Union, and keeping the lid on the Middle East. Ford's image as a strong international leader gained some luster with his handling of the Mayaguez incident, and in his campaign he continually stressed that America was at last at peace.

In spite of all this, Americans felt a sense of uneasiness about international affairs. The Arab oil boycott had provided a dramatic and frightening example of America's vulnerability to forces beyond her borders. The strategic arms limitation talks with the Soviets were suspected of undermining U.S. security, and the role of Henry Kissinger's diplomacy was continually attacked by Carter as overly secretive, too independent of the President, and questionable on moral grounds.

Perhaps the best summary of the foreign policy area in 1976 would be to call it a standoff. Only one American in 20 felt that foreign policy was America's most important problem. Ford's natural advantage as an incumbent Republican was further diminished by the experience with the oil boycott and by the perception that it was really Kissinger, and not Ford, who possessed all the expertise. The Republicans enjoyed an edge of less than 0.5 percent in this area in 1976.

Party Performance. The attitudes held by the electorate in the area of party performance involve the perception of how well a party has done or might do in running the government. As you can see in Figure 12.4, the Republicans usually enjoy a slight edge in this department, perhaps because of the view among the voters that running the government must be something like running a large corporation and that businessmen tend to be Republican.

There have been three departures from the typical 1-to-2 point Republican advantage in this area over the past 24 years. In 1952 one of the charges made against the Truman administration was corruption. While Truman was in no way implicated in the misdeeds of a few subordinates and was not even the Democratic candidate, the feeling of mismanage-

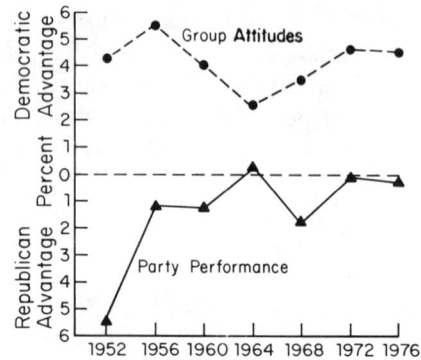

Figure 12.4. The Electoral Impact of Party Performance and Group Attitudes, 1952–1976.

Source: Reprinted by permission of the publisher, from Michael Kagay and Greg Caldeira, "A 'Reformed' Electorate? Well, At Least, a Changed Electorate, 1952–1976." In the forthcoming book by William Crotty (ed.), *Paths to Political Reform*, to be published by Lexington Books, Lexington, Mass. Copyright © 1979, D. C. Heath and Company.

ment by the Democrats stuck in the voters' minds. The result was a much larger than usual preference for Republican management.

The second exception came in 1964. This was clearly the result of a fear that if Goldwater was elected, he would wreak havoc on certain well-established federal programs, like Social Security. Johnson's candidacy also helped the Democratic reputation for good management, since he was known as a wily politician who could get along with Congress.

The third deviation in the pattern has stretched over both the 1972 and 1976 elections. In 1972 the reasons for the Republicans' failure to gain their accustomed advantage probably revolved around Vietnam. The foreign policy element of this issue was on the wane; that is, by 1972 the major concern was no longer "what to do" but "how to get out." Vietnam, in other words, had become an administrative problem, and the Republicans, month after month, proved themselves incapable of finding a way to stop American involvement in the war. Their reputations as managers was tarnished considerably.

In 1976 the source of the Republican weakness in the party performance area was obviously Watergate. The image of Nixon's coarse language and his contempt for other people—and perhaps even more, the stupidity of getting caught—seriously damaged the electorate's ability to view the Republican Party as good managers of government. Even though Nixon had been out of office for two years, the memories of corruption and illegal acts hurt Ford's campaign.

Group-Related Attitudes. The most consistently pro-Democratic attitude of this set of six comes from the association of that party with certain groups in society. Over the years the Democrats have benefited consistently from their identification as the party of the little man. By contrast, the Republicans have suffered from the identification with wealthy businessmen.

The Democratic gain from its group affiliations diminished somewhat during the early 1960s. Stokes concludes that this reflects the white electorate's hesitation with the Democrats' backing of the civil rights movement.[30] However, the restoration of the 4 or 5 percent advantage that had occurred by 1972 indicates that, *in principle,* the attachment of the Democrats to the civil rights movement has not diminished the party's popularity in the area of group identification. This view is simply reinforced by the 1976 figure, which shows the Democrats maintaining their accustomed strong advantage in this area.

SUMMARY

This chapter details how various attitudes influence turnout in elections and the partisan choice of the voter. The overall impression, I suspect, is that these behaviors are produced by an incredible tangle of motives, and that we should despair of ever finding clear-cut explanations. I admit this is true to some extent, but at the same time this is precisely what makes politics so fascinating. I do not admit, however, that we can never find patterns among the elements I have discussed in this chapter. Patterns—very regular and dependable patterns, in fact—do exist. They are the topic of Chapter 13.

NOTES

1. Raymond E. Wolfinger and Steven J. Rosenstone, "Who Votes?" Paper presented at the annual meeting of the American Political Science Association, Washington, D.C., September 1–4, 1977. This paper provides a thorough and up-to-date analysis of the determinants of turnout.

2. Walter Dean Burnham, "The Changing Shape of the American Political Universe," *American Political Science Review,* vol. 59, no. 1 (March 1965), 7–28; W. D. Burnham, "Theory and Voting Research: Some Reflections on Converse's 'Change in the American Electorate,'" *American Political Science Review,* vol. 68, no. 3 (September 1974), 1002–1023; W. D. Burnham, *Critical Elections and the Mainsprings of American Politics* (New York: Norton, 1970).

3. Philip E. Converse, "Change in the American Electorate," in A. Campbell and P. E. Converse (Eds.), *The Human Meaning of Social Change* (New York: Russell Sage, 1972), chap. 8.

4. *Ibid.,* p. 282.

5. This measure was originally developed in Angus Campbell, Gerald Gurin, and Warren E. Miller, *The Voter Decides* (New York: Harper & Row, 1954), Appendix A.

6. Morris Rosenberg, "Some Determinants of Political Apathy," *Public Opinion Quarterly*, vol. 18, no. 4 (Winter 1954–55), 349–366.

7. This measure was originally developed in Campbell, Gurin, and Miller, *op. cit.*, Appendix B.

8. Angus Campbell, Philip E. Converse, Warren E. Miller, and Donald E. Stokes, *The American Voter* (New York: J. Wiley, 1960).

9. William H. Flanagan and Nancy H. Zingale, *Political Behavior of the American Electorate*, 3d ed. (Boston: Allyn and Bacon, 1975), p. 50.

10. Donald E. Stokes, Angus Campbell and Warren E. Miller, "Components of Electoral Decisions," *American Political Science Review*, vol. 52, no. 2 (June 1958), 378.

11. Herbert Asher, *Presidential Elections and American Politics: Voters, Candidates and Campaigns Since 1952* (Homewood, Ill.: Dorsey, 1976), p. 147.

12. Cited from the SRC 1960 Presidential Study by Asher, *op. cit.*, pp. 147–151.

13. Philip E. Converse et al., "Stability and Change in 1960: A Reinstating Election," in A. Campbell, P. E. Converse, W. E. Miller, and D. E. Stokes, *Elections and the Political Order* (New York: J. Wiley, 1966), p. 92.

14. Ithiel de Sola Pool, Robert P. Abelson and Samuel Popkin, *Candidates, Issues and Strategies* (Cambridge, Mass.: M.I.T. Press, 1965), pp. 115–118.

15. Quoted from Goldwater's acceptance speech by Marvin R. Weisbord, *Campaigning for President* (New York: Washington Square Press, 1966), p. 421.

16. Rowland Evans and Robert Novak, "Inside Report," *Newark Sunday News*, October 27, 1968, p. C2.

17. Timothy Crouse, *The Boys on the Bus* (New York: Random House, 1973), pp. 340–341.

18. See Philip E. Converse, Aage R. Clausen, and Warren E. Miller, "Electoral Myth and Reality: The 1964 Election," *American Political Science Review*, vol. 59, no. 2 (June 1965), 321–336.

19. Richard M. Scammon and Ben J. Wattenberg, *The Real Majority* (New York: Coward-McCann, 1970), pp. 40–44.

20. SRC 1968 Presidential Election Study.

21. Philip E. Converse, Warren E. Miller, Jerrold G. Rusk, and Arthur C. Wolfe, "Continuity and Change in American Politics: Parties and Issues in the 1968 Election," *American Political Science Review*, vol. 63, no. 4 (December 1969), 1083–1104.

22. Quoted in Asher, *op. cit.*, pp. 177–178.

23. Campbell et al., *The American Voter*, *op. cit.*, p. 49.

24. SRC 1960 Presidential Election Study.

25. Asher, *op. cit.*, p. 153.

26. Benjamin E. Page and Richard A. Brody, "Policy Voting and the Electoral Process: The Vietnam War Issue," *American Political Science Review*, vol. 66, no. 3 (September 1972), 979–995.

27. Theodore H. White, *The Making of the President 1968* (New York: Atheneum, 1969), p. 447.

28. Gerald M. Pomper, *Voter's Choice: Varieties of American Electoral Behavior* (New York: Dodd, Mead, 1975), p. 189.

29. Arthur H. Miller, Warren E. Miller, Alden S. Raine, and Thad A. Brown, "A Majority Party in Disarray: Policy Polarization in the 1972 Election," *American Political Science Review*, vol. 70, no. 3 (September 1976), 753–778.

30. Donald E. Stokes, "Some Dynamic Elements of Contests for the Presidency," *American Political Science Review*, vol. 60, no. 1 (March 1966), 19–28.

13
The Voting Outcome: Attitudes Combined

You have no doubt noticed by this time that Democratic identifiers outnumber Republican identifiers in the electorate by almost a two-to-one margin. Yet since 1952 the Democrats have won the presidency only three times to the Republican's four. Clearly, something needs explaining here. The key to this mystery lies in a fact we discovered in the previous chapter. The vote is not simply the reflection of party identification. It is the product of the combination of two sets of attitudes: party identification, or the standing commitment, on the one hand and short-term forces on the other. The natural question to ask, then, is "How do these attitudes combine to produce the vote?"

THE COMBINATION OF PARTY IDENTIFICATION AND THE VOTE

In order to discuss how political attitudes combine to produce the vote, I want to present a slightly magnified portion of Figure 11.1. The arrows in this diagram represent influence, or a cause-and-effect relationship. You can readily see how the three sets of attitudes combine. Party identification is the central element. It has a direct influence on the vote, as we have seen. Its influence is also indirect, for it has an effect on how we perceive the issues and the candidates. These short-term forces (issues and candidates) both have a direct impact on the vote. In other words, a voter may vote for the man or on the basis of the issues and ignore his other attitudes. In addition, the issues may have an influence on how the candidates are perceived.[1]

Figure 13.1 remains a bit technical and remote. Fortunately, Kelley and Mirer have studied the processes by which these attitudes combine, and their description may be a bit easier to grasp.

> The voter canvasses his likes and dislikes of the leading candidates and major parties involved in an election. Weighing each like and dislike equally, he votes for the candidate for whom he has the greatest net number of favorable attitudes, if there is such a candidate. If no candidate has such an advantage, the voter votes consistently with his party affiliation, if he has one.[2]

This description may strike you as a little silly, being as simple as it is. But in simplicity there is virtue. The voting act for most Americans is not one they agonize over. People generally go to the polls, add up the pluses and minuses in a very uncomplicated way, and pull the lever.

The Kelley-Mirer approach has another virtue: It works. Applying their rule to the elections from 1952 to 1968, they could predict the vote more than 98 percent of the time. (That is, 98 percent of the people in the Michigan studies which were analyzed had either issue or candidate likes or dislikes, or had a party identification, or had some combination of these.) More impressively, however, these predictions were *right* 85 to 90 percent of the time between 1952 and 1968, slipping to 82 percent in 1968. Margolis has replicated the analysis for 1972 and found a 99 percent predictability rate, with 87 percent correct.[3]

Now we are beginning to get close to an understanding of how Republicans like Eisenhower and Nixon can be elected by an electorate whose party identification favors the Democrats. We can clarify the picture even further if we split the electorate into partisan groups: strong Democrat, weak Democrat, Independent, weak Republican, and strong Republican. The differences in the ways these groups react to short-term forces in different elections tell us much about the dynamics of the individual's vote decision.

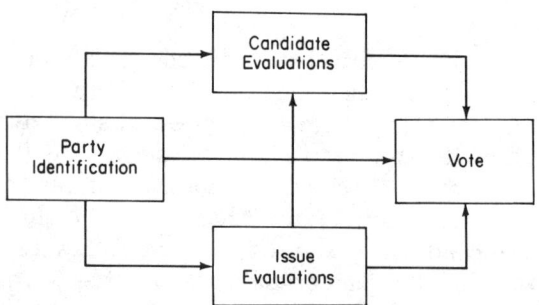

Figure 13.1. A Causal Model of the Vote Decision.

The Normal Vote

In order to illuminate these differences, we must have some way to separate the effects of short-term forces from those due to the standing commitment. This breakdown is provided by the normal vote. The normal vote is a concept originally proposed by Angus Campbell, who defined it as "the basic underlying division of standing commitments to the two parties."[4] Put in another way, it is the proportion of the vote *that would be cast* for the Republican candidate *if* short-term forces were not a factor. That is, it is the Republican proportion of the vote cast either if there are no short-term forces or if the short-term forces favoring the Democrats balance precisely with short-term forces favoring the Republicans. It is the vote motivated by party identification alone.

The Flow of the Vote

These ideas can be most effectively discussed by means of a set of diagrams.[5] In the first instance we have a hypothetical election in which short-term forces balance out. In Figure 13.2 the position of the arrows on the bottom line represents the vote as it would be produced by the party identification, or standing commitment, motive alone. The fact that all the arrows stand directly upright illustrates the idea that the standing commitment is not at all deflected in either a pro-Republican or a pro-Democratic direction when the vote decision is made. Short-term forces have had no effect in this case. The position of the arrows along the upper line represents the actual vote, and as you can see, these are identical to the vote expected from party identification alone. This is the normal vote.

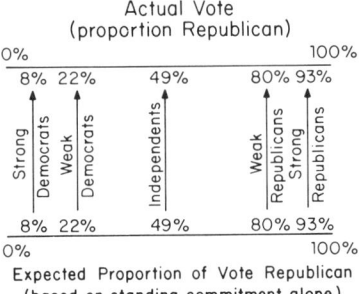

Figure 13.2. The Vote of Party Identification Groups When No Short-Term Forces Are Present or Short-Term Forces Are Balanced.

Source: Adapted from Philip E. Converse, "The Concept of the Normal Vote," in Angus Campbell et al., *Elections and the Political Order* (New York: Wiley, 1966), pp. 17 and 27. Copyright © 1966 by John Wiley & Sons, Inc. Reprinted by permission of John Wiley & Sons, Inc. The expected vote proportions are calculated for the 1964–1976 period from parameters supplied by Arthur H. Miller of the University of Michigan.

In Figure 13.3 I have used this kind of diagram to display what actually happened in three recent presidential elections. Look first at the 1956 election. This was a case of strong pro-Republican short-term forces. Notice especially the different reactions of the partisan groups. While the vote of each group is deflected in the Republican direction, the groups least affected are the strong partisans. Of course, this is the consequence of the fact that strong partisans hold their party identification attitude most intensely. It is therefore less easily changed by the new information provided during the course of the campaign.

Since weak partisans hold their loyalty to party less intensely than strong partisans, they are more prone to be affected by short-term forces. As you can see, weak Democrats were deflected 19 points in the Republican direction in 1956, from an expected vote of 18 percent to an actual vote of 37 percent. Weak Republicans became 9 points more Republican than their loyalty would have predicted, moving from 84 percent to 93 percent.

Independents, without any standing commitment, are motivated totally by short-term forces.[6] In 1956, the vote of 51 percent, which would have been expected to occur in the absence of short-term forces, was deflected to a 73 percent Republican vote. As a rule of thumb, the role of short-term forces in any election can be gauged roughly by looking at the vote of the Independents. We know that in a balanced year their vote will split about 50-50 between the Republicans and the Democrats. So when we see a 10- or 20-point deviation in favor of one party or the other, we have an immediate sense of the flow of short-term forces in that particular campaign.

The second part of Figure 13.3 presents the 1964 election, in which the Democrats enjoyed very strong short-term forces in their favor. You can easily observe that the pattern is almost exactly like the one above it except that the flow of the vote is in the opposite direction. Most stable are the strong partisans, followed by the weak partisans, and then the Independents. (Goldwater apparently offended large numbers of weak Republicans, because in this year they reacted even more to short-term forces than did the Independents.)

The election of 1976 is truly remarkable for it is one of those rare cases in which short-term forces were nearly evenly balanced. There were advantages on both sides: Ford was the incumbent, a fact that often enhances the credibility of a campaign, and Carter was a Southerner, a fact that allowed him to redeem the heavy losses in that region suffered by the Democrats in the three previous presidential elections. Although short-term forces existed, on the whole the low turnout rate reflected an election that lacked the passion of either a burning issue or a charismatic leader. The result was a fairly even balancing of short-term forces, and a vote that fairly accurately reflected the party loyalties of the electorate.

This model of the interrelationship between party loyalty, short-term forces, and the vote helps us to understand a problem which I mentioned

THE VOTING OUTCOME: ATTITUDES COMBINED   263

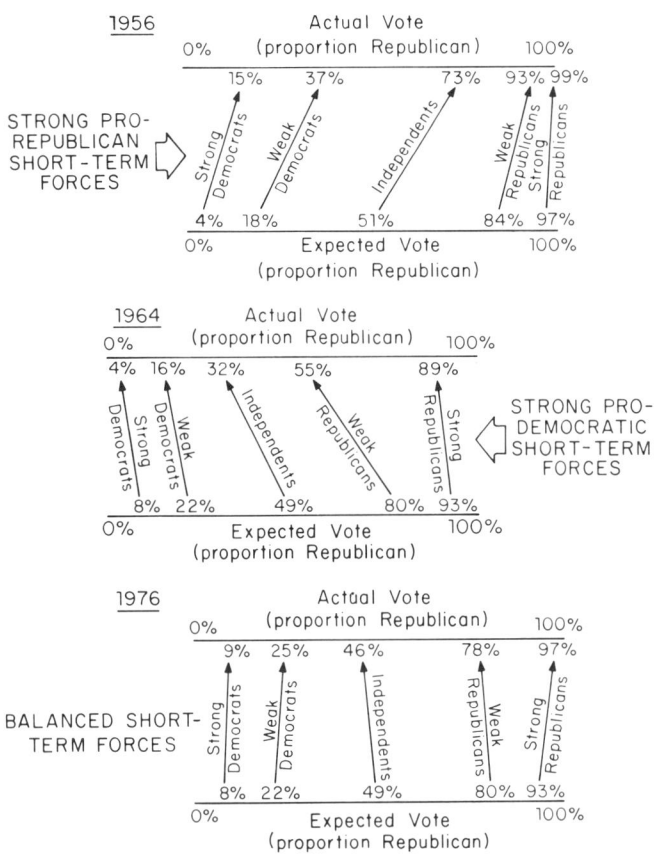

Figure 13.3. The Vote of Party Identification Groups When Different Types of Short-Term Forces Are Present.

Source: Adapted from Philip E. Converse, "The Concept of the Normal Vote," in Angus Campbell et al., *Elections and the Political Order* (New York: Wiley, 1966), pp. 17 and 27. Copyright © 1966 by John Wiley & Sons, Inc. Reprinted by permission of John Wiley & Sons, Inc. The expected vote proportions are calculated for the 1964–1976 period from parameters supplied by Arthur H. Miller of the University of Michigan.

a moment ago. How, considering that they are outnumbered by Democratic identifiers nearly two-to-one, do the Republicans ever win a presidential election? Obviously the answer is in the play of short-term forces. The Republicans can and do win, but only when short-term forces are running strongly in their favor. (They also enjoy an advantage arising from their higher turnout rates.) The Democrats, on the other hand, do not need such an advantage. Their numerical superiority means that they will win when short-term forces are balanced and can even prevail in the face of mildly pro-Republican short-term forces. Kennedy's victory in 1960 is an excellent example of the case where Democratic partisanship overcame a Republican advantage in attitudes about the candidate.

The diagrams in Figures 13.2 and 13.3 illustrate a second point that I made when I discussed the impact of political campaigns: the central importance of the Independents in the determination of the outcome of an election. No matter how strong the short-term forces, the strong partisans deviate only a few percentage points one way or the other. The votes that swing an election one way or the other come from the center. The Republicans know that to win they must bring these votes to their side.

Issue Voting

Once we have concluded that the vote is produced by a combination of factors the natural question that comes up is *which* of the factors is most important. This question has a number of aspects and deserves our attention for a moment. Classical democratic theory tells us that the citizen in a democracy should be able to make wise and informed choices between candidates competing for office. He should know his own stand on the issues of the day and should pick his preferred candidate on the basis of

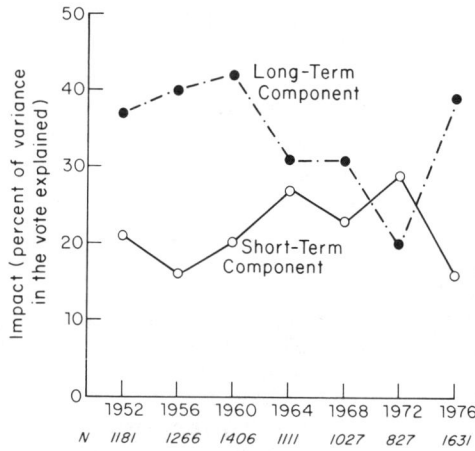

Figure 13.4. The Relative Impact of Party Identification and Short-Term Forces on the Presidential Vote, 1952–1976.

Source: Reprinted by permission of the publisher, from Michael Kagay and Greg Caldeira, "A 'Reformed' Electorate? Well, At Least, a Changed Electorate, 1952–1976." In the forthcoming book by William Crotty (ed.), *Paths to Political Reform*, to be published by Lexington Books, Lexington, Mass. Copyright © 1979, D. C. Heath and Company.

the candidate's positions on those issues. In the early days of the Republic, political parties were thought to threaten democracy, precisely because they sought to substitute party loyalty for the thoughtful evaluation of the issues proposed by the theorists.

Of course, in contemporary America, precisely what our forebears feared has come to pass. Many voters do no more than pull the party lever. Some do not even know the names of the candidates. In recent years, however, there have been signs that the American electorate is becoming less dependent on party loyalty, and more sensitive to the issues, as it chooses its elected representatives. Some evidence of such a trend has been gathered by Kagay and Caldeira.[7] Their findings are summarized in Figure 13.4.

This figure shows that the importance of party identification as a force motivating the vote did decline markedly between 1960 and 1972. As the short-term component (issues and candidates) increased in importance, the American electorate passed through a period of three elections in which short-term forces rivaled party loyalty as a source of the vote choice, finally moving past party loyalty to become the more important source in 1972.

You can easily understand how scholars, studying these data in 1973 or 1974, would have been led to conclude that a major change was coming about in the nature of the voting act. This electorate was seen to be throwing off the yoke of party loyalty and liberating its powers of intellect in a new surge toward a consideration of what really mattered in politics: the candidates and the issues.

This was a very exciting period for political scientists, who thought they were witnessing the birth of a new breed of voters. The results for 1976, however, deflated that hope almost totally. In the latter year the reliance that voters placed on the issues and candidates in making up their minds how to vote fell to the lowest level since 1952. At the same time, the importance of party identification rose markedly to levels similar to those of the 1950s. What this pattern suggests is the operation of the dynamic equilibrium process. When issues are on the voters' minds, as in 1964, 1968, and 1972, they tend to displace party loyalties as the source of the vote. When an election is relatively free of issues, as in the 1950s and again in 1976, the underlying importance of party identification will reemerge.

DIRECTIONS IN THE ELECTORATE

In the second half of this chapter, I am going to shift focus a bit from the individual voting decision, which has held our attention up to this point, to the electorate as a whole. In particular, I want to look at the shifts in the partisanship of the electorate over the past 24 years, and the question of partisan realignment that has attracted so much attention recently. Once again, the normal vote concept proves most useful in illustrating the important patterns.

Patterns of Partisanship

Table 13.1 presents the actual vote for each presidential election since 1952, along with the normal vote. The short-term force component, by definition, is the difference between the actual vote and the normal vote. In this case, I have calculated the normal vote as the expected proportion Democratic of the two-party vote.

There are two patterns in this table which are particularly worthy of mention. First, look at the normal vote. The stability of this indicator is absolutely amazing. From a mean of about 55½ percent Democratic, the average variation from election to election over these 24 years is less than 1 percent.

The second pattern involves the short-term forces. All but one of them is negative. This means that in every year but 1964 the Democrats did less well than party identification alone would have led us to expect. In other words, short-term forces have favored the Republicans with enormous

TABLE 13.1. Actual Vote, Normal Vote, and Short-Term-Force Component of the Vote in Presidential Elections, 1952–1976

Year	Actual Vote[a] (% Democratic)	Normal Vote (% Democratic)	Short-Term-Force Component[b] (Difference)
1952	44.6	56.3	−11.7
1956	42.2	54.0	−11.8
1960	50.1	55.7	−5.6
1964	61.3	58.2	3.1
1968	49.6	55.9	−6.3
1972	38.2	53.9	−15.7
1976	51.1	54.2	−3.1

Sources: Actual vote: 1952–1972: Herbert Asher, *Presidential Elections and American Politics* (Homewood, Ill.: Dorsey, 1976), p. 34; 1976: *Congressional Quarterly Weekly Report*, vol. 34, no. 45 (November 6, 1976), p. 3118. Normal vote: Calculated from SRC/CPS 1952–1976 Presidential Election Studies. Parameters for the 1952–1960 period are from Philip E. Converse, "The Concept of a Normal Vote," in Angus Campbell, et al., *Elections and the Political Order* (New York: Wiley, 1966), chap. 2. Parameters for the 1964–1976 period were provided by Arthur H. Miller of the University of Michigan.

[a] Percentage of the two-party vote.
[b] A negative number indicates a pro-Republican short-term force.

consistency. Even the victories of Kennedy and Carter came in the face of mild pro-Republican short-term forces.

What, then, do we make of all this? In 1960 it was fairly easy to look at the two Eisenhower elections and think of them as exceptions. We can explain them in terms of the strong pro-Republican short-term forces which were generated by the sheer attractiveness of the candidate. Even the 1960 election can be seen as a temporary deviation from a basically pro-Democratic pattern, which was produced by Kennedy's religion. But now, from the post-1976 perspective, we have a string of seven elections, six of which show pro-Republican short-term forces. It becomes more and more difficult to assume that these deviations have been produced by idiosyncratic factors that are new and unique with each election. Instead, it seems impossible to avoid the thought that there is some dynamic that is acting in some consistent way on the electorate to produce those short-term forces in election after election.

The puzzle of the strong pro-Republican short-term forces has attracted the attention of numerous scholars. Some of them have looked at tables like the one above and arrived at a number of rather radical conclusions about the future shape of the American electorate. One of the more popular predictions involves a basic realignment of party strength. That is, it expects that the Republican Party will again become the majority party, as it was before 1932.[8] Another projection foresees a time when parties lose their place in American politics altogether, and voters make their decisions without any sense of party identification.[9] This outcome has often been called "dealignment." However these arguments are couched, they all revolve around one group: the Independents.

The Increasing Importance of Independents

The figures in Table 13.1 suggest that party identification has remained virtually unchanged over the past 24 years. Compared to most other political attitudes, this is certainly true. Nevertheless, in recent years we have seen a steady alteration in the partisan profile of the electorate which the calculation of the normal vote conceals. This alteration, as we have already discovered, involves the Independents. In Table 13.2 it can be seen that between 1964 and 1976 the number of Independents increased by more than 50 percent, to a point where about one person in three refuses to claim a loyalty to either of the major parties.

Let us consider for a moment the question of what this can be expected to do to the vote. Remembering how party identification and short-term forces combine, the more numerous the Independents the more important will short-term forces be in determining the party choice. This means two things. First, we are likely to see greater instability in the partisan division of the vote. Nixon's 1972 victory was the second largest in history,

TABLE 13.2. Proportion of the Electorate Claiming an Independent Party Identification, 1952–1976

	1952	1956	1960	1964	1968	1972	1976
Pure Independents	5%	9%	8%	8%	11%	13%	15%
All Independents[a]	22	24	23	23	29	35	36
N (total):	(1614)	(1772)	(3021)	(1571)	(1531)	(2659)	(2824)

Source: ICPSR Archive: SRC/CPS Presidential Election Studies, 1952–1976.
[a] Includes Independents leaning toward the Democrats or the Republicans.

and was easily the largest ever scored by a candidate of the minority party (that is, the party with the fewer identifiers).

The second result is the advantage that large numbers of Independents present to third parties. The presence of millions of people in the electorate who have rejected allegiance to either of the major parties must constitute a huge temptation for politicians. How easy it is to think that all one has to do is send the right message to those millions, and the White House could be the prize. That is a far more difficult task than many may think, and in 1968 not even George Wallace could come close. But here the feeling lingers that sooner or later those Independents will find a cause around which they can rally.

Where do these new Independents come from? Partly, they are the youth of the electorate. The inclusion of 18-, 19-, and 20-year olds, which first occurred in 1972, brought millions of young voters into the electorate. Since the youngest voters are the least likely to identify with a party, some of the increase in independence can be attributed to that source. To the extent that this is true, we can expect the proportion of the electorate that considers itself to be Independent to decrease over the years as these voters mature and begin to establish partisan loyalties.[10] However, it seems clear that the increase measured in Table 13.2 goes far beyond anything produced by the 18-year-old vote. Many of these new Independents are adults who were formerly identifiers with one or the other of the two major parties.

There is some evidence that the lack of loyalty to party that characterizes the young may be overtaking older partisans as well as the years pass. Table 13.3 shows that during the 1950s desertion rates among strong partisans ran around 4 percent. That is, about one strong partisan in 25 would vote for the other party in a presidential election. In the 1960s, those desertion rates doubled. There was one desertion for every 12 or 14 strong partisan votes during this decade. And the desertion rates among weak partisans increased to the point where one vote in every five was for the opposite party.

The data from the 1970s should be taken with a grain of salt, because one of the two elections was the Nixon landslide. Nevertheless, these

TABLE 13.3. Defection Rates for Strong and Weak Partisan Identifiers

	Strong Democrats	Weak Democrats	Weak Republicans	Strong Republicans
1950s	4.3%	18.2%	16.2%	3.7%
1960s	8.0	22.4	19.6	7.2
1970s	17.8	38.3	15.5	3.2

Source: 1950s and 1960s: Arthur H. Miller et al., "A Majority Party in Disarray: Policy Polarization in the 1972 Election," *American Political Science Review*, vol. 70, no. 3 (September 1976), 753–788; 1970s: ICPSR Archive: CPS Presidential Election Studies, 1972 and 1976.

figures document a continuing decay in the loyalty of Democratic identifiers. Well over a third of the weak Democrats deserted to the Republican side in these elections, and more than one strong Democrat in six cannot be counted on to vote for his party.

On the Republican side, the Nixon victory in 1972 did wonders for the loyalty of the rank and file. Their rates of desertion fell below those recorded in the 1950s. However, if we look only at 1976, we find that 22 percent of the weak Republicans deserted to Carter, compared to only a 9 percent desertion rate to McGovern in 1972.

Overall, these figures suggest that among every partisan group, except perhaps strong Republicans, party identification exercises a weaker influence on the vote with each passing decade. This trend was violated in 1976, however, as party loyalties reemerged as the dominant element of the vote choice. Whether this single election allows us to conclude that the trend has been reversed remains problematic. We must still recognize the impact that the increasing numbers of voters with no party loyalty at all will have on the vote, which suggests that we may well be entering a period of great electoral instability.

The Prospects for Realignment

The different things we have discovered about the electorate, the increasing number of Independents, the increasing importance of issues and candidates, and the increasing desertion rates among partisans all suggest one thing. The stability of the presidential vote in the electorate, which arose from the presence of party identification as the dominant influence, must be lessening. If this is true, then we immediately begin to wonder whether the shape of the American political universe is going to change —and if so, how. You may remember our discussion a bit earlier, where the decline in turnout in the electorate was attributed by Burnham to an increased cynicism about politics, a feeling that participation doesn't do any good anyway, so why bother.[11] This argument also has relevance as far as party identification is concerned. If Burnham's thesis is correct, people are turning away from party loyalty for the same reasons they are failing to vote at all; the parties simply don't represent their interests anymore. This notion has enjoyed considerable popularity in recent years. Burnham has extended his argument to conclude that if the parties cannot realign themselves to represent the electorate more effectively, then the electorate will simply begin to ignore parties in its voting decisions. He predicts a partyless society, the logical outcome of the process of dealignment.

While dealignment is popular as a prediction of the future, I don't think it will happen, for two reasons. In the first place, Burnham's whole thesis rests on one basic assumption: that the electorate has certain policy preferences, that it attempts to vote for a party because of the belief that the party will fight for those policy preferences, and finally, that if the party fails, the voter will turn away and vote for a different party the next time.

Analysis by RePass does indeed suggest that something like this is happening in the electorate.[12] Specifically, he shows that where voters have strong issue orientations (issues that they say are "on their minds a lot" or cause them "extreme worry"), and when they can see a different between the parties, they will vote for the party that matches their issue preference. In 1964, out of about 1500 people in the SRC sample, there were five strong Democrats with high Republican issue orientations. They all voted Republican. Similarly, 22 of 30 weak or strong Democrats with medium or high Republican issue orientation voted Republican. And 14 of the 18 weak or strong Republicans with medium or high Democratic issue orientation voted Democratic.

Beyond any doubt, this is issue voting. But RePass's conclusions are misleading because of the small number of voters who have strong issue orientations, who know the parties' positions on these issues, *and* whose party identification conflicts with their issue orientations. There were only 48 such voters out of a total of 1500 in the 1964 sample. Issue voting, by RePass's definition, involved only about 3 percent of the electorate in that year.

Thus, it appears that the assumption that the electorate as a whole votes according to its policy preferences cannot be confirmed from this evidence.[13] This is not to say that there is no relationship between what happens in society and the electoral fortunes of the political parties. It simply says that *specific* issues do not move many voters. It leaves open the possibility of a broad and gut-level kind of reaction by voters to events. Good times and bad times, war and peace, the issue of corruption in government or desegregation in the South move the electorate from one party to the other. But I would hesitate to call this issue voting.

My conclusion that few voters look to their parties to execute certain specific policies leaves us with an uncomfortable feeling. If parties don't perform issue-related functions, then why do the voters bother with party loyalty at all? To what are they loyal? The answer to this question arises very directly from our original discussion of attitudes. Attitudes perform functions for us, and party loyalty is no different. Voters have a sense of partisanship because it *serves* them to do so. People have a need for order and understanding in their world; they seek to adopt certain viewpoints, certain attitudes, that will do this. At best, politics is a terribly confusing business. The possession of some organizing principle becomes vitally important for anyone who wants to make sense of it all. (Of course, there are those who solve the problem by paying no attention to politics whatsoever.) We have discussed earlier how a sense of partisanship serves as an extremely efficient organizer. The voter has merely to label an incoming stimulus as "Democratic" or "Republican." He then compares that evaluation with his own sense of partisanship; if they match, he evaluates the stimulus positively. If they do not match, he evaluates it negatively.

Now clearly, there is more to political thinking than this. My point is that at a very basic and important level, party identification is *useful.* So long as this is true, it will remain a central political attitude.

The preceding paragraphs lead us to conclude that we can probably reject dealignment as predictive of the future. But what about realignment—a major and lasting shift in the strength of the two parties? The jury is still out on that one, but one thing seems clear: Realignment is certainly a possibility.

The most obvious reason to suspect a realignment is the huge number of Independents that presently exists. A little arithmetic tells us that if about one-half of those Independents were to decide to become Republicans, the Republicans would take over as the largest party in the electorate.

Whether this will happen will depend on events. However, the prospects for realignment get stronger with every passing year. This is true because, as you know, partisanship is rooted in socialization, and the socialization experiences of the electorate have changed dramatically over the years.[14] The Great Depression and the New Deal essentially divided the electorate into three groups. Those who had completed their socialization by 1929 (that is, those born around the turn of the century and before), form one group. As we have seen, this is a relatively Republican group, but today these people are in their seventies and eighties and are no longer a strong political force.

The second group contains those who were socialized into politics during the depression (those who were born between about 1905 and 1923). For these people, politics was terribly important because of the critical atmosphere of that period. What the government did or did not do was vital to the welfare of millions of Americans. The outcome of this experience was to create a majority of Democrats. But more than this, it created voters with extremely strong and durable party loyalties. Today, these people are in their mid-fifties to mid-seventies.

The third group is the cohort which Beck calls "ripe for realignment." These individuals were born after 1923, and therefore had no direct experience with the Depression. (The oldest members of this group would have been six when the stock market crashed.) They were insulated by their youth from the sense of urgency and the fierce political loyalties that were produced during that period. The "glue" holding them to their party loyalty is therefore a good deal weaker than that of their elders. In part, the increase in the number of Independents can be attributed to this difference in socialization experience.

Yet a fourth group of voters has begun to enter the electorate during the 1970s. These will be people whose *parents* had no direct experience with the Depression. They are twice as insulated from the effects that period had on partisanship. Presumably they will have even less reason to maintain a party loyalty passed on to them through parental socialization and will be even freer to shift their allegiance.

In sum, the turnover of the generations contains within it forces that weaken party loyalties. However, this weakening does not guarantee realignment. An electorate ripe for realignment must still *be* realigned by some force that pushes loyalties from one party to the other. On the whole, no such forces have yet emerged on the political scene.[15] Not even Vietnam or Watergate, as serious as they were, caused much net change. These issues were too clouded, and neither party could claim to be on the "right" side, thereby attracting converts.

At the national level, therefore, we must simply wait and see what happens. However, in one region of the country, realignment has taken place already, and may provide a model for the rest of the country. That region is the South.

Realignment in the South

From the beginning of this century until about 1948, the Democratic Party dominated southern politics. So complete was this dominance that the "Solid South" was, in effect, a one-party system. Since the Truman campaign of 1948, however, the Solid South has slowly crumbled until, in 1972, the Democratic Party did not win a single electoral vote in the region.

This shift in electoral success can also be traced in the normal vote of the region. Table 13.4 gives the actual and normal votes for the South since 1952.[16]

TABLE 13.4. Actual Vote, Normal Vote and Short-Term Force Component of the Vote in Presidential Elections in the South, 1952–1976

Year	Normal Vote (Percent Democratic)	Actual Vote (Percent Democratic)	Impact of Short-Term Forces[a]
1952	71.7	50.2	−21.2
1956	67.5	46.6	−20.9
1960	62.1	49.9	−12.2
1964	70.6	52.9	−17.7
1968[b]	68.6	47.4	−21.2
1972	59.3	30.5	−28.8
1976	58.7	54.7	−3.1

Source: Bruce A. Campbell, "Change in the Southern Electorate," *American Journal of Political Science*, Vol. 21, no. 1 (February 1977), 37–64. Table appears on p. 43. Reprinted by permission of the University of Texas Press. 1976 data are from the CPS 1976 Presidential Election Study.

[a] A negative number indicates that the short-term forces favor the Republicans.

[b] In 1968 the Democratic percent of the two-party vote was used because of the biasing effect of Wallace's candidacy. If the total vote (Wallace included) is used, the percent Democratic of the total vote was 33.0%, giving an impact of −35.6 attributed to short-term forces.

This table displays even more clearly a pattern that was suggested by the nationwide data in Table 13.1. Two related phenomena can be identified here. First, we see an uninterrupted period of strong and unrelenting pro-Republican short-term forces. The only exception is the most recent election, when native son Jimmy Carter managed to offset most of the Republican advantages.

The second, and possibly more interesting, change involves the normal vote. While the normal vote has held steady at the national level, the same is not true of the South. Beginning with the remarkable score of 71.7 percent expected Democratic vote in 1952, by 1976 the figure had dropped to 58.7 percent.

Obviously, these juxtaposed patterns suggest that there is a relationship between the two phenomena. Specifically, we must ask whether the source of change in party loyalties (reflected in the normal vote) is not the consequence of an increasing pressure of short-term forces. This, I hasten to point out, is a rather radical idea. In Figure 13.1 you learned that party identification is the taproot of the vote decision. The issues and candidates might deflect it from time to time, but this basic standing commitment should be counted upon to reemerge in election after election, moving the voter to behave in the same way time and again. Moreover, we have seen the theoretical basis of the expectation: the grounding of party loyalties in childhood socialization, which produce an attitude of almost unshakable stability.

274 ATTITUDES IN ACTION: POLITICAL PARTICIPATION

Now we discover that party loyalties are perhaps not entirely unchanging. Party loyalties may be stable enough to withstand an Eisenhower or a Watergate every so often. But for some reason, in every election in the South for over 20 years there seem to have been persuasive reasons to vote for the Republicans. Over that long period, it makes sense to think that even the staunchest Democrat would begin to feel that perhaps loyalty had been misplaced.

To investigate the possibility that the short-term forces have altered partisanship, we need to find out what, specifically, the short-term forces have been over this period. In order to do that, I have divided the electorate into whites and blacks, since the political experience of the two races differs so tremendously, as shown in Figure 13.5.

Consider first the case of southern blacks.[17] During the Eisenhower years, blacks were even more Republican than whites, reflecting the old Civil War division of the electorate. The major shift in the partisanship of this group occurred in 1964 when blacks abruptly became far more Democratic than whites. In a very real way, the election of 1964 was for southern blacks what the Depression was for Americans generally. For the first time, one of the major parties took a strong position in favor of civil rights, while the other party was perceived to favor the white supremacists. (Senator Goldwater's vote against the 1964 Civil Rights Act is probably the most well-known vote ever cast by a Senator.) Black opinion was crystallized by Lyndon Johnson. It suddenly became clear that it was the Democratic party that would defend black interests. The result was a tremendous shift, both by black Republicans who became Democrats, and by previously apolitical blacks who also adopted a Democratic loyalty.

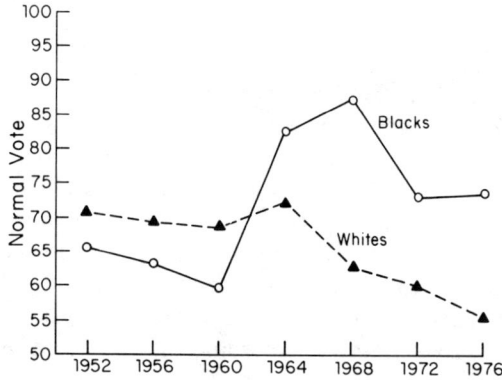

Figure 13.5. Normal Vote of Southerners by Race, 1952–1976.

Source: ICPSR Archive: SRC/CPS Presidential Election Studies.

(The proportion of southern blacks who gave no partisan identification—Democrat, Republican, or Independent—dropped from 32 percent in 1956 to 6 percent in 1964.)

This assumption that shifts in black partisanship were related to civil rights between 1960 and 1964 can be tested by looking separately at those blacks who felt neutral or negative about federal involvement in integration and those who were strongly in favor of such involvement. Of those few who were neutral or negative, the normal vote shifted slightly in the *Republican* direction from 1960 to 1964. For the vast majority who favored involvement, the normal vote shifted nearly 40 points toward the Democrats, from about 46 to 84! In sum, we can conclude that the general issue of integration and civil rights has been primarily responsible for shifts in southern black partisanship.

White partisanship does not yield so easily to explanation. The first thing we can observe about white change is how smooth and continuous it has been over the past 24 years. Only the Johnson-Goldwater campaign reversed the slow, steady trend of southern whites away from their traditional Democratic loyalties.

The fact that change in white partisanship takes this slow, continuous form does tell us something about the forces that have produced it, however.[18] Specifically, it is not likely that a single controversy like civil rights, no matter how broad, could have brought it about.[19] Rather, this type of change is created by forces that act continuously, at about the same level of magnitude, over long periods of time. The civil rights excitement of 1964 and 1968, which so profoundly affected blacks, had only a passing influence on white partisanship.

For whites, the forces of change have not been unique and identifiable events. They have arisen instead from the increasing strain between the policies of integration and federal power that the national Democratic Party had come to support, and the attitudes of many southern whites, which opposed those policies. I am speaking here not of any particular issue but rather of disagreement in basic philosophy, which has been building in many ways over a number of years. This "philosophical estrangement," based on the voters' opposition to federal interference of all kinds at the state level, and abetted by the migration into the region of many northern Republicans, has brought about the slow transfer of party loyalty away from the Democrats.

The shift in white Southerners' party loyalties will not cease, therefore, until the imbalance brought on by these individuals' rejections of the liberalism of the national Democratic party has been removed. Partly, the Democratic party may help to resolve the imbalance by backing away from some of its more liberal positions (on school busing, for instance). But ultimately, the imbalance will be resolved when the most conservative voters have abandoned the Democrats and have become Republicans.

1952–1976: An Electorate in Transition?

Not only in the South, but across the country, the increasing numbers of Independents indicates that voters are coming unglued from their earlier sense of party loyalty. In broad terms, this is happening for two reasons. The first is that the young people in the electorate are by now two generations removed from the experience of the Depression. The urgency of party loyalty that their parents or grandparents knew during that period has been largely forgotten. Partisanship for the young has, when it exists, become simply a habit, unrelated to the questions of economic survival.

The second reason for the decrease in partisanship has to do with the changing nature of society. In Chapter 12 we discussed how the basis of political debate was primarily economic before about 1964. Between 1964 and 1972, however, the "social issue"—the fear of crime, the breakdown of morality, drugs, integration, and all the rest—captured the voters' attention. The problem is that neither party has been able to shift out of its old economically oriented alignments to provide comfort for those millions of voters who now want redress not for economic needs but in the area of the social issue. Many blue-collar workers, for instance, who were once staunch supporters of the Democratic Party on economic grounds, view with great alarm the open association between the Democrats and all manner of outgroups: hippies, women's libbers, and blacks, for instance. They voted for Wallace in 1968 and for Nixon in 1972. On the other hand, the college-educated, who were once solidly in the Republican camp because of their connections with business and the professions, are beginning to reject the identification of the Republican as the servant of big business. Their concerns with social reform, pollution, and the environment have turned many of them toward the Democrats.

However, these disenchanted voters have not really found a comfortable home in the opposite party. Neither major party is anxious to abandon its traditional basis of power in order to curry favor with groups that do not belong to its traditional coalition.[20] Also, neither party is willing to be branded as "soft" on crime, or drugs, or Communism. In essence, everybody is in favor of doing something about the social issue, but the parties are not yet distinguishable in this area. And of course, we must not neglect the resurgence of the economic issue as the number one problem on the voters' minds, which has come about since the recession of 1973. The social issue remains the second largest concern, but we cannot tell at this time whether the latter development will effectively defuse the social issue as a possible source of realignment.

What the experience of the past few years has taught us is that the issues and cleavages of the past have so far failed to form the basis for a new realignment. The economy, the social issue, and race (outside the South) are all unpromising sources of realignment. Asher and Strong have specu-

THE VOTING OUTCOME: ATTITUDES COMBINED   277

lated that older class cleavages will be replaced by cultural cleavages, and political divisions will be formed around alternate life-styles. Questions of sex, pornography, and censorship are certainly in the news these days, but in Asher's words "they seem an unlikely foundation for realignment since it is rare that parties will be on opposite sides on such issues, especially when the overwhelming majority of the population is on one side."[21]

The hard fact of the matter is that while we know that the potential for realignment of the electorate is very great, we simply have no idea whether or how that realignment will come about. Greeley's view is probably the most realistic. He feels that the outcome will be given shape and form by the next generation of leadership.[22] What this implies is that we are in a period of tremendous opportunity. The electorate, it seems to me, stands to exercise great influence in the basic shaping of American politics over the next decades. It needs simply to be made aware of its opportunity and of its power to choose the leaders who will accomplish that realignment.

SUMMARY

This chapter has presented the coming together of a number of threads that I have discussed in different places throughout this book. The overall context is an attitudinal one. This reflects the primary role I assign to attitudes in the determination of political behavior. The concept of intensity emerges when we discover that strong partisans are more loyal to the candidate of their party, while weak partisans are less loyal in their vote for President. The idea that attitudes are functional helps explain why party loyalty remains such a powerful force in the voting behavior of Americans. Finally, the notion of dynamic equilibrium gives a framework in which the interplay of party identification and short-term forces becomes understandable.

The dynamic equilibrium concept simply says that the greater the strength of party identification in determining the vote, the weaker the importance of short-term forces. Specifically, in the 1950s we saw that party identification was the primary attitude underlying the vote. This was true because this was a period during which there were relatively few issues to divide the electorate. (Although the influence of Eisenhower was a sufficiently strong short-term force to win the presidency twice, three of the four Houses were Democratic between 1952 and 1960.) During the 1960s, however, certain issues attracted a great deal of attention in the electorate. Their impact on the vote consequently increased, which in turn resulted in a reduction of the importance of party identification.

Looking into the future, the dynamic equilibrium concept should caution us against any prediction that because party identification seems to have been less important recently, it will continue to lose importance in the future. Anyone who understands that the importance of party loyalty depends on the salience of the issues in a given election will know that such a prediction is not necessarily correct at all. The resurgence of party loyalty as a determinant of the vote in 1976 serves to underscore this point.

This chapter has been written from the perspective of the individual who seeks to deepen his understanding of human behavior to the greatest possible extent. However, what I have presented here is also valuable for another group: politicians, or others whose main interest is winning elections. The politician, above all else, needs to know where to look for votes. This intelligence comes directly from knowledge of what motivates the voters. For instance, a politician of the majority party (the Democrats if we are discussing the national electorate), will stress his party endorsement and might tend to downplay the issues. The candidate of the minority party, on the other hand, knows he will lose unless the campaign generates a good deal of excitement about the issues. He will therefore do everything possible to stir up excitement in an attempt to use the issues to convince some of the loyalists of the majority party to desert to his side.

The second rule that politicians should remember is that the campaign will have its greatest potential effect in the center of the party identification distribution. That is, the strong partisans can usually be taken for granted: They will support their party's candidate almost regardless of the positions he takes. The candidates therefore are wise to aim their campaigns at the weak partisans and Independents. The Democratic candidate will win if he can hang onto his own weak identifiers and win about half of the Independents. The Republican, on the other hand, will sleep in the White House only if he can capture the bulk of the Independent vote as well as a good slice of the weak Democratic group.

These truths help to explain why presidential campaigns tend to be so lackluster. Both candidates spend most of their time wooing the voters in the middle. The Democrat tries to sound just a little like the Republican in order to win some weak Republican votes, and the Republican candidate does just the opposite in order to win some of those weak Democratic votes that are so vital for his victory. Neither one, on the other hand, dares to stray too far toward the center, for fear that the strong partisans may eventually desert the cause. And, of course, no candidate can afford to move *away* from the center, unless he wants to end up like Goldwater or McGovern.

McGovern's campaign of 1972, as dismal a failure as it was, did reveal one interesting example of these principles. Early in the campaign, McGovern's television spots ended with a standard shot showing nothing but the candidate's name, while the announcer solemnly intoned "McGovern." As time went on, however, it became increasingly clear that McGovern was not even appealing to Democrat identifiers, many of whom were planning to vote for Nixon. The TV spots were therefore changed in a small way.

The final shot now contained the word "McGovern" as before, in boldface in the center of the screen. Then, however, the word "Democrat" appeared in the lower right-hand corner. A small change, but it reflected the basic theoretical view of voting that I have presented in these pages. The Democrats knew that party loyalty produces at least some votes, and they wanted to be sure to appeal to that sense of loyalty in every way possible.

NOTES

1. This model is a simplified version of one presented by Gerald Pomper, *Voter's Choice: Varieties of American Electoral Behavior* (New York: Dodd, Mead, 1975). This type of model was originally developed in Arthur Goldberg, "Discerning a Causal Pattern among Data on Voting Behavior," *American Political Science Review*, vol. 60, no. 4 (December 1966), 913–922. We should note that John E. Jackson, "Issues, Party Choices, and Presidential Votes," *American Journal of Political Science*, vol. 9, no. 2 (May 1975), 161–185, takes the position that issue position actually causes party identification, and not the other way around.

2. Stanley Kelley, Jr., and Thad W. Mirer, "The Simple Act of Voting," *American Political Science Review*, vol. 68, no. 2 (June 1974), 572–591. Quote from p. 574.

3. Michael Margolis, "From Confusion to Confusion: Issues and the American Voter (1956–1972)," *American Political Science Review*, vol. 71, no. 1 (March 1977), 31–43.

4. Angus Campbell, "Voters and Elections: Past and Present," *Journal of Politics*, vol. 26, no. 4 (November 1964), 745–757.

5. The following figures appeared originally in Philip E. Converse, "The Concept of a Normal Vote," in Angus Campbell, Philip E. Converse, Warren E. Miller and Donald E. Stokes, *Elections and the Political Order* (New York: Wiley, 1966), chap. 2. Figures are on p. 17.

6. Let me remind you that this statement is limited to the attitudinal model under consideration. Independents are still subject to group-based forces, historical forces, and election day occurrences in making their vote decisions.

7. Michael R. Kagay and Greg A. Caldeira, "A 'Reformed' Electorate? Well, At Least, A Changed Electorate, 1952–1976," in William J. Crotty (Ed.), *Paths to Political Reform* (Lexington, Mass.: Heath, forthcoming.)

8. For one of the more forceful statements of this thesis, see Kevin P. Phillips, *The Emerging Republican Majority* (Garden City, N.Y.: Anchor Books, 1970).

9. The principal exponent of this view is Walter Dean Burnham, "The Changing Shape of the American Political Universe," *American Political Science Review*, vol. 59, no. 1 (March 1965), 7–28.

10. See Nelson W. Polsby, "An Emerging Republican Majority?" *Public Interest*, no. 17 (Fall 1969), 119–126.

11. Burnham, *op. cit.*

12. David E. RePass, "Issue Salience and Party Choice," *American Political Science Review*, vol. 65, no. 2 (June 1971), 389–400.

13. For more on this, see Margolis, *op. cit.*

14. Elements of this analysis have been drawn from Paul Allen Beck, "A Socialization Theory of Partisan Realignment," in Richard G. Niemi (Ed.), *The Politics of Future Citizens* (San Francisco: Jossey-Bass, 1974), chap. 10.

15. On this point, see the interesting discussion by Donald S. Strong, *Issue Voting and Party Realignment* (University, Ala.: University of Alabama Press, 1977).

16. This discussion refers to the 16-state Census South: the eleven states of the old Confederacy plus Delaware, Maryland, West Virginia, Kentucky, and Oklahoma.

17. The analysis to follow is taken from Bruce A. Campbell, "Patterns of Change in the Partisanship of Native Southerners: 1952–1972," *Journal of Politics*, vol. 39, no. 3 (August 1977), 730–761.

18. For a cogent discussion of the meaning of patterns of change, see V. O. Key, Jr., "A Theory of Critical Elections," *Journal of Politics*, vol. 17, no. 1 (February 1955), 3–18; V. O. Key, Jr., "Secular Realignment and the Party System," *Journal of Politics*, vol. 21, no. 2 (May 1959), 198–210.

19. Bruce A. Campbell, *op. cit.*

20. They may, however, pay lip service to new alignments. You may have heard comments as astounding as that made by Matt Mattingly, chairman of the Republican Party of Georgia. He noted how Carter and Bert Lance, former director of the Office of Management and Budget (OMB), are both wealthy men. He concluded that the Democratic Party is the party of millionaires, while the Republican Party is the party of the little people.

21. Herbert Asher, *Presidential Elections and American Politics: Voters, Candidates and Campaigns since 1952* (Homewood, Ill.: Dorsey, 1976), p. 307; Strong, *op. cit,* chap. 4.

22. Andrew M. Greeley, *Building Coalitions* (New York: F. Watts, 1974), pp. 272–273.

Part V

Epilogue: The Impact of the American Electorate on Public Policy

From time to time throughout this book we have encountered instances in which the American electorate has exercised meaningful political influence. In this epilogue I want to take a more formal look at the question of the impact the mass citizenry does have, or might potentially have, on public policy. Let me begin, however, with a caveat. Many volumes have been written about the origins of public policy, and I shall be able to say only a few words about a very large field in these last pages. My goal is clearly not to present the subject in its entirety. Rather, the focus will be on the attitudes of the common man. My hope is to leave you with a sense of political self-awareness and a feeling for the possibilities existing in the political realm for a democratic electorate that is determined to take its proper place in the affairs of its government.

The phrase "public policy" has been used to mean a great many different things. Perhaps most commonly it refers to the detailed plans written up by a federal agency to implement a broad mandate from Congress. The Occupational Safety and Health Administration, for example, has developed a long list of highly detailed criteria to which a business must conform in order to be considered safe. In this sense, public policy includes the rule that a fire extinguisher must be a certain number of inches from the floor.

At quite another level, public policy means the legislation passed by Congress. For instance, the Voting Rights Act of 1965 made it policy for federal registrars to place blacks on the lists of registered voters in certain counties. Or, in another case, each year the Congress votes a new tax law, and it then becomes policy to allow deductions for home insulation or to reduce the oil depletion allowance.

The President himself creates public policy either through the proposal of programs (which must of course be ratified by Congress in order actually to become policy), or through the device of executive orders. Kennedy created policy in the former way with both the Peace Corps and the commitment to send a man to the moon. Franklin Roosevelt was one of the more creative users of executive orders (commitments to actions by the federal bureaucracy that do not need the approval of Congress), which he employed to send American aid to Great Britain in the early years of World War II, at a time when Congress was very hostile to any American involvement.

Even the courts may set policy, even though their role is formally confined to the adjudication of disputes. As an example, the area of school desegregation has proved most difficult to resolve by our elected representatives. Consequently, the Supreme Court has in effect made policy over the years, from the *Brown* decision outlawing segregated schools in 1954, to the *Bakke* decision limiting the use of racial quotas for admission to medical school in 1978.

So we see that the policy analyst needs to define his terms with some care before he begins to talk about public policy. In this book our basic concern has been with the electorate and with the *impact* the common people have on government. Given this perspective, I am not so concerned with the particular content of policy or with the way policy is administered. Whatever impact the common citizen may have comes mainly during the process that *creates* policy.[1] When I say public policy, therefore, I confine my meaning rather narrowly to the *decision-making process by which policy is made.* When I speak of the electorate's impact on public policy, I mean that for some reason or another, a decision maker somewhere in government feels that he must take the electorate into account as he decides which of the alternatives open to him he will choose.

Naturally, not all decision makers feel equally obligated to listen to the electorate, although we can conceive of circumstances in which the electorate could exercise a powerful influence on virtually *any* policy decision. For the moment, let me simply present a figure in which political decision makers might be arranged, according to how much attention they must pay to input from the electorate.

Figure V.1 shows that there are two sorts of circumstance that can bring a decision maker more directly under the electorate's influence. First, an elected official will be more likely to take the electorate's wishes into account than an appointed official, for obvious reasons. Moreover, officials

EPILOGUE: THE IMPACT OF THE AMERICAN ELECTORATE ON PUBLIC POLICY

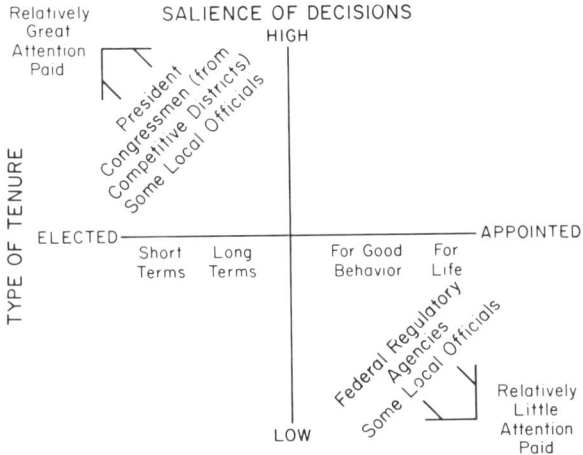

Figure V.1. Schema Explaining the Attention Public Officials Pay to Popular Demands.

elected for a short term will be more sensitive to the public than those elected to long terms. Among the appointed officials, those appointed for good behavior will be more careful to take the popular will into account than those appointed for life. (With lifetime appointments I include lame-duck elected officials, that is, those who are serving the end of their term of office.)

I should point out that this arrangement represents only a theoretical ordering, and is not always observed in practice. Many representatives in Congress pay little attention to their constituents' desires. If we consider, however, that these representatives are elected time after time in noncompetitive districts, it would probably be more correct to place them somewhere among the appointed officials. The formality of their election does not really threaten them with early retirement almost no matter what they do.

The second dimension in Figure V.1 tells us that the more important and visible the decisions are to the electorate, the more the decision maker must take the views of the public into account. The logic of this statement is straightforward: The public is not going to take action against any decision maker unless it is aware of his or her decisions.

What sorts of decision makers would be likely to be found in the various parts of this diagram? At the federal level, the Representative has the shortest term, followed by the President. Moreover, these officials tend to make high-salience decisions, both because of the amount of money they control and the coverage their decisions receive in the media. At the local level, the most vulnerable decision maker is probably the school board member. These people are not only elected for short terms but must often deal with extremely high-salience issues like busing.

In the opposite corner we find policymakers who are relatively free from the need to be concerned with what the mass citizenry wants. Members of federal regulatory agencies often occupy this position. They are appointed to long, fixed terms, and the decisions they make are generally perceived only by those in the regulated industry. Local appointed officials also fall into this category with great frequency. The administrator of the county airport, for instance, rarely runs afoul of an aroused public.

You might wonder why any official with a lifetime appointment would ever worry about public opinion. To be sure, such people are not greatly threatened by the loss of their position should they make an unpopular decision. However, wise policymakers are also concerned about whether their decisions will be effectively implemented. The justices of the Supreme Court recognize this explicitly. During the Second World War, the Court upheld the notoriously unconstitutional movement of all persons of Japanese ancestry who lived on the West Coast to inland detention centers.[2] The Court realized that the intensity of public feeling about the Japanese after Pearl Harbor meant that to overturn the relocation policy might have resulted in acts of violence; and it might have eroded the authority of the Court itself. As Justice Cardozo once said: "The great tides and currents which engulf the rest of mankind do not turn aside in their course and pass the judges idly by."[3]

Let me conclude my discussion of Figure V.1 by observing how it explains why the Court has been in the forefront in the area of civil rights. While the Court must sometimes bow to public opinion, it is also well-insulated from that pressure. This is why the task of desegregation has fallen on its shoulders. What was required under the Constitution, namely, equality under the law, was opposed by a large sector of the populace, which effectively handcuffed the elected decision makers in government. Action by many of these representatives would have meant political suicide, and in addition, the Southern delegation in Congress held trump cards with their chairmanships of crucial committees and their use of the filibuster. Only the Court could act and be effective.

In the sections to follow, I want to discuss how each of the three major areas that I have discussed in this book has an impact on policy. Before I begin, however, I want to recall the diagram in Chapter 1 that presented the linkages between mass political attitudes, behavior, and the actions of government. What this diagram tells us is that the impact of the American electorate on public policy occurs in a variety of ways. We must not imagine that the public's influence occurs only when a decision maker is compelled to commit a certain act. This might be true in the case of a referendum, but such influence is only the tip of the iceberg. Most of the political muscle of the common people is flexed in indirect ways. A decision maker may feel compelled to make his choice from a restricted range of alternatives because he fears that decisions outside that range might arouse the public's anger. At a more basic level, the very structure of decision making, how policy is made—with public hearings, for instance—is determined in large measure by what is universally seen as legitimate. I hope that in the sections to follow I shall succeed in illustrating the many ways in which the mass electorate can exercise influence in government.

THE STRUCTURE OF DEMAND: HOW POLITICAL SOCIALIZATION INFLUENCES POLICY

Political socialization and its companion, political culture, influence policy in four ways. The most general of these we might call "the orderliness of political competition." I have discussed at length the consensus that exists on fundamental political issues. The authority of the Constitution and of the political rules of the game that it sets out are virtually unchallenged. This ensures a certain stability in the structures of political competition. We know that elections will be held on schedule and that legislation is basically the product of debate and not of bribery or of violence. We know that the military will not overthrow the government. To be sure, there is much in American politics that is unpredictable. But the structure of competition remains the same, and this is true in large part because any major violation of these basic norms would be totally rejected by the great majority of the public.

The consequence of orderliness of political competition for policy is twofold. First, it frees political officials from the continual necessity to ensure their tenure in office. A leadership that has to be concerned with preventing coups d'état will not have much energy left over for any kind of coherent policy planning or execution. In addition to freeing their energies for policymaking, secure tenure in office also enables officials to engage in long-term planning. While shifts in personnel from election to election do bring alterations in the directions of more controversial policies, the fact that the federal bureaucracy endures from one administration to the next makes it possible for the President and Congress to contemplate and to implement programs that span not only presidential administrations but generations. The program to put men on the moon could never have been successful, for example, unless President Kennedy had had a reasonable assurance that subsequent Congresses would continue to vote the necessary funds, or that the National Aeronautical and Space Administration would continue to exist for the required period of time. An even better example of the effect of orderliness on planning is Social Security. Without the confidence that Social Security would pay a pension 30 years hence, few would be willing to submit to the Social Security tax on present income.

Socialization patterns influence policy in a second way through their relationship to the sorts of demands placed on government and the modes of behavior deemed appropriate to use in placing these demands. In the latter case, there is a strong rule in our political culture that demands for favorable policy decisions shall be made in peaceful and well-defined ways. Most explicitly, violence or the threat of violence is ruled out as a way to secure a decision. If anything, our culture expects that the use of violence will be counterproductive, stiffening resistance to the demanded policy. Unfortunately, we are currently in a period when terrorists are seeking to use violence for political ends. To date they have most often failed, but the political structures of several nations have been sorely tested, and it remains to be seen whether terrorism will become a viable political tool in this country.

The kinds of demands that various segments of the American electorate make on policymakers are also limited by the political culture. In terms of content, we generally accept the current welfare liberalism of American public policy, and demands remain within those boundaries. On the liberal side, the federal government may face a demand for national health insurance, but no one has proposed that the government take over the medical profession. The government may be asked to provide price supports for milk, but it does not consider the communalization of agriculture. On the conservative end, government is pressured to increase the defense budget but not to give the military a dominant role in government. There are demands to limit the power of trade unions, but not to abolish them. All in all, the more extreme demands simply cannot be made in our culture, because they are not taken seriously even by those who would be advantaged by them.

The third way in which socialization impacts on policy is through the passivity it encourages in the acceptance of policy outputs. A strong element of compromise exists in our culture. Few people expect to get everything they ask from government. The failure to secure the desired decision in one case is offset by the anticipation of a favorable action in the future. As long as policy is perceived as more or less equitable, most groups will not insist on winning any particular fight.

Finally, patterns of socialization influence policy because of the strong element of patriotism and national unity that binds Americans together. Faced with a threat from some external enemy, Americans have traditionally come together in a common cause instead of splintering into opposing camps. This solidarity affects our international policy in obvious ways. It allows the government to engage in an armed conflict like Vietnam with very little initial criticism. This unity has another face, however. The dissention that Vietnam produced about the execution of our foreign policy has led to unaccustomed restraints on the President's ability to control foreign policy. Our noninvolvement in the Angolan civil war can probably be attributed to the backlash from Vietnam.

THE STRUCTURE OF COMMUNICATION: HOW PUBLIC OPINION INFLUENCES POLICY

Like political socialization and political culture, public opinion tends to have a passive effect on public policy. That is, public opinion rarely compels a decision maker to choose one alternative over another. Instead, public opinion sets limits on the kinds of decisions policymakers may make. This sort of influence is what I have earlier called the "boundary-setting function." So long as public officials make decisions within a broad range of acceptability, the electorate will remain generally passive and accepting. However, on the rare occasions when an unfortunate public official should stray across the boundary of acceptable behavior, public opinion may translate into retribution at the next election.

One of the best examples of the boundary-setting function of the electorate occurred in the 5th Congressional District of Arkansas in 1958. Brooks Hays held this seat before 1958 and, as was typical of southern Congressmen at that time, had taken consistently negative positions on civil rights legislation. In that year, however, President Eisenhower declared that Little Rock High School should be integrated, and in a complicated set of exchanges with Governor Faubus, nationalized the Arkansas Guard to assure the safety of the black students attending the school. Representative Hays had no direct part in this exchange, and he certainly did not favor integration. He did, however, agree to serve as an intermediary between Governor Faubus and President Eisenhower during the process of bringing the Guard under federal authority. Unhappily for Hays, in doing this service, he stepped over one of the invisible boundaries that had been erected by public opinion. He became seen in his constituency as someone who had aided the cause of school desegregation, and his transgression was punished in a rather remarkable way. Brooks Hays was defeated in 1958 by a write-in candidate, Dale Alford, who campaigned solely on the issue of school integration.[4]

A second way in which public opinion affects policy is through the definition of feasible alternatives. This is really a special type of boundary setting. It refers to the case in which the public makes it clear through its expression of opinion that a certain kind of decision would be acceptable should the decision maker choose to make it.

The most phenomenal example of the power of public opinion in this century is a case of the definition of feasible alternatives. Of course, I am referring to the Watergate affair and the link between public opinion and President Nixon's resignation. In Figure V.2 I have traced the record of Nixon's popularity throughout his presidency. (The entries are the percentages of the electorate approving of the way Nixon was handling his job.) Compared to his predecessors, Nixon was never a terribly popular President. Nevertheless, he managed to maintain an approval rating of over 50 percent for nearly all of his first term. His all-time high came in early 1973, at the time of the Vietnam settlement, when 68 percent of the electorate gave him its approval. There followed an unprecedented 18 months, during which the Watergate affair ran its course. Nixon's support plummeted 44 points from its peak, ending up at a mere 24 percent when he resigned in August 1974.

One obvious conclusion which comes from Figure V.2 is the extent to which the public's support of the President depends on current events. You can easily see how Nixon's successes, primarily in foreign policy, came shortly before the peaks of his popularity. And of course the downhill slide of 1973 and 1974 is marked by the various Watergate episodes as well as by economic bad news, which is traditionally hard on presidential popularity.

One is tempted to infer from this pattern that the decline in Nixon's popular support was one of the major factors that led to his resignation. Now this is a weak argument to make on the basis of the information in Figure V.2. Just because the decline in support preceded the resignation does not mean it caused the resignation. However, when we recall what the various members of Congress were doing and saying from the summer of 1973 through August 1974, it becomes clear that public opinion was one of the central factors that allowed them to decide to vote for impeachment and conviction. Throughout this period the Representatives made repeated checks on their constituencies to see whether a vote for impeach-

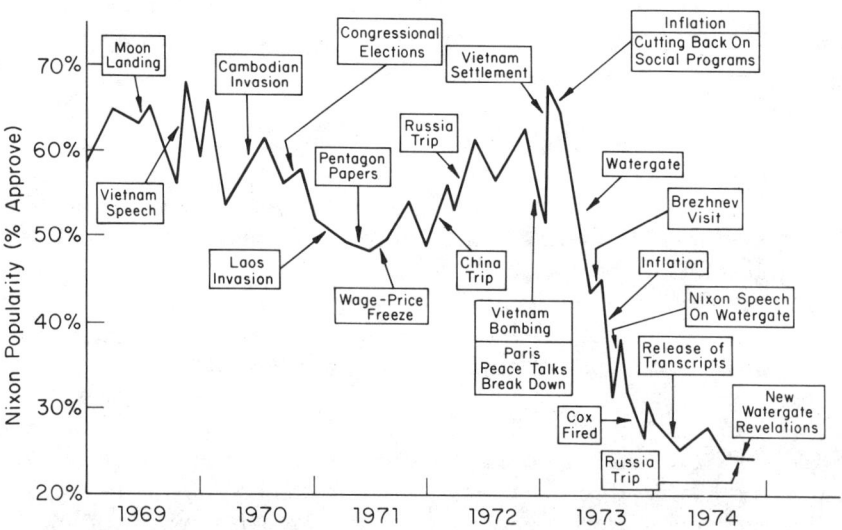

Figure V.2. President Nixon's Approval Ratings.

Source: *Gallup Opinion Index*, Report No. 111 (September 1974), p. 12.

EPILOGUE: THE IMPACT OF THE AMERICAN ELECTORATE ON PUBLIC POLICY   289

ment would be tolerated. In the early stages it was clear that impeachment would not be acceptable to the American public. It was too drastic a step and represented too strong an attack on the institution of the presidency. However, as time went along, and the evidence began to build up, a new alternative emerged in the public mind. Impeachment began to be discussed, written about in the papers—in short, accepted as one possible outcome to the affair. This was the catalyst that allowed the Congress to move ahead, to vote the Articles of Impeachment in committee, and to make it clear that unless he resigned, Nixon would have been impeached and convicted.

The Nixon case was of course extraordinary, since removal from office is almost never at issue. No matter how unpopular a President is, his right to serve out his term is not challenged in our political culture without due cause. This does not prevent a President from becoming unpopular, of course, as the experience of President Carter illustrates. In Figure V.3, you can easily see the phenomenal slide in approval rating that Carter experienced during his first year and a half in office. His postinauguration honeymoon boosted his approval rating to 75 percent in March 1977, but between then and July 1978, he lost 36 points, nearly the equivalent of Nixon's loss four years earlier.

Such a drop in popularity has three broad impacts on policy. First, presidential approval ratings have a relationship to the congressional vote in the off-year elections. Clearly, a charismatic President in the White House, one who is capable of campaigning effectively for Congressmen, will draw votes to his party's ticket even when he is not running. One

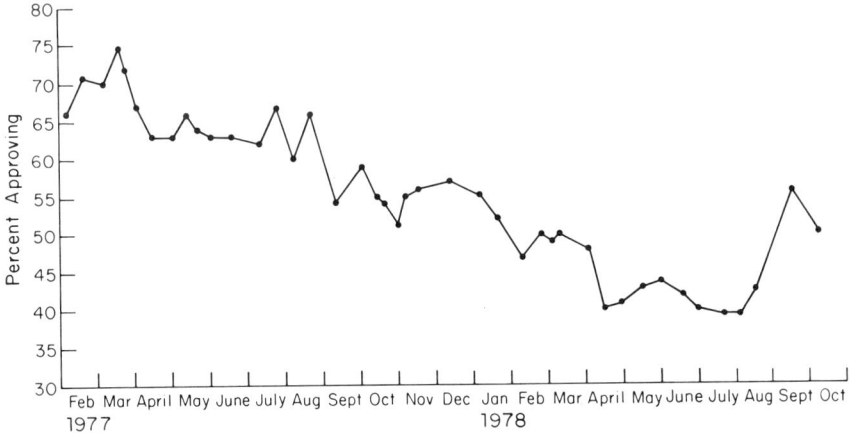

Figure V.3.   President Carter's Approval Rating.

Source: *Gallup Opinion Index*, Report No. 152 (March 1978), pp. 16–17. Later entries are by personal communication with the American Institute of Public Opinion.

study has attempted to calculate the actual effect that presidential popularity had on the congressional vote in 1970. It found that among Independents, for instance, 50 percent of those who approved of the way Nixon was handling his job voted Republican for Congress, compared to only 35 percent of those who disapproved.[5] Translating these calculations to 1978, we might predict that a Carter approval rating of 75 would have resulted in the election of roughly 15 more Democratic Representatives to Congress than a rating of 38.

The second policy implication of Carter's poor approval rating is closely related to the first. A poor approval rating leads to a weakening of presidential authority, for two reasons. First, an unpopular President is seen as less legitimate than a popular one. Kennedy might have been able to talk the steel industry out of raising prices, but Carter could not in early 1978. The steel industry, or whatever group I might name, feels that it will not suffer widespread disapproval in the mind of the public if it defies an unpopular President and will therefore be more willing to do so.

The second reason is that an unpopular President is less able to offer political rewards, especially to Congressmen. Congressmen know that a weak President cannot help them at the polls. Such a President may even hurt their chances for reelection, and they may go out of their way to dissociate themselves from him for that reason. Either way, the ability of the President to influence legislation through his influence on Congressmen from his own party is reduced.

Finally, the third impact that low presidential popularity has on policy arises from the fact that an unpopular President will do things calculated to increase his popularity. We can see this happening in Figure V.3 with the upturn in Carter's approval rating, which began in August 1978. I do not mean to imply that Carter's motive in calling the Camp David summit in early September sprang from his concern with his public image. However, the breakthroughs in the Middle East situation that were achieved at Camp David had a clear impact on the electorate's approval of the way Carter was handling his job.

Other activities in the White House reveal President Carter's desire to improve his standing in the public eye. One such move was the appointment in early summer of Gerald Rafshoon, Carter's 1976 media consultant, to the newly created post of assistant to the President in charge of communication. By communication, the White House evidently meant the communication of good news about Jimmy Carter to a doubting electorate.

At a more substantive level, Carter showed strong support for positions with broad popular appeal in the fall of 1978. The obvious sympathy across the country for lower taxes and an easing of inflation undoubtedly influenced his decision to veto two major appropriations bills, one for the military and the other for public works. In this, Carter followed in the footsteps of President Ford before him, who advocated an expansion of the national park system and new educational legislation in the weeks before the election of 1976.

To conclude this section, I want to point out some obvious limits on the process of boundary setting. In general, most limits the American electorate places on policymakers are so broad as to be virtually nonexistent. This arises from the typically low levels of interest that Americans have in politics. Low levels of interest mean that most people do not care about policy outcomes in most areas. Only in the most extraordinary of circumstances would a large enough attentive public be generated to make policymakers aware of their influence. And in order for public opinion to influence policy direction it must set boundaries that exclude the policies being pursued or those about to be pursued. The Vietnam situation provides an excellent and important example of an instance in which all the necessary elements did occur. However, such events are rare.

THE STRUCTURE OF ALTERNATIVES: HOW PARTICIPATION INFLUENCES POLICY

There are three basic ways in which participation influences policy. The first and most important type, of course, is elections. Voting is by far the most common form of political behavior in this country and is also potentially the most effective. However, there are two main reasons why the election of one candidate over another does not result in perfect representation of the electing constituency. The first of these is the simple fact that many Representatives do not think they should represent their constituents' opinions. Such Representatives have been labeled "trustees," and they approach decision making with the conviction that they should let their own judgments prevail. This style contrasts with the "delegate," who relies on his constituents' opinions to guide his decisions, and the "politico," who shifts between his own judgment and constituency opinion, depending on the issue. Davidson's study of the House of Representatives in the 1960s found that 46 percent of the members called themselves politicos, 28 percent claimed to be trustees, and only 23 percent said that they were delegates.[6]

When we begin to ask why so many U.S. Representatives seem to violate the basic democratic norm that they should represent their constituents' wishes, we come upon the second reason that elections do not effectively control policy. In many instances the trustee role is forced upon legislators because they can find no consensus of opinion in their constituencies. The effect of such a situation is illustrated by Figure V.4, which shows the role that constituency attitudes play in the determination of their Representatives' behavior on roll-call votes. The link between the constituency

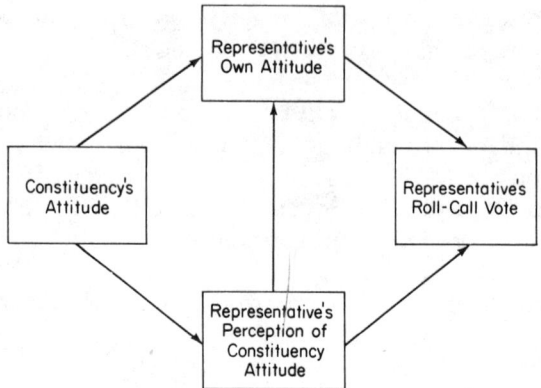

Figure V.4. A Model of the Influence of Constituents on Congressmen.

Source: Charles F. Cnudde and Donald V. McCrone, "The Linkage between Constituency Attitudes and Congressional Voting Behavior: A Causal Model," *American Political Science Review*, Vol. 60, No. 1 (March 1966), 69.

attitude and the Representative's attitude is the result of the electoral process: In theory, people tend to elect Representatives who think as they do. In practice, of course, this link is very weak. Partly this is because constituencies are often large and very heterogeneous, with the result that no elected Representative could possibly hold attitudes that corresponded to those of all his constituents.

A fine example of this can be drawn from the 1964 presidential election. Vietnam first became an issue in that election, and Johnson's victory was generally interpreted by journalists and academics as a mandate for military restraint. But did Johnson's subsequent policy of escalating the war really violate an electoral mandate? When we look at the data, we find that LBJ did receive 63 percent of the vote of those who favored withdrawal from Vietnam. But he also won 52 percent of the "hawk" vote, those who wanted a more aggressive military posture. And fully 82 percent of those who wanted to keep U.S. troops in Vietnam while at the same time trying to end the fighting voted for Johnson. What did the mandate of 1964 mean to Johnson? It could have meant anything he wanted it to mean.[7]

There is also evidence that even when there is a clear choice between candidates, and the voters *do* have identifiable issue preferences, they still fail to elect the person who best represents them.[8] The voters simply fail to gather the information necessary to make the link between what they want and what the candidates propose to do. The Miller-Stokes study found that typically half the electorate in a constituency knew nothing about either candidate, and only a quarter had heard or read something about both candidates.[9]

What this information suggests, of course, is that Representatives do not take their constituents' opinions into account, either because they cannot or because they do not have to. This conclusion leads in turn to a theme that I first set out in the introductory chapter. The electorate has the ability to secure greater influence on its Representatives. All it has to do is to take identifiable positions on issues and to vote according to those positions.

Once the election has taken place, there is still a great deal that members of the electorate can do to influence Representatives as well as nonelected policymakers. Such influence is represented in Figure V.4 by the link between the constituency's attitude and the Representative's perception of the constituency's attitude. There is a wide variety of ways in which constituents can make their views known to policymakers. Most often these ways involve the intermediate structures of interest groups or the political parties. A few interest groups have a mass membership or a membership that seeks to represent the mass interest, like Common Cause or Nader's public interest research groups. The potential for such organized participation by the common citizenry is very great, for the citizens' major political resource is their numbers. However, most interest groups represent *very* small segments of the population and should more properly be seen as elite institutions. So in spite of their undeniable influence on policy, I shall not discuss them here.

Even limiting our discussions to modes of input that do not involve organized groups, there are at least three ways in which the common man can attempt to influence policymakers. The first is by mail, the second through congressional polls, and the third is by referendum.

Congressmen tend to attach great importance to their mail.[10] In the first place, they receive a great deal of it. Typical Representatives in Congress receive over 500 pieces of mail per week, and a Senator may receive over 10,000 per week. Of this, as much as one-third to one-half may be concerned with legislative issues (the rest are personal service matters). Second, Representatives claim to pay attention to their mail. One study found that over half the Congressmen polled placed either "quite a bit" or "great" reliance on their mail as a source of information about their constituency's positions. Only 3 percent said they placed no reliance on their mail.[11]

Of course, the mail does not come from all constituents and therefore cannot represent opinion accurately. Only about 15 percent of the public say that they have ever written a letter to a public official, and about two-thirds of all letters are written by only 3 percent of the electorate.[12] How misleading this can be was demonstrated by Goldwater's campaign in 1964. By mistaking letter opinion for public opinion, Goldwater was led to believe that he held an appreciable lead over Johnson in midcampaign, that the majority of Americans were basically conservative and that they were thoroughly upset over the growing size of the federal government. Goldwater's defeat clearly illustrated how biased a representation letter opinion is of public opinion.

On the other hand, the mail a Representative receives is useful precisely because it is biased. Letters come from the most interested and articulate segment of the population, who are also likely to be influential in their communities. While the mail cannot give an accurate estimate of the distribution of opinion in the electorate as a whole, it does provide a rather sensitive gauge of the salience of old issues and the emergence of new ones among the elites in a constituency.[13]

In theory, the way a Representative can learn the total opinion of his district, rather than just the letter opinion, is through polling. Congressmen enjoy the free use of the mail, and so questionnaires can be sent out for only the cost of the printing. Unfortunately, most Congressmen know little about the technique of survey research, and their results are usually so poor that they learn little more than they could learn for free by reading their mail. To cite only one example, the typical response rate to questionnaires sent out by members of Congress is less than 17 percent. In other words, only about one constituent in six bothers to send back the questionnaire he receives from his Congressman. This level of response suggests strongly that the information provided has come from an unusual segment of the electorate, one that is probably more informed and more active politically, or perhaps more angry, than the majority of the voters.

Low response rates, in addition to biasing poll results, set another limitation on the usefulness of polling. Representatives naturally interpret the failure to return questionnaires as a sign of popular disinterest in an issue and an encouragement to adopt the trustee role. The impact of polls on policymakers would undoubtedly increase if five-sixths of those polled responded, instead of only one-sixth. Some evidence supporting this hypothesis comes from the national study conducted by Verba and Nie.[14] These scholars studied 64 communities, interviewing both common citizens and the community leaders. Their analysis led them to conclude that the best way to measure the influence of the electorate on its policymakers was to examine the extent to which the two groups agreed on their "agenda" of community priorities.[15] They found that the level of participation in a district related strongly to the measure of concurrence between mass and leadership priorities. In fact, people living in communities with the highest levels of political activity enjoyed twice the level of concurrence with their political leaders as those who lived in the communities with the lowest levels of activity.

The interpretation of these findings concurs with our earlier conclusions. The actively participating community is the one in which more information is communicated to the leadership. It is also the one in which the electorate is more vigilant, sets boundaries more narrowly on acceptable policy decisions, and has a more credible threat that if these boundaries are trespassed, there will be consequences at the next election.

One final mode of influence that the electorate can use between elections is the referendum. Introduced in many states by the political reform movement around the turn of the century, this mode of political input has long played a prominent role in decision-making on state and local bond issues and state constitutional amendments. However, the referendum has burst upon the public's consciousness in recent months after widespread media coverage of the repeal of homosexual rights ordinances in several cities and by the astounding victory of drastic tax reform legislation in California in the summer of 1978. It is still too early to tell just what use the voters will make of their newly discovered powers. There is some reason to think, however, that citizen discontent with high taxes and general government misdoings will find a sudden release in a spate of fairly fundamental alterations of governmental politics.

Considering only the area of tax reform, we know that the proportion of people in the United States who feel that the government wastes a lot of money they pay in taxes has climbed from 42 percent in 1958 to 78 percent in 1978.[16] Concurrently, we find that 57 percent of the population would prefer smaller government with fewer services, and 41 percent would be willing to cut welfare and social services "a lot" in exchange for a tax cut. These opinions may presage support for a broad range of tax-cutting referenda that will probably find their way onto the ballots in numerous states over the next few years.

On the Difficulty of Mass Political Influence

Over the past 10 or 20 years, books claiming that the common people have little influence on our governing elites, and that a military-industrial complex or some other conspiratorial cabal really makes all the important decisions in American politics, have enjoyed great popularity. These works are accompanied by examples in which the public interest has been neglected or abused, evidence that is cited as proof of the inevitable domination of public policy by the elites. While it must be clear by now that I do not support the ramification of this view, which is that the public can *never* have any meaningful influence on public policy no matter what it does, there are nevertheless numerous ways in which the influence of the common man in the political arena is limited.

The first limit on the public's influence on political decision making stems from the complexity of many of the issues facing government today. Without extensive information and a good deal of thought, not even the most well-meaning citizen can take a wise position on some issues. Indeed, when Representatives say that they sometimes follow their own judgment rather than their constituency's desires, they often justify their behavior by explaining how complex the issues in question are. Their constituents, without reading long staff reports and listening to many witnesses, probably don't really know where their own interests lie. Emotionalism tends to outweigh information in many such cases, and the public sometimes ends up supporting positions that would do exactly the opposite of what they want to accomplish. In such situations the Representative is probably justified in taking the trustee role, and voting his own convictions.

A more serious problem for the Representative arises when his constituency's opinion is split on an issue. In some cases, it is not possible to detect which of several opinions is favored by a majority of the electorate because the most preferred option for one group is the least preferred for another group. Again, the Representative has little choice but to follow his own judgment.

The second limit on the electorate's impact on public policy is the unavoidable fact that resources are finite. Deficit financing dulls the edge of this problem at the federal level, but for many states and localities the situation is very real. Particularly in sparsely populated counties, government simply does not have sufficient revenue to do anything but provide the most basic consensually approved services. In essence, there is no public impact on decision making because there is no decision making. No amount of popular outrage can get a street paved if there are no funds to hire a paving contractor.

At the national level, with the immense federal budget, the situation is less severe, partly because there is adequate income and partly because in a half-trillion-dollar budget it is not too difficult to find a few million dollars for some special project. But at a higher level, federal decision makers still confront the same quandary. The most basic confrontation is between spending for the military and spending for social services. Both sides have their strong advocates who want to fund increases by reducing allocations to the other. Until some consensus emerges that one of these policy areas is less deserving than the other, those on either side of the issue will be forced to accept compromise solutions.

The third factor limiting the impact of the public on policy is the inability we have to foresee issues. This has two consequences. First, it means that the direct influence of elections on decision making is completely eliminated if a totally new issue arises after the election that does not relate to any of the positions contained in the electoral mandate. A Representative elected to deal in a certain way with inflation and unemployment, for example, might not have much sense of his constituency's desires regarding student protests at the local university. The problem is exacerbated by the fact that the constituency itself will very likely not have a coherent position on a completely new issue. If a previously quiet town suddenly experiences a series of rapes, it will probably be some time before a coherent idea emerges in the minds of the citizenry about how to confront the problem. In the interim, the city council and the police are on their own and may follow courses of action that are later rebuked by their constituents.

Finally, a new limit on the power of the American electorate to influence public policy has arisen in the past several years. It derives from the increasing dependence of the American economy on events outside the United States and generally beyond the control of our government. The most obvious example is the lack of control we have over the price of oil, but there are many others. The policies established by foreign governments cannot fail to touch all of us. Imported products may be less expensive than the domestic products they compete against because of lower foreign labor costs or because of preferential policies accorded the involved industries by foreign governments. The price we pay for foreign goods, many of which, like oil, are near-necessities for the functioning of our economy, contributes to a staggering balance-of-payments deficit. This in turn influences inflation and the rate of employment. In short, we live in a world that is exerting greater and greater control over our domestic affairs. Popular control over these affairs must necessarily decline in proportion.

On Making America More Democratic

I now return to the central question. We have a sense of the ways in which the electorate can influence policy and a sense of the limitations on that influence. We also know that in fact the contemporary electorate exercises relatively little of its potential. Why? Because people do not care to make the necessary effort. This apathy arises both from a real lack of interest in politics and from experience with unsuccessful attempts to influence public policy.

How can this apathy be overcome? It is essentially a matter of political self-awareness. People, to be politically active, must see politics as an important arena for action and must see themselves as effective political actors. Unfortunately, to instill these attitudes in the minds of millions of voters presents an imposing task. Education may make people aware of the impact that government has on their lives and the reasons why they should therefore seek to control government as much as possible. But if the policies of government are primarily beneficent, as they were almost continuously for the 20 years following World War II, no amount of exhortation is likely to convince many people to make the effort. However, in the past 10 or 15 years the outputs of government have not been nearly as favorable. More discontent has arisen, and this may be the catalyst that will lead the electorate to seek ways of expanding its control over public policy.

Once the motivation to control policy exists, success depends on the electorate's ability to channel its efforts effectively. First, it should concentrate on the decision makers who are most vulnerable to influence: those who face frequent elections and who make important decisions. This means, of course, that the voters must become aware of the issues. They must know their own position, and they must know the positions of the competing candidates. Once it becomes clear to a Representative that his tenure in office depends on the policy decisions he makes, you can be sure he will move away from the independent role of the trustee and become a much more attentive delegate.

In addition to arming itself with information, the electorate must realize that its strength is in numbers. Its greatest chance to influence policy lies in its ability to act in concert, in large aggregates. Only in this way can the voters contest the advantages of time, money, skill, and access enjoyed by many interest groups. Furthermore, the voters must understand the virtue of patience. Sudden, wholesale, direct alterations in policy occur rarely. They must understand the limits on their power and avoid diminishing their morale by taking on impossible tasks.

You belong to this electorate. Perhaps this book has helped you to understand your own political identity and your place in the American political order. Perhaps you will now conclude that the role which the American electorate will play in our political future is in no one's hands but your own, in concert with your fellow citizens. I hope you will act to make that future a good one.

Notes

1. Exactly when policy is really made is a complex issue. The initial decision that creates a particular policy is the most obvious moment. It goes without saying, however, that decisions are made regarding the administration of policy which are far from routine and which may also create policy in a very real way. Unfortunately, we do not have the space to consider the latter possibility.

2. *Korematsu v. United States*, 323 U.S. 214 (1944).

3. Henry J. Abraham, *Justices and Presidents* (New York: Oxford, 1974), p. 270.

4. Warren E. Miller and Donald E. Stokes, "Constituency Influence in Congress," *American Political Science Review*, vol. 57, no. 1 (March 1963), 45–56.

5. James E. Piereson, "Presidential Popularity and Midterm Voting at Different Electoral Levels," *American Journal of Political Science*, vol. 19, no. 4 (November 1975), 683–694.

6. Roger H. Davidson, *The Role of the Congressman* (New York: Pegasus, 1969), pp. 110–142.

7. Richard W. Boyd, "Popular Control of Public Policy: A Normal Vote Analysis of the 1968 Election," *American Political Science Review*, vol. 66, no. 2 (June 1972), 429–449.

8. John L. Sullivan and Robert E. O'Connor, "Electoral Choice and Popular Control of Public Policy: The Case of the 1966 House Elections," *American Political Science Review*, vol. 66, no. 4 (December 1972), 1256–1268.

9. Warren E. Miller and Donald E. Stokes, *op. cit.*

10. Lewis Anthony Dexter, "What Do Congressmen Hear?" in Nelson Polsby (Ed.), *Congressional Behavior* (New York: Random House, 1971), p. 28.

11. Warren E. Miller, "Policy Preferences of Congressional Candidates and Constituents," paper presented at the annual meeting of the American Political Science Association, September 1961.

12. Philip E. Converse, Aage R. Clausen, and Warren E. Miller, "Electoral Myth and Reality: The 1964 Election," *American Political Science Review*, vol. 59, no. 2 (June 1965), 321–336.

13. Dennis Ippolito, Thomas G. Walker, and Kenneth Kolson, *Public Opinion and Responsible Democracy* (Englewood Cliffs, N.J.: Prentice-Hall, 1976), p. 290.

14. Sidney Verba and Norman Nie, *Participation in America: Political Democracy and Social Equality* (New York: Harper & Row, 1972).

15. *Ibid.*, p. 302.

16. Adam Clymer, "Poll Discloses Property Tax Cuts Are Widely Backed around Nation," *The New York Times*, Wednesday, June 28, 1978, p. 1.

Bibliography

Abraham, Henry J. *Justices and Presidents* (New York: Oxford, 1974).
Adelson, Joseph, & Beall, Lynette. "Adolescent Perspectives on Law and Government," *Law and Society Review,* vol. 4, no. 4 (May 1970), 495–504.
Adelson, Joseph; Green, Bernard; & O'Neil, Robert P. "Growth of the Idea of Law in Adolescence," *Developmental Psychology,* vol. 1, no. 4 (July 1969), 327–332.
Adelson, Joseph, & O'Neil, Robert P. "Growth of Political Ideas in Adolescence: The Sense of Community," *Journal of Personality and Social Psychology,* vol. 4, no. 3 (1966), 295–306.
Adorno, T. W.; Frenkel-Brunswik, Else; Levinson, Daniel J.; & Sanford, R. Nevitt. *The Authoritarian Personality* (New York: Harper & Row, 1950).
Alexander, Herbert E. *Financing Politics* (Washington, D.C.: Congressional Quarterly Press, 1976).
Almond, Gabriel A., & Verba, Sidney. *The Civic Culture* (Princeton, N.J.: Princeton University Press, 1963).
Ardrey, Robert. *The Territorial Imperative* (New York: Atheneum, 1967).
Asher, Herbert. *Presidential Elections and American Politics: Voters, Candidates and Campaigns since 1952* (Homewood, Ill.: Dorsey, 1976).
Atlanta Journal-Constitution, September 26, 1976, p. 20A
Bandura, Albert, & Walters, Richard H. *Social Learning and Personality Development* (New York: Holt, Rinehart and Winston, 1963).
Barghoorn, Frederic C. *Politics in the USSR* (Boston: Little, Brown, 1966).
Batlin, Robert. "San Francisco Newspapers' Campaign Coverage: 1896, 1952," *Journalism Quarterly,* vol. 31 (Summer 1954), 297–303.
Beck, Paul Allen. "A Socialization Theory of Partisan Realignment," in R. G. Niemi (Ed.), *The Politics of Future Citizens* (San Francisco: Jossey-Bass, 1974) chap. 10.

Berkowitz, Leonard (Ed.). *Roots of Aggression* (New York: Atherton, 1969).
Best, James J. *Public Opinion: Micro and Macro* (Homewood, Ill.: Dorsey, 1973).
Blalock, Hubert. *Social Statistics,* 2d ed. (New York: McGraw-Hill, 1972).
Boorstin, Daniel J. *The Genius of American Politics* (Chicago: University of Chicago Press, 1953).
Boyd, Richard W. "Popular Control of Public Policy: A Normal Vote Analysis of the 1968 Election," *American Political Science Review,* vol. 66, no. 2 (June 1972), 429-449.
Brittain, Clay V. "Adolescent Choices and Parent-Peer Cross-Pressures," *American Sociological Review,* vol. 28, no. 3 (June 1963), 385-391.
Burnham, Walter Dean. "The Changing Shape of the American Political Universe," *American Political Science Review,* vol. 59, no. 1 (March 1965), 7-28.
Burnham, Walter Dean. *Critical Elections and the Mainsprings of American Politics* (New York: Norton, 1970).
Burnham, Walter Dean. "Theory and Voting Research: Some Reflections on Converse's 'Change in the American Electorate,' " *American Political Science Review,* vol. 68, no. 3 (September 1974), 1002-1023.
Campbell, Angus. "Voters and Elections: Past and Present," *Journal of Politics,* vol. 26, no. 4 (November 1964), 745-757.
Campbell, Angus. *White Attitudes toward Black People* (Ann Arbor, Mich.: Institute for Social Research, 1971).
Campbell, Angus, & Converse, Philip E. (Eds.). *The Human Meaning of Social Change* (New York: Russell Sage, 1972).
Campbell, Angus; Converse, Philip E.; Miller, Warren E.; & Stokes, Donald E. *The American Voter* (New York: Wiley, 1960).
Campbell, Angus; Converse, Philip E.; Miller, Warren E.; & Stokes, Donald E. *Elections and the Political Order* (New York: Wiley, 1966).
Campbell, Angus; Gurin, Gerald; & Miller, Warren E. *The Voter Decides* (New York: Harper & Row, 1954).
Campbell, Angus, & Schuman, Howard. *Racial Attitudes in Fifteen American Cities* (Washington, D.C.: GPO, 1968).
Campbell, Bruce A. "Peer Influence in Political Socialization," paper presented at the annual meeting of the Southern Political Science Association, Nashville, Tenn., November 6-8, 1975.
Campbell, Bruce A. "Racial Differences in the Reaction to Watergate: Some Implications for System Support," *Youth and Society,* vol. 7, no. 4 (June 1976), 439-460.
Campbell, Bruce A. "Patterns of Change in the Partisanship of Native Southerners: 1952-1972," *Journal of Politics,* vol. 39, no. 3 (August 1977), 730-761.
Cartwright, Dorwin, & Zander, Alvin. "Group Pressures and Group Standards: Introduction," in D. Cartwright & A. Zander (Eds.), *Group Dynamics: Research and Theory,* 2d ed. (New York: Harper & Row, 1960), chap. 9.
Cartwright, Dorwin, & Zander, Alvin (Eds.) *Group Dynamics: Research and Theory,* 2d ed. (New York: Harper & Row, 1960).
Catt, Carrie Chapman, & Shuler, Nellie Rodgers. *Woman Suffrage and Politics* (New York: Scribner's, 1926).
Chandler, Robert. *Public Opinion: Changing Attitudes on Contemporary Political and Social Issues* (New York: Bowker, 1972).

Chute, Marchette. *The First Liberty: A History of the Right to Vote in America, 1619–1850* (New York: Dutton, 1969).
Cirino, Robert. *Don't Blame the People* (New York: Vintage, 1971).
Cirino, Robert. *Power to Persuade: Mass Media and the News* (New York: Bantam, 1974).
Citrin, Jack. "Comment: The Political Relevance of Trust in Government," *American Political Science Review*, vol. 68, no. 3 (September 1974), 973–988.
Clausen, John A. (Ed.) *Socialization and Society* (Boston: Little, Brown, 1968).
Clymer, Adam. "Poll Discloses Property Tax Cuts Are Widely Backed around Nation," *The New York Times*, Wednesday, June 28, 1978, p. 1.
Coleman, James S. *The Adolescent Society* (New York: Free Press, 1961).
Comisión Nacional Cubana de la UNESCO, "Cuba y la conferencia de educación y desarrollo económico y social" (Havana: Editorial Nacional de Cuba, 1962).
Converse, Philip E. "The Concept of a Normal Vote," in A. Campbell, P. E. Converse, W. E. Miller, & D. E. Stokes, *Elections and the Political Order* (New York: Wiley, 1966), chap. 2.
Converse, Philip E. "Public Opinion and Voting Behavior," in N. W. Polsby & F. I. Greenstein, *Handbook of Political Science*, Vol. 4 (Reading, Mass.: Addison-Wesley, 1975).
Converse, Philip E. "Change in the American Electorate," in A. Campbell & P. E. Converse (Eds.)., *The Human Meaning of Social Change* (New York: Russell Sage, 1972), chap. 8.
Converse, Philip E., et al. "Stability and Change in 1960: A Reinstating Election," in A. Campbell, P. E. Converse, W. E. Miller, & D. E. Stokes *Elections and the Political Order* (New York: Wiley, 1966).
Converse, Philip E.; Clausen, Aage R.; & Miller, Warren E. "Electoral Myth and Reality: The 1964 Election," *American Political Science Review*, vol. 59, no. 2 (June 1965), 321–336.
Converse, Philip E.; Miller, Warren E.; Rusk, Jerrold G.; & Wolfe, Arthur C. "Continuity and Change in American Politics: Parties and Issues in the 1968 Election," *American Political Science Review*, vol. 63, no. 4 (December 1969), 1083–1104.
Coombs, Steven. "Editorial Endorsements and Election Outcomes" (unpublished Ph.D. dissertation, University of Michigan, 1978).
Crotty, William J. (Ed.). *Paths to Political Reform* (Lexington, Mass: Heath, forthcoming).
Crowne, D., & Marlowe, D. "A New Scale of Social Desirability Independent of Psychopathology," *Journal of Consulting Psychology*, vol. 24, no. 4 (1960), 349–354.
Current Population Reports. *Population Characteristics*, Voter Participation in November 1976 (advance report, Series P-20, no. 304 (December 1976).
Crouse, Timothy. *The Boys on the Bus* (New York: Random House, 1973).
Davidson, Roger H. *The Role of the Congressman* (New York: Pegasus, 1969).
Dawson, Richard E., & Prewitt, Kenneth. *Political Socialization* (Boston: Little, Brown, 1969).
Devine, Donald J. *The Political Culture of the United States* (Boston: Little, Brown, 1972).
Dexter, Louis Anthony. "What Do Congressmen Hear?" in N. Polsby (Ed.), *Congressional Behavior* (New York: Random House, 1971).

Dollard, John; Doob, Leonard W.; Miller, Neal E.; Mowrer, O. H.; & Sears, Robert R. *Frustration and Aggression* (New Haven: Yale University Press, 1939).
Easton, David, & Dennis, Jack. *Children in the Political System: Origins of Political Legitimacy* (New York: McGraw-Hill, 1969).
Easton, David, & Hess, Robert D. "The Child's Political World," *Midwest Journal of Political Science*, vol. 6, no. 3 (August 1962), 229–246.
Efron, Edith. *The News Twisters* (Los Angeles: Nash Publishing, 1971).
Electing Congress (Washington, D.C.: Congressional Quarterly, Inc., 1978)
Erikson, Robert S., "The Influence of Newspaper Endorsements in Presidential Elections: The Case of 1964," *American Journal of Political Science*, vol. 20, no. 2 (May 1976), 207–233.
Erikson, Robert S., & Luttbeg, Norman R. *American Public Opinion: Its Origins, Content, and Impact* (New York: Wiley, 1973).
Evans, Rowland, & Novak, Robert. "Inside Report," *Newark Sunday News*, October 27, 1968, p. C2.
"Extremists Using Media, Pulitzer Recipient Warns," *Red and Black*, vol. 83, no. 82 (Athens, Ga.: University of Georgia), March 29, 1977, p. 1.
Fagen, Richard R. *Cuba: The Political Content of Adult Education* (Stanford, Calif.: The Hoover Institution of War and Peace, 1964).
Flanigan, William H., & Zingale, Nancy H. *Political Behavior of the American Electorate*, 3d ed. (Boston: Allyn and Bacon, 1975).
Free, Lloyd A., & Cantril, Hadley. *The Political Beliefs of Americans* (New Brunswick, N.J.: Rutgers University Press, 1967).
Gabriel, Ralph Henry. *The Course of American Democratic Thought*, 2d ed. (New York: Ronald, 1956).
Gallatin, Judith, & Adelson, Joseph. "Individual Rights and Public Good, a Cross-National Study of Adolescence," *Comparative Political Studies*, vol. 3, no. 2 (July 1970), 226–242.
Gallup Opinion Index. Various reports.
Gamson, William A., & McEvoy, James. "Police Violence and Its Public Support," *Annuals of the American Academy of Political and Social Science*, 391 (September 1970), 97–110.
Ginsparg, Sylvia; Moriarty, Alice; & Murphey, Lois B. "Young Teenagers' Responses to the Assassination of President Kennedy: Relation to Previous Life Experiences," in M. Wolfenstein & G. Kliman (Eds.), *Children and the Death of a President* (Garden City, N.Y.: Anchor Books, 1966), chap. 1.
Glamser, Francis D. "The Importance of Age to Conservative Opinions: A Multivariate Analysis," *Journal of Gerontology*, vol. 29, no. 5 (September 1974), 549–594.
Goldberg, Arthur. "Discerning a Causal Pattern among Data on Voting Behavior," *American Political Science Review*, vol. 60, no. 4 (December 1966), 913–922.
Goodwin, William L., & Klausmeir, Herbert J. *Facilitating Student Learning: An Introduction to Educational Psychology* (New York: Harper & Row, 1975).
Gosnell, Harold F. *Democracy: The Threshold of Freedom* (New York: Ronald, 1948).
Greeley, Andrew M. *Building Coalitions* (New York: F. Watts, 1974).
Greenberg, Edward S. "Political Socialization and Support of the System," (unpublished Ph.D. dissertation, Department of Political Science, University of Wisconsin, 1969).

Greenstein, Fred I. "The Benevolent Leader," *American Political Science Review,* vol. 54, no. 4 (December 1960), 934–943.
Greenstein, Fred I. *Children and Politics* (New Haven: Yale University Press, 1965).
Greenstein, Fred I. *Personality and Politics: Problems of Evidence, Inference, and Conceptualization* (Chicago: Markham, 1969).
Greenstein, Fred I. "The Benevolent Leader Revisited: Children's Images of Political Leaders in Three Democracies," *American Political Science Review,* vol. 69, no. 4 (December 1975), 1371–1398.
Grovey v. Townsend, 295 U.S. 45 (1935).
Guinn and Beal v. United States, 238 U.S. 348 (1915).
Harris, Louis. *The Anguish of Change* (New York: Norton, 1973).
Hart, Albert Bushnell. "The Exercise of the Suffrage," *Political Science Quarterly,* vol. 7, no. 2 (June 1892), 307–329.
Harter, Susan. "Piaget's Theory of Intellectual Development: The Changing World of the Child," in E. Zigler & I. L. Child (Eds.), *Socialization and Personality Development* (Reading, Mass.: Addison-Wesley, 1973), chap. 3.
Hartz, Louis. *The Liberal Tradition in America* (New York: Harcourt, 1955).
Heider, Fritz. *The Psychology of Interpersonal Relations* (New York: Wiley, 1958).
Hennessy, Bernard C. *Public Opinion,* 3d ed. (Belmont, Calif.: Wadsworth, 1975).
Henry, Jules. "Docility, or Giving the Teacher What She Wants," *Journal of Social Issues,* vol. 2, no. 2 (1955), 33–41.
Hess, Robert D., & Torney, Judith V. *The Development of Basic Attitudes and Values toward Government and Citizenship during the Elementary School Years,* Part I, Cooperative Research Project No. 1078 (Chicago: University of Chicago, 1965).
Hess, Robert D., & Torney, Judith V. *The Development of Political Attitudes in Children* (Chicago: Aldine, 1967).
Higbie, Charles E. "Wisconsin Dailies in the 1952 Campaign: Space vs. Display," *Journalism Quarterly,* vol. 31 (Winter 1952), 56–60.
Hoffman, Martin L., & Hoffman, Lois W. (Eds.) *Review of Child Development Research,* Vol. 1 (New York: Russell Sage, 1964).
Hovland, Carl I. (Ed.). *The Order of Presentation in Persuasion* (New Haven: Yale University Press, 1957).
Hovland, Carl I.; Janis, Irving L.; & Kelley, Harold H. *Communication and Persuasion* (New Haven: Yale University Press, 1953).
Hovland, Carl I., & Weiss, Walter. "The Influence of Source Credibility on Communication Effectiveness," *Public Opinion Quarterly,* vol. 15, no. 4 (Winter 1951–52), 635–650.
Huntington, Samuel P. *Political Order in Changing Societies* (New Haven: Yale University Press, 1968).
Ippolito, Dennis; Walker, Thomas G.; & Kolson, Kenneth. *Public Opinion and Responsible Democracy* (Englewood Cliffs, N.J.: Prentice-Hall, 1976).
Jacobson, Gary C. "The Effects of Campaign Spending in Congressional Elections," *American Political Science Review,* vol. 72, no. 2 (June 1978), 469–491.
Jackson, John E. "Issues, Party Choices, and Presidential Votes," *American Journal of Political Science,* vol. 19, no. 2 (May 1975), 161–185.

Jaros, Dean; Hirsch, Herbert; & Fleron, Frederic, Jr. "The Malevolent Leader: Political Socialization in an American Subculture," *American Political Science Review*, vol. 62, no. 2 (June 1968), 564–575.
Jaros, Dean, & Kolson, Kenneth L. "The Multifarious Leader: Political Socialization of Amish, 'Yanks,' Blacks," in R. G. Niemi (Ed.), *The Politics of Future Citizens* (San Francisco: Jossey-Bass, 1974), chap. 3.
Jennings, M. Kent, & Niemi, Richard G. "The Transmission of Political Values from Parent to Child," *The American Political Science Review*, vol. 62, no. 1 (March 1968), 169–184.
Jennings, M. Kent, & Niemi, Richard G. *The Political Character of Adolescence: The Influence of Families and Schools* (Princeton, N.J.: Princeton University Press, 1974).
Jennings, M. Kent, & Niemi, Richard G. "Continuity and Change in Political Orientations: A Longitudinal Study of Two Generations," *American Political Science Review*, vol. 69, no. 4 (December 1975), 1316–1335.
Johnson, Gerald W. "The Superficial Aspect," *New Republic* (May 2, 1955).
Kagay, Michael R., & Caldeira, Greg A. "A 'Reformed' Electorate? Well, at Least a Changed Electorate," in William J. Crotty (Ed.), *Paths to Political Reform* (Lexington, Mass.: Heath, forthcoming.)
Katz, Daniel. "The Functional Approach to the Study of Attitudes," *Public Opinion Quarterly*, vol. 24, no. 2 (Summer 1960), 163–204.
Katz, Elihu, & Feldman, Jacob J. "The Debates in the Light of Research: A Survey of Surveys," in S. Kraus, (Ed.), *The Great Debates* (Bloomington: Indiana University Press, 1962.)
Katzenstein, Caroline. *Lifting the Curtain* (Philadelphia: Dorrance, 1955).
Kelley, Stanley, Jr., & Mirer, Thad W. "The Simple Act of Voting," *American Political Science Review*, vol. 68, no. 2 (June 1974), 572–591.
Key, V. O., Jr. "A Theory of Critical Elections," *Journal of Politics*, vol. 17, no. 1 (February 1955), 3–18.
Key, V. O., Jr. "Secular Realignment and the Party System," *Journal of Politics*, vol. 21, no. 2 (May 1959), 198–210.
Key, V. O., Jr. *Politics, Parties and Pressure Groups*, 5th ed. (New York: Crowell, 1964).
Key, V. O., Jr. *Public Opinion and American Democracy* (New York: Knopf, 1965).
Key, V. O., Jr. *The Responsible Electorate* (Cambridge, Mass.: Harvard University Press, 1966).
Klapper, Joseph T. *The Effects of Mass Communication* (New York: Free Press, 1960).
Kobre, Sidney, "How Florida Dailies Handled the 1952 Presidential Campaign," *Journalism Quarterly*, vol. 30 (Spring 1953), 163–169.
Koeppen, Sheilah, "Children and Compliance: A Comparative Analysis of Socialization Studies," *Law and Society Review*, vol. 4, no. 4 (May 1970), 545–564.
Kohlberg, Lawrence. "Implications of Developmental Psychology for Education—Examples from Moral Education," *Educational Psychologist*, vol. 10, no. 1 (Winter 1973), 5.
Kohlberg, Lawrence, "Moral Stages and Moralization: The Cognitive Developmental Approach," in T. Lickona (Ed.), *Moral Development and Behavior* (New York: Holt, Rinehart and Winston, 1976), chap. 2.

Kohlberg, Lawrence, "Development of Moral Character and Moral Ideology," in M. L. Hoffman & L. W. Hoffman (Eds.), *Review of Child Development Research*, Vol. 1 (New York: Russell Sage, 1964), pp. 383–432.

Kohn, Melvin L. "Social Class and Parent-Child Relationships: An Interpretation," *American Journal of Sociology*, vol. 68, no. 4 (January 1963), 471–480.

Korematsu v. *United States*, 323 U.S. 214 (1944).

Kraus, Sidney (Ed.) *The Great Debates* (Bloomington: Indiana University Press, 1962).

Kraus, Sidney (Ed.) *Great Debates, Carter vs. Ford, 1976* (Bloomington: Indiana University Press, forthcoming).

Kroeber, Alfred, & Kluckhohn, Clyde. *Culture: A Critical Review of Concepts and Definitions* (New York: Random House, 1952).

Lane, Robert. *Political Life: Why People Get Involved in Politics* (New York: Free Press, 1959).

Lane, Robert E. "Fathers and Sons: Foundations of Political Belief," *American Sociological Review*, vol. 24, no. 4 (August 1959), 502–511.

Langton, Kenneth P., & Jennings, M. Kent. "Political Socialization and the High School Civics Curriculum in the United States," *American Political Science Review*, vol. 62, no. 3 (September 1968), 852–867.

LaPiere, Richard T. "Attitudes vs. Actions," *Social Forces*, vol. 13, no. 2 (December 1934), 230–237.

Laurence, Joan E. "White Socialization: Black Reality," *Psychiatry*, vol. 23, no. 2 (May 1970), 174–194.

Lawson, Edwin D. "Development of Patriotism in Children: A Second Look," *Journal of Psychology*, vol. 55 (1963), 279–286.

Lazarsfeld, Paul; Berelson, Bernard; & Gaudet, Hazel. *The People's Choice: How the Voter Makes Up His Mind in a Presidential Election*, 3d ed. (New York: Columbia University Press, 1968).

Lewis, Anthony. *Portrait of a Decade* (New York: Random House, 1964).

Lewis, Helen. "The Teen-age Joiner and His Orientation toward Public Affairs" (unpublished Ph.D. dissertation, Department of Political Science, Michigan State University, 1962).

"Liberal Bias" as a Factor in Network Television News Reporting (Washington: The American Institute for Political Communications, 1972).

Lickona, Thomas (Ed.) *Moral Development and Behavior* (New York: Holt, Rinehart and Winston, 1976).

Liebert, Robert, & Baron, Robert. "Short-Term Effects of Televised Aggression on Children's Aggressive Behavior," *Television and Social Behavior: Report to the Surgeon General*, Vol. 2 (Washington, D.C.: GPO, 1972).

Likert, Rensis. "A Technique for the Measurement of Attitudes," *Archives of Psychology*, no. 140 (June 1932), 1–55.

Lindzey, Gardner, & Aronson, Elliot (Eds.) *The Handbook of Social Psychology*, 2d ed., Vol. 3 (Reading, Mass.: Addison-Wesley 1969).

Lipsitz, Lewis. "If, as Verba Says, the State Functions as a Religion, What Are We to Do Then To Save Our Souls?", *American Political Science Review*, vol. 62, no. 2 (June 1968), 527–535.

Litt, Edgar. "Civic Education, Community Norms and Political Indoctrination," *American Sociological Review*, vol. 28, no. 1 (February 1963).

Lorenz, Konrad. *On Aggression,* Marjorie Wilson, transl. (New York: Harcourt, 1966).
LoSciuto, Leonard A. "A National Inventory of Television Viewing Behavior," in E. Rubenstein, G. A. Comstock, & J. P. Murray (Eds.), *Television and Social Behavior,* vol. 4 (Washington, D.C.: GPO, no date).
Maccoby, Eleanor E. "The Development of Moral Values and Behavior in Childhood," in J. A. Clausen (Ed.), *Socialization and Society* (Boston: Little, Brown, 1968), pp. 227–269.
Maccoby, Eleanor E. (Ed.). *Readings in Social Psychology,* 3d ed. (New York: Holt, Rinehart and Winston, 1958).
Margolis, Michael. "From Confusion to Confusion: Issues and the American Voter (1956–1972)," *American Political Science Review,* vol. 71, no. 1 (March 1977), 31–43.
Marsh, David. "Political Socialization: The Implicit Assumptions Questioned," *British Journal of Political Science,* vol. 1, pt. 4 (October 1971), 453–465.
Matthews, Donald R., & Protho, James W. *Negroes and the New Southern Politics* (New York: Harcourt, 1966).
McGinniss, Joe. *The Selling of the President 1968* (New York: Trident Press, 1969).
McGuire, William J. "The Nature of Attitudes and Attitude Change," in G. Lindzey & E. Aronson (Eds.), *The Handbook of Social Psychology,* 2d ed., vol. 3 (Reading, Mass.: Addison-Wesley, 1969).
Merelman, Richard M. *Political Socialization and Educational Climates* (New York: Holt, Rinehart and Winston, 1971).
Merritt, Richard L. *Symbols of American Community, 1735–1775* (New Haven: Yale University Press, 1966).
Milbrath, Lester W. *Political Participation* (Chicago: Rand McNally, 1965).
Miller, Arthur H. "Political Issues and Trust in Government: 1964–1970," *American Political Science Review,* vol. 68, no. 3 (September 1974), 951–972.
Miller, Arthur H.; Miller, Warren E.; Raine, Alden S.; & Brown, Thad A. "A Majority Party in Disarray: Policy Polarization in the 1972 Election," *American Political Science Review,* vol. 70, no. 3 (September 1976), 753–778.
Miller, Neal, & Dollard, John. *Social Learning and Imitation* (New Haven: Yale University Press, 1941).
Miller, Warren E. "Policy Preferences of Congressional Candidates and Constituents," paper presented at the annual meeting of the American Political Science Association, September 1961.
Miller, Warren E., & Levitin, Teresa F. *Leadership and Change: The New Politics and the American Electorate* (Cambridge, Mass.: Winthrop Publishers, 1976).
Miller, Warren E., & Stokes, Donald E. "Constituency Influence in Congress," *American Political Science Review,* vol. 57, no. 1 (March 1963), 45–56.
Mischel, Walter. "Toward a Cognitive Social Learning Reconceptualization of Personality," *Psychological Review,* vol. 80, no. 4 (July 1973), 253–283.
Monroe, Alan D. *Public Opinion in America* (New York: Dodd, Mead, 1975).
Napolitan, Joseph. *The Election Game and How to Win It* (New York: Doubleday, 1972).
Newcomb, Theodore. "Attitude Development as a Function of Reference Groups: The Bennington Study," in E. Maccoby (Ed.), *Readings in Social Psychology,* 3d ed. (New York: Holt, Rinehart and Winston, 1958), pp. 265–275.

Newsweek, February 21, 1977, 67.
Nielson, A. C. Report in *Newsweek*, February 21, 1977, 63.
Niemi, Richard G. (Ed.) *The Politics of Future Citizens* (San Francisco: Jossey-Bass, 1974).
Orlansky, Harold. "Reactions to the Death of President Roosevelt," *Journal of Social Psychology*, vol. 26 (November 1947), 235–266.
Page, Benjamin I., & Brody, Richard A. "Policy Voting and the Electoral Process: The Vietnam War Issue," *American Political Science Review*, vol. 66, no. 3 (September 1972), 979–995.
Paletz, David L., & Dunn, Robert. "Press Coverage of Civil Disorders: A Case Study of Winston-Salem, 1967," *Public Opinion Quarterly*, vol. 33, no. 3 (Fall 1969), 328–345.
Paletz, David L.; Reichert, Peggy; & McIntyre, Barbara. "How the Media Support Local Governmental Authority," *Public Opinion Quarterly*, vol. 35, no. 1 (Spring 1971), 80–92.
Phillips, Kevin P. *The Emerging Republican Majority* (Garden City, N.Y.: Anchor Books, 1970).
Piaget, Jean. *The Origins of Intelligence in Children* (New York: Norton, 1963).
Piaget, Jean. *The Moral Judgment of the Child* (New York: Free Press, 1966).
Piereson, James E. "Presidential Popularity and Midterm Voting at Different Electoral Levels," *American Journal of Political Science*, vol. 19, no. 4 (November 1975), 683–694.
Polsby, Nelson (Ed.) *Congressional Behavior* (New York: Random House, 1971).
Polsby, Nelson W. "An Emerging Republican Majority?" *Public Interest*, no. 17 (Fall 1969), 119–126.
Polsby, Nelson W., & Greenstein, Fred I. *Handbook of Political Science*, Vol. 4 (Reading, Mass.: Addison-Wesley, 1975).
Pomper, Gerald M. *Elections in America: Control and Influence in Democratic Politics* (New York: Dodd, Mead, 1970).
Pomper, Gerald M. *Voter's Choice: Varieties of American Electoral Behavior* (New York: Dodd, Mead, 1975).
Pomper, Gerald M. *The Election of 1976: Reports and Interpretations* (New York: McKay, 1977).
Pool, Ithiel de Sola; Abelson, Robert P.; & Popkin, Samuel. *Candidates, Issues and Strategies* (Cambridge, Mass.: M.I.T. Press, 1965).
Porter, Kirk Harold. *A History of Suffrage in the United States* (New York: AMS Press, Inc., 1971).
Prothro, James W., & Grigg, Charles M. "Fundamental Principles of Democracy: Bases of Agreement and Disagreement," *Journal of Politics*, vol. 22, no. 2 (May 1960), 276–294.
Psathas, George. "Ethnicity, Social Class and Adolescent Independence from Parental Control," *American Sociological Review*, vol. 22, no. 4 (August 1957), 415–423.
RePass, David E. "Issue Salience and Party Choice," *American Political Science Review*, vol. 65, no. 2 (June 1971), 389–400.
Reynolds, H. T. *Politics and the Common Man: An Introduction to Political Behavior* (Homewood, Ill.: Dorsey, 1974).

Robinson, John P. "The Press as King-Maker: What Surveys From the Last Five Campaigns Show," *Journalism Quarterly*, vol. 51, no. 4 (Winter 1974), 587–594, 606.

Robinson, John P. "Public Reaction to Political Protest: Chicago, 1968," *Public Opinion Quarterly*, vol. 34, no. 1 (Spring 1970), 1–9.

Rodgers, Harrell R., & Bullock, Charles S., III. *Law and Social Change: Civil Rights and Their Consequences* (New York: McGraw-Hill, 1972).

Rosenberg, Morris, "Some Determinants of Political Apathy," *Public Opinion Quarterly*, vol. 18, no. 4 (Winter 1954–55), 349–366.

Rubenstein, Eli; Comstock, George A.; & Murray, John P. (Eds.) *Television and Social Behavior: Television in Day-to-Day Life: Patterns of Use*, Vol. 4 (Washington, D.C.: GPO, no date).

Salant, Richard S. "The Television Debates: A Revolution That Deserves a Future," *Public Opinion Quarterly*, vol. 26, no. 3 (Fall 1962), 335–350.

The Sampler (Princeton, N.J.: Response Analysis), no. 8 (Spring 1977), 4.

Scammon, Richard M., & Wattenberg, Ben J. *The Real Majority* (New York: Coward-McCann, 1970).

Sears, David O., & McConahay, John B. "Participation in the Los Angeles Riot," *Social Problems*, vol. 17, no. 1 (Summer 1969), 3–20.

Sears, Robert D. "Identification as a Form of Behavioral Development," in D. Harris, (Ed.), *The Concept of Development* (Minneapolis: University of Minnesota Press, 1957).

Sebert, Suzanne Koprince. "The Political Texture of Peer Groups," in M. K. Jennings & R. G. Niemi, *The Political Character of Adolescence: The Influence of Families and Schools* (Princeton, N.J.: Princeton University Press, 1974), chap. 9.

Sigel, Roberta S. "Image of a President: Some Insights into the Political Views of School Children," *American Political Science Review*, vol. 62, no. 1 (March 1968), 216–226.

Sigel, Roberta S. "An Exploration into Some Aspects of Political Socialization: School Children's Reaction to the Death of a President," in M. Wolfenstein & G. Kliman (Eds.), *Children and the Death of a President* (Garden City, N.Y.: Anchor Books, 1966), chap. 2.

Smith v. *Allwright*, 321 U.S. 649 (1944).

Smith, M. Brewster. "A Map for the Analysis of Personality and Politics," *Journal of Social Issues*, vol. 24, no. 3 (July 1968), 15–28.

Stempel, Guido, III. "The Prestige Press Covers the 1960 Presidential Campaign," *Journalism Quarterly*, vol. 38 (Spring 1961), 157–163.

Stempel, Guido, III. "The Prestige Press in Two Presidential Elections," *Journalism Quarterly*, vol. 42 (Winter 1965), 15–21.

Stokes, Donald E. "Some Dynamic Elements of Contests for the Presidency," *American Political Science Review*, vol. 60, no. 1 (March 1966), 19–28.

Stokes, Donald E.; Campbell, Angus; & Miller, Warren E. "Components of Electoral Decisions," *American Political Science Review*, vol. 52, no. 2 (June 1958), 378.

Strong, Donald S. *Issue Voting and Party Realignment* (University, Ala.: University of Alabama Press, 1977).

Sullivan, John L., & O'Connor, Robert E. "Electoral Choice and Popular Control of Public Policy: The Case of the 1966 House Elections," *American Political Science Review,* vol. 66, no. 4 (December 1972), 1258–1268.

Television and Growing Up: The Impact of Televised Violence. Report to the Surgeon General, U.S. Public Health Service (Washington, D.C.: GPO 1972).

Truman, David B. *The Governmental Process,* 2d ed. (New York: Knopf, 1971).

U.S. Commission on Civil Rights. *1959 Report* (Washington, D.C.: GPO, 1960), 80.

U.S. Commission on Civil Rights. *Voting in Mississippi* (Washington, D.C.: GPO 1965), 14–15.

U.S. Commission on Civil Rights. *The Voting Rights Act* (Washington, D.C.: GPO, 1965), 8.

U.S. v. *Lynd,* 301 F.2d 818 (1962).

Verba, Sidney, & Nie, Norman H. *Participation in America* (New York: Harper & Row, 1972).

Watters, Pat, & Cleghorn, Reese. *Climbing Jacob's Ladder: The Arrival of Negroes in Southern Politics* (New York: Harcourt, 1967).

Weisbord, Marvin R. *Campaigning for President* (New York: Washington Square Press, 1966).

Weissberg, Robert. *Political Learning, Political Choice, and Democratic Citizenship* (Englewood Cliffs, N.J.: Prentice-Hall, 1974).

Weissberg, Robert. *Public Opinion and Popular Government* (Englewood Cliffs, N.J.: Prentice-Hall, 1976).

White, Theodore H. *The Making of the President 1968.* (New York: Atheneum, 1969).

Wicker, Allan W. "Attitudes versus Actions: The Relationship of Verbal and Overt Behavioral Responses to Attitude Objects," *Journal of Social Issues,* vol. 25, no. 4 (Autumn 1969), 41–78.

Williamson, Chilton. *American Suffrage from Property to Democracy: 1760–1860* (Princeton, N.J.: Princeton University Press, 1960).

Wolfenstein, Martha. "Death of a Parent and Death of a President: Children's Reactions to Two Kinds of Loss," in M. Wolfenstein and G. Kliman (Eds.), *Children and the Death of a President* (Garden City, N.Y.: Anchor Books, 1966), chap. 3.

Wolfenstein, Martha, & Kliman, Gilbert (Eds.) *Children and the Death of a President* (Garden City, N.Y.: Anchor Books, 1966).

Wolfinger, Raymond E., & Rosenstone, Steven J. "Who Votes?" Paper presented at the annual meeting of the American Political Science Association, Washington, D.C., September 1–4, 1977.

Wood, Forrest G. *Black Scare: The Racist to Emancipation and Reconstruction* (Berkeley: University of California Press, 1968).

Woodward, C. Vann. *The Strange Career of Jim Crow* (New York: Oxford, 1955).

Ziblatt, David. "High School Extracurricular Activities and Political Socialization," *Annals of the American Academy of Political and Social Science,* vol. 361 (September 1965), 21.

Zigler, Edward, & Child, Irvin L. (Eds.) *Socialization and Personality Development* (Reading, Mass.: Addison-Wesley, 1973).

INDEXES

NAME INDEX

Adams, Abigail, 15
Adams, John, 12, 15
Adelson, Joseph, 59, 60, 61, 62
Agnew, Spiro, 181, 182, 246
Alford, Dale, 287
Allport, Gordon, 157
Almond, Gabriel A., 77, 82, 88, 123
Anthony, Susan B., 18, 21
Asher, Herbert, 276, 277

Beck, Paul Allen, 272
Blaine, James G., 139, 140
Boorstin, Daniel, 107
Brent, Margaret, 15
Brinkley, David, 181
Brittain, Clay V., 126
Brown, Joseph E., 17
Bryan, William Jennings, 235
Burchard, Samuel D., 139
Burnham, W. D., 235, 269, 270

Caldeira, Greg A., 264
Campbell, Angus, 133, 240, 261
Cardozo, Benjamin, 284
Carter, Jimmy, 1, 38, 39, 40, 42, 44, 46, 48, 49, 63, 64, 66, 87, 101, 107, 129, 143, 144, 148, 159, 179, 182, 183, 185, 198, 216, 221, 223, 225, 227, 228, 232, 241, 242, 248, 252, 253, 255, 262, 267, 269, 273, 289, 290
Cartwright, Dorwin, 126
Chandler, Robert, 85
Cirino, Robert, 181
Citrin, Jack, 89
Cleveland, Grover, 99
Coleman, James S., 126
Connor, Eugene "Bull", 27
Converse, Philip, 235, 236, 245
Coombs, Steven, 180
Cox, William Harold, 30
Crouse, Timothy, 247

Daley, Richard, 251
Davidson, Roger H., 291
Dennis, Jack, 8, 70, 103
Dorr, Thomas, 14

Eagleton, Thomas, 247
Eastland, James, 30
Easton, David, 8, 70, 103
Edison, Thomas, 78
Efron, Edith, 181
Eisenhower, Dwight D., 56, 87, 100, 101, 151, 228, 239, 242, 243, 244, 249, 253, 254, 260, 267, 274, 277, 287

Faubus, Orville, 287
Flanigan, William H., 241
Ford, Gerald, 1, 40, 44, 45, 46, 48, 49, 63, 64, 87, 107, 148, 159, 182, 185, 216, 223, 242, 247, 248, 249, 252, 253, 255, 262, 291
Franklin, Benjamin, 1, 12

Gabriel, Ralph Henry, 79
Gamson, William A., 83, 84
Ginsparg, Sylvia, 54
Glamser, Francis D., 175
Goldwater, Barry, 97, 100, 101, 128, 179, 197, 224, 242, 246, 249, 250, 254, 256, 262, 274, 275, 278, 293, 294
Greeley, Andrew M., 277
Greeley, Horace, 17
Greenstein, Fred I., 87, 89, 102, 103, 131
Grigg, Charles M., 80, 82
Grimke, Angelina, 17
Guttierrez, Armand, 103

Hall, Leonard, 178
Hamilton, Alexander, 12
Harding, Warren G., 21
Harris, Louis, 166, 172

NAME INDEX

Hayes, Rutherford B., 23
Hays, Brooks, 287
Heider, Fritz, 42
Hennessy, Bernard C., 179
Hess, Robert D., 76, 77, 82, 86, 97, 103
Hirsch, Herbert, 103
Hitler, Adolf, 72, 146, 158, 220
Hovland, Carl I., 160
Hughes, Charles Evans, 20
Humphrey, Hubert, 101, 181, 218, 225, 227, 246, 247, 251, 253, 254
Huntley, Chet, 181

Jackson, Andrew, 13, 221
Jacobson, Gary C., 183
Jaros, Dean, 103, 105
Jarvis, Howard, 3, 156
Jay, John, 12
Jefferson, Thomas, 12
Jennings, M. Kent, 94, 98, 111, 116, 121, 122, 133
Johnson, Andrew, 22
Johnson, Lyndon B., 5, 22, 97, 100, 101, 128, 149, 203, 221, 224, 230, 242, 243, 246, 250, 254, 256, 274, 275, 292, 293

Kagay, Michael R., 264
Katz, Daniel, 145, 146, 147, 157, 158, 162
Kelley, Stanley, 260
Kennedy, John, 5, 27, 54, 62, 87, 93, 100, 101, 131, 184, 185, 186, 220, 230, 245, 246, 249, 264, 267, 282, 285, 290
Kennedy, Robert, 5, 246
Key, V. O., 14, 140, 141
King, Martin Luther, 5, 27, 28
Kissinger, Henry, 255
Kluckhohn, Clyde, 71
Kolson, Kenneth L., 105
Kovenock, David, 217, 218, 219

LaFollette, Robert, 243
Lane, Robert E., 55, 56, 57
Langton, Kenneth P., 121, 122
LaPiere, Richard, 45
Lawson, Edwin D., 51, 77
Lazarsfeld, Paul, 218, 219, 220, 221, 223, 230
Lincoln, Abraham, 22, 79, 223
Lipsitz, Lewis, 74, 75

Litt, Edgar, 119, 120
Liuzzo, Viola, 28

MacArthur, Douglas, 253
McCarthy, Eugene, 149, 247
McEvoy, James, 83, 84
McGinnis, Joe, 178
McGovern, George, 101, 179, 180, 181, 226, 227, 229, 232, 247, 252, 255, 269, 278, 279
Madison, James, 12
Margolis, Michael, 260
Markel, Lester, 186
Marx, Karl, 129, 166
Mencken, H. L., 148
Milbrath, Lester W., 210, 214
Miller, Arthur H., 88, 89, 133, 196
Miller, Warren E., 292
Mirer, Thad, 260
Mitchell, John, 5
Moriarty, Alice, 54
Moro, Aldo, 187
Mott, Lucretia, 16
Murphey, Lois B., 54

Nader, Ralph, 293
Napolitan, Joseph, 159, 161
Nie, Norman H., 212, 213, 294
Niemi, Richard G., 98, 111, 116
Nixon, Richard, 4, 42, 43, 44, 87, 100, 101, 106, 107, 108, 140, 141, 151, 152, 157, 178, 181, 182, 183, 184, 185, 227, 244, 246, 247, 249, 251, 252, 255, 256, 260, 267, 268, 269, 276, 278, 287, 288, 289, 290

Orlansky, Harold, 54
Orwell, George, 6
Oppenheimer, Robert, 160
Oswald, Lee Harvey, 62

Paine, Thomas, 12
Paletz, David L., 178
Passman, Leo, 157
Peabody, Endicott, 159, 160
Piaget, Jean, 57, 58, 59, 60, 61, 68
Prothro, James W., 80, 82

Rafshoon, Gerald, 290
Reagan, Ronald, 242, 248
RePass, David E., 270
Reynolds, H. T., 157
Robinson, John P., 180

Romney, George, 186, 187
Roosevelt, Franklin, 25, 26, 54, 73, 78, 87, 99, 114, 131, 220, 222, 249, 282
Roosevelt, Theodore, 99, 243
Roper, Elmo, 184

Scammon, Richard M., 166, 200
Schuman, Howard, 133
Shaw, Raymond, 37
Sigel, Roberta S., 62, 130
Skinner, B. F., 67
Smith, Al, 245
Stanton, Elizabeth Cady, 16
Stevens, Thaddeus, 17
Stevenson, Adlai, 228, 239, 244
Stokes, Donald E., 244, 257, 292
Strong, Donald, 276
Sumner, Charles, 17

Taft, Robert, 56
Taft, William H., 243
Thieu, Nguyen Van, 181
Thoreau, Henry David, 75
Tilden, Samuel, 23

Tito, Josip, 114
Torney, Judith V., 76, 77, 82, 86, 97, 103
Truman, David, 87
Truman, Harry, 249, 253, 255, 272

Verba, Sidney, 77, 82, 88, 123, 212, 213, 294

Wallace, George, 5, 28, 149, 168, 170, 181, 225, 243, 246, 251, 252, 268, 276
Washington, George, 13, 93
Watson, Tom, 24
Wattenberg, Ben, 166, 200
Weiss, Walter, 160
Weissberg, Robert, 132
Wicker, Allen W., 45
Wilson, Woodrow, 19, 20, 21, 25, 99, 243

Zander, Alvin, 126
Ziblatt, David, 125
Zingale, Nancy H., 241

SUBJECT INDEX

Abolitionists, 16
Affect (*see* Attitudes)
Age effects, on turnout and partisanship, 228–229
   See also Public opinion
Amendment, Thirteenth, 22
   Fifteenth, 17, 21, 23
   Eighteenth, 20
   Nineteenth, 19, 20, 21
   Twenty-Fourth, 31
   Twenty-Sixth, 31
Anthony Amendment (*see* Amendment, Nineteenth)
"Attentive" public (*see* Public opinion)
Attitudes, acquisition of (*see* Socialization)
   affective component of, 38
   belief systems of, 41: balance of, 42; constraint of, 42, 150
   centrality of, 39
   cognitive component of, 36
   definition of, 36
   direction of, 38
   expression of, 6, 7
   intensity of, 38–39
   origins of, 6, 7
   political, 35
   relationship to behavior, 45–49
   relationship to voter turnout, 232–240
Authoritarianism, 56, 161–162
   See also Public opinion
Authority, benevolent leader phenomenon, 103
   child's view of, 55, 93, 94, 104
   malevolent leader phenomenon, 102, 103
   negative, 56, 103
   of teachers, 123
   See also School

Bill of Rights, definition of, 79
Brown vs. Board of Education, 282

Bureaucracy, 5
   bureaucrats, 1
   and public policy, 281, 282

Campaigns, Carter-Ford campaign, 1, 182, 247–249, 252–253, 255
   and the media, 178, 182–186
   and spending, 182
   the "two step flow" hypothesis, 186
   See also Short-term forces
Citizenship roles, 115, 116
   definition of, 115
   socialization of, 115–116
Civil Rights Act of 1957, 29
   of 1960, 29
   of 1964, 30
Civil War, 17
   and black suffrage, 21
   and women's suffrage, 17
Cognitive developmental theory, 89, 92–93, 110
   See also Political socialization; Attitudes
Constitution, 79, 80
Constitutional Convention of 1787, 12
Control, levels of, aggregate, 3, 4, 6, 32
   direct, 5
   indirect, 3, 4, 5, 6
   popular, 5, 6
   single, 3, 5
Culture, 11, 84
   concept of, 71
   political, 72, 76: definition of, 71; government and, 86–95; persistence of, 73; political religion in, 74–75, 87, 107, 122, 133; shaping of social processes in, 72
   See also Political community; Regime; Government
Debates, of Ford-Carter, 148, 185, 248

SUBJECT INDEX

Debates (*cont.*)
    of Kennedy-Nixon, 184, 245
Democracy, 11, 297, 298
    definition of, 1
Depression of 1929, 25, 72, 80, 221–222, 226, 271
Dorr War, 14

Editorial endorsements (*see* Media)
Education, influence on voter turnout and partisanship, 225–227
    level of, 168
    See also Public opinion
Efficacy (*see* Political efficacy)
Emancipation Proclamation, 22

Family (*see* Political socialization)
Franchise, 233
    definition of, 12
Freehold, 14, 15
    definition of, 12
    proportion of, 13
    requirements of, 13, 14

Government, attitudes toward, 86–95
Grandfather Clause, 25
Grovey vs. Townsend, 25

Impeachment, of Andrew Johnson, 22
    of Richard Nixon, 87, 288–289
Independents, increase in, 101
    in presidential elections, 265–267
    reaction to short-term forces, 262, 264
    socialization of, 112
Instrumental conditioning (*see* Political socialization)
Issue voting (*see* Voting)

Jarvis-Gann Referendum, 3, 156, 295

Ku Klux Klan, 27, 159

Levels of conceptualization (*see* Public opinion)

Media, 7, 177–187
    bias in the, 179–182: editorial endorsements, 179, 180
    interpretation of politics by, 177–179
    and political campaigns, 182–186

National American Women's Suffrage Association (NAWSA), 19
    and World War II, 20
National Women's Party (NWP), 19, 20
    picketing of the White House by, 19, 20, 32
New Deal, 25, 226, 249, 250, 271
New Deal Coalition, 100, 101
Normal vote, 261
    in presidential elections, 265–266
    in the South, 273

Opinion (*see* Public opinion)

Parents, 7
    See also Political socialization
Party identification, 40
    class differences in, 131
    historical patterns of, 99–102
    influence on party choice, 241–243, 259–269
    influence on voter turnout, 239–240
    origins in the family, 111–113
    in presidential elections, 265–267
    as stereotypes, 148
Peer group, 7
    extent of influence by, 127–128
    reasons for influence by, 126
    See also Political socialization
Perceptual screen (*see* Public opinion)
Police, and civil rights, 127, 128
    as figures of authority, 82–84
Political community, attitudes toward, 76–79, 84
    identification with, 76
    as symbols of, 77
Political efficacy, 95–99
    definition of, 95, 96
    influence on voter turnout, 237–238
    trends in, 96
    socialization of, 97–99, 116–117
Political knowledge, 113–115
    class differences of, 131
    levels of, 113, 114, 148–149
    socialization of, 114, 115
Political participation, 6, 11
    definition of, 209
    levels of, 210–214
    racial differences in, 133–134
Political religion (*see* Culture)

Political socialization, 7, 8, 51, 68
  agents of, 110–129: family, 110–118; peer group, 126–128; school, 118–126
  cognitive-developmental approach to, 57–62
  definition of, 52
  group differences in, 129–134: race, 132–134; social class, 129–132
  psychoanalytic approach to, 53–57
  social learning theory approach to, 63–67: conditions facilitating, 66–67; instrumental conditioning of, 64
  sugar-coating the political pill, 92, 103
  See also Attitudes; Citizenship roles; Party identification; Political knowledge; Public policy; Trust
Political trust (*see* Trust)
Popular control (*see* Control)
Populism, definition of, 24
President, 3
  admiration for, 55, 86, 87, 93, 103, 107
  as father image, 87
  grief for, 54
Public opinion, 6, 7, 11
  attentive public, definition of, 141
  definition of (public opinion), 140
  domestic-economic issues of, 196–199
  formation and change of, 143–156, 165: concept of function, 145–148, 157
  group differences in, 165–177: by age, 172–176; by education, 168; by race, 171–172; by socioeconomic status, 165–171
  perceptual screen, 156–158: characteristics of the message, 158–160; individual characteristics of, 157–158
  impact of personality on, 160–162: intelligence, 160–161; traits, 161–162
  power of, 32
  and public policy, 193–196
  rationality of, 148–156: constraint, 150; inter-opinion consistency,

Public opinion (*cont.*)
  152–156; levels of conceptualization, 150–152; levels of information, 148–149
Public policy, 5
  definition of, 281–282
  impact of mass participation on, 291–297
  impact of public opinion on, 287–291
  impact of socialization on, 285–286
Psychoanalytic theory, 89, 104, 110
  See also Political socialization

Realignment, prospects for, 269–272
  in the South, 272–275
Race, influence on voter turnout and voting, 223–225
  See also Public opinion; Political socialization
Reconstruction Act of 1867, 22
  and black suffrage, 21
Reconstruction period, 22
Redemption period, 23, 24
Redundancy effect (*see* School)
Regime, attitudes toward, 79–84
  constitution as symbol of, 79
  cynicism towards, 89
  rules of game, 79
Region, influence on voter turnout and partisanship, 227–228
Registration, effect on voter turnout, 233–236
  of southern blacks, 29–32
Religion, influence in 1960 election, 245–246
  influence on voter turnout and partisanship, 220–221
Revolution, 12

School, 7
  direct socialization in, 118–122: classroom ritual, 122; impact of civics curriculum, 121, 122; redundancy effect on learning, 122, 126
  indirect socialization in, 123–126: compliance to authority, 123; and participatory experience, 124–125
  See also Authority; Culture; Political socialization

SUBJECT INDEX

Sense of citizen duty, influence on voter turnout, 238–239
Short-term forces, 236
  influence on party choice, 243–257, 259–269: candidate attitudes, 244–249; domestic policy, 249–253; foreign policy, 253–255; party performance, 255–256
  influence on voter turnout, 236–237
Smith vs. Allwright, 26
Social class, influence on voter turnout and partisanship, 221–223
"Social issue," 200, 250–251, 252, 276
Socialization (*see* Political socialization)
Social learning theory, 89, 92, 103, 111
  See also Attitudes; Political socialization
Southern Christian Leadership Conference, 28
Suffrage, 32
  black, 21–32
  women's, 14–21: opponents of, 18
  universal male, 11–14

Trust, 2, 88, 125
  political, 87–95: decline of, 88–89, 94–95; racial differences in, 133; socialization of, 89, 116–117

Veto, presidential, 5
Vietnam, 1, 78, 141, 166, 170, 175, 254–255, 286, 292
  See also Public opinion
Voting, 8, 11, 210, 212–214
  attitudinal bases of, 8
  group bases of, 8
  issue voting, 264–265, 270
  and political efficacy, 97
  primary group influence on, 217–218
  secondary group influence on, 218–229: index of political predisposition, 218–220
  See also Age effects; Education; Region; Religion; Social class
Voting Rights Act of 1965, 31
  1975 amendment to, 31

Watergate, 1, 43, 44, 101, 141, 241
  effect on political culture, 97, 106, 197
  and political trust, 88, 89
  and Richard Nixon, 87, 157, 256, 287–289
White primary, 25, 26
Women's Rights Convention of 1848, 16
World War I, and women's suffrage, 20
World War II, 70, 72, 73